# RSF: The Russell Sage Foundation Journal of the Social Sciences

*The Criminal Justice System as a Labor Market Institution*

**VOLUME 6, NUMBER 1, MARCH 2020**

**RSF: The Russell Sage Foundation Journal of the Social Sciences**     ISSN 2377-8261

## The Russell Sage Foundation

The Russell Sage Foundation, one of the oldest of America's general purpose foundations, was established in 1907 by Mrs. Margaret Olivia Sage for "the improvement of social and living conditions in the United States." The foundation seeks to fulfill this mandate by fostering the development and dissemination of knowledge about the country's political, social, and economic problems. While the foundation endeavors to assure the accuracy and objectivity of each book it publishes, the conclusions and interpretations in Russell Sage Foundation publications are those of the authors and not of the foundation, its trustees, or its staff. Publication by Russell Sage, therefore, does not imply foundation endorsement.

## Board of Trustees

Claude M. Steele, *Chair*
Larry M. Bartels
Marianne Bertrand
Cathy J. Cohen
Karen S. Cook
Sheldon Danziger
Kathryn Edin
Jason Furman
Michael Jones-Correa
David Laibson
Nicholas Lemann
Hazel Rose Markus
Martha Minow
Jennifer Richeson
Mario Luis Small
Hirokazu Yoshikawa

## Mission Statement

*RSF: The Russell Sage Foundation Journal of the Social Sciences* is a peer-reviewed, open-access journal of original empirical research articles by both established and emerging scholars. It is designed to promote cross-disciplinary collaborations on timely issues of interest to academics, policymakers, and the public at large. Each issue is thematic in nature and focuses on a specific research question or area of interest. The introduction to each issue will include an accessible, broad, and synthetic overview of the research question under consideration and the current thinking from the various social sciences.

## RSF Journal Editorial Board

Toni C. Antonucci, University of Michigan
Sheldon H. Danziger, Russell Sage Foundation
Shigeo Hirano, Columbia University
Chinhui Juhn, University of Houston
Maria Krysan, University of Illinois, Chicago
Michal Kurlaender, University of California, Davis
Helen Levy, University of Michigan
Cecilia Menjivar, University of California, Los Angeles
Martha Minow, Harvard University
Sandra Susan Smith, University of California, Berkeley
Christopher Wildeman, Cornell University

Copyright © 2020 by Russell Sage Foundation. All rights reserved. Printed in the United States of America. No part of this publication may be reproduced, stored in a retrieval system, or transmitted in any form or by any means, electronic, mechanical, photocopying, recording, or otherwise, without the prior written permission of the publisher. Reproduction by the United States Government in whole or in part is permitted for any purpose.

Opinions expressed in this journal are not necessarily those of the editors, editorial board, trustees, the Russell Sage Foundation, or the W.K. Kellogg Foundation.

We invite scholars to submit proposals for potential issues to journal@rsage.org. Submissions should be addressed to Suzanne Nichols, Director of Publications.

To view the complete text and additional features online please go to **www.rsfjournal.org**.

## Open Access Policy

*RSF: The Russell Sage Foundation Journal of the Social Sciences* is an open access journal. It is published under a Creative Commons Attribution-NonCommercial-No Derivs 3.0 Unported License.

**Russell Sage Foundation**
112 East 64th Street
New York, NY 10065

**ISSN (print):**       2377-8253
**ISSN (electronic):**  2377-8261
**ISBN:**               978-0-87154-790-3

# The Criminal Justice System as a Labor Market Institution

ISSUE EDITORS
Sandra Susan Smith, University of California, Berkeley
Jonathan Simon, University of California, Berkeley

## CONTENTS

Exclusion and Extraction: Criminal Justice Contact and the Reallocation of Labor  **1**
*Sandra Susan Smith and Jonathan Simon*

### Part I. Consequences for Mass Incarceration of Intersecting Labor Market Institutions

Institutional Castling: Military Enlistment and Mass Incarceration in the United States  **30**
*Bryan L. Sykes and Amy Kate Bailey*

Working to Avoid Incarceration: Jail Threat and Labor Market Outcomes for Noncustodial Fathers Facing Child Support Enforcement  **55**
*Noah D. Zatz and Michael A. Stoll*

### Part II. Criminal Justice Policies as Structural Barriers to Employment

Providing After Prison: Nonresident Fathers' Formal and Informal Contributions to Children  **84**
*Allison Dwyer Emory, Lenna Nepomnyaschy, Maureen R. Waller, Daniel P. Miller, and Alexandra Haralampoudis*

On Thin Ice: Bureaucratic Processes of Monetary Sanctions and Job Insecurity  **113**
*Michele Cadigan and Gabriela Kirk*

Locked Out of the Labor Market? State-Level Hidden Sentences and the Labor Market Outcomes of Recently Incarcerated Young Adults  **132**
*Cody Warner, Joshua Kaiser, and Jason N. Houle*

### Part III. The Effects of Post-prison Employment on Future Criminal Justice Involvement

Post-prison Employment Quality and Future Criminal Justice Contact  **154**
*Joe LaBriola*

Parolefare: Post-prison Supervision and Low-Wage Work  **173**
*Josh Seim and David J. Harding*

### Part IV. Work and Identity in and After Prison

Sandpiles of Dignity: Labor Status and Boundary-Making in the Contemporary American Prison  **198**
*Michael Gibson-Light*

# Exclusion and Extraction: Criminal Justice Contact and the Reallocation of Labor

SANDRA SUSAN SMITH AND JONATHAN SIMON

In the United States, almost seven million people are under correctional control. This includes 2.3 million held in the nation's jails, prisons, detention centers, and involuntary commitment facilities. It also includes 4.5 million people in community corrections—3.7 million on probation and more than eight hundred thousand on parole (Sawyer and Wagner 2019). That works out to be roughly 2,160 per hundred thousand adult residents (Kaeble and Cowhig 2018). Among low-income people of color, who are far more likely to be caught in the system's web, the rate is much higher.[1] Although these figures represent modest declines over the past decade in the population under supervision, by historical standards, current rates are still extraordinarily high. They are roughly seven times higher than at any other period in the United States between 1900 and 1975 (and probably since the genesis of the prison in the nineteenth century), and higher per capita than any other nation, including China and Russia.

The dramatic expansion of the criminal justice system, with its attendant collateral consequences, has left no major institution untouched. Perhaps nowhere, however, have effects of the system's growing reach been studied more than in the labor market. As is by now well known, contact with the criminal justice system is associated with significantly poorer employment outcomes. Arrest, conviction, and incarceration reduce the odds of searching for work (Sugie 2018; Smith and Broege 2019), and, contingent on a search, of getting a job (Apel and Sweeten 2010). When employed, individuals who have had criminal justice contact struggle with job stability, annually working many fewer weeks and earning significantly lower wages (Freeman 1991a; Grogger 1992; Waldfogel 1994; Nagin and Waldfogel 1995; Western 2006; for exceptions, see Kling 2002;

---

**Sandra Susan Smith** is professor and chair of the Department of Sociology at the University of California, Berkeley. **Jonathan Simon** is associate dean of the Jurisprudence and Social Policy Program at the Berkeley School of Law at the University of California.

© 2020 Russell Sage Foundation. Smith, Sandra Susan, and Jonathan Simon. 2020. "Exclusion and Extraction: Criminal Justice Contact and the Reallocation of Labor." *RSF: The Russell Sage Foundation Journal of the Social Sciences* 6(1): 1–27. DOI: 10.7758/RSF.2020.6.1.01. Direct correspondence to: Sandra Susan Smith at sandra_smith@berkeley.edu, Department of Sociology, University of California-Berkeley, 410 Barrows Hall, Berkeley, CA 94720; and Jonathan Simon at jssimon@berkeley.edu, Boalt Law School, University of California-Berkeley, 592 Simon Hall, Berkeley, CA 94720.

Open Access Policy: *RSF: The Russell Sage Foundation Journal of the Social Sciences* is an open access journal. This article is published under a Creative Commons Attribution-NonCommercial-NoDerivs 3.0 Unported License.

1. For instance, the incarceration rate for whites has hovered around 380 per hundred thousand, but that for Latinos is 966 and that for blacks is roughly 2,207 (Wagner 2012).

Pettit and Lyons 2007; Sabol 2007). This is in part because for many individuals, employment typically amounts to day labor with no real prospects of further employment, let alone benefits (Sugie 2018). Thus the criminal justice system not only affects aggregate labor market participation, employment rates, and employment stability, but also erodes wages and earnings while driving up rates of poverty among the employed (Western and Beckett 1999; Western 2002; Western and Pettit 2005).

We draw from the economic and sociological bodies of research to define what we mean by labor market institutions and then explain how criminal justice policies serve as such, focusing on the role these policies have played to both exclude justice-involved individuals from labor market opportunities, but also to extract labor from the same population, often under oppressive conditions. We end our discussion by asking whether the United States is unique in its use of the criminal justice system as a key labor market institution? Is this yet another case of American exceptionalism?

## WHAT ARE LABOR MARKET INSTITUTIONS?

Broadly defined, labor market institutions are organizations and policy interventions that have significant effects on short- and long-term wage and employment outcomes and on economic performance generally. According to Gordon Betcherman (2012, 2), "The laws, practices, policies, and conventions that fall under the umbrella of 'labor market institutions' determine *inter alia* [emphasis in the original] what kinds of employment contracts are permissible; set boundaries for wages and benefits, hours, and working conditions; define the rules for collective representation and bargaining; proscribe certain employment practices; and provide for social protection for workers" (see also Holmlund 2014).

Collectively, these institutional arrangements have a profound effect on individuals' well-being, shaping patterns of social and economic stability over the life course. They affect individuals' access to jobs and shape aggregate labor market participation, employment status, security, stability, and compensation, including wages and benefits. To the extent that labor market institutions affect training, the adoption of new technologies, the size and structure of firms, and the efficient reallocation of labor, they also affect productivity. And, insofar as labor market institutions contribute significantly to individuals' sense of economic security and stability, they also indirectly influence social cohesion, including individuals' sense of belonging to their community, their sense that equality of opportunities exists, and their civic engagement, among other things (Sampson 2011).

Employment protection laws, labor unions, minimum wage laws, and social insurance programs, most notably unemployment insurance, are the most often studied labor market institutions (Freeman 2007; DiPrete et al. 1997; DiPrete 2002; Gangl 2004a, 2004b, 2006; Cigagna and Sulis 2013; Jaumotte and Buitron 2015). *Employment protection laws* regulate the hiring and firing of workers as well as the terms of temporary and fixed-term employment contracts. They can make it very difficult for employers to dismiss workers, thus providing the foundation for greater job security and greater labor market stability over the life course (DiPrete 2002).[2] *Strong unions*, which negotiate with employers for better wages, benefits, and working conditions, can also push to secure stronger employment protections for their members as well. As a result, union workers earn higher wages than their non-union counterparts. Fur-

---

2. The relatively high labor market stability that workers in Germany experience is attributable in part to the strong protections that German workers receive from employment protection laws and from extremely high rates of collective bargaining coverage—upward of 80 to 90 percent (Freeman 2002; DiPrete 2002). According to Thomas DiPrete (2002), German workers' pronounced labor market stability is also attributable to their tight coupling of education and job training, between school and work. Such strong protections, however, also discourage employers from hiring for fear that they might be stuck with bad employees or unable to dismiss workers during periods of economic shocks.

ther, in industries and communities with higher union density, workers, no matter their union affiliation, earn higher wages, and levels of intergenerational economic mobility are much higher, even for children of non-union workers (Western and Rosenfeld 2011; Freeman et al. 2015). *The minimum wage* sets a floor under which most workers should not fall. Recent studies of local and state minimum wage increases reveal significant earnings increases for targeted and nontargeted workers, but a minimal effect on local unemployment rates (Allegretto et al. 2018); a growing body of evidence also indicates that higher minimum wage floors reduce racial gaps in earnings (Derenoncourt and Montialoux 2018). *Collective social insurance programs* can protect workers who experience triggering events, including job loss, from significant declines in living conditions (DiPrete 2002). For instance, through public pension systems for those retiring because of old age, unemployment insurance for those displaced through no fault of their own, and disability for those who fall ill, social insurance programs help manage the risks that families experiencing employment exits face by smoothing income streams during periods of income volatility (DiPrete et al. 1997, 323; Brady 2009; Gangl 2004b, 2006). In so doing, they help decouple workers' living conditions and life chances from labor market fluctuations (DiPrete 2002; Gangl 2004a, 2004b, 2006). Thus, labor market institutions shape economic performance and the flow of workers into and out of the labor market by altering incentives, as with minimum wage increases; by facilitating efficient bargaining, as with strong unions; and by increasing information and communication flows inside firms, which can facilitate better decision making by both managers and labor.

The massive expansion and reach of the penal state—the set of institutions that have control over the power to punish (Garland 2013), including but not limited to those that adjudicate guilt and punish wrongdoers (Beckett and Murakawa 2012)—has altered the incentives of labor market participants, employers, and the state. In so doing, it has also profoundly and negatively affected employment and wages (Western and Beckett 1999), disproportionately so for low-income communities of color. Indeed, with its expansion, the penal state has come to play an outsized role in the reproduction of inequalities, increasing racial and class disparities across a number of important indicators (Western and Beckett 1999). It has also helped obscure the lack of progress the country has made toward racial equality (Western and Beckett 1999). Further, to the extent that penal expansion has removed individuals at high risk of unemployment, underemployment, or pure joblessness from the labor force, it has also helped conceal just how much the U.S. economy struggles to provide adequate employment for all who want it, in absolute terms and relative to other advanced capitalist economies (Western and Beckett 1999). Indeed, with few exceptions, mainstream economic analysis continues to ignore the impact that high rates of criminal justice involvement has, not only on rates of employment, but also on labor-force participation. Thus, the criminal justice system legitimizes a political economic system that increasingly fails to provide opportunities to achieve social and economic stability, security, and inclusion.

Just as the penal state shapes the flow of individuals into and out of the labor market, so the labor market shapes the flow of individuals into and out of the criminal justice system—employment laws and labor market agents surveilling, identifying, and penalizing individuals for perceived or actual criminal behavior (Levin 2018; Simon 2007). Because expanding incarceration also creates employment for some potential workers, often racially and geographically quite different than the communities from which the incarcerated are taken, this complex interaction has arguably become one of the major anchors for the enduring racial stratification in the labor market (Harcourt 2011). Further, the criminal justice system does not limit its moonlighting to its role in shaping labor market flow. In a society that relies heavily on the penal state to address rather than resolve its most pressing and seemingly intractable problems of poverty and race, it comes as little surprise that the penal system also functions as quasi-welfare, education, and healthcare institutions, providing housing, education and training, and treatment for many among the poor who struggle with the effects of poverty and social exclusion.

## THE CRIMINAL JUSTICE SYSTEM AS A LABOR MARKET INSTITUTION

In a pivotal article, "How Unregulated Is the U.S. Labor Market? The Penal System as a Labor Market Institution," Bruce Western and Katherine Beckett (1999) note that by making significant investments in the expansion of the carceral system, the state through its criminal justice policy had a substantial, and dynamic effect on employment trends. In the short term, they argue, warehousing socially and economically marginalized, able-bodied men of working age artificially lowered conventional measures of unemployment by removing individuals at high risk of joblessness from the labor force. Indeed, independent of the actual volume of criminal activity, increases in unemployment rates tend to yield higher rates of incarceration (Yeager 1979; Chiricos and Delone 1992; D'Alessio and Stolzenberg 2002).[3] In this way, incarceration is for Western and Beckett a "hidden joblessness" of sorts.[4] They contend, however, that incarceration in the long term actually increases conventional unemployment rates by constructing serious barriers to employment for those returning home after time served. In the following section, we discuss the meaningful ways that policies related to criminal justice contact profoundly shape employment trends and economic performance. In some cases, exclusions and extractions appear coterminous, given that justice-involved individuals are directed away from promising employment opportunities while being coerced into taking some of the worst jobs at the low end of the labor market.

### Labor Market Exclusion and Marginalization After Criminal Justice Contact

Even before penal contact, justice-involved people, who are disproportionately poor, uneducated, and of color (Western 2006; Wacquant 2009), generally struggle with higher rates of unemployment, and when employed garner lower hourly wages, work relatively few weeks per year, and have annual earnings that place them below the poverty line (Western and Beckett 1999; Western, Kling, and Weiman 2001; Western 2002, 2006).[5] After penal contact, however, their employment prospects dim further still (Western 2006; Visher and Kachnowski 2007).

On criminal convictions, courts impose punishment with sentences of varying degrees of severity, but sometimes even before their cases are fully adjudicated, the convicted face another set of sanctions—the formal and informal collateral consequences of criminal justice contact, which combine to erect significant barriers to employment. Formal collateral consequences, most of which are stipulated in criminal employment law, restrict or limit the rights that individuals with criminal records have to participate in social, political, and economic domains of life. This includes but is not limited to voting, parenting, holding public office, serving on a jury, and working.[6]

---

3. This has been interpreted to mean that in anticipation of the social, political, and economic disorder that can emerge during periods of high unemployment, criminal justice authorities incarcerate individuals at risk for joblessness at higher rates than normal to head off potential troubles (D'Alessio and Stolzenberg 2002).

4. Many institutionalized populations—the incarcerated and military personnel—are not counted in official statistics on labor market participation, and thus incarcerated individuals are not counted in conventional measures of employment either. Because the justice-involved would likely experience unemployment, underemployment, or joblessness at much higher rates, counting them in official statistics would not only produce higher rates of unemployment, but also significantly lower average wages and earnings.

5. For this reason, many point to justice-involved job seekers' pre-offense, individual-level attributes to explain poor employment outcomes post-contact, in that the characteristics that predict criminal behavior also help explain poor employment outcomes, post-offense (Grogger 1995; Useem and Piehl 2008).

6. Some restrictions are deployed unambiguously as an additional form of punishment; voting bans are an example. The appeal of others is that they protect society; for example, persons with convictions for theft, including identity theft, embezzlement, and fraud, cannot be hired for positions requiring fiduciary responsibility.

In the realm of employment, federal and state governments have not only restricted individuals' access to government employment, they have also enacted numerous provisions against extending licenses to justice-involved people for government-regulated, private occupations, with distressing results (Dale 1976; May 1995; Olivares, Burton, and Cullen 1996; Petersilia 2003; Bushway and Sweeten 2007; Mills 2008). Nationwide, roughly eight hundred occupations are formally off limits to ex-felons because of such statutes (Bushway and Sweeten 2007). And, as Cody Warner, Joshua Kaiser, and Jason Houle (2020) report in this volume, the accumulation of these penalties, what they call "hidden sentences," has serious consequences for employment and earnings. Analyzing the National Longitudinal Survey of Youth 97 (NLSY97) and the National Inventory of the Collateral Consequence of Conviction datasets, the authors find that state-level hidden sentences have a significant and negative effect on the employment prospects of justice-involved young adults. Relative to individuals residing in states with low levels of hidden sentences, those living in states with high levels experience greater unemployment and, when employed, lower earnings. This was especially so for black formerly incarcerated individuals for whom employment and earnings penalties were largest.

Unfortunately, individuals' efforts to engage the courts around the barriers created by hidden sentences also contribute to rupturing their connection to the formal labor market. In this volume, Michele Cadigan and Gabriela Kirk (2020) highlight the hurdles that individuals face when attempting to resolve issues relating to court-ordered debt. Drawing from hours of observations of court hearings in Illinois and Washington State, as well as in-depth interviews with residents of those states who had been sentenced to pay court-ordered monetary sanctions, Cadigan and Kirk deftly describe the bureaucratic procedural pressure points that individuals must negotiate to successfully navigate encounters with the courts and to keep their jobs. Not surprisingly, the barriers created by race, class, and gender disadvantaged many, and in the process severed all the more profoundly individuals' ties to the formal labor market.

Although studied less often, informal collateral consequences, including the loss of employment opportunities resulting from employers' efforts to avoid legal liabilities associated with criminal records, can also have pernicious effects, magnifying the social, political, psychological, and economic costs of criminal justice contact. As extensions of punishments meted out by the courts, both formal and informal collateral consequences raise serious concerns insofar as they indicate a lack of consideration made for proportionality, parsimony, citizenship, and social inclusion, ideals for how justice in any context should be meted out (Travis, Western, and Redburne 2014).

## Civil Death: State and Federal Restrictions on Employment

Federal and state governments have not only restricted access to government employment for individuals with criminal records, but also enacted numerous provisions against extending licenses to justice-involved people for government-regulated, private occupations (Dale 1976; May 1995; Olivares, Burton, and Cullen 1996; Petersilia 2003; Bushway and Sweeten 2007; Mills 2008). For instance, in New York, ex-felons are restricted from owning barber shops, distributing commercial feed, and acting as emergency medical technicians (Uggen et al. 2006). In Florida, speech–language pathology and cosmetology are off limits. According to Kathleen Olivares, Velmer Burton Jr., and Francis Cullen (1996), six states have permanently denied access to public employment—Alabama, Delaware, Iowa, Mississippi, Rhode Island, and South Carolina. For the remaining states, restrictions in access vary in length and by given contingencies. For instance, in ten states, public sector employers have discretion to hire justice-involved individuals; in twelve states, hiring is contingent on whether the conviction is occupation-related; and in seventeen states, individuals are able to access public employment once they have completed their sentences.

Perhaps more profoundly damaging the employment prospects of the justice-involved are the numerous provisions against extending licenses to justice-involved people for government-regulated private occupations.

Trade or occupational licenses represent the formal permission that a government body gives to individuals, which allow them to engage in activities, including professional, skilled, or semi- and unskilled work, that would otherwise be off limits if not for the state's permission (Dale 1976; Rodriguez and Avery 2016). The number of occupations requiring licenses has grown significantly over the past half century, presumably for public protection. According to Morris Kleiner (2015), fewer than 5 percent of workers in the United States required state permission to work in their chosen profession seventy years ago, but today more than one in four workers must have a license to perform their occupational duties (see also Kleiner and Krueger 2010). Rates vary by state, however, the lowest share (12.4 percent) is in South Carolina and the highest (fully 33 percent) is in Iowa (Kleiner 2015).

Although the statutory requirements for obtaining occupational licenses vary widely by state and across occupations, all states have numerous provisions that effectively exclude the justice-involved from engaging in various forms of employment. Indeed, the American Bar Association's (ABA) inventory of penalties documents more than twenty-seven thousand state occupational licensing restrictions against individuals with a criminal record. These restrictions without question significantly reduce the quantity and quality of employment available to those with criminal records (Dale 1976; May 1995; Rodriguez and Avery 2016), impacts varying by race and ethnicity (Rodriguez and Avery 2016). According to one study, for instance, occupational restrictions are estimated to reduce by almost three million the number of people employed across the nation (Kleiner, Humphris, and Koumenta 2011; Kleiner 2015; Blair and Chung 2018). This would seem to have clear implications for the justice-involved.

Two types of requirements in occupational licensing statutes create the greatest barriers to obtaining licenses for the justice-involved (Dale 1976; May 1995; Rodriguez and Avery 2016). The first are blanket bans, which automatically disqualify individuals with certain records. According to the ABA Inventory, individuals found guilty of any felony face more than twelve thousand restrictions in occupational, professional, and business licenses categories; those with any type of misdemeanor face more than six thousand such restrictions. Further, permanent, or lifetime, disqualifications number more than nineteen thousand; mandatory disqualifications, for which licensing agencies have no choice but to deny a license, total more than eleven thousand (Rodriguez and Avery 2016). Statutes requiring good moral character and the like also erect significant barriers to justice-involved individuals' ability to get occupational licenses and find employment. Embedded in many licensing laws is a character component (May 1995). As highlighted in the literature, however, requiring *good moral character* raises at least two issues. The term is itself vague and subjective, leaving decisions about who qualifies as having such character to the discretion of licensing agencies. Also, having been convicted of a crime can easily be marshaled as evidence that one lacks good moral character, an argument with which both the courts and licensing agencies have generally agreed (May 1995). Statutes that require a "good reputation," "reputable character," or "honest and trustworthy character" are less demanding insofar as they allow for the possibility of rehabilitation and redemption. The plethora of vague statutory terms (such as good moral character) and widely varying requirements and procedures, both across states and within occupations, creates a lack of transparency and predictability in licensing systems, magnifying the burdens that the justice-involved face as they undergo the process to become licensed and to find work (Rodriguez and Avery 2016). In terms of restricting licensing boards' ability to take criminal records into consideration, a comprehensive evaluation of states' licensing laws revealed generally poor standards across the board (Rodriguez and Avery 2016).

Although it remains unclear what impact occupational licensing restrictions, and the failure of many states to check them, have had on employment, evidence indicates that the effects are significant. In Florida, for instance, 40 percent of jobs have been subject to state-mandated criminal background checks or employment restrictions based on having a criminal record (Mills 2008). Even for defendants, legal stigma forecloses access to some jobs while their cases remain open, and thus they are also vulnerable to sanction even before their cases are adjudicated and even if their cases are eventually dismissed (Kohler-Hausmann 2013).

## The Impact of Legal Liabilities on Employers' Hiring and Retention Practices

Although most attention on the collateral consequences of criminal justice involvement focus on its formal aspects, the result of statutory restrictions enforced by state or public actors, Benjamin Levin (2018) makes a compelling argument for researchers' focused attention on the informal, where nonstatutory legal frameworks shape the actions and decision making of private actors, namely, private employers. Specifically, Levin argues that private employers have also become key players in extending the punishments meted out to the justice-involved. The reason is simple. Because some of the liability they face is tied to their employees' criminal justice involvement, the legal system incentivizes employers to both surveil and sanction their employees' behavior, both on and off the job. In effect, they become agents of criminal justice.

The primary routes through which the penal system does so are tort doctrines of negligent hiring and retention (Glynn 1998; Holzer 1996; Holzer et al. 2001; Levin 2018). These doctrines link employers' liability to employees' identities and histories of criminal justice involvement, making employers responsible for employees' misconduct wherever this misconduct occurs. As examples, employers can be held liable if, without investigating potential red flags, they hire someone who then goes on to cause harm in the workplace. Employers can be held responsible for negligent retention if they retain employees with reputations for misconduct that could put others in harm's way, even if patterns of misconduct occur outside the employment context and regardless of whether the employer has acted to prevent employees' misconduct on the job.

Such liabilities create strong incentives for employers to discover and weed out applicants with criminal records. According to Ben Goldberg (2016), 72 percent of companies perform background checks on every new employee; among these, 82 percent screen potential employees for their criminal histories. They do so in good part to avoid claims of negligent hiring, but also to avoid other threats to the workplace.[7] But these liabilities also incentivize employers to monitor and sanction, where necessary, the behaviors of current employees, both on and off the job, for signs of misconduct. Levin points to employee conduct policies that ban criminal conduct that occurs off duty and away from the workplace, which, along with or instead of state sanction, privately punishes individuals. Both sets of actions are attempts to safeguard against being held legally responsible for their employees' actions. To do otherwise could be quite costly. Levin points to a 2001 study revealing that the overwhelming majority of employers lose negligent hiring cases that go to trial, settlements averaging more than $1.5 million. Although it is unclear just how much such doctrines indirectly depress the employment opportunities available to the justice-involved by disincentivizing employers to hire and retain justice-involved individuals, one doubts that their effects are negligible.

## Employers' (and Job Contacts') Aversion to Justice-Involved Individuals

Employers do not want to hire individuals with criminal records. In absolute terms, employer surveys indicate that more than 40 percent would not knowingly hire them, and fewer than 12 percent report that they would definitely hire them (Holzer 1996; Holzer et al. 2007). These figures are likely overestimates of employers' willingness, however. Devah Pager and Lincoln Quillian (2005) report that many employers who say that they are willing to hire individuals

---

7. The use of criminal background checks has skyrocketed, despite the significant flaws associated with the system, including inaccurate criminal records data that would almost certainly disqualify applicants who might otherwise be great prospects (Duane, Reimal, and Lynch 2017).

with criminal records are no more likely to do so than those who report being unwilling.[8]

In relative terms, employers much prefer applicants without criminal records to those who have had criminal justice contact (Schwartz and Skolnick 1964; Boshier and Johnson 1974; Pager 2003). Two studies are worth highlighting. One, by Richard Schwartz and Jerome Skolnick in 1964, revealed that any type of criminal justice contact would reduce the odds of employer interest in hiring lesser-skilled workers. The authors designed a field experiment in which one hundred employers were randomly assigned to one of four treatments: an application from someone with no criminal record, an arrest for assault with acquittal and letter from judge, an arrest for assault and acquittal without a letter, and an arrest and conviction for assault. All else about applicants' details were the same. Rates of positive responses by employers varied substantially by level of criminal justice contact. Thirty-six percent of employers who received applications indicating no criminal record responded positively, relative to 24 percent of employers who received applications indicating acquittal with a letter, 12 percent who received applications indicating acquittal without a letter, and 4 percent who received applications from those convicted. Thus, even when criminal justice contact did not result in conviction, Schwartz and Skolnick's research indicates that it would significantly diminish individuals' employment prospects.

Devah Pager's (2003) field study has advanced our understanding of the effect of the criminal record on employment outcomes by highlighting how felony conviction status and race affected employer callback rates. She discovered that whites without a criminal record were twice as likely to receive a callback than equally qualified whites with a felony conviction. Among blacks, the ratio was worse, at 3:1. Further, blacks *without a felony conviction* appeared no more likely than whites *with a conviction* to get a positive response. Regardless of race, then, having a criminal record has a substantial and negative effect on making it through the hiring process, but those odds are far worse for blacks than for their white justice-involved counterparts (see also Pager, Western, and Sugie 2009; Pager, Western, and Bonikowski 2009).[9] As discussed earlier, some of employers' reluctance to hire can be attributed to fears of being found liable for negligent hiring, but employers are also clearly driven by a general distrust of a pool of applicants who have essentially been certified untrustworthy by the penal system (Schwartz and Skolnick 1964; Boshier and Johnson 1974; Holzer et al. 2007; Ispa-Landa and Loeffler 2016; but see Atkin and Armstrong 2013), a negative effect amplified by the race of justice-involved individuals (Pager 2003, 2007). Most employers generally perceive the justice-involved to be too risky to trust with business operation and assets (Schwartz and Skolnick 1964; Boshier and Johnson 1974; Pager 2003; Pager and Quillian 2005; Holzer et al. 2007).

Referrals from trusted individuals, such as current employees, can go far in convincing employers to hire the justice-involved (Fahey et al. 2006), but it is unclear under what circumstances current employees would act in this capacity for job seekers tainted by a criminal record. After all, the stigma that informs employers' perceptions of former prisoners likely also shapes the way potential job contacts perceive them. Indeed, public opinion about ex-offenders tends to be quite negative. A number of older studies indicate that because most contacts would be uncomfortable having formerly incarcerated individuals as coworkers, fearing

---

8. Many, however, is not all. For instance, in industries—such as manufacturing—where workers have little contact with customers, employers express a greater willingness to hire them. During tight labor markets, too, employers' willingness to hire increases modestly, as evidenced by the greater demand during such times for these job seekers (Holzer et al. 2001, 2007). Indeed, recent reports indicate that, in the expanding markets and low unemployment of the current labor market, and given public discussion about the need to reduce the barriers to employment that individuals with criminal records have (Garsd 2019), employer views about hiring justice-involved individuals might be changing, to the benefit of those with records.

9. Here again, exceptions exist because some employers prefer to hire recently released former prisoners because they perceive them as more motivated, hard working, and willing to perform dirty tasks (Pager 2003).

their own safety and that of their coworkers, they would also be unwilling to help them during the hiring process (Conklin 1975; Kutchinsky 1968; Simmons 1965). This is because diverse populations see offenders as outsiders, low-class, unattractive and prone to violence (Reed and Reed 1973; Roberts 1992, 1997; Saladin et al. 1988; Shoemaker and South 1978; Simmons 1965). They also assume that those who have been convicted of crime have several priors and are quite likely to commit new crimes in the future (Roberts 1997). In the minds of most, past is prologue.

To varying degrees, then, concerns about former prisoners' trustworthiness and fears about their risk of reoffending would likely animate the thoughts of many potential job contacts and affect their decisions to act as personal intermediaries. After all, individuals' perceptions of the justice-involved also affect their behaviors toward them. In general, although flexible and modifiable (Cullen et al. 1990; Flanagan and Caufield 1984; Sandys and McGarrell 1995), the American public's attitudes about crime and punishment tend toward punitiveness. Despite some support for rehabilitative measures, including counseling and educational and vocational training programs for individuals with some types of offenses, the last four decades have been characterized by a general tenor of harshness and a clear focus on retribution, constant surveillance, and incapacitation (Garland 2001; McCorkle 1993; Simon 2014). Still, levels of support for such punitive criminal justice policies and practices vary, and variations have been linked to cultural frames about punishment, deterrence, rehabilitation, and racial injustice (Bobo and Johnson 2004; Bobo and Thompson 2006; Cullen et al. 1990; McCorkle 1993).

But cultural frames—the meanings that we attribute to events or situations—do more than shape support for criminal justice policies. They also shape whether or to what extent potential job contacts help formerly incarcerated job seekers to find work. Drawing from in-depth interviews with 126 racially and ethnically diverse jobholders at one large, public sector employer, Sandra Smith (2018) shows that jobholders' willingness to assist depended in good part on whether they embraced one of two cultural frames—the second chance frame and the signaling change frame. Jobholders who argued that all individuals were capable of change and entitled to more chances to prove themselves were strongly inclined to help the formerly incarcerated to find work. Jobholders who tended to be noncommittal either referenced the nature of offenses for which job seekers were punished—a proxy for their ability to change—or evidence that job seekers had changed—a proxy for former prisoners' commitment to do better. Without strong evidence that job seekers had been rehabilitated and become oriented more toward the job market, these jobholders were too uncomfortable to offer much in the form of job-matching assistance. Racial and ethnic background also informed the extent, nature, and quality of jobholders' experiences with the formerly incarcerated and shaped which frame or set of frames jobholders deployed when considering whether they might provide help with job search.

The findings reported in Smith (2018) suggest that, as with employers, formerly incarcerated individuals' friends, relatives, and acquaintances also want assurances that they have changed, that they are committed to work in the formal wage economy, and that they are no more likely than those without criminal records to cause harm to the physical, financial, or reputational well-being of the workplace.[10] Without these assurances, potential job contacts would be far less open to offer help, even when they are able to do so. Such assurances,

---

10. Alfred Blumstein and Kiminori Nakamura (2009) estimate a "point of redemption" and find that for individuals with nonviolent offenses, it takes roughly 4.8 years without a new arrest to achieve a risk of re-arrest that is comparable to, or lower than that for, an individual of the same age in the general population; for individuals with violent offenses, eight years clean achieves a risk similar to that of the generation population (see also Bushway, Nieuwbeerta, and Blokland 2011). Few employers know about these points of redemption, however, and many laypeople would struggle to provide job-matching assistance to the justice-involved without evidence that an individual's risk of reoffending had declined significantly (Smith 2018).

however, are difficult to come by. Potential job contacts do not often know enough about job seekers to make informed decisions about who is work-ready and who, for whatever reasons, might not yet be there, increasing the odds of facilitating poor employment matches.

Community corrections could offer a remedy for the asymmetric information problem faced by the friends, relatives, and acquaintances. Potential job contacts need strong and effective signals to differentiate between those who are and are not work-ready; additionally, through transitional employment-based reentry programs, members of probation and parole departments can be trained to provide the institutional supports needed for differentiation to happen. The point of a signaling program is not to effect desistance but to identify those who are likely to be good bets for desistance and employment stability. As Shawn Bushway and Robert Apel (2012) contend, even if such programs do not have a causal impact on employment and recidivism, because those who choose to participate and complete such programs are likely distinct from those who do not, the programs can play an important role in the reentry process by signaling who is work-ready and who is not. In the process, they provide employers and potential job contacts with the information they need to make hiring and job-matching assistance decisions, respectively.

To be an effective signal of change and work-readiness, however, signaling programs would have to have at least three key features. First, they would have to be voluntary, because interested parties would have difficulty assessing change and work-readiness among those coerced into participation. Second, because work program requirements are likely more costly to individuals who are not yet ready to give up criminal offending or to earn income legitimately, opportunity costs must be high enough to weed out those who are not yet ready but not so high as to discourage participation among those who are truly committed. Third, participants must actively participate and successfully complete the program. According to Bushway and Apel (2012, 33), these "explicit mechanisms . . . will allow the 20% to 30% of returning prisoners who have desisted from crime to self-identify to employers or other decision makers[potential job contacts] as soon as they step beyond the prison walls, or very shortly after release from prison." After voluntary enrollment, active participation, and successful completion, program graduates can receive a certificate of completion—perhaps offered at a formal graduation that family members and friends can attend—that they can then share not only with employers but also with potential job contacts from their personal networks. Further, not only should employers be encouraged to hire those certified as work-ready, as is already done in many probation and parole departments across the country, community members should be encouraged to help as well, providing whatever assistance they can, including word of mouth, to help graduates to find work.

## Consequences for Justice-Involved Individuals' Employment and Wages

In part because of the legal and social barriers formerly incarcerated individuals face, their probability of being employed is reduced significantly (Freeman 1991a, 1991b; Waldfogel 1994; Western 2006), and they work many fewer weeks per year (Freeman 1991a, 1991b). Indeed, almost two-thirds remain without work one year after release (Travis 2002; Finlay 2008). It is not only the formerly incarcerated, however, who have diminishing employment prospects. Several studies also link arrest, conviction, and probation to employment problems as well. For instance, using data from a random sample of Philadelphia residents, Terrence Thornberry and R.L. Christenson (1984) sought to test the hypothesis that crime and the factors presumed to cause it (that is, unemployment) are actually instead mutually reinforcing. The evidence supported their hypothesis. Not only did unemployment appear to increase the probability of getting arrested, but having been arrested also increased the probability of being unemployed. Grogger's 1992 study had two objectives—to determine the effect that arrest had on employment and to ascertain the extent to which black-white gaps in employment could be explained by racial differences in their rates of arrest. Analyzing two datasets—merged arrest and employment records of men arrested in California and the 1980 wave of the National Longitudinal Survey Youth Cohort—Grogger finds that arrest did reduce employment prospects. Further, racial differences in arrest rates also helped explain why blacks had lower rates of employment relative to whites. In a more recent study, Bushway (1998) analyzes the National Youth Survey data and found that first-time arrest had a strong and negative effect on employment stability, reducing by almost eleven weeks the amount of time an individual spent at their main job.

Several studies have also found a causal link between conviction and employment problems. Researchers have found that having a conviction can reduce the probability of employment by between 2 and 6 percentage points (Freeman 1991b; Waldfogel 1994). It can also negatively affect employment stability. For instance, Daniel Nagin and Joel Waldfogel (1995) examine the effect of conviction on the number of weeks and found that conviction added two additional weeks of unemployment.

Research also indicates that probation also negatively affects employment, reducing the probability of employment by up to 10 percentage points (Freeman 1991a; Waldfogel 1994). In this volume, Josh Seim and David Harding (2020) examine the effect of parole, not probation, on employment. Specifically, they investigate whether parole supervision increases the odds of employment and, importantly, whether employment while on parole reduces the odds of recidivism. Analyzing administrative data from the Michigan Department of Corrections matched with data on employment and earnings from Michigan's Unemployment Insurance Agency, Seim and Harding find that though parole supervision did increase the odds of employment, parole employment did not reduce the likelihood that individuals would recidivate, as has been hypothesized. That supervised parolees did not desist calls into question arguments that parole-related employment acts as a protective factor against future criminal involvement.

Perhaps, instead, the issue with parole-related employment is one of job quality. Even when employed, the quality of jobs that are available to the justice-involved is generally poor (for a general discussion of bad jobs, see Kalleberg, Reskin, and Hudson 2011). Despite their general desire to work in jobs with regular hours, a guaranteed income, and benefits (Ispa-Landa and Loeffler 2016, 399; Sugie 2018; Kalleberg, Reskin, and Hudson 2011), the justice-involved are often relegated to informal, temporary, and part-time work (Ispa-Landa and Loeffler 2016). According to Christy Visher and Vera Kachnowski (2007), of the minority of former prisoners from Illinois employed within eight months of release, the overwhelming majority worked in construction, manual labor, and maintenance—among the few industries still generally open to hiring them—and earned between $750 and $900 per month; only among childless, single adults making the upper range would these earnings break the poverty threshold (see also Western 2002, 2006; Western and Pettit 2005).

In this volume, Joe LaBriola (2020) explores the issue of post-prison employment quality and its effects on recidivism, using data on the employment outcomes of all prisoners paroled in Michigan in 2003. LaBriola finds that job quality matters. Parolees who found work in high-quality industries—those with above average earnings, job tenure, firm-level earnings, and state-level union coverage—were six times less likely to recidivate than parolees who found work in low-quality industries—industries below average on these four indicators. Further, those in low-quality industries were no more likely to desist than unemployed parolees. Insofar as low-income people of color are more likely to reside in and return to neighborhoods and communities where relatively few job opportunities exist, much less "good jobs," their probability of employment, regardless of penal disposition, will be further compromised and the likelihood of recidivism will be greater (Sabol 2007; Wang, Mears, and Bales 2010; Bellair and Kowalski 2011).

## Reform Efforts

Reform efforts are under way, and they take many forms. According to the Institute for Justice, since 2015, eighteen states have reformed their occupational licensing laws to make it easier for ex-offenders to find work in state-licensed fields. Reforms include new rules preventing licensing boards from blanket bans (ten states), instituting new reporting requirements (five states), prohibiting the use of vague language related to moral character (four states), and allowing individuals to petition licensing boards at any time to determine whether their record will disqualify them from being licensed (eight states).[11]

Further, to remove some of the barriers to employment that the justice-involved face, more than 150 cities and counties, thirty-four states, and the District of Columbia have also adopted ban-the-box (BtB) policies, a part of a larger fair chance employment initiative. These policies, which began appearing in the mid-2000s, are intended to improve employment outcomes of the justice-involved by preventing employers from taking criminal records into consideration until the latter stages of the hiring process (Doleac and Hansen 2016; Rodriguez and Avery 2016; Vuolo et al. 2017). For instance, California's new statewide policy, effective January 2018, prohibits employers from inquiring about arrest or conviction records until after a conditional job offer is made. Thus, employers, public and private, are disallowed asking whether applicants have a criminal record on applications or during interviews; nor are they allowed to run a criminal background check until after a conditional offer is made. With criminal records in hand, employers cannot discriminate at all about arrests that did not lead to convictions, participation in diversion or deferral of judgment programs, or convictions older than seven years (a few exceptions aside). If, after background checks, employers decide against completing the hiring process, they must provide the applicant with a copy of the background check, explain how the conviction informed the hiring decision, and provide the applicant with an opportunity to respond.

To date, research on the effectiveness of such policies is limited. What does exist suggests that such policies do affect employers' behavior, increasing the callback rates and hiring for people with criminal records (Atkinson and Lockwood 2014; Agan and Starr 2016; Berracasa et al. 2016; Shoag and Veuger 2016). However, whether BtB works appears contingent on the race of the applicants and the sector of employment in question. For instance, in the private sector, BtB policies actually reduce the likelihood that justice-involved applicants who are black and Latino receive callbacks or are offered jobs (Agan and Starr 2016; Doleac and Hansen 2016). Consistent with prior research (Holzer, Raphael, and Stoll 2001), this finding suggests that when a person's criminal history is unavailable, employers in the private sector engage in statistical discrimination.[12] In the public sector, however, BtB policies increase the likelihood that formerly incarcerated individuals will receive callbacks and job offers (Craigie 2017). Still, the effects of BtB policies are relatively small, and it is therefore not clear how much such policies can improve the labor market outcomes of justice-involved job seekers. Significant limitations in the scope and reach of such policies, the general lack of awareness that the justice-involved have about

---

11. Institute for Justice, "State Occupational Licensing Reforms for Workers with Criminal Records," https://ij.org/activism/legislation/state-occupational-licensing-reforms-for-people-with-criminal-records (accessed September 23, 2019).

12. Harry Holzer, Steven Raphael, and Michael Stoll (2001) report that, ironically, when employers did conduct criminal background checks, black applicants had a higher likelihood of being offered employment because many fewer had criminal records than employers assumed. When employers did not check, they would assume that black applicants likely had criminal records and so would be less likely to offer them employment. Employers' willingness to hire ex-offenders affected the size of the gap. Among employers willing to hire ex-offenders, those who conducted criminal background checks were only 4.8 percentage points more likely than employers who did not to have recently hired a black applicant. Among employers who are unwilling to hire ex-offenders, the gap is larger. Those who run background checks were 10.7 percentage points more likely to have recently hired a black applicant than employers who did not check. In general, Holzer and colleagues find this pattern of decision making for stigmatized workers—welfare recipients, high school noncompleters, workers with spotty work histories, and the long-term unemployed.

such policies, and the lack of accountability systems to ensure employers' compliance, will almost certainly limit their effectiveness.

The reform of laws that allow individuals to seal or expunge their criminal records (expungement) is another pathway by which some have sought to block the devastating effects of formal and informal collateral consequences. Expungement limits public access to arrest and conviction records, thus allowing the justice-involved to pursue opportunities, including employment and housing, that might otherwise be off limits. Today, the overwhelming majority of states have procedures in place to permit sealing or expunging criminal records. Typically, one must petition the court, often after a waiting period, and judges are empowered to decide, with determinations based on the type, severity, or number of convictions on an individuals' record. Expungements, however, can also be automatic or, on request, mandatory.

In an era of mass criminalization and easy public access to those records, various efforts are afoot to deploy expungement as a weapon against the collateral consequences of criminal records (Roberts 2015). Perhaps pushed by advocacy organizations and think tanks, numerous states have considered either adopting new expungement laws or expanding those they already have. In 2018 alone, twenty states reformed their expungement laws to further limit public access to criminal records. Pennsylvania was one, becoming the first state to automatically expunge criminal convictions of minor, nonviolent misdemeanors after ten years of desistance (Prescott and Starr 2019). Multiple efforts are under way, however, to expand the number of expunged cases. As Jenny Roberts (2015) explains, public defenders, civil legal aid offices, and reentry clinics are increasingly aiding clients through the expungement process, and law school training is more likely now to include modules on expungement.

Increasingly, too, researchers are studying how sealing and expungement affects individuals' outcomes. Early evidence indicates that expungement makes a significant difference, offering the justice-involved a second (or first) chance in a social, political, and economic landscape that is otherwise extremely difficult to navigate. In a compelling new study, for instance, J. J. Prescott and Sonja Starr (2019) study the effects of expungement laws on rates of recidivism and employment outcomes. They combined criminal records data from the Michigan State Police—which included individuals whose criminal records had been set aside because of expungement as well as the criminal history records for similarly situated individuals whose convictions were not set aside—with detailed wage and employment data from the state's unemployment insurance program for the same individuals. Although few who were eligible applied for expungement (just 6.5 percent), among those who did, set-aside crime rates were comparable to that of the general population. Their rates of recidivism were so low that they could not be considered a public safety threat. In addition, set-asides were more likely to be employed and had better jobs than their counterparts whose records had not been expunged (Prescott and Starr 2019).

Still, in an era when criminal records are readily available and at low cost online, expungement laws will likely be of limited utility, unless a number of other steps are taken. According to Roberts (2015), to maximize the effectiveness of expungement laws, we must also guarantee the accuracy of criminal records, restrict how decision makers can use criminal records, and effectively regulate companies that profit from providing access to such records.

Policy interventions that seek to improve the employment prospects of the justice-involved should also shape how well they can support their families. In this volume, Allison Dwyer Emory and her colleagues (2020) draw from both the Fragile Families Study data and a dataset of state employment protection laws to examine the effect of incarceration on noncustodial fathers' ability to contribute formally and informally to their children's household economy. As might be expected, the authors find that incarceration reduces these odds, but they also report that state policies implemented to protect the justice-involved from employment discrimination moderated these effects in noteworthy but complicated ways.

Other policy interventions with greater

reach and more teeth will be needed to fundamentally improve the employment prospects of the justice-involved. The Legal Action Center advocates taking four steps to fully embrace fair chance hiring. These include eliminating unreasonable legal restrictions on hiring, improving background checking systems and processes, providing strong antidiscrimination protections for workers with criminal records, and limiting negligent hiring liability for employers who follow fair hiring practices.[13] Anything short of these combined steps will not likely make a huge difference in the employment chances of the justice-involved.

Further, other labor market institutions might militate against incarceration for individuals otherwise at high risk of criminal justice contact. In this volume, Bryan Sykes and Amy Bailey (2020) examine how military employment affected the risk of confinement for black and white men. They show that among black, male, high school dropouts, veterans' status was a protective factor against contact with the criminal justice system. Black veterans without a high school diploma were significantly less likely than their nonveteran counterparts to experience incarceration. The authors point to evidence of "institutional castling," where shifts in the prominence of competing institutions—the military and the criminal justice system—affected the underlying risk of military enlistment and penal confinement for different demographic groups. This important work highlights the role that various institutions have played, independently and in concert, in profoundly shaping the social and economic fortunes of society's most vulnerable.

**Implications for Job Search**

Given the number and nature of the demand-side constraints described, job search costs are unquestionably higher for justice-involved job seekers (McCall 1970). They would have to expend more effort to find work than those who have not had criminal justice contact, and much more effort for "good" jobs. They know this. The majority seem well aware that penal contact substantially diminishes the quantity and quality of employment opportunities, and so they expect that job-finding will be very difficult (Sullivan 1989; Harding 2003; Visher and Kachnowski 2007; Goffman 2009). In general, such perceptions among job seekers are associated with reduced search effort and withdrawal from search entirely (Kanfer, Wanberg, and Kantrowitz 2001); in this way, the justice-involved are no different.

A growing body of research suggests that because of discouragement borne from the anticipation of stigma, and because of frustration borne from early job search failures, many do not put in the amount of effort required to find a job (Apel and Sweeten 2010; Sugie 2018). Using the NLSY97, for instance, Robert Apel and Gary Sweeten (2010) investigated the factors that lay behind incarceration's apparent effect on employment outcomes, contrasting the experiences of convicted young men who had been incarcerated with convicted young men who had not. They showed that formerly incarcerated young men were less likely to be employed in good part because they were less likely than their nonincarcerated counterparts to search for work. For Apel and Sweeten, this detachment from the labor market contributed significantly to the lower wages that formerly incarcerated individuals earned when employed. Time without employment further eroded the skills, education, and training they brought to the labor market, which negatively affected wage outcomes as well. More recently, Naomi Sugie (2018) reports that immediately after release from prison, the formerly incarcerated in her sample overwhelmingly searched for work, but within one month their search efforts plummeted, likely also the result of frustration and discouragement (see also Visher and O'Connell 2012).[14]

Finally, to investigate whether and how criminal justice contact—arrest, conviction,

---

13. Legal Action Center, "Beyond 'Ban the Box': Four Steps to Build on Fair Chance Hiring," https://lac.org/beyond-ban-the-box-four-steps-to-build-on-fair-chance-hiring (accessed September 23, 2019).

14. It is unclear, however, whether or to what extent this pattern of job search—high levels of search intensity at the early stages of search followed by a significant curtailment of search activity—is unique to formerly incarcerated individuals. Examining the job-search strategies of unemployed, white-collar job seekers, Ofer Sharone

and incarceration—altered search patterns and, through search, affected search success, Sandra Smith and Nora Broege (2019) analyze the 2001–2011 panels of the 1997 cohort of the National Longitudinal Survey of Youth (NLSY97). Focusing solely on men, who still make up the vast majority of those who have had penal contact, they examine whether and how young, justice-involved blacks, Latinos, and whites searched for work. In the process, the authors implicate both nonsearch engagement and the use of ineffective search methods in job seekers' relative lack of success in finding jobs. After penal contact, individuals were less likely to search for work; for whatever reasons, they appeared to detach from labor-force participation. Those who did search tended to use fewer methods of job search and abandoned search methods that were more effective and efficient at producing jobs, such as direct application.[15] This resulted in less successful job search episodes and more frequent unemployment. Smith and Broege also show that whether and how individuals searched mattered not only for former prisoners, but also for arrestees and nonincarcerated convicts. For the full sample, all three penal dispositions showed patterns of search that differed from the search efforts observed before contact with the criminal justice system. Further, these changes in job search patterns contributed significantly to justice-involved individuals' lower odds of search success, especially for blacks. Thus, although we continue to study the proportion of justice-involved individuals who continue to search for work, more research needs to be done to better understand the process by which some individuals opt out of labor-force participation altogether or alter their search patterns to the point of ineffectiveness.

## EXTRACTING AND EXPLOITING LABOR AFTER CRIMINAL JUSTICE CONTACT

Over the past three decades, the bulk of research at the intersection of labor market outcomes and criminal justice contact has focused on how such contact contributes to individuals' exclusion and marginalization from labor market opportunities, as well as the short- and long-term consequences borne from such exclusions. Historically speaking, however, labor extraction and exploitation after contact have been the rule, servicing not only the needs of political and ideological forces (Garland 1990), but also of economic production (Rusche and Kirschheimer 2009), producing not only goods but also potentially more tractable, docile, and useful workers (Foucault 1977; Melossi and Pavarini 2018). Early criminologists and religious promoters of improving the habits of the poor perceived idleness as the major cause of criminality in the poor and advocated hard physical labor and tight regulation on the leisure lives of the poor to stem the problem (Melossi and Pavarini 2018, 121). From its origins in the nineteenth century (McLennan 2008), U.S. prisons across the country sought to defray a significant portion of the total costs of imprisonment through forced extraction of labor from prisoners. In some instances, the prisoners were contracted out to private employers; in others, prison officials supervised the labor and sold the output. Outside the South, the era of profitable labor began to decline in the late nineteenth century as unions and private competitors won legislation limiting the market for prison-made goods. In the South, however, the end of slavery led to the widespread adoption of the convict lease system in which prisoners, essentially only black prisoners, were leased out to private contractors for ruthless exploitation (Lichtenstein 1996; Oshinsky 1996). Even after the convict lease system ended at the turn to the twentieth century, many southern and western states retained an extensive focus on agricultural labor. It was not until the federal courts began to intervene against the harsh conditions in the 1970s that this changed in meaningful ways (Feeley and Rubin 1998). As mass imprisonment took off at

---

(2013) finds a similar pattern in the United States (but not Israel, his other site of study) and linked this to the messages job seekers received in the labor market institutions in which they were embedded.

15. Post-contact, job seekers are generally less inclined to apply directly to employers, to go-it-alone, despite greater odds of search success when using this method. In prior work, David Harding (2003) suggests that

the end of the twentieth century, labor in most prisons was limited to service functions for the prison itself and deemphasized as a way of either paying costs or "training" prisoners. However, as Eric Hatton (2018) cogently argues, most prisoners in most states are still working and the labor they perform is essentially forced labor.

Insofar as punishment, or the threat of it, has compelled individuals to work specifically in service of economic production, the criminal justice system acts as a labor market institution, facilitating the reallocation of labor and doing so on terms quite favorable to economic and political elites. In the following section, we discuss efforts to compel or coerce labor from the justice-involved, in and outside the prison context, where work, often uncompensated or poorly compensated, is used as punishment or as the threat of punishment.

**Prison Labor**
Georg Rusche and Otto Kirschheimer (2009) were perhaps the first to put forward a clearly articulated thesis, neo-Marxist in nature, that the criminal justice system operated as a labor market institution. In *Punishment and Social Structure*, first published in 1939, they drew on historical material that spanned the Middle Ages to the turn of the twentieth century to explain why specific forms of punishment were deployed or cast aside in specific historical moments. Embedded in their question was the assumption that, although all systems of punishment were at least in part a response to crime, they were also always designed in response to some other social, political, and, perhaps most important, economic project, and in particular projects aimed at controlling the behavior of the poor.

It is through this theoretical lens that we are to understand the birth of the modern prison. The house of correction, which Rusche and Kirschheimer (2009) describe as combination poorhouse, workhouse, and penal institution, emerged in response to problems of early capitalism. Toward the end of the mercantilist period, markets were expanding rapidly at home and abroad, but population stagnation meant that labor reserves were too low to meet demand. There were simply not enough workers, at the wages and work conditions that labor could insist on, empowered in the moment by tight labor markets. With the upper hand in labor negotiations, workers would either garner the high wages and improved working conditions they desired, or they could choose to withhold their labor power. For capitalists, the situation was untenable.

According to Rusche and Kirschheimer, to resolve their labor shortage crisis, capitalists sought assistance from the state. The state responded in numerous ways, including the deployment of relatively new forms of punishment, which essentially made withholding one's labor power impermissible. In addition to galley slavery and transportation, Rusche and Kirschheimer offered the house of correction, whose purpose was to force unwilling, able-bodied people to work. By exploiting labor and training new labor reserves, early prisons helped solve problems inherent to early capitalism, and, in the process, to varying degrees served the needs of the penal institution itself, of capital production, and of the national economy.

---

justice-involved men who successfully searched alone adopted different impression management strategies, including failing to disclose their criminal justice status, in an effort to either completely eliminate the negative consequences for employment of having a criminal record, or to blunt its negative effect, and he linked impression management strategies to individuals' employment outcomes. Not everyone can so easily manipulate employers' impressions for their own benefit, however; race matters in how employers respond when justice-involved men disclose (Pager 2007). Increasingly, too, the justice-involved have much less control over the impressions they make. As employers gain ever greater access to applicants' personal records (SEARCH Group 2005; Bushway and Sweeten 2007)—criminal records and credit histories—it would seem that attempts to manage impressions by not disclosing one's contact with the penal system will fail to achieve its intended goal, since most employers are both loathe to hire the justice-involved and strongly inclined to verify their status and creditworthiness. For this reason, despite the potential benefits associated with using this method of job search, job seekers may perceive that with less control over the impressions they make, they are less likely to get the results they are hoping for.

During the Industrial Revolution, efficient systems of mass production and effectively organized labor movements made precarious the role that houses of corrections played in helping to produce new labor reserves easily exploitable for industry, and so prison work was transformed from a productive, profitable form of training into a rational system of deterrence. Indeed, Rusche and Kirschheimer (2009) predicted that insofar as the prison had become obsolete in solving important problems in the economic realm, it might also soon be cast aside as a useful form of punishment. It did not.

Building on Rusche and Kirchheimer (2009), historian Michel Foucault (1977) suggests that even where the prison abandoned the goal of economic productivity, the core elements of the prison—its cellular structure and its emphasis on precise controls over the body—reproduced the disciplinary form of power that was itself essential to the emergence of capitalist production and mass democracies. Dario Melossi and Massimo Pavarini (2018) point as well to the merging of punishment and a capitalist vision of the laboring body. The prison was less a factory to produce goods than a factory to produce obedient and pliable labor.

Despite some challenges, prisons have avoided the extinction that Rusche and Kirchheimer had predicted. Indeed, prison industries have been thriving. As evidence, from 1980 to 1994, although the number of federal and state prisoners increased by 221 percent, both the number of inmates employed in prison industries and the amount of prison industry sales grew by more than 350 percent, the latter growing to $1.3 billion (Erlich 1995). Whether operating in prisons or in collaboration with prison industries, corporations are clearly and increasingly profiting from punishment.

Still, not everyone in prison engages in productive labor. One of the distinctive features of mass incarceration is the frequency with which idleness rather than overwork now constitutes one of the pains of imprisonment (Travis, Western, and Redburne 2014). The overwhelming majority of those who do work have "regular" jobs that do not generate profit for industry. Instead, they provide institutional support in the form of maintenance, food preparation, laundry services, and the like, work that aids in the operation of the prison (Sawyer 2017). For these nonindustry jobs, prisoner-workers in 2001 were paid between $0.86 and $3.45 per hour, a decline because a growing number of states, all southern, chose not to pay inmates anything for performing in these positions (Sawyer 2017).[16]

Work release programs, work camps, and community work centers offer additional options for low-risk inmates and those preparing to be released, and in these situations it is not unusual for employers from the community to pay inmates' wages.

Roughly 6 percent of prison inmates work in state-owned businesses, which provide goods and services that are typically sold to government agencies (Sawyer 2017). UNICOR, the trade name for the Federal Prison Industries program, is perhaps the oldest such organization. Established in 1934, it currently has more than seventy factory locations across the United States with a diverse portfolio of products and services.[17] Through UNICOR, roughly eighteen thousand prisoners annually produce apparel and accessories, electronics, eyewear, food service products, license plates, office furniture, print products, awards and plaques, mattresses and bedding, office seating, and signage. The services they offer include computer-aided design; data services; distribution, warehousing, and logistics; electronic recycling; call center solutions; and printing and bindery services.[18] In 2017, from more than $450 million in sales these operations combined to yield almost $17 million in net income, an increase of roughly $13 million in net income from the prior fiscal

16. Alabama, Arkansas, Florida, Georgia, and Texas continue the practice of not paying inmates who work "regular" jobs in prison (Sawyer 2017).

17. UNICOR, "Factory Locations," March 2019, https://www.unicor.gov/about.aspx#FactoryMap (accessed September 23, 2019).

18. UNICOR, "Shopping," https://www.unicor.gov/Category.aspx?iStore=UNI&idCategory=1 (accessed September 23, 2019).

year. Meanwhile, during the same period, state-owned businesses like UNICOR paid their prisoner-workers on average between $0.33 cents and $1.41 per hour.[19] Although these amounts are approximately twice what the same prisoner-workers would make in regular prison jobs or privately run facilities, the significant profits they help generate would seem to warrant a greater piece of the prison industries pie. Unlike in Europe, where human rights conventions require that prisoners receive minimum wage, the United States has no laws protecting prisoners against forced labor, and, notoriously, the Thirteenth Amendment of the U.S. Constitution, which bars "involuntary servitude" or slavery, explicitly excludes those convicted of crimes.

Finally, a small number of incarcerated people work for businesses that contract with correctional agencies through the Prisoner Industry Enhancement Certification Program (Bureau of Justice Assistance 2018), a program that allows private companies to run aspects of their business operations inside prison walls using prison labor. At least thirty-seven states have legalized this practice, and a number of prominent companies are taking advantage.[20] Although these companies are mandated to pay prisoner-workers the "prevailing wages" for these jobs in the local area (Pelaez 2018), in the end, workers might see only a small fraction of the gross. Up to 80 percent of their earnings will likely be deducted mandatorily for various fees, including deductions for court-assessed fees, fines, and surcharges; victim restitution; room and board; and family support (Sawyer 2017).

In such contexts, how do prisoners gain a sense of dignity, especially as it relates to work? In this volume, Michael Gibson-Light (2020) reports on the discursive strategies that inmates in one medium-security men's prison deployed to claim self-worth in prison. Drawing from ethnographic fieldwork data and eighty-two in-depth interviews with prisoners and staffers, Gibson-Light offers the "sandpile of dignity" metaphor to describe a context in which work roles are constantly shifting and prisoners attempt to make claims to legitimacy in part by erecting symbolic boundaries between themselves and the prisoners in lower status jobs, those whose dedication, motivation, and work ethic could be challenged by virtue of their lower position. In the process, they are able to justify their standing in the ever-shifting prison-work hierarchy.

Given that prison labor typically lacks employment protections, does not qualify for minimum wage, and is ineligible for overtime pay, and that prisoner-workers are prohibited from organizing and collectively bargaining for improved wages and working conditions, they are stuck as one of the most vulnerable and exploitable sources of cheap labor in the Global North and their conditions appear comparable to some in the Global South. Indeed, many contend that with the loss of economic citizenship, prison labor in the United States is socially, politically, and economically equivalent to working in free enterprise zones in Africa, Asia, and Latin America,[21] a reality made all the worse by the fact that the vast majority of labor performed in prisons fails to translate into marketable or transferable skills on the outside. Thus, most will be released with almost no financial resources, despite hours of labor, and skills no more developed than when they arrived, making the prospect of finding work after release that much more difficult.

## Coercing Labor from Nonincarcerated Workers

When considering the collateral consequences of criminal justice contact, we tend to think specifically of those consequences, formal and informal, that create barriers to employment, such as occupational licensing restrictions or

---

19. Prison Policy Initiative, "Section III: The Prison Economy," https://www.prisonpolicy.org/prisonindex/prisonlabor.html (accessed September 23, 2019).

20. This includes the following: IBM, Boeing, Motorola, Microsoft, AT&T, Wireless, Texas Instrument, Dell, Compaq, Honeywell, Hewlett-Packard, Nortel, Lucent Technologies, 3Com, Intel, Northern Telecom, TWA, Nordstrom's, Revlon, Macy's, Pierre Cardin, Target Stores, and many more.

21. Jaron Browne, "Rooted in Slavery: Prison Labor Exploitation," *Reimagine*, Spring 2007, http://www.reimaginerpe.org/node/856 (accessed September 23, 2019).

employer liabilities for negligent hiring. As a small but growing body of research indicates, however, collateral consequences of criminal justice contact might also have the opposite effect, forcing work from the justice-involved under the threat of further punishment, including the loss of freedom (Zatz et al. 2016). To the extent that penal contact threatens individuals' economic citizenship rights, it also makes the justice-involved vulnerable to labor exploitation and extraction, and in the process, deepens the precariousness that many of these individuals already face.

In important new work, Noah Zatz and his colleagues tackle this very issue, identifying the routes of legal authority through which the justice-involved become vulnerable, and then highlighting the negative consequences for them and non-justice-involved coworkers, including deteriorating conditions of labor for the working class and the working poor generally. Probation and parole are one route. The vast majority of probationers and parolees are required to abide by multiple conditions to remain free from further sanction. Indeed, virtually no offenders are released on probation without stipulation, and almost all (99 percent) had one or more conditions to their probation sentence (Travis and Petersilia 2001; Rainville and Reaves 2003; Siegel and Senna 2007). Of those released conditionally, approximately 84 percent were required to pay some sort of fee or fine; 35 percent were required to find employment or enroll in some type of educational or job training program—41 percent of those convicted of felonies and 27 percent of those convicted of misdemeanors (Bonczar 1997). The courts are the other route. As with probation and parole, the courts have the power to mandate that the justice-involved pay their criminal justice and child support payments or face the consequences. Zatz and his colleagues (2016) explain that to please the court or probation officers and to avoid sanction for noncompliance, including possible jail time, justice-involved individuals are required to pay or to find a job, a better job, or two or more jobs. For those who cannot pay their fines or fees, it is fairly typical for the courts to mandate community service to work off the debt or jail time.

These are not idle threats, and, unsurprisingly, they disproportionately affect low-wage workers of color. According to a 2016 report (Zatz et al. 2016), approximately nine thousand individuals nationwide were jailed for violating probation or parole requirements that they hold a job; roughly two-thirds of those sanctioned were black or Latino. Five percent of all fathers in major cities were jailed for failure to pay child support; the figure for black fathers was 15 percent. Further, African American fathers make up nearly 80 percent of those incarcerated by the child support enforcement system and are incarcerated at a rate ten times higher than other fathers. In Los Angeles, the authors report that between fifty thousand and one hundred thousand residents were court-ordered to engage in community service to work off their legal debt. In other words, they must work to remain free. Most of these were from Los Angeles County, where residents are disproportionately of color and low-income.

The problem, of course, is that many who face these mandates lack the resources to do better. Take, as an example, payment of legal financial obligations and child support. Amounts vary somewhat by state, but analysis of data from Washington State revealed court assessments ranging from a minimum of $500 (mandatory for all felony convictions) to a maximum of $256,257; the median amount assessed per felon was $5,254; the mean $11,471 (Harris, Evans, and Beckett 2010). Many justice-involved fathers are weighed down by child support arrears as well. One in five incarcerated parents has a child support obligation, and these, too, can be daunting. In Boston, for instance, parents entering prison with a child support case owed roughly $10,000 in arrears; upon release, their average debt had doubled (Thoennes 2002).

These figures are not inconsequential. The vast majority of justice-involved men and women are poor or near poor (Western 2006). According to Alexes Harris, Heather Evans, and Katherine Beckett (2010, 1776), white, Hispanic, and black male felons have median legal debt loads that are roughly 60 percent, 36 percent, and 50 percent of their annual incomes, respectively; mean debt loads are roughly 10 percent, 69 percent, and 222 percent of their average annual earnings, respectively (see also Evans

2014). Thus, most simply could not afford to fulfill their obligations in the short term, and given the accumulation of interest on court-imposed sanctions, fulfillment over the long term is unlikely. Even small monthly payments could reduce take-home pay substantially, but most states have the authority to garnish much more—as much as 35 percent of wages for legal fines and fees and as much as 65 percent for back child support debt (Sandberg 2010). Such deductions from already-meager earnings would make it near impossible to meet other needs and obligations, such as buying groceries and paying rent. In this situation, even if already employed, poor or near poor parents would either have to accept community service that forced them to work for free, or they would have to serve time in jail, encouraging system avoidance (Brayne 2014).

In addition, the mandate to pay, work, or to go to jail puts pressure on those already in precarious economic circumstances to accept employment arrangements that they might otherwise forsake, including jobs offering low pay, no benefits, few employment protections, and poor working conditions.[22] By deferring to employers and allowing them to report on whether the justice-involved workers are in compliance with work requirements, the state essentially bestows on employers the power not only to hire and fire, but to jail as well. Thus, workers might feel pressure to silence their dissent and to accept employers' demands, no matter how unreasonable or illegal, deepening the sense of precarity that many caught up in the criminal justice system already face. Recent empirical evidence suggests that this is the case (see Hatton 2018). In this volume, Noah Zatz and Michael Stoll (2020) explore the question, examining the extent to which child support enforcement techniques, especially punitive ones such as incarceration, affect noncustodial fathers' employment outcomes. Analyzing from the Fragile Families Study data, they find that in cities that rely heavily on incarceration sanctions, noncustodial fathers who are most vulnerable to incarceration work more hours and at lower wages than those who are not so vulnerable. Thus, their study is one of the first to provide empirical support for the hypothesis that the threat of liberty lost will push vulnerable individuals to take on jobs with significantly poorer work arrangements and, likely, poor work conditions as well. Through the criminal justice system, it seems, we have created multiple mechanisms through which to trap justice-involved individuals in poverty.

## CONCLUSION: IS THE UNITED STATES UNIQUE?

As is true of many policies, organizations, and institutions, the criminal justice system has a hand in shaping the flow of individuals, especially those in the lower classes, into and out of the labor market as well as affecting economic performance generally. The United States is not unique in this regard. Perhaps what is unique is the scale at which the penal state is deployed at least in part in service of a winner-take-all economy, where worker protections, social insurance programs, and active labor market systems are weak. In such a context, the twin actions of exclusion and extraction, though seemingly at odds, make sense. What is also unique is the degree to which, in an otherwise largely unregulated labor market, where workers receive few protections against unemployment and antidiscrimination laws are systematically underenforced, the criminal justice system stands out as an aggressive form of state intervention in the labor market. With criminal justice contact, individuals are automatically excluded from a large swath of employment op-

---

22. These large debt liabilities can discourage work, even with the threat of jail. Harris, Evans, and Beckett (2010) report that 80 percent of their respondents found their legal debt obligations to be "unduly burdensome," and their heightened financial stress actually had the unintended consequence of reducing commitment to work and related search effort. Despite the possibility of jail time for nonpayment, some of their respondents chose not to work, relying on crime, or, where this was allowable for legal debtors, cash assistance. High child support arrears balances and aggressive enforcement policies have also been found to have similar effects on fathers' work effort (Pate 2002; Bartfeld 2003; Meyer, Ha, and Hu 2008; Cancian, Heinrich, and Chung 2009). Thus, in the form of heavy monetary sanctions, penal interventions can worsen before-search options to the point of eroding commitments to work and thus engaged job search.

portunities, most irrelevant to the offense for which individuals have been punished. Now struggling to find work and to make ends meet, the same individuals are often then pressured into taking any job, or even working for free, under the threat of additional sanctions, including the loss of freedom. With these twin actions of exclusion and extraction, the criminal justice system in the United States plays a heavy role in creating a vast pool of surplus labor, most often in low-income communities of color, that can be tapped whether inside prison walls or on the streets of neighborhoods and communities.

## REFERENCES

Agan, Amanda Y., and Sonja B. Starr. 2016. "Ban the Box, Criminal Records, and Statistical Discrimination: A Field Experiment." *University of Michigan Law and Economics* research paper no. 16-012. Ann Arbor: University of Michigan.

Allegretto, Sylvia, Anna Godoey, Carl Nadler, and Michael Reich. 2018. "The New Wave of Local Minimum Wage Policies: Evidence from Six Cities." *CWED* Policy Report. Berkeley: University of California, Institute for Research on Labor and Employment.

Apel, Robert, and Gary Sweeten. 2010. "The Impact of Incarceration on Employment During the Transition to Adulthood." *Social Problems* 57(3): 448–79.

Atkin, Cassandra, and Gaylene S. Armstrong. 2013. "Does the Concentration of Parolees in a Community Impact Employer Attitudes Toward the Hiring of Ex-offenders?" *Criminal Justice Policy Review* 24(1): 71–93.

Atkinson, Daryl V., and Kathleen Lockwood. 2014. "The Benefits of Ban the Box: A Case Study of Durham, NC." Durham, N.C.: Southern Coalition for Social Justice.

Bartfeld, Judi. 2003. "Falling Through the Cracks: Gaps in Child Support Among Welfare Recipients." *Journal of Marriage and Family* 65(1): 72–89.

Beckett, Katherine, and Naomi Murakawa. 2012. "Mapping the Shadow Carceral State: Toward an Institutionally Capacious Approach to Punishment." *Theoretical Criminology* 16(2): 221–44.

Bellair, Paul, and Brian R. Kowalski. 2011. "Low-Skill Employment Opportunity and African American-White Difference in Recidivism." *Journal of Research in Crime and Delinquency* 48(2): 176–208.

Berracasa, Colenn, Alexis Estevez, Charlotte Nugent, Kelly Roesing, and Jerry Wei. 2016. "The Impact of 'Ban the Box' in the District of Columbia." Washington, D.C.: Office of the District of Columbia Auditor.

Betcherman, Gordon. 2012. *Labor Market Institutions: A Review of the Literature*. Policy Research working paper no. 6276. Washington, D.C.: The World Bank.

Blair, Peter Q., and Bobby W. Chung. 2018. "Job Market Signaling Through Occupational Licensing." *NBER* working paper no. 24791. Cambridge, Mass.: National Bureau of Economic Research.

Blumstein, Alfred, and Kiminori Nakamura. 2009. "Redemption in the Presence of Widespread Background Checks." *Criminology* 47(2): 327–59.

Bobo, Lawrence D., and Devon Johnson. 2004. "A Taste for Punishment: Black and White Americans' Views on the Death Penalty and the War on Drugs." *Du Bois Review* 1(1): 151–80.

Bobo, Lawrence D., and Victor Thompson. 2006. "Unfair by Design: The War on Drugs, Race, and the Legitimacy of the Criminal Justice System." *Social Research* 73(2): 445–72.

Bonczar, Thomas P. 1997. "Characteristics of Adults on Probation, 1995." Washington: U.S. Department of Justice.

Boshier, Roger, and Derek Johnson. 1974. "Does Conviction Affect Employment Opportunities?" *British Journal of Criminology* 14(3): 264–68.

Brady, David. 2009. *Rich Democracies, Poor People: How Politics Explain Poverty*. New York: Oxford University Press.

Brayne, Sarah. 2014. "Surveillance and System Avoidance: Criminal Justice Contact and Institutional Attachment." *American Sociological Review* 79(3): 367–91.

Bureau of Justice Assistance. 2018. "Prison Industry Enhancement Certification Program." Program Brief, August. Washington: U.S. Department of Justice.

Bushway, Shawn D. 1998. "The Impact of an Arrest on the Job Stability of Young White American Men." *Journal of Research in Crime and Delinquency* 35:454–79.

Bushway, Shawn D., and Robert Apel. 2012. "A Signaling Perspective on Employment-Based Reentry Programming: Training Completion as a Desistance Signal." *Criminology and Public Policy* 11(1): 21–50.

Bushway, Shawn, Paul Nieuwbeerta, and Arjan Blokland. 2011. "The Predictive Value of Criminal Background Checks: Do Age and Criminal History Affect Time to Redemption?" *Criminology* 49(1): 27–60.

Bushway, Shawn D., and Gary Sweeten. 2007. "Abolish Lifetime Bans for Ex-Felons." *Criminology and Public Policy* 6(4): 697–706.

Cadigan, Michele, and Gabriela Kirk. 2020. "On Thin Ice: Bureaucratic Processes of Monetary Sanctions and Job Insecurity." *RSF: The Russell Sage Foundation Journal of the Social Sciences* 6(1): 113–31. DOI: 10.7758/RSF.2020.6.1.05.

Cancian, Maria, Carolyn Heinrich, and Yiyoon Chung. 2009. "Does Debt Discourage Employment and Payment of Child Support? Evidence from a Natural Experiment." *Institute for Research on Poverty* discussion paper no. 1366-09. Madison: University of Wisconsin-Madison.

Chiricos, Theodore G., and Miriam A. Delone. 1992. "Labor Surplus and Punishment: A Review and Assessment of Theory and Evidence." *Social Problems* 39(4): 421–46.

Cigagna, Claudia, and Giovanni Sulis. 2013. "On the Potential Interaction Between Labour Market Institutions and Immigration Policies." *SEARCH* working paper no. WP3/02. Barcelona: University of Barcelona, AQR-IREA Research Group.

Conklin, John. 1975. *The Impact of Crime*. New York: Macmillan.

Craigie, Terry-Ann. 2017. "Ban the Box, Convictions, and Public Sector Employment." *SSRN* working paper. Accessed September 20, 2019. https://papers.ssrn.com/sol3/papers.cfm?abstract_id=2906893.

Cullen, Francis T., Sandra Skovron, Joseph Scott, and Velmer Burton Jr. 1990. "Public Support for Correctional Treatment: The Tenacity of the Rehabilitative Ideology." *Criminal Justice and Behavior* 17(1): 6–18.

D'Alessio, Stewart J., and Lisa Stolzenberg. 2002. "A Multilevel Analysis of the Relationship between Labor Surplus and Pretrial Incarceration." *Social Problems* 49(2): 178–93.

Dale, Mitchell W. 1976. "Barriers to the Rehabilitation of Ex-Offenders." *Crime and Delinquency* 22(3): 322–37.

Derenoncourt, Ellora, and Claire Montialoux. 2018. "Minimum Wages and Racial Inequality." Working paper, University of California, Berkeley.

DiPrete, Thomas. 2002. "Life Course Risks, Mobility Regimes, and Mobility Consequences: A Comparison of Sweden, Germany, and the United States." *American Journal of Sociology* 108(2): 267–309.

DiPrete, Thomas. A., Paul M. de Graaf, Ruud Luijkx, Michael Tåhlin, and Hans-Peter Blossfeld. 1997. "Collectivist Versus Individualist Mobility Regimes? Structural Change and Job Mobility in Four Countries." *American Journal of Sociology* 103(2): 318–58.

Doleac, Jennifer, and Benjamin Hansen. 2016. "Does 'Ban the Box' Help or Hurt Low-Skilled Workers? Statistical Discrimination and Employment Outcomes When Criminal Histories Are Hidden." *NBER* Working Paper no. 22469. Cambridge, Mass.: National Bureau of Economic Research.

Duane, Marina, Emily Reimal, and Mathew Lynch. 2017. "Criminal Background Checks and Access to Jobs: A Case Study of Washington, DC." *Justice Policy Center* research report. Washington, D.C.: The Urban Institute. Accessed September 20, 2019. https://www.urban.org/sites/default/files/publication/91456/2001377-criminal-background-checks-and-access-to-jobs_2.pdf.

Dwyer Emory, Allison, Lenna Nepomnyaschy, Maureen R. Waller, Daniel P. Miller, and Alexandra Haralampoudis. 2020. "Providing After Prison: Nonresident Fathers' Formal and Informal Contributions to Children." *RSF: The Russell Sage Foundation Journal of the Social Sciences* 6(1): 84–112. DOI: 10.7758/RSF.2020.6.1.04.

Erlich, Reese. 1995. "Prison Labor: Workin' for the Man." *Covert Action Quarterly* 54: 58–64.

Evans, Douglas N. 2014. "The Debt Penalty: Exposing the Financial Barriers to Offender Reintegration." New York: John Jay College of Criminal Justice, Research and Evaluation Center.

Fahey, Jennifer, Cheryl Roberts, and Len Engel. 2006. *Employment of Ex-Offenders: Employer Perspectives*. Boston, Mass.: Crime and Justice Institute.

Feeley, Malcolm, and Edward Rubin. 1998. *Judicial Policy Making and the Modern State: How Courts Reformed America's Prisons*. Cambridge: Cambridge University Press.

Finlay, Keith. 2008. "Effect of Employer Access to Criminal History Data on the Labor Market Outcomes of Ex-Offenders and Non-Offenders."

NBER working paper no. 13935. Cambridge, Mass.: National Bureau of Economic Research.

Flanagan, Timothy J., and Susan L. Caufield. 1984. "Public Opinion and Prison Policy: A Review." *Prison Journal* 64(1): 39–59.

Foucault, Michel. 1977. *Discipline and Punish: The Birth of the Prison*. New York: Pantheon.

Freeman, Richard B. 1991a. "Crime and the Employment of Disadvantaged Youth." *NBER* working paper no. 3875. Cambridge, Mass.: National Bureau of Economic Research. Accessed September 20, 2019. https://www.nber.org/papers/w3875.pdf.

———. 1991b. "Employment and Earnings of Disadvantaged Young Men in a Labor Shortage Economy." In *The Urban Underclass*, edited by Christopher Jencks and Paul E. Petersen. Washington, D.C.: Brookings Institution Press.

———. 2002. 'Single Peaked vs. Diversified Capitalism: The Relation Between Economic Institutions and Outcomes." In *Inequality Around the World*, edited by Richard B. Freeman. London: Palgrave.

———. 2007. "Labor Market Institutions Around the World." *NBER* working paper no. 13242. Cambridge, Mass.: National Bureau of Economic Research. Accessed October 10, 2019. https://www.nber.org/papers/w13242.

Freeman, Richard B., Eunice Han, David Madland, and Brendan V. Duke. 2015. "How Does Declining Unionism Affect the American Middle Class and Intergenerational Mobility?" *NBER* working paper no. 21638. Cambridge, Mass.: National Bureau of Economic Research. Accessed October 10, 2019. https://www.nber.org/papers/w21638.

Gangl, Markus. 2004a. "Institutions and the Structure of Labour Market Matching in the United States and West Germany." *European Sociological Review* 20(3): 171–87.

———. 2004b. "Welfare States and the Scar Effects of Unemployment: A Comparative Analysis of the United States and West Germany." *American Journal of Sociology* 109(6): 1319–64.

———. 2006. "Scar Effects of Unemployment: An Assessment of Institutional Complementarities." *American Sociological Review* 71(6): 986–1013.

Garland, David. 1990. *Punishment and Modern Society: A Study in Social Theory*. Chicago: University of Chicago Press.

———. 2001. *Mass Imprisonment: Social Causes and Consequences*. Thousand Oaks, Calif.: Sage Publications.

———. 2013. "Penality and the State: The 2012 Sutherland Address." *Criminology* 51(3): 475–517.

Garsd, Jasmine. 2019. "Former Inmates Are Getting Jobs as Employers Ignore Stigma in Bright Economy." National Public Radio, May 23. Accessed September 23, 2019, https://www.npr.org/2019/05/23/718737833/former-inmates-are-getting-jobs-as-employers-ignore-stigma-in-bright-economy.

Gibson-Light, Michael. 2020. "Sandpiles of Dignity: Labor Status and Boundary-Making in the Contemporary American Prison." *RSF: The Russell Sage Foundation Journal of the Social Sciences* 6(1): 198–216. DOI: 10.7758/RSF.2020.6.1.09.

Glynn, Timothy P. 1998. "The Limited Viability of Negligent Supervision, Retention, Hiring, and Infliction of Emotional Distress Claims in Employment Discrimination Cases in Minnesota." *William Mitchell Law Review* 24(3): 581–633.

Goffman, Alice. 2009. "On the Run: Wanted Men in a Philadelphia Ghetto." *American Sociological Review* 74(3): 339–57.

Goldberg, Ben. 2016. "Majority of Employers Background Check Employees . . . Here's Why." CareerBuilder, November 17. Accessed October 10, 2019. https://www.careerbuilder.com/advice/majority-of-employers-background-check-employees.

Grogger, Jeff. 1992. "Arrests, Persistent Youth Joblessness, and Black/White Employment Differentials." *Review of Economics and Statistics* 74(1): 100–106.

———. 1995. "The Effect of Arrests on the Employment and Earnings of Young Men." *Quarterly Journal of Economics* 110(10): 51–71.

Harcourt, Bernard E. 2011. *The Illusion of Free Markets*. Cambridge, Mass.: Harvard University Press.

Harding, David J. 2003. "Jean Valjean's Dilemma: The Management of Ex-Convict Identity in the Search for Employment." *Deviant Behavior* 24(6): 571–95.

Harris, Alexes, Heather Evans, and Katherine Beckett. 2010. "Drawing Blood from Stones: Legal Debt and Social Inequality in the Contemporary United States." *American Journal of Sociology* 115(6): 1753–99.

Hatton, Erin. 2018. "When Work Is Punishment: Penal Subjectivities in Punitive Labor Regimes." *Punishment and Society* 20(2): 174–91.

Holmlund, Bertil. 2014. "What Do Labor Market Institutions Do?" *CESifo* working paper series no. 4582. Munich: Center for Economic Studies.

Holzer, Harry J. 1996. *What Employers Want: Job Prospects for Less-Educated Workers*. New York: Russell Sage Foundation.

Holzer, Harry J., Steven Raphael, and Michael A. Stoll. 2001. "Will Employers Hire Ex-Offenders? Employer Checks, Background Checks, and Their Determinants." *Program on Housing and Urban Policy* working paper no. W01–005. Berkeley: University of California.

———. 2007. "The Effect of an Applicant's Criminal History on Employer Hiring Decisions and Screening Practices: Evidence from Los Angeles." In *Barriers to Reentry? The Labor Market for Released Prisoners in Post-Industrial America*, edited by Shawn Bushway, Michael A. Stoll, and David F. Weiman. New York: Russell Sage Foundation.

Ispa-Landa, Simone, and Charles E. Loeffler. 2016. "Indefinite Punishment and the Criminal Record: Stigma Reports among Expungement Seekers in Illinois." *Criminology* 54(3): 387–412.

Jaumotte, Florence, and Carolina Osorio Buitron. 2015. "Inequality and Labor Market Institutions." *IMF Staff Discussion Note* no. 15/14. Washington, D.C.: International Monetary Fund.

Kaeble, Danielle, and Mary Cowhig. 2018. "Correctional Populations in the United States, 2016." Washington: U.S. Department of Justice, Bureau of Justice Statistics.

Kalleberg, Arne L., Barbara F. Reskin, and Ken Hudson. 2011. "Bad Jobs in America: Standard and Nonstandard Employment Relations and Job Quality in the United States." *American Sociological Review* 65(2): 256–78.

Kanfer, Ruth, Connie R. Wanberg, and Tracy M. Kantrowitz. 2001. "Job Search and Employment: A Personality-Motivational Analysis and Meta-Analytic Review." *Journal of Applied Psychology* 86(5): 837–55.

Kleiner, Morris M. 2015. "Reforming Occupational Licensing Policies." *Hamilton Project* discussion paper no. 2015-01. Washington, D.C.: Brookings Institution.

Kleiner, Morris M., Amy Humphris, and Maria Koumenta. 2011. "How Does Government Regulate Occupations in the UK and US? Issues and Policy Implications." In *Employment in the Lean Years: Policy and Prospects for the Next Decade*, edited by David Marsden. New York: Oxford University Press.

Kleiner, Morris M., and Alan B. Krueger. 2010. "The Prevalence and Effects of Occupational Licensing." *British Journal of Industrial Relations* 48(4): 676–87.

Kling, Jeffrey R. 2002. "The Effect of Prison Sentence Length on the Subsequent Employment and Earnings of Criminal Defendants." Unpublished manuscript, Princeton University.

Kohler-Hausmann, Issa. 2013. "Misdemeanor Justice: Control Without Conviction." *American Journal of Sociology* 119(2): 351–93.

Kutchinsky, Berl. 1968. "Knowledge and Attitudes Regarding Legal Phenomena in Denmark." In *Scandinavian Studies in Criminology*, vol. 2: *Aspects of Social Control in Welfare States*, edited by Nils Christie. London: Tavistock.

LaBriola, Joe. 2020. "Post-prison Employment Quality and Future Criminal Justice Contact." *RSF: The Russell Sage Foundation Journal of the Social Sciences* 6(1): 154–72. DOI: 10.7758/RSF.2020.6.1.07.

Levin, Benjamin. 2018. "Criminal Employment Law." *Harvard Public Law* working paper no. 17-05. Cambridge, Mass.: Harvard University.

Lichtenstein, Alexander. 1996. *Twice the Work of Free Labor: The Political Economy of Convict Labor in the New South*. New York: Verso.

May, Bruce E. 1995. "The Character Component of Occupational Licensing Laws: A Continuing Barrier to the Ex-Felon's Employment Opportunities." *North Dakota Law Review* 71: 187–93.

McCall, John J. 1970. "Economics of Information and Job Search." *Quarterly Journal of Economics* 84 (July): 300–317.

McCorkle, Richard C. 1993. "Research Note: Punish and Rehabilitate? Public Attitudes Toward Six Common Crimes." *Crime and Delinquency* 39(2): 240–52.

McLennan, Rebecca. 2008. *The Crisis of Imprisonment: Protest, Politics, and the Making of the American Penal State, 1776–1941*. Cambridge: Cambridge University Press.

Melossi, Dario, and Massimo Pavarini. 2018. *The Prison and the Factory: Origins of the Penitentiary System*. New York: Springer.

Meyer, Daniel, Yoonsook Ha, and Mei-Chen Hu. 2008. "Do High Child Support Orders Discourage Child Support Payments?" *Social Service Review* 82(1): 93–118.

Mills, Linda. 2008. *Inventorying and Reforming State-Created Employment Restrictions Based on Criminal Records: A Policy Brief and Guide*. Baltimore, Md.: Annie E. Casey Foundation.

Nagin, Daniel, and Joel Waldfogel. 1995. "The Effects of Criminality and Conviction on the Labor Market Status of Young British Offenders." *International Review of Law and Economics* 15(1): 109–26.

Olivares, Kathleen M., Velmer S. Burton Jr., and Francis Cullen. 1996. "The Collateral Consequences of a Felony Conviction: A National Study of State Legal Codes 10 Years Later." *Federal Probation* 60: 10–17.

Oshinsky, David. 1996. *Worse Than Slavery: Parchman Farm and the Ordeal of Jim Crow Justice*. New York: Free Press.

Pager, Devah. 2003. "The Mark of a Criminal Record." *American Journal of Sociology* 108(5): 937–75.

———. 2007. "Two Strikes and You're Out: The Intensification of Racial and Criminal Stigma." In *Barriers to Reentry? The Labor Market for Released Prisoners in Post-Industrial America*, edited by Shawn D. Bushway, Michael A. Stoll, and David Weiman. New York: Russell Sage Foundation.

Pager, Devah, and Lincoln Quillian. 2005. "Walking the Talk? What Employers Say Versus What They Do." *American Sociological Review* 70(3): 355–80.

Pager, Devah, Bruce Western, and Bart Bonikowski. 2009. "Discrimination in a Low-Wage Labor Market: A Field Experiment." *American Sociological Review* 74(5): 777–99.

Pager, Devah, Bruce Western, and Naomi Sugie. 2009. "Sequencing Disadvantage: Barriers to Employment Facing Young Black and White Men with Criminal Records." *Annals of the American Academy of Political and Social Science* 623(1): 195–213.

Pate, David J., Jr. 2002. "An Ethnographic Inquiry into the Life Experiences of African American Fathers with Children on W-2." In *Nonexperimental Analyses of the Full Disregard and Pass-Through*, vol. 2, edited by Daniel R. Meyer and Maria Cancian. Madison: Wisconsin Department of Workforce Development.

Pelaez, Vicki. 2018. "The Prison Industry in the United States: Big Business or a New Form of Slavery?" *Global Research*, September 13. Accessed September 23, 2019. https://www.globalresearch.ca/the-prison-industry-in-the-united-states-big-business-or-a-new-form-of-slavery/8289.

Petersilia, Joan. 2003. *When Prisoners Come Home: Parole and Prisoner Reentry*. New York: Oxford University Press.

Pettit, Becky, and Christopher J. Lyons. 2007. "Status and the Stigma of Incarceration: The Labor Market Effects of Incarceration, by Race, Class, and Criminal Involvement." In *Barriers to Reentry? The Labor Market for Released Prisoners in Post-Industrial America*, edited by Shawn Bushway, Michael A. Stoll, and David F. Weiman. New York: Russell Sage Foundation.

Prescott, J. J., and Sonja B. Starr. 2019. "Expungement of Criminal Convictions: An Empirical Study." *Harvard Law Review* 133(1)(November).

Rainville, Gerard, and Brian Reeves. 2003. "Felony Defendants in Large Urban Counties, 2000." NCJ 202021. Washington, D.C.: Bureau of Justice Statistics.

Reed, John P., and Robin S. Reed. 1973. "Status, Images and Consequence: Once a Criminal Always a Criminal." *Sociology and Social Science* 57(4): 460–72.

Roberts, Jenny. 2015. "Expunging America's Rap Sheet in the Information Age." *Wisconsin Law Review* 2(May): 321–47.

Roberts, Julian V. 1992. "Public Opinion, Crime, and Criminal Justice." *Crime and Justice* 16:99–180.

———. 1997. "The Role of Criminal Record in the Sentencing Process." *Crime and Justice* 22:303–62.

Rodriguez, Michelle Natividad, and Beth Avery. 2016. "Unlicensed and Untapped: Removing Barriers to State Occupational Licenses for People with Records." Fact Sheet. Washington, D.C.: National Employment Law Project. Accessed September 23, 2019. https://www.nelp.org/publication/nationwide-trend-reform-unfair-occupational-licensing-laws.

Rusche, Georg, and Otto Kirschheimer. 2009. *Punishment and Social Structure*, 5th ed. New Brunswick, N.J.: Transaction Publishers.

Sabol, William J. 2007. "Local Labor Market Conditions and Post-Prison Employment Experiences of Offenders Released from Ohio State Prisons." In *Barriers to Reentry? The Labor Market for Released Prisoners in Post-Industrial America*, edited by Shawn Bushway, Michael A. Stoll, and

David F. Weiman. New York: Russell Sage Foundation.

Saladin, Michael, Zalman Saper, and Lawrence Breen. 1988. "Perceived Attractiveness and Attributions of Criminality: What Is Beautiful Is Not Criminal." *Canadian Journal of Criminology* 30:251–59.

Sampson, Robert. 2011. *Great American City: Chicago and the Enduring Neighborhood Effect.* Chicago: University of Chicago Press.

Sandberg, Erica. 2010. "Ex-offenders Face Big Debt Challenges after Prison." CreditCards.com, August 30. Accessed October 9, 2019. http://www.creditcards.com/credit-card-news/ex-offenders-felons-prisoners-jail-in-debt-1264.php.

Sandys, Marla, and Edmund F. McGarrell. 1995. "Attitudes Toward Capital Punishment: Preference for the Penalty or Mere Acceptance?" *Journal of Research in Crime and Delinquency* 32(2): 191–213.

Sawyer, Wendy. 2017. "How Much Do Incarcerated People Earn in Each State?" *Prison Policy Initiative* (blog), April 10. Accessed September 23, 2019. https://www.prisonpolicy.org/blog/2017/04/10/wages.

Sawyer, Wendy, and Peter Wagner. 2019. "Mass Incarceration: The Whole Pie 2019." Northampton, Mass.: Prison Policy Initiative. Accessed July 19, 2019. https://www.prisonpolicy.org/reports/pie2019.html.

Schwartz, Richard D., and Jerome H. Skolnick. 1964. "Two Studies of Legal Stigma." *Social Problems* 10(2): 133–42.

SEARCH Group. 2005. *1988 Standards for the Security and Privacy of Criminal History Record Information*, 3d ed. Technical Report No. 13. Sacramento, Calif.: SEARCH Group.

Seim, Josh, and David J. Harding. 2020. "Parolefare: Post-prison Supervision and Low-Wage Work." *RSF: The Russell Sage Foundation Journal of the Social Sciences* 6(1): 173–95. DOI: 10.7758/RSF.2020.6.1.08.

Sharone, Ofer. 2013. *Flawed System/Flawed Self: Job Searching and Unemployment Experiences.* Chicago: University of Chicago Press.

Shoag, Daniel, and Stan Veuger. 2016. "Banning the Box: The Labor Market Consequences of Bans on Criminal Record Screening in Employment Application." Working paper, Harvard University. Accessed September 23, 2019. https://scholar.harvard.edu/files/shoag/files/banning-the-box-september-2016.pdf.

Shoemaker, Donald J., and Donald R. South. 1978. "Nonverbal Images of Criminality and Deviance: Existence and Consequence." *Criminal Justice Review* 3(1): 65–80.

Siegel, Larry, and Joseph Senna. 2007. *Essentials of Criminal Justice.* Belmont, Calif.: Thompson Wadsworth.

Simmons, Jeri Lynn. 1965. "Public Stereotypes of Deviants." *Social Problems* 13(2): 223–32.

Simon, Jonathan. 2007. *Governing Through Crime: How the War on Crime Transformed American Democracy and Created a Culture of Fear.* New York: Oxford University Press.

———. 2014. *Mass Incarceration on Trial: A Remarkable Court Decision and the Future of American Prisons.* New York: New Press.

Smith, Sandra Susan. 2018. "'Change' Frames and the Mobilization of Social Capital for Formerly Incarcerated Job Seekers." *DuBois Review* 15(2): 387–416.

Smith, Sandra Susan, and Nora Broege. 2019. "Searching for Work with a Criminal Record." *Social Problems.* First published online May 6, 2019. DOI: 10.1093/socpro/spz009.

Sugie, Naomi F. 2018. "Work as Foraging: A Smartphone Study of Job Search and Employment After Prison." *American Journal of Sociology* 123(5): 1453–91.

Sullivan, Mercer L. 1989. *Getting Paid: Youth, Crime and Work in the Inner City.* Ithaca, N.Y.: Cornell University Press.

Sykes, Bryan L., and Amy Kate Bailey. 2020. "Institutional Castling: Military Enlistment and Mass Incarceration in the United States." *RSF: The Russell Sage Foundation Journal of the Social Sciences* 6(1): 30–54. DOI: 10.7758/RSF.2020.6.1.02.

Thoennes, Nancy. 2002. "Child Support Profile: Massachusetts Incarcerated and Paroled Parents." Denver, Colo.: Center for Policy Research. Accessed September 23, 2019. http://cntrpolres.qwestoffice.net/reports/profile%20of%20CS%20among%20incarcerated%20&%20paroled%20parents.pdf.

Thornberry, Terence P., and R. L. Christenson. 1984. "Unemployment and Criminal Involvement: An Investigation of Reciprocal Causal Structures." *American Sociological Review* 49(3): 398–411.

Travis, Jeremy. 2002. "Invisible Punishment: An Instrument of Social Inclusion." Washington, D.C.: The Urban Institute.

Travis, Jeremy, and Joan Petersilia. 2001. "Reentry Reconsidered: A New Look at an Old Question." *Crime and Delinquency* 47(3): 291–313.

Travis, Jeremy, Bruce Western, and F. Stevens Redburn. 2014. *The Growth of Incarceration in the United States: Exploring Causes and Consequences*. Washington, D.C.: National Academy of Sciences.

Uggen, Christopher, Jeff Manza, and Melissa Thompson. 2006. "Citizenship, Democracy and the Civic Reintegration of Criminal Offenders." *Annals of the American Academy of Political and Social Science* 605(1): 281–310.

Useem, Bert, and Anne Morrison Piehl. 2008. *Prison State: The Challenge of Mass Incarceration*. New York: Cambridge University Press.

Visher, Christy A., and Vera Kachnowski. 2007. "Finding Work on the Outside: Results from the 'Returning Home' Project in Chicago." In *Barriers to Reentry? The Labor Market for Released Prisoners in Post-Industrial America*, edited by Shawn Bushway, Michael A. Stoll, and David F. Weiman. New York: Russell Sage Foundation.

Visher, Christy A., and Daniel J. O'Connell. 2012. "Incarceration and Inmates' Self Perceptions about Returning Home." *Journal of Criminal Justice* 40(5): 386–93.

Vuolo, Mike, Sarah Lageson, and Christopher Uggen. 2017. "Criminal Record Questions in the Era of 'Ban the Box.'" *Criminology and Public Policy* 16(1): 139–65.

Wacquant, Loic. 2009. *Punishing the Poor: The Neoliberal Government of Social Insecurity*. Durham, N.C.: Duke University Press.

Wagner, Peter. 2012. "Incarceration Is Not an Equal Opportunity Punishment." Northampton, Mass.: Prison Policy Initiative. Accessed September 23, 2019. https://www.prisonpolicy.org/articles/notequal.html.

Waldfogel, Joel. 1994. "The Effect of Criminal Conviction on Income and the Trust 'Reposed in the Workmen.'" *Journal of Human Resources* 29(1): 62–81.

Wang, Xia, Daniel P. Mears, and William D. Bales. 2010. "Race Specific Employment Contexts and Recidivism." *Criminology* 48(4): 201–41.

Warner, Cody, Joshua Kaiser, and Jason N. Houle. 2020. "Locked Out of the Labor Market? State-Level Hidden Sentences and the Labor-Market Outcomes of Recently Incarcerated Young Adults." *RSF: The Russell Sage Foundation Journal of the Social Sciences* 6(1): 132–51. DOI: 10.7758/RSF.2020.6.1.06

Western, Bruce. 2002. "The Impact of Incarceration on Wage Mobility and Inequality." *American Sociological Review* 67(4): 526–46.

———. 2006. *Punishment and Inequality in America*. New York: Russell Sage Foundation.

Western, Bruce, and Katherine Beckett. 1999. "How Unregulated Is the U.S. Labor Market? The Penal System as a Labor Market Institution." *American Sociological Review* 104(4): 1030–60.

Western, Bruce, Jeffrey Kling, and David Weiman. 2001. "The Labor Market Consequences of Incarceration." *Crime and Delinquency* 47: 410–27.

Western, Bruce, and Becky Pettit. 2005. "Black-White Wage Inequality, Employment Rates, and Incarceration." *American Journal of Sociology* 111(2): 553–78.

Western, Bruce, and Jake Rosenfeld. 2011. "Unions, Norms, and the Rise in U.S. Wage Inequality." *American Sociological Review* 76(4): 513–37.

Yeager, Matthew G. 1979. "Unemployment and Imprisonment." *Journal of Criminal Law and Criminology* 70(4): 586–88.

Zatz, Noah D., Tia Koonse, Theresa Zhen, Lucero Herrera, Han Lu, Steven Shafer, and Blake Valenta. 2016. "Get to Work or Go to Jail: Workplace Rights Under Threat." Research Brief. Los Angeles: UCLA Institute for Research on Labor and Employment.

Zatz, Noah D., and Michael A. Stoll. 2020. "Working to Avoid Incarceration: Jail Threat and Labor Market Outcomes for Noncustodial Fathers Facing Child Support Enforcement." *RSF: The Russell Sage Foundation Journal of the Social Sciences* 6(1): 55–81. DOI: 10.7758/RSF.2020.6.1.03

# PART I

## Consequences for Mass Incarceration of Intersecting Labor Market Institutions

# Institutional Castling: Military Enlistment and Mass Incarceration in the United States

BRYAN L. SYKES AND AMY KATE BAILEY

*The military is a major state provider of employment, occupational training, and educational subsidies. Yet military downsizing and its increased selectivity during penal expansion may have cleaved off employment opportunities for disadvantaged men. We show how* institutional castling—*the shifting prominence of competing institutions in the lives of specific demographic groups—has affected the underlying risk of military employment and penal confinement. Black veterans who have dropped out of high school are less likely to be incarcerated than their nonveteran counterparts, and declines in the employment rates of military servicemembers with less than a high school education are associated with large increases in incarceration rates. The military's critical role in providing institutional protection from the penal system has eroded for young, undereducated African American men.*

**Keywords:** institutional castling, incarceration, military, employment, race

The United States has seen tremendous growth in incarceration since 1970. Although crime rates are at historic lows, incarceration rates remain at unprecedented highs (Travis, Western, and Redburn 2014). Mass incarceration—rates of imprisonment significantly above historical and societal levels that lead to the systematic incapacitation of particular sociodemographic groups within a society (Garland 2001a)—has been fueled by a set of social policies that disproportionately affect young, undereducated, nonwhite men. Changes in mandatory minimum sentencing laws, increased prosecutorial discretion, and more severe crim-

---

**Bryan L. Sykes** is assistant professor in the Department of Criminology, Law and Society and Sociology and Public Health, by courtesy, at the University of California, Irvine. **Amy Kate Bailey** is associate professor in the Department of Sociology at the University of Illinois–Chicago and visiting faculty affiliate at the University of Washington's Center for Studies in Demography and Ecology.

© 2020 Russell Sage Foundation. Sykes, Bryan L., and Amy Kate Bailey. 2020. "Institutional Castling: Military Enlistment and Mass Incarceration in the United States." *RSF: The Russell Sage Foundation Journal of the Social Sciences* 6(1): 30–54. DOI: 10.7758/RSF.2020.6.1.02. We thank Sandra Susan Smith, Jonathan Simon, Sheldon Danziger, Elizabeth Ananat, Emily Marshall, Christine Percheski, Becky Pettit, Hana Shepherd, LaTonya Trotter, three anonymous reviewers, and participants of the Russell Sage Foundation's Criminal Justice System as a Labor Market Institution meeting for their time and helpful comments on previous versions of this manuscript. We are also indebted to Josh Seim and Joshua A. Kaiser for pointing us to additional readings and various legal codes, respectively. An earlier version of this paper was presented at the 2014 Annual Meeting of the Population Association of America. Direct correspondence to: Bryan L. Sykes at blsykes@uci.edu, Department of Criminology, Law and Society, 3317 Social Ecology II, Irvine, CA 92697; and Amy Kate Bailey at akbailey@uic.edu.

Open Access Policy: *RSF: The Russell Sage Foundation Journal of the Social Sciences* is an open access journal. This article is published under a Creative Commons Attribution-NonCommercial-NoDerivs 3.0 Unported License.

inal sanctions for low-level drug offenses have contributed to the expansion of the criminal justice system, creating staggering race and class inequality in incarceration (Western 2006; Alexander 2010; Pettit 2012). On any given day, more than one-third of young black men who dropped out of high school are behind bars and face a lifetime risk of spending time in prison or jail at close to 70 percent (Pettit and Western 2004; Pettit, Sykes, and Western 2009; Pettit 2012; Sykes and Pettit 2014).

At the same time, the U.S. military changed profoundly in the size and composition of its personnel. Beginning in 1973, for example, the American armed forces transitioned from a staffing policy based on a selective service draft to one that positioned the military as a competitor for volunteers within the civilian labor market (Fredland et al. 1996). For the first time in the nation's history, black men came to be overrepresented in uniform relative to their concentration in the civilian population (Fernandez 1996; Oi 1996; Segal and Segal 2004), and military employment emerged as a major player in the labor market for young men of color. By 1979, one in four working black men age sixteen to twenty-four were employed by the armed forces, as were one in six of their Latino counterparts (Grissmer 1992, 37).

Yet, conventional wisdom holds that the armed forces and the criminal justice system are two distinct arms of the state performing separate and isolated functions. This perception persists despite evidence linking military participation with subsequent criminal activity (Culp et al. 2013; Tsai et al. 2013) and the potential loss of turning points from crime and social disadvantage (Elder 1986; Sampson and Laub 1993; 1996). Importantly, the armed forces have played a key role in employing large percentages of moderately skilled men from disadvantaged backgrounds (Grissmer 1992; Segal and Segal 2004) and, until 2015, were the largest employer in the United States (DMDC 2015; Lundquist, Pager, and Strader 2018). We believe that these institutions are directly connected by virtue of their relationship to the labor market experiences of young black men because changes in the processes that govern selection into one of these institutions are likely to reverberate across other institutions (Han 2018; Mare and Winship 1984).

This article examines the historical relationship between penal confinement and military employment. The degree to which these institutions intersect and the way that rapid and simultaneous policy shifts during the 1960s and 1970s have interacted to affect the risk of incarceration among particular sociodemographic groups have garnered limited scholarly attention. This neglect persists despite the fact that the state establishes admissions criteria for both institutions, and the carceral system and the armed forces have been separately identified as deeply intertwined with the labor market for young men of color (Pettit and Western 2004; Western and Pettit 2005). We join Pierre Bourdieu in invoking "hyperbolic doubt" (1994, 1)—a rethinking of state institutional functions that appear distinct from one another, as well as the synergistic ways in which those institutions may operate in concert to influence and obscure patterns of social inequality. The correctional system and the military are institutional expressions of the state's coercive power and symbolic violence (Bourdieu 1994, 4–5), representing the polarities of the internal (penal system) and external (military) application of state force. To comprehend the state, we must understand the interrelated functioning of its bureaucratic institutions, as well as the synchronistic consequences of its actions.

We draw on a wealth of data from various sources to examine how the demographic composition of these social institutions have changed in the wake of policies enacted during the mid- to late twentieth century. We contribute to the literature on social inequality and to the body of work on the consequences of military service by assessing the changing risks of incarceration among veterans. Our reasoning is that, as a larger share of men with minimal formal education were excluded from the armed forces, the incarceration patterns among veterans and nonveterans should diverge, particularly among young, black high school dropouts. Specifically, we investigate whether and to what extent changes in the racial, educational, and population distributions of active duty military personnel are associated with racial and educational inequality in incarceration. Using standardization and decomposition techniques (Kitagwa 1955; Preston, Heuveline, and Guillot 2001) and other statistical methods, our analysis quantifies levels of incarceration associated with shifts in the race and class distribution of military enlistment across generations. In doing so, we demonstrate the demographic consequences of *institutional castling*—the shifting prominence of state institutions in the lives of particular demographic groups following changes in social policies or judicial decisions, allowing more prominent, protective, and integrative institutions to exchange their risk of exposure with less active and more punitive agencies across generations.

## LABOR MARKET STRUCTURE, THE MILITARY, AND PENAL SYSTEM EXPOSURE

Much has been written about the connection between crime, incarceration, and labor-force participation. Marxian approaches understand the prison system as a means of managing surplus labor (Spitzer 1975), as the connection between labor market structure, crime, and the criminal justice system can be complex and multilayered (Cantor and Land 1985; Bellair and Roscigno 2000; Phillips and Land 2012; Wadsworth 2004). Research suggests that the structure of the labor market (that is, the relative concentration of primary and secondary sector jobs), and not the overall supply of jobs, drives rates of imprisonment (Sutton 2004). Similarly, scholarship is mixed on whether crime rates are more responsive to the quantity of jobs (relative to the population) or to the quality of jobs available (Doeringer and Piore 1971; Crutchfield 1989, 2014). The labor stratification perspective that Robert Crutchfield (1989, 2014) advances finds that communities plagued by higher levels of crime experience labor market instability and possess a concentration of secondary sector jobs. This relationship may be particularly salient for young adult men, who make up roughly 90 percent of new military accessions (Krivo and Peterson 2004; Office of the Under Secretary of Defense, Personnel and Readiness 2017).

Additionally, workers who have jobs with characteristics that mark them as being in the primary sector, such as anticipating that their current job will last for a longer period of time (Crutchfield and Pitchford 1997) or reporting receiving benefits and emotional rewards from their employment (Wadsworth 2006), are less likely to engage in criminal activity.[1] Work in the military and in the civilian sector of the labor market are known to operate as turning points from crime, delinquency, and social disadvantage (Shattuck 1945; Mattick 1960; Dressler 1946; Elder 1986, 1999; Sampson and Laub 1993; Uggen 2000), particularly for those who secure high-quality jobs that provide them with a level of professional satisfaction (Uggen 1999; Van der Geest, Bijleveld, and Blokland 2011). The deterrent effect of work may also operate via an emotional dimension because formerly incarcerated men who are employed report less criminal activity when they feel committed to their jobs, regardless of job characteristics (Apel and Horney 2017).

A more limited body of research investigates the link between service in the armed forces and subsequent criminality. Although veterans have lower criminal justice involvement overall relative to nonveterans (Teachman and Tedrow 2016), a history of military employment does appear to increase violent offending (Bouffard 2005; Crutchfield and Pitchford 1997; Wadsworth 2006). However, the circumstances of each tour of duty, including the era of service and the selectivity of enlistment, shape that association (Bouffard 2014; Culp et al. 2013), given that mental health problems and substance abuse could prevail after discharge (Erickson et al. 2008; Tanielian and Jaycox 2008; Tsai et al. 2013).

Despite the benefits and costs associated with military employment, disadvantaged men who aspired to enlist saw their enlistment opportunities diminished twice. The first time was in 1980 and 1981, when the previously misnormed (that is, inaccurately calibrated) Armed Forces Qualifying Test (AFQT)—the standard-

---

1. Interestingly, both of these articles control for prior military employment and find higher levels of violent crime, but no effect on nonviolent offenses, among veterans relative to other workers in the civilian sector, net of social background characteristics.

ized entrance examination used to both establish eligibility for enlistment and to assign new service personnel to a military occupational specialty—was replaced (U.S. Congress 1989). Wide racial disparities emerged in AFQT scores (Kilburn, Hanser, and Klerman 1998), and large percentages of black men who would have previously qualified for the armed forces no longer met the minimum requirements (Angrist 1993). In the wake of this error, the Department of Defense struggled to find what it termed "highly qualified" applicants—those possessing both a diploma (rather than a GED or no certification) and an AFQT score above the median (Office of the Under Secretary of Personnel and Readiness 2000). By 1985, for example, only in the Air Force did a majority of enlistees clear these criteria (Office of the Undersecretary of Defense, Personnel and Readiness 2017, table D-9).

The second diminished opportunity for military employment occurred a decade later, when concerns over the capabilities of those in uniform converged with moves toward privatization, resulting in a "drawdown" of military personnel in the early 1990s (Lytell et al. 2015). The armed forces increased enlistment criteria in anticipation of military downsizing, virtually eliminating opportunities for enlistment among young men who lacked either a high school diploma (or GED) and a standardized test score in the middle range (Boesel 1992). The number of new accessions shrank rapidly, from 313,777 in 1986 to 205,501 in 1991, and down further to 160,511 by 2010 (Office of the Undersecretary of Defense, Personnel and Readiness 2017, table D-8). The total number of active duty enlisted personnel declined by roughly seven hundred thousand during the same period (Office of the Undersecretary of Defense, Personnel and Readiness 2017, table D-11). Joshua Angrist (1993, 2) finds that changes in minimum enlistment criteria in the early decades of the All-Volunteer Force "had an adverse effect on service opportunities for minority applicants." We suggest that the shrinking availability of primary sector employment offered by the U.S. military and the changes in their enlistment criteria may have altered the demographic composition of both the armed forces and the penal system via a set of social policy changes during the mid- to late twentieth century.

## INSTITUTIONAL CASTLING: RACE, LABOR STRATIFICATION, AND THE MILITARY AND PENAL SYSTEMS

We explore the demographic consequences of what we term institutional castling—the shifting prominence of state institutions in the lives of particular demographic groups following a change in social policy or judicial decisions, allowing more prominent, protective, and integrative institutions to exchange their risk of exposure with less active and more punitive agencies across generations.[2] Institutional castling may be a result of either disparate treatment (intentionality), disparate impact (unintentional consequences), or unconscious bias following the enactment of a particular social policy or judicial decision. State priorities may be revealed through legislation and budget allocations; the joint effect of new and large federal resource allocations and the creation of new social policies that upend and reconstitute the hierarchal stratification of institutions in the lives of particular demographic groups facilitates the castling of government agencies tasked with both integrating the American underclass into normative-based conceptions of society and punishing the particular types of behaviors associated with poverty and inequality. There have been two moments in American history when the military and penal systems have cas-

---

2. In chess, castling is a special defensive move in which the king and rook shift simultaneously in opposite directions, trading places in their relative positions on the board. As the only move in chess where a player can shift two pieces at the same time, castling enables the king to lessen the risk of checkmate by moving to a safer location, while the rook plays a more active role throughout the game. Although several conditions must be met before a player can castle—neither piece has been moved from its initial position; the space between the pieces must be empty; and the king cannot move into or out of check—the value of castling is highly subjective because the significance of the defensive move depends on the current position and potential movement of other pieces. Yet the strategic decision to castle remains an indispensable tool to ensure the king's safety. Although castling may require intentionality in the game of chess, the same need not be true of institutional castling.

tled: the Civil War and, in analyses that follow, the mid- to late twentieth century.

## Institutional Castling in U.S. History

A longer read of historical labor stratification points to an unassailable truth: prior to deindustrialization, penal growth, a drawdown in the size of the armed forces, and an increase in the selectivity of military enlistees during the close of the twentieth century, the first instance of institutional castling (between the military and carceral systems) took place during the era of slavery.[3] In *Black Reconstruction in America*, W.E.B. DuBois (1998) highlights the ways in which shifting Northern interpretations of two key policies led to the institutional castling of the military and criminal justice system for slaves and freedmen, given that fugitives from slavery and free Negroes were precluded from joining the Union Army. First, the Fugitive Slave Act of 1850 decreed that people who escaped slavery had to be returned to their masters, and the *Dred Scott v. Sandford* decision of 1857 ruled that the U.S. Constitution did not apply to blacks, whether enslaved or free.[4] Despite these laws and judicial decisions, Union Army generals routinely employed fugitive and freed slaves as "soldiers, spies, servants, military laborers, and laborers on plantations" (DuBois 1998, 66). Although initially supportive of excluding fugitive and enslaved men from the Union Army, President Lincoln "faced the truth front forward . . . the Negro was to be allowed to fight or the draft itself would not bring enough white men into the army to keep up the war" (82). Thus, the initial *disparate treatment* of slaves and free men under the Fugitive Slave Act and the *Dred Scott* decision were set aside to ensure that the Union Army had sufficient soldiers and resources throughout the war, providing the first instance of institutional castling where "fugitives became organized and formed a great labor force for the army" (65).

Second, the military policy to integrate fugitive and freed slaves into the Union Army also produced a set of *disparate impacts* that segregated formerly enslaved blacks and their families from white Union servicemembers, despite fighting alongside each other. For instance, DuBois (1998, 70) writes that "There were new and strange problems of the social contract. The white soldiers, for the most part, were opposed to serving Negroes in any manner, and were even unwilling to guard the camps where they were segregated or protect them against violence." The disparate impact of integrating freed slaves into the military but holding them at arm's length, facilitated a de facto system of racial segregation that would engender the disbandment of blacks and freed slaves from specific units of the armed forces after the Civil War ended, recastling the institutions of the military and penal system during Reconstruction in Southern states where "black codes" emerged to control the labor and criminalize the behavior of former slaves and African Americans (Roediger 2014).

## Institutional Castling During the Mid- to Late Twentieth Century

We argue that the mid- to late twentieth century was another turning point in the American lifecycle of institutional castling between the military and penal spheres for young, undereducated black men. Race-neutral social policies enacted by Congress and state agencies since the late 1960s may have shifted institutional castling from being predicated on (mostly) disparate treatment during the Civil War to new forms of normalization that are rooted in disparate impacts and unconscious biases.

On February 27, 1877, Congress passed an act whereby "no minor under the age of sixteen years, no insane or intoxicated person, no deserter from the service, and no person who has been convicted of a felony shall be enlisted or mustered into the military service."[5] This law remained unchanged until 1968, when Congress amended and expanded it to specify, in 10 USC§504(a), that "No person who is insane,

---

3. We conceive of slavery as both a labor market institution and a system whereby people who sought to free themselves became carceral subjects. In this article, we use language referring to the carceral aspects of slavery, but we recognize that this system of labor stratification also controlled the labor-power of enslaved people.

4. Fugitive Slave Act of 1850, 9 Stat. 462; *Dred Scott v. Sandford*, 60 U.S. (19 How.) 393 (1857).

5. Rev. Stat. Sec. 1118, Sec. 1, 19 Stat. 242 (1877).

intoxicated, or a deserter from an armed force, or who has been convicted of a felony, may be enlisted in any armed force. However, the Secretary [of Defense] concerned may authorize exceptions, in meritorious cases, for the enlistment of deserters and persons convicted of felonies."[6] The amendment is important because it carves out exceptions in the U.S. Code allowing for the possibility of felony and conduct waivers during the enlistment process. Between 1948 and 1968, the percentage of non–African Americans with a felony record had nearly doubled (from 1 to 2 percent); among African Americans, the percentage grew from 5 to 8 percent over the same period, with men bearing the brunt of this institutional growth (Shannon et al. 2017). Yet contemporary research shows that the military personnel granted these felony waivers do not reflect the racial and educational distribution of people with a felony record (Lundquist, Pager, and Strader 2018; Travis, Western, and Redburn 2014).

The same year that the 1877 law was amended to create 10 USC§504(a), to carve out provisions for felony and conduct waivers that would subsequently disproportionately favor whites and those with a higher education in enlistment decisions, Congress passed the Omnibus Crime Control and Safe Streets Act of 1968,[7] which established the Law Enforcement Assistance Administration (LEAA), now known as the Office of Justice Programs, which allocated $100 million in block grants to states, with half of the money going to local law enforcement (Office of Justice Programs 1996). The LEAA also provided resources to develop alternative sanctions for the punishment of young offenders and to deal with rioting and organized crime (Office of Justice Programs 1996). The Safe Streets Act also expanded the use of surveillance at the local level and provided for closer training between local law enforcement and the FBI (Office of Justice Programs 1996).

The coterminous creation of 10 USC§504(a), aimed at excluding people with felony records from the military unless waived, and the enactment of crime control legislation (and its authorized funding apparatus) were not accidental; these decisions represent intentional actions to reconstitute the functioning of particular American institutions.[8] Jonathan Simon (2007, 75) observes that "it is not just the scope of this wave of lawmaking [starting in the late 1960s] that makes it impressive, it is also the coherence of this body of law as reflecting a vision of how institutions govern through crime." Similarly, Elizabeth Hinton (2016, 340) notes that "Questions of intent, or the degree to which federal policymakers foresaw the consequences of the choices they made with respect to urban social programs in black communities, are only relevant to a certain extent. The issue is to uncover the series of decisions that made contemporary mass incarceration possible in order to discover our own actual history." Thus the functioning of state institutions since the late 1960s and their demographic reconstitutions must be understood through the

---

6. 10 USC§504 "Persons Not Qualified", Public L. No. 90-235, 81 Stat. 753 (1968).

7. Omnibus Crime Control and Safe Streets Act of 1968, Public L. No. 90-351, 82 Stat. 197 (1968).

8. For example, during Nixon's 1970 State of the Union address, wherein he laid out his vision for a War on Crime, he highlighted that "while state and local law enforcement agencies are the cutting edge in the effort to eliminate crime, the Federal Government should play a greater role," and to further that role, he intended to double the 1971 federal spending for local law enforcement beyond that which was budgeted in 1970 (Nixon 1970). Additionally, between 1969 and 1972, the federal government's law enforcement budget tripled; federal aid to state and local law enforcement grew from $63 million to almost $700 million, and the LEAA saw its budget increase tenfold between 1969 and 1972 (Mitchell 1971; Office of Justice Programs 1996).

Furthermore, the language used to describe the rising tide of unrest and crime in the 1960s mixes the metaphors of the military and penal institutions. For example, during then Attorney General John Mitchell's 1971 conference on crime reduction in the United States (Mitchell 1971, 4), he unequivocally stated, "To go back to my analogy, the enemy's advance [crime] has been slowed, but he is not yet retreating. I'd like to think the situation can be described in Winston Churchill's cautious words when the Allies had stalled Nazi expansion and opened a new front in Africa in the fall of 1942. 'Now this is not the end,' he said. 'It is not even the beginning of the end. But it is, perhaps, the end of the beginning.'"

refracted prism of governing through crime and social control following the civil rights movement (Garland 2001b; Simon 2007).

It is our contention that race-neutral policies such as 10 USC§504(a) may have had a disparate impact on the ability of African American men to enlist in the military—a trend that was exacerbated by other policy changes that increased the educational and testing requirements for enlistment during military downsizing. Despite moments in American history when felons have been allowed to enlist, particularly during World Wars I and II, the men who served underwent extensive assessments and reviews by parole boards, Selective Service personnel, and psychologists, and the military considered their enlistment an experiment (Shattuck 1945; Mattick 1960; Dressler 1946). Even now, felons may obtain conduct and felony waivers for military employment; however, research shows that these waivers are selectively administered across military branches and vary inversely with civilian labor market trends, disproportionately favoring whites, men, and individuals with a high school degree or more, much to the exclusion of blacks and high school dropouts (see Lundquist, Pager, and Strader 2018).

These changes may have jointly cleaved off potential turning points in the life course of young, undereducated black men, allowing the military and penal institutions to castle in ways that would elevate the risk of criminal justice contact for African American men during labor market restructuring. The combination of increasing requirements for eligibility and the exclusion of those with prior criminal records intersect to deny large segments of the young, black male population access to the protective or corrective benefits of military employment. These federal codes and legislation were intentionally amended, enacted, and funded, regardless of whether the resulting biases were unconscious, unintended, or deliberate. Local, state, and federal governments began to govern through crime in ways that may have portended the castling of major institutions in the lives of specific disadvantaged men. The generational shift in these modalities of governance, in relation to the military and penal institutions, may mean that the same demographic group will have radically different experiences with these social institutions over time. Our conceptual framework and empirical inquiry seeks to examine whether the military is protected from demographic groups with the highest risks of incarceration, given their lower rates of felony waiver issuance (Lundquist, Pager, and Strader 2018).

To underscore the plausibility of our inquiry into the changing composition of the civilian and military labor markets, figure 1 displays employment trends since the early 1970s for young, non-Hispanic white and black men who did and did not graduate from high school. As panel A illustrates, the percentage of young men on active duty has declined since the 1970s, particularly among black men without a secondary education. Blacks with less than a high school education saw their relative employment presence in the armed forces eliminated by 1986, but white men who dropped out of high school maintained a small presence. At the same time, civilian labor-force statistics, presented in panel B, also underscore the growing disadvantage of young, African American men with less than a high school education. At the beginning of the series, educational and racial parity in employment rates was higher. Yet, deindustrialization (Wilson 1987) and penal expansion (Western and Pettit 2005; Western 2002, 2006; Pettit 2012) led to sharply declining employment rates among black men with little formal education.

Panels C and D of figure 1 convey complementary stories about labor inactivity for young, undereducated men. Panel C shows trends in the unemployment rate by race and education level. Young black men who have dropped out of high school have the highest unemployment rates, whereas white men with a high school diploma have the lowest unemployment rates. African American men with a secondary education and white men who have dropped out of high school tend to have similar unemployment rates.

Panel D displays the percentage of each demographic group that has given up its search for work. Black men who did not complete high school have the highest rates of removal from the labor force, reaching almost 50 percent by the close of the first decade of millennium, a

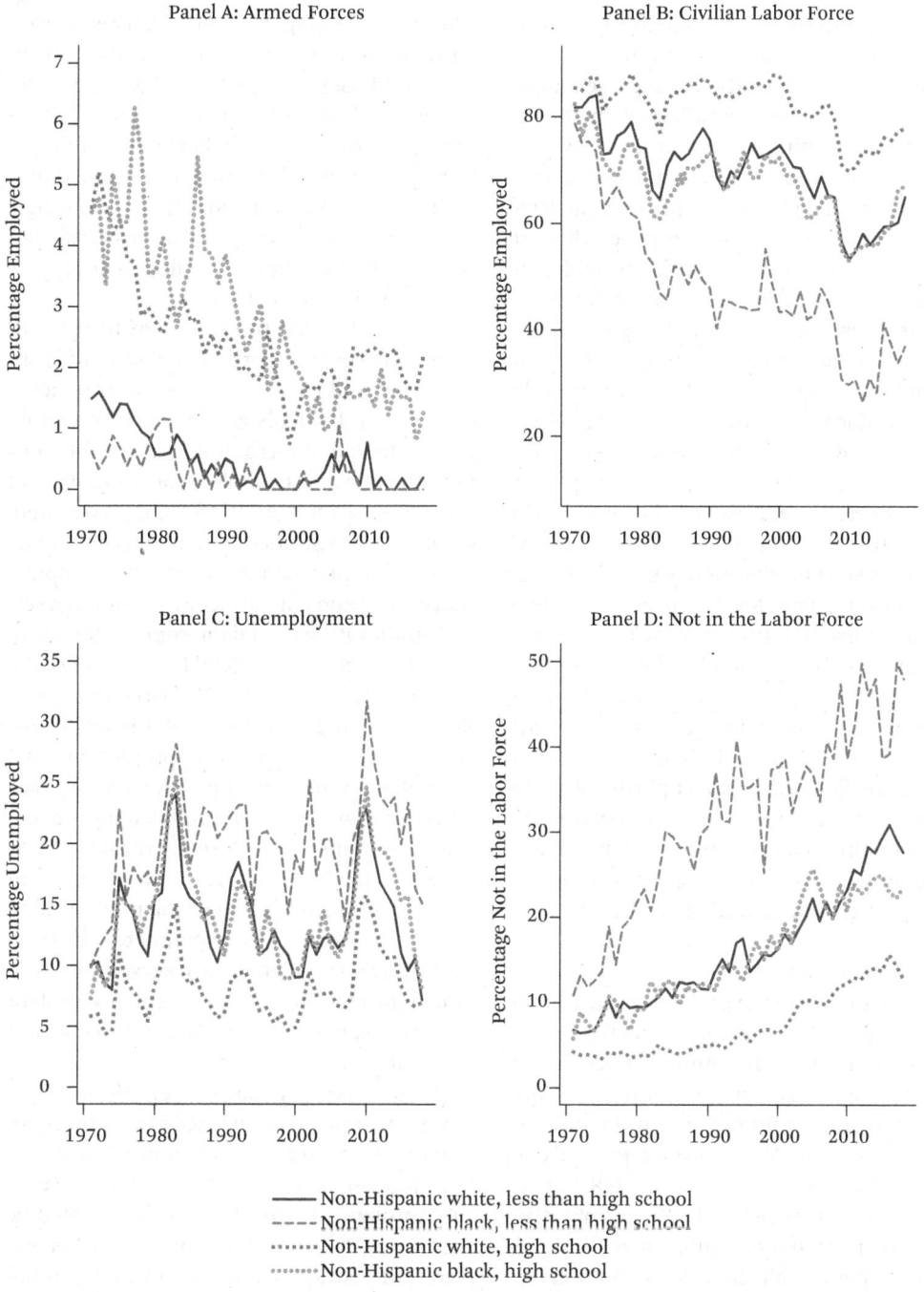

**Figure 1.** Trends in Employment Status for U.S. Men Age Twenty to Thirty-Four, by Race and Educational Attainment, 1971–2018

*Source:* Authors' calculations based on the Annual Social and Economic Supplement of the Current Population Survey.

rate double that of white high school dropouts. Again, black high school graduates and white dropouts generally have similar levels of employment hopelessness, though the trends vary in the last two decades of our time series.

Historically, men without a high school diploma had more military enlistment and labor market opportunities than they do today (Carnevale, Smith, and Strohl 2010). The mass unemployment and joblessness of undereducated men may have differentially exposed them to the criminal justice system during penal expansion and military downsizing. We therefore begin our investigation into contemporary institutional castling by documenting veteran and nonveteran incarceration rates over time by race and educational attainment. Our analyses focus on a "downstream" measure—changes in the incarceration rates of veterans and nonveterans over time. Next, we decompose the change in the incarceration rate that is due to changes in veteran educational attainment over time, allowing for a closer inspection into how military enlistment policies may have severed a conduit to upward mobility for severely disadvantaged men. Then, we examine how decades of penal expansion are associated with compositional changes (in both size and educational quality) in military employment across generations. Finally, we illustrate how contemporary institutional castling between the military and penal institutions severely disadvantaged young, undereducated black men.

## DATA AND CODING

To understand how the protective role of military service castled with the carceral institutions of punishment for young, African American men, we begin by compiling a unique dataset to analyze immersion in the military and penal systems. We use twelve waves of data from twin sources collected by the U.S. Census Bureau and distributed by the Bureau of Justice Statistics. The Survey of Inmates in Local Jails series has periodically collected nationally representative data on individuals held in local correctional facilities across the span of four decades. Respondents include those being held pretrial, those serving local sentences, and those awaiting transfer into the custody of another correctional facility. The survey was fielded in 1972, 1978, 1983, 1989, 1996, and 2002. Although prior research on veteran incarceration has excluded inmates in local custody when investigating differences between veterans and nonveterans (Culp et al. 2013; Greenberg and Rosenheck 2007), including data on inmates in local jails has increased in importance, as extended periods of pretrial detention, prison overcrowding, and other policy shifts (such as AB109 in California) increasingly mean that inmates will spend at least a fraction of their sentenced time in local and county jails (Turney and Connor 2019).

We also include the Survey of Inmates in State and Federal Correctional Facilities. In 1974, 1979, and 1986, this survey was conducted only with individuals at state correctional facilities. In 1991, it was administered to inmates in both state and federal prisons. In 1997 and again in 2004, the state and federal surveys were combined. These surveys were designed to be nationally representative of the inmate population in state and federal facilities. Although several studies have used data from the Survey of Inmates in State and Federal Facilities since the mid-1980s (Culp et al. 2013; Greenberg and Rosenheck 2012), no study systematically uses all inmate data since 1972 to present national estimates of veteran incarceration rates by race and education. However, Sanjiv Gupta and Jennifer Lundquist (2012) use aggregate data to show how the fraction of service personnel and inmates has stabilized since the mid-1990s. In total, the fifteen facility-year inmate series covers 121,554 respondents. Each survey wave contains information on whether the respondent has ever been or is currently employed by the armed forces.

To allow a comparison between the incarcerated and noninstitutionalized populations, we also use the March Current Population Survey (also known as the March CPS) for the years 1972 through 2012, inclusive. It is collected by the Census Bureau and the Bureau of Labor Statistics, surveys approximately fifty to sixty thousand noninstitutionalized respondents in settled households, and collects data on a variety of socioeconomic and demographic characteristics, including race and veteran status. In all, our analysis draws on almost 6.9 million records over the forty-one years in this study. All analyses use sample weights for national representation.

## METHODS

The rate at which veterans are siphoned into the criminal justice system is critical to understanding the changing sociodemographic distribution of each institution over time, and how the military's capacity to protect at-risk men from criminal justice contact may have shifted after periods of increased enlistment criteria. We follow methods outlined in previous studies to generate race and class estimates of incarceration (Pettit and Western 2004; Western 2006; Pettit, Sykes, and Western 2009; Pettit 2012; Ewert, Sykes, and Pettit 2014; Sykes and Pettit 2014). We begin by constructing annual estimates of grouped incarceration rates for each year beginning in 1972. We calculate the cross-classified proportion of inmates in each demographic group—race, sex, age, educational level, and veteran status—within facility type, and use survey weights to obtain nationally representative estimates. We then linearly interpolate weighted group means between survey years and through 2012 to obtain a complete time series. Finally, we apply the weighted proportion for each group to annual correctional counts within facility type, as reported by the Bureau of Justice Statistics, and sum the total number of inmates within each group across different facility types (jails and prisons).

Data from the Current Population Survey and the Survey of Inmates have been analyzed systematically to ensure that our estimates of veteran and nonveteran incarceration rates do not reflect the sample selectivity associated with household based surveys. The weighted counts derived from the Survey of Inmates and the Bureau of Justice Statistics are used in the numerator of the incarceration rate. To avoid sample selection bias reported in Pettit (2012) and other studies, denominators for the incarceration rate are obtained by combining noninstitutionalized population counts (from CPS) and inmate counts (used in the numerator).

We use a standard demographic technique to understand racial and educational inequality in military enlistment and incarceration. Evelyn Kitagawa's (1955) standardization and decomposition method allows us to examine how the changing size of the veteran population and the increased educational selectivity for enlistment converge to explain differences in the veteran and nonveteran incarceration rates for particular demographic groups. Essentially, the decomposition quantifies how much of the difference in incarceration rates, between veterans and nonveterans, is explained by the compositional differences in the (racial and educational) distribution of veterans and nonveterans over time, net of the underlying population incarceration rate across demographic groups.

CPS population counts (c) and the incarceration rate (M) for veterans (v) and nonveterans (nv) during year (t) can be decomposed into two parts: the contribution of compositional differences in the veteran population (the first term) and the contribution of differences in the incarceration rate (the second term), as presented in equation (1).

$$\Delta = \sum_t^n \left(c_t^v - c_t^{nv}\right) \left[\frac{M_t^v + M_t^{nv}}{2}\right] \\ + \sum_t^n \left(M_t^v - M_t^{nv}\right) \left[\frac{c_t^v + c_t^{nv}}{2}\right]. \quad (1)$$

The first term (before the plus sign) measures the relative difference in the composition of the veteran and nonveteran population, weighted by the average incarceration rate. The second term (after the plus sign) captures the difference in the incarceration rate schedule (when the two groups are incarcerated), weighted by the average population size of veterans and nonveterans. In the decomposition, we hold constant age and examine men age twenty through thirty four because the turning points literature focuses on young men during ages at risk of military employment, criminal delinquency, and incarceration (Elder 1986; Sampson and Laub 1993, 1996).

The decomposition captures the average cohort effect in compositional and rate differences across periods for a fixed age group (such as men age twenty through thirty-four). We perform race-specific decompositions between veterans and nonveterans to uncover the patterns of educational inequality in enlistment and incarceration for white and black males. We apply this technique twice across each level of educational attainment (less than high school and high school graduates who have not completed any college coursework).

Second, we explore how demographic change in military employment across generations is associated with penal expansion using ordinary least squares regression analysis. We construct a panel dataset—using aggregated individual observations—and estimate a model of how logged adjusted incarceration rates (which includes inmates into the population denominator of the rate) for $r$ race (white or black), $e$ education group (dropout or high school graduate), and $v$ veteran status (veteran or nonveteran) during year $t$ are associated with a vector of $X$ demographic variables, as displayed in equation (2).

$$\ln(\textit{Adjusted Incarceration Rate}_{revt}) = \beta_0 + \beta X_{revt} + \gamma D_{ret-20} + \lambda_t + \varepsilon_{revt}. \quad (2)$$

We also include a vector of lagged military employment rates from two decades before ($D_{ret-20}$) to estimate how the compositional shift to a smaller, more educated military affected incarceration rates across generations. A two-decade lag was selected to provide a few years for the implementation of military enlistment policies and to measure the association across a complete generation (eighteen years). Year fixed-effects ($\lambda_t$) are included in the model to capture period-specific events that are not directly measured in the regression equation (such as crime rates, changes in the economy, educational expansion, military actions, and other national conditions that are associated with that year, relative to other years in the data). Standard errors have been clustered on year. Because equation (3) is a log-level regression model, to calculate the percentage change in the adjusted incarceration rate, the coefficients for $\beta$ and $\gamma$ must be retransformed, such that %$\Delta y = 100 * (e^\beta - 1)$ If the military provided protection against incarceration for specific demographic groups, we expect that the coefficients for $\beta$ and $\gamma$ will be negative.

## FINDINGS

Figure 2 presents the prevalence of incarceration and veteran status among the American adult population. In 1972, nearly 308,000 Americans (or 150 per hundred thousand) were behind bars. By 2012, more than 2.2 million men and women were in prison or jail, with the incarceration rate peaking at 764 inmates per hundred thousand in 2008 (Glaze and Kaeble 2014; West and Sabol 2009). Current Population Survey data indicate that in 1972 more than twenty-five million U.S. veterans, roughly one in eight American adults and nearly one in four men, had been employed by the military. Although the number of active duty personnel increased slightly during the 1970s, the deceleration in enlistment after the implementation of an All-Volunteer Force in 1973 was rapid. Increased population growth, higher death rates for veterans of earlier service periods, and a smaller active duty population with longer average terms of service have substantially decreased the rate of veterans returning to civilian life over the last four decades. These trends suggest the relative risk of an American adult participating in either the armed forces or the penal system have become chiral (the mirror image of these trends), with the rate of change (slope) remaining relatively constant for both trends, despite differences in their absolute levels. Figure 2 highlights contemporary institutional castling.

Trends in figure 2 suggest a compositional change among the veteran and incarcerated population by race and education. Much research shows the lifetime risk of incarceration has changed for white and black men with low levels of education born during the mid- to late twentieth century (Pettit and Western, 2004; Pettit et al. 2009; Heckman and LaFontaine 2010; Pettit, 2012; Ewert, Sykes, and Pettit 2014; Neal and Rick 2014). Figure 3 shows the percentage of men age eighteen through sixty-four who are veterans, by race and education. In 1972, almost 43 percent of white male dropouts were veterans. By 2012, that number had declined to 4.3 percent—a 90 percent reduction. Among black men who did not complete high school, 28.7 percent were veterans in 1972, but only 5.5 percent were by the close of 2012, a reduction of 80.8 percent.

For more educated men, the percentage of veterans in the population is higher and the decline occurs more slowly. For white men who completed high school, 55.4 percent were vet-

**Figure 2.** Veteran and Incarceration Rates for U.S. Adults Age Eighteen to Sixty-Four, 1972–2012

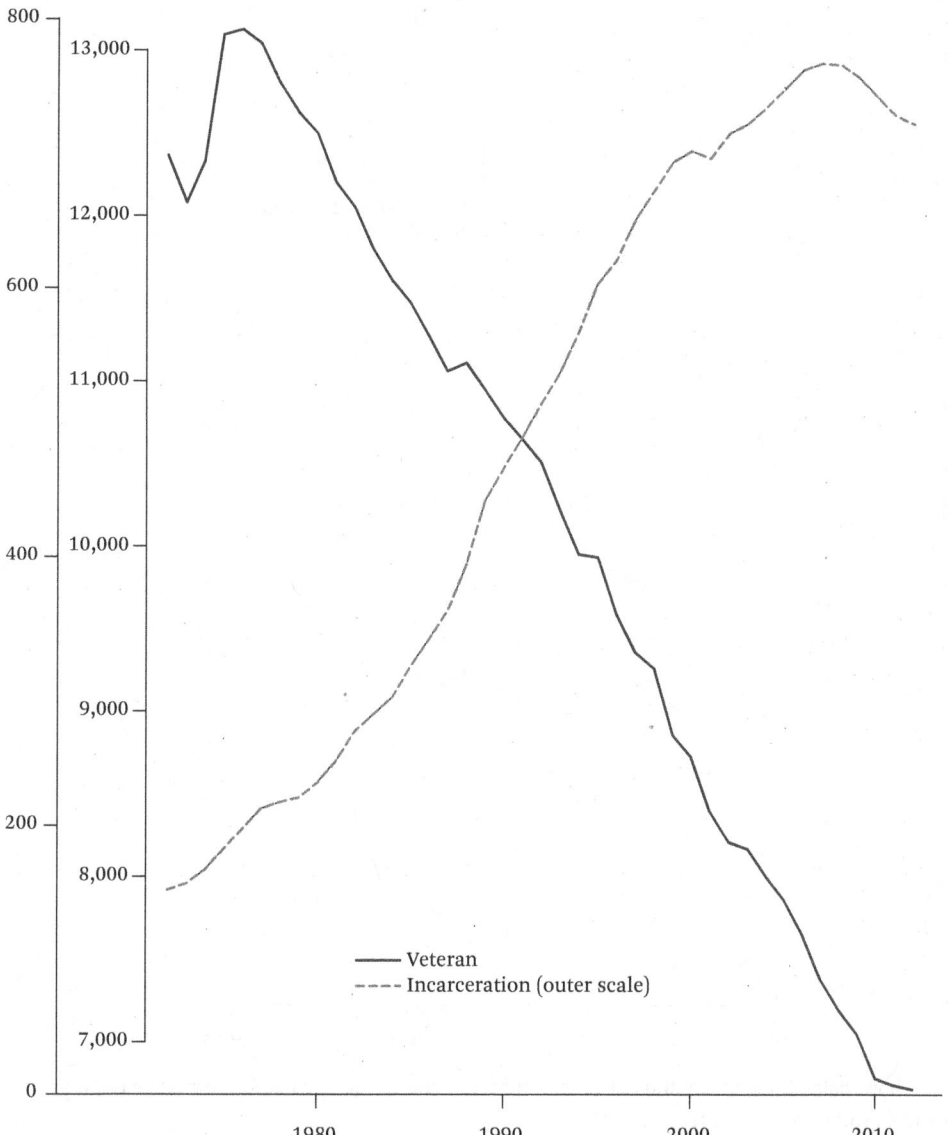

*Source:* Authors' calculations from the Surveys of Inmates, the Bureau of Justice Statistics population counts, and Current Population Survey data.
*Note:* Rate is per one hundred thousand.

erans in 1972 versus 13.9 percent in 2012. For blacks with a high school diploma, the percentage declines from 44.8 percent to 13.4 percent. Interestingly, figure 3 shows approximate racial parity in the proportion of high school dropouts and high school graduates with and without prior military employment by 2012. Such convergence for both racial groups across levels of education may be the result of both the downsizing of the military and a shift toward a more educated personnel over time.

Figure 4 displays veteran and nonveteran incarceration rates by race for men age eighteen through sixty-four between 1972 and 2012. In the earliest year (1972), these men were born between 1908 and 1954, and would have been at

**Figure 3.** Veteran Percentage of U.S. Men Age Eighteen to Sixty-Four, by Race and Education, 1972–2012

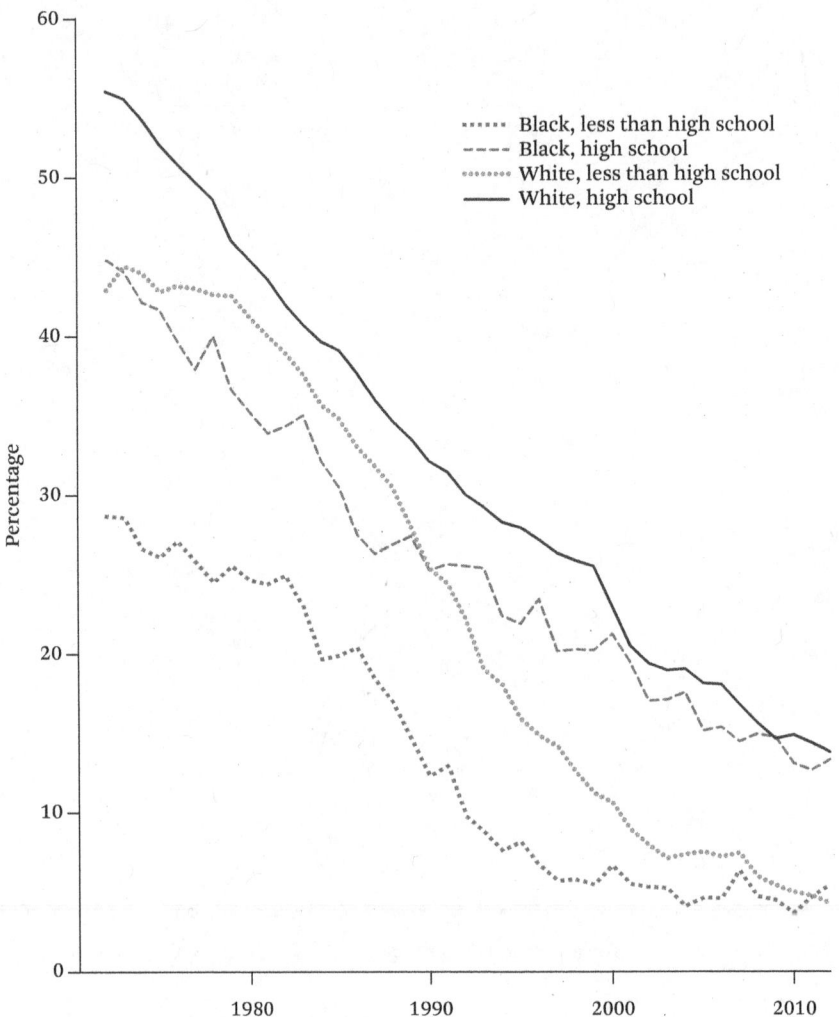

*Source:* Authors' calculations from the Surveys of Inmates, the Bureau of Justice Statistics population counts, and Current Population Survey data.

the highest risk of serving in World War II, Korea, and Vietnam. Their counterparts in 2012 would have been born between 1948 and 1994 and were most likely to have served in Vietnam, during the early years of the All-Volunteer Force, or in recent U.S. engagements in the Middle East. Incarceration rates for black men have soared since 1972 and the gap in incarceration rates by veteran status has increased. In 1972, black nonveterans were incarcerated at a rate of 1,054 per hundred thousand. By 2012, that number had more than tripled, to 3,252 per hundred thousand. Similarly, the veteran incarceration rate among black men quintupled over this period, increasing from 490 in 1972 to 2,054 in 2012. This difference between groups suggests that the gap in incarceration rates by veteran status was 564 per hundred thousand among black men in 1972. By 2012, the veteran status gap had nearly doubled, to 1,198. Among black men, across all four decades of our data, being a veteran clearly served as protection

**Figure 4.** Incarceration Rates by Race and Veteran Status for U.S. Men Age Eighteen to Sixty-Four, 1972–2012

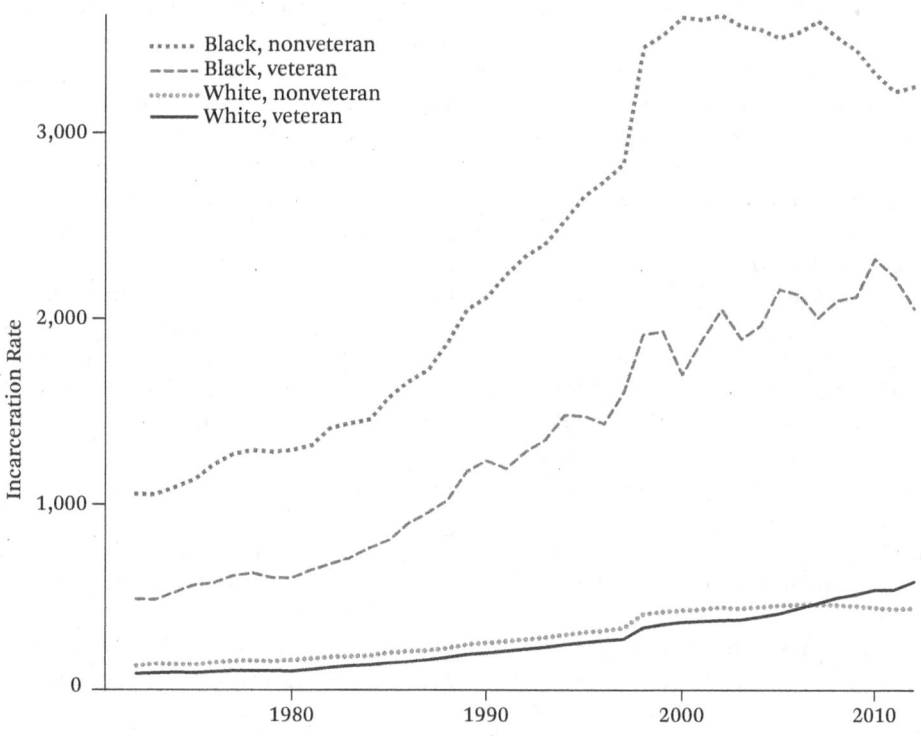

*Source:* Authors' calculations from the Surveys of Inmates, the Bureau of Justice Statistics population counts, and Current Population Survey data.

against involvement with the criminal justice system.[9]

White men, however, had lower rates of incarceration for both veterans and nonveterans. The rate increased more gradually for white men than it did for blacks, and the gap between veterans and nonveterans is much smaller. For instance, white nonveteran incarceration rates increased from 130 per hundred thousand in 1972 to 442 in 2012. Comparatively, veteran incarceration rates among white men rose by a factor of 6.7, from 87 to 584 between 1972 and 2012. We estimate that, among whites, veteran incarceration rates now outpace those for nonveterans for the first time in the All-Volunteer era, and have done so since 2007. This finding suggests that veteran status operates as a protective shield against involvement with the criminal justice system for black men but not for white men.

Next, we present results from the decomposition of the intersection between the shifting educational distribution and the changing rate of incarceration between veterans and nonveterans in the American population. Our presentation in figure 3 of the changing concentration of veterans, by race and education, among the male working-age population, and the percentage of black and white men who are incarcerated, by veteran status, depicted in figure 4, are animated by research that documents how penal growth obscures the measurement of social inequality by excluding inmates from household-based surveys. This exclusion has led

---

9. We thank an anonymous reviewer for pointing out that an unknown percentage of respondents in the Current Population Survey have been previously incarcerated. The results we discuss should be interpreted conservatively, as they reflect point-in-time, rather than lifetime, rates of incarceration.

scholars to adjust measures of social inequality to include institutionalized populations.[10] Because data from the CPS are used to construct our rates, the trends we present for veteran status, educational attainment, and incarceration are adjusted for the exclusion of inmates from household surveys, allowing for more precise estimates of within-group educational differences for veterans and between-group incarceration rate differences among veterans and nonveterans.[11] Our focus here is identifying the unique contributions of each component in explaining racial and educational differences in incarceration. Because the goal of this decomposition is to explain the unique contribution of each factor to the observed change or difference, the effects should sum to 100 percent, and in most cases, both numbers are positive.

Samuel Preston, Patrick Heuveline, and Michelle Guillot (2001, 29) argue that in many applications, however, one factor—either differences in compositional effects or in rate schedules—"will account for more than 100% of the original difference," particularly when "two factors work in opposite directions and there is no reason to believe such phenomena should operate in concert." This implicitly means that one factor will be negative.[12] We contend that such processes may be at work (as displayed in figure 2) for young, African American men with low levels of education, who do not meet military enlistment criteria, face difficulties in the civilian labor market, and experience an increased risk of criminal justice contact. If this is true (as shown in figures 1, 3, and 4), then among black men only, we expect to find a positive value in excess of 100 percent for the veteran compositional difference, rendering the incarceration rate schedule for black men largely negative to offset the difference between these two components of change.

Table 1 shows that for white high school dropouts, changes in the characteristics of veterans over time account for 85.9 percent of the changes in institutional composition. Incarceration rates for poorly educated whites explain 14.1 percent of the difference. For black dropouts, however, the role of the military is more pronounced: the educational distribution of veterans accounts for 135.6 percent of the compositional change in institutions. Because the difference in the incarceration rate underexplains 35.6 percent of the change, this finding suggests that many of the poorly educated black men who have been incarcerated may have been at risk for enlistment in the military as a competing institution to criminal justice contact. These estimates—+14.1 percent (for white dropouts) and -35.6 percent (for black dropouts)—are closely aligned with research that estimates contemporary civilian incarceration rates for white and black dropouts to be 12 percent and 37.2 percent, respectively (Pettit, Sykes, and Western 2009, 13; Pettit 2012, 15). Findings from the decomposition support our contention that the negative incar-

---

10. A substantial body of literature suggests that failure to account for changes in social policy can distort research findings on labor market processes. For example, the liberalization of eligibility requirements and the increased real value of benefits led to expanded Social Security Disability enrollment among poorly educated, working-age Americans—a trend that artificially deflated official unemployment rates (Autor and Duggan 2003). Penal expansion has been shown to produce similar obscuring estimates of labor market participation, wage growth, and wealth (Western and Beckett 1999; Western 2002; Western and Pettit 2000, 2005; Holzer, Offner, and Sorenson 2005; Western 2006; Pettit 2012; Pettit and Sykes 2015; Sykes and Maroto 2016). Official estimates touting an increase in high school graduation have also been shown to be deceptively optimistic due to reliance on household-based surveys that fail to include institutionalized populations (Pettit 2012; Ewert et al. 2014; Heckman and LaFontaine 2010; Neal and Rick 2014; Pettit and Sykes 2015).

11. Contact the authors for a reference figure and its narrative documenting the growth in selection bias associated with these measures due to the exclusion of inmates from household-based sample surveys of the population.

12. These components are likely to be in excess whenever the trend in one of the two factors is strongly influenced by specific legislative policies or social norms that govern that population process (such as age-specific contraceptive use rates and their corresponding birth rates).

**Table 1.** Decomposition of the Differences in U.S. Veteran Composition and Adjusted Incarceration Rates for Men Age Twenty to Thirty-Four, by Education and Race, 1972–2012

|  | Less Than High School | | High School | |
| --- | --- | --- | --- | --- |
|  | Non-Hispanic White | Non-Hispanic Black | Non-Hispanic White | Non-Hispanic Black |
| Veteran compositional difference | 85.9 | 135.6 | 85.2 | 102.1 |
| Incarceration rate difference | 14.1 | −35.6 | 14.8 | −2.1 |

*Source:* Authors' calculations from the Surveys of Inmates, the Bureau of Justice Statistics population counts, and Current Population Survey data.

ceration effect in table 1 for black high school dropouts points to the differential enlistment patterns for severely disadvantaged men over time. Put simply, military enlistment may have been a protective factor for poorly educated blacks against rising levels of incarceration given that this group experienced significantly more positive compositional effects in enlistment than their white counterparts.

Blacks who completed high school, however, were not significantly harmed by these compositional shifts, as indicated by numerical estimates in the last column of table 1. Because the new enlistment criteria did not exclude them, black men who had graduated from high school remained able to use the armed forces as a protective institution against the criminal justice system.[13]

Finally, table 2 presents estimates from our log-level regression model examining how veteran status is associated with incarceration for young black and white men between 1972 and 2012. Not surprisingly, the baseline model (model 1) shows that incarceration rates for black men are three times ($301.1\% = 100 * (e^{1.389} - 1)$) higher than the incarceration rates of white men. Similarly, young men who have dropped out of high school have incarceration rates 2.3 times ($230.7\% = 100 * (e^{1.196} - 1)$) larger than men with a high school diploma.

Veteran status is not associated with incarceration (model 2); however, on fully interacting veteran status with race and education (model 3), the main effect of veteran status is positively associated with incarceration rates for white men. Model 3 also shows that black veterans and veterans with low levels of education have incarceration rates 19.6 to 32.2 percent lower than their reference groups. This association is so strong that the three-way interaction involving race, education, and veteran status increases by 72.1 percent in logged-units, going from a coefficient of −0.215 (in model 3) to −0.370 (in model 4), when military employment rates from a generation ago are controlled (model 4). The same interaction for black veterans with less than a high school education shows that their incarceration rates were 30.9 percent ($= 100 * (e^{0.370} - 1)$) lower than their same-race counterparts with similar formal education who were not veterans, when the percentage of military personnel from a generation ago is included in the model, pointing to both the changing size and evolving composition of military enlistees. The increased educational requirements for employment in the military are evident in model 5: a 1 percentage point increase in the employment of military servicemembers with less than a high school education a generation ago is associated with a 21.4 percent ($-100 * (e^{0.241} - 1)$) reduction in incarceration rates.

---

13. The negative incarceration component for black men with a high school degree may represent qualitative educational distinctions between servicemen who graduated from high school and servicemen who obtained GEDs (as discussed in Heckman and LaFontaine 2010). We are unable to test this proposition because of the nature of the data. Testing this proposition would require knowing the exact dates of incarceration, military enlistment, high school completion, and GED acquisition. CPS and Survey of Inmates data do not provide this detailed information.

**Table 2.** Estimates from a Model Predicting the Natural Log of the Adjusted Incarceration Rate for U.S. Men Age Twenty to Thirty-Four, by Race, Education, Veteran Status, and Enlistment Rates, 1972–2016

|  | Baseline (1) | $M_1$ + Veteran (2) | $M_2$ + Interactions (3) | $M_3$ + % Employed in Military (4) | $M_4$ + Education Interaction (5) |
|---|---|---|---|---|---|
| Non-Hispanic black | 1.389*** | 1.389*** | 1.744*** | 1.646*** | 1.654*** |
|  | (0.0361) | (0.0361) | (0.0249) | (0.0360) | (0.0372) |
| Less than high school (LTHS) | 1.196*** | 1.196*** | 1.465*** | 1.654*** | 1.755*** |
|  | (0.0517) | (0.0518) | (0.0647) | (0.0945) | (0.104) |
| Veteran |  | -0.0247 | 0.332*** | 0.392*** | 0.392*** |
|  |  | (0.0384) | (0.0407) | (0.0413) | (0.0414) |
| Non-Hispanic black x LTHS |  |  | -0.213*** | -0.105* | -0.162* |
|  |  |  | (0.0285) | (0.0450) | (0.0643) |
| Non-Hispanic black x veteran |  |  | -0.388*** | -0.376*** | -0.376*** |
|  |  |  | (0.0487) | (0.0615) | (0.0616) |
| LTHS x veteran |  |  | -0.218*** | -0.248** | -0.248** |
|  |  |  | (0.0594) | (0.0741) | (0.0742) |
| Non-Hispanic black x LTHS x veteran |  |  | -0.215+ | -0.370* | -0.370* |
|  |  |  | (0.121) | (0.143) | (0.143) |
| Percent employed by military twenty years ago |  |  |  | 0.0699* | 0.0573+ |
|  |  |  |  | (0.0288) | (0.0330) |
| LTHS x percent employed in military twenty years ago |  |  |  |  | -0.241* |
|  |  |  |  |  | (0.102) |
| Constant | 5.192*** | 5.205*** | 4.946*** | 5.184*** | 5.298*** |
|  | (0.0228) | (0.0382) | (0.0380) | (0.104) | (0.111) |
| Observations | 360 | 360 | 360 | 280 | 280 |
| $R^2$ | 0.913 | 0.913 | 0.935 | 0.917 | 0.919 |

*Source:* Authors' compilation of data based on the Surveys of Inmates, the Bureau of Justice Statistics, the March Current Population Survey, and the Annual Social and Economic Supplement of the Current Population Survey.
*Note:* Authors' calculations from a OLS regression model predicting the natural log of the adjusted incarceration rate. All models include year fixed effects (to control for period-specific events such as crime rates, changes in the economy, educational expansion, military actions, and other national conditions associated with that year, relative to other years in the data), and standard errors have been clustered on year. Non-Hispanic whites, those with a high school diploma, and nonveterans are the reference groups. All coefficients must be retransformed to estimate percentage changes ($\%\Delta y = 100*(e^\beta - 1)$).
+$p < .1$; *$p < .05$; **$p < .01$; ***$p < .001$

Figure 5 displays the predicted incarceration trends from model 5 of table 2, with shaded 95 percent confidence intervals. Of particular importance is that changes in enlistment selectivity over time did not produce statistically significant differences between veterans and nonveterans who were white dropouts or black high school graduates. However, among white high school graduates, incarceration rates for veterans were higher than for nonveterans for nearly twenty years (from 1987 through 2006). Among young black men who dropped out of high school, differences in incarceration rates among veterans and nonveterans prior to the mid-1970s were not measurable. Yet, beginning around 1977, nearly four years after the transi-

**Figure 5.** Fitted Linear Model of Incarceration Rates by Veteran Status Across Race and Educational Levels, 1972–2012

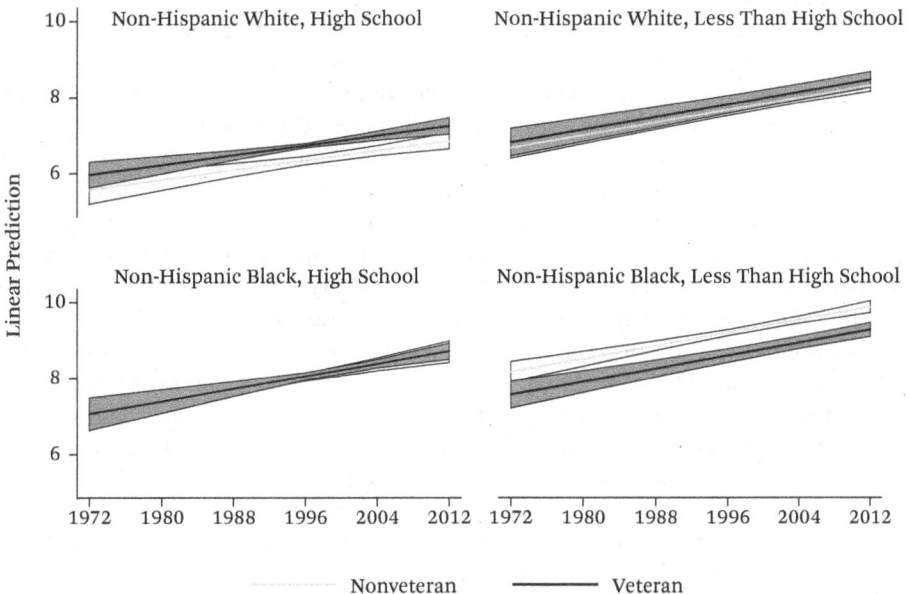

*Source:* Authors' calculations from the Surveys of Inmates, the Bureau of Justice Statistics population counts, and Current Population Survey data.

tion to the All-Volunteer Force and almost a decade after 10 USC§504(a)—incarceration rates increased for black nonveterans who dropped out of high school. This trend diverges significantly from the trend associated with black veterans who dropped out of high school, confirming results from the decomposition of incarceration by race and education (presented in table 1). These findings speak to the role of contemporary institutional castling following a series of policy changes that, within a decade, would cleave off military enlistment as a potential turning point in the lives of young, undereducated black men.

## CONCLUSIONS AND IMPLICATIONS

In the opening line of *Rethinking the State*, Bourdieu (1994, 1) argues that "to endeavor to think the state is to take the risk of taking over (or being taken over by) a thought of the state, i.e. of applying to the state categories of thought produced and guaranteed by the state and hence to misrecognize its most profound truth." The misrecognition of truth occurs when social scientists do not employ a radical rethinking of the state through *hyperbolic doubt*—striving "to question all the presuppositions and preconstructions inscribed in the reality under analysis as well as in the very thoughts of the analyst" (1). Hyperbolic doubt facilitates the rethinking and reimagining of social problems through a critical examination of the state and its processes, functions, conventions, and teachings. Although Bourdieu's case examined the role of state in matters of orthography (that is, correct spelling), he states that social artifacts in one realm under examination are "the product of a work of normalization and codification, quite analogous to that which the state effects concurrently in other realms of social life" (2).

In this article, we have sought to employ Bourdieuan hyperbolic doubt by reexamining the presuppositions and preconstructions of racial and educational inequalities in incarceration by exploring an often underexamined explanation for the disproportionate representation of young, undereducated men in the correctional system: the role of the military industrial complex. Growth in the penal system and diminished opportunities for enlistment among the disadvantaged during the late twentieth century have profoundly changed the contemporary demographic composition of American penal and military institutions.

In the early 1970s, increasing punishment and inequality occurred in tandem with a decline in military employment rates and a shifting educational composition of the armed forces. At the same time, an increasing share of veterans reentering civilian life meant elevated risks for criminal justice contact, depending on their race and education. Spending time in the armed forces can provide a critical opportunity for positive redirection in the life course of economically disadvantaged (Elder 1999) or delinquent (Sampson and Laub 1996) young people. If adolescents and young adults are to benefit from this institutionally driven course correction, however, they must first apply and be accepted for admittance. Yet, for the first time, the 1973 transition to the All-Volunteer Force positioned the U.S. armed forces as an active competitor in the entry-level labor market, even in the presence of shifting restrictions on enlistment among those with prior criminal justice contact (10 USC§504(a)). Black men who were admitted to the armed forces in the wake of the All-Volunteer Force tended to be positively, educationally selected relative to other blacks (Angrist and Krueger 1994; Elder 1987; Moskos and Butler 1996; Fernandez 1996; Teachman, Call, and Segal 1993; Mare and Winship 1984), and whites who found themselves in uniform typically had lower social class origins than other whites (Appy 1993).

Indeed, until recently, the Department of Defense was the nation's largest employer as well as the largest employer of black high school graduates (Lundquist, Pager, and Strader 2018; Segal and Segal 2004). In the early years of the All-Volunteer Force, the low pay scale and limited opportunities for educational advancement effectively made the military an employer of last resort for young men (and some women) who had limited alternative educational or occupational opportunities. During the All-Volunteer Force era, the average length of enlistment more than tripled, from fewer than two years to more than six (Morin 2011), and the share of blacks among those in uniform grew, meaning that blacks were overrepresented in the armed forces for the first time in U.S. history (Nalty 1986; Segal and Segal 2004).

Rising levels of educational attainment among the U.S. population during the closing decades of the twentieth century meant that the military was able to institute and maintain high school graduation or GED certification as a nearly universal requirement for enlistment (Asch, Hosek, and Warner 2001; Day and Bauman 2000). In 1984, the armed forces instituted the Montgomery GI Bill and other benefits to provide college assistance for a limited number of veterans (Fredland et al. 1996; Thirtle 2001), a program retroactively made available to virtually all veterans who have served since 2001 (Steele, Salcedo, and Coley 2010).[14] Potential college funding, as recruitment and enlistment tools, allows the armed forces to continue to target young adults who have the aptitude to perform academically but cannot independently fund higher education—and perhaps also lack the sociocultural resources to identify alternate funding for postsecondary education (Bachman, Freedman-Doan, and O'Malley 2001; Houle 2013; Thirtle 2001).

A practical consequence of this selected recruitment has been the partial and institutional reshuffling of young, undereducated men from the military to the penal sphere by institutional castling. We show that the generational divide in who was employed by the military is related to incarceration rates two decades later, given that a 1 percentage point increase in the employment rate of military servicemembers with less than a high school education a generation ago is associated with a 21.4 percent reduction in incarceration rates. Military employment reduces incarceration rates among black and undereducated men for two reasons. First, blacks have longer military careers, on average, than whites (Moskos and Butler 1996), providing stable primary sector employment during their prime criminogenic years (Office of the Deputy Assistant Secretary of Defense, Military Community and Family Policy 2013). Longer tenure in the military also insulates men of color from the vicissitudes of the civilian labor market.

---

14. Supplemental Appropriations Act, Public L. No. 110-252 (2008).

A second reason the military's protective effects are concentrated among blacks and undereducated men is due to perceptions about military employment; blacks and whites appear to have different orientations to military service. Whereas black men are drawn to military occupational specialties that provide a high degree of convergence with the civilian labor market, white men are overrepresented in combat arms specialties, which have fewer analogous occupations outside the military (Gifford 2005; MacLean and Parsons 2010) and that place them at risk for incarceration if exposure to violence, and its physical and psychological consequences, elevates the risk of subsequent criminal offending. Blacks in the military are also significantly more likely than whites to take advantage of training and educational opportunities (Barley 1998) and are more likely to apply for promotion than to voluntarily exit the armed forces under its "up or out" structure (Moskos and Butler 1996; Asch, Miller, and Malchiodi 2012). In short, the military historically provided a path for upward mobility for disadvantaged men during distinct phases of military staffing, even though contemporary research shows that the positive benefits of enlistment have largely vanished (Bailey and Sykes 2018).

The conscription of fugitive slaves and freedmen during the Civil War set the stage for institutional castling (and recastling) in the lives of young, undereducated black men across periods of American history. Yet, contemporary institutional castling is not localized solely to the military and penal systems, palimpsests of a particular epoch, or a particular race or gender; the durability of institutional castling can be observed for other demographic groups in research on institutions (directly and indirectly) tied to the penal system and labor market. For instance, Bernard Harcourt (2006, 2011a, 2011b) shows that the deinstitutionalization of mental hospitals and asylums coincided with the growth of the penal system, suggesting that medical and penal institutions castled in the lives of disadvantaged people suffering from various health and mental afflictions. Similarly, Loïc Wacquant (2001) argues that the ghetto and penal system share a symbiotic relationship (they castled) in ways that make the ghetto look more like a prison and the prison look more like a ghetto, drawing attention to the chiral relationship between residential location and systems of surveillance and punishment for poor communities of color. Wacquant (2010) also illustrates how welfare reform at the close of the twentieth century castled the institutions of the social safety net (welfare) and the low-wage labor market (workfare) for poor, disadvantaged women, many of whom were African American and Latina. Subsequent to the period of institutional castling between welfare and workfare, the specter of penality and punishment was always lurking beneath the surface, giving rise to what Wacquant (2010) termed *prisonfare*, given that welfare fraud investigations and prosecutions rose after the passage of the *Personal Responsibility and Work Opportunity Reconciliation Act of 1996* (Gustfason 2011). Thus, contemporary institutional castling in the lives of disadvantaged men and women has now become a normative feature of the American underclass and can be readily observed in a variety of social contexts. Military enlistment and penal confinement are but one configuration.

In sum, given the high rates of enlistment and veteran status among African American men, our findings suggest that ignoring differences in veteran status and military employment rates conceals a key aspect of racial inequality in the criminal justice system across generations. Bruce Western and his colleagues (Western and Beckett 1999; Western and Pettit 2005) show that ignoring the effects of incarceration—and specifically the omission of incarcerated men from statistics on employment and income—distorts our understanding of the true nature of racial inequality in labor market outcomes. We concur, and show that the military—as an independent, bureaucratic institution—has remarkable protective effects against the penal institution for men with low levels of education, in general, and for African American men, in particular. Bourdieu (1994, 4) powerfully wrote that "the instituted institution makes us forget that it issues out of a long series of acts of *institution* (in the active sense) and hence has all the appearances of the *natural*." Secondary educational attainment and nonfelony status for military employment were not historically natural for servicemembers of the armed forces, particularly during World Wars I and II (Dressler 1946; Mattick 1960; Shattuck 1945). The expansion of the criminal justice apparatus under the Safe Streets Act, the simultaneous barring of felons from military enlistment under 10 USC§504(a), and the subsequent requirements of a high school diploma or GED during military downsizing meant that young men with criminal records or those who did not graduate from high school were at an increased risk of civilian labor market exclusion (during periods of deindustrialization) and correctional custody (during periods of criminal justice expansion). The castling of these two institutions in the lives of disadvantaged men requires hyperbolic doubt to reimagine how state power is exercised to shape (and reshape) the composition of the armed forces, the penal system, and the civilian labor market synchronistically.

## REFERENCES

Alexander, Michelle. 2010. *The New Jim Crow: Mass Incarceration in the Age of Colorblindness*. New York: The New Press.

Angrist, Joshua D. 1993. "The 'Misnorming' of the U.S. Military's Entrance Examination and Its Effect on Minority Enlistments." *Institute for Research on Poverty* discussion paper no. 1017-93. Madison: University of Wisconsin.

Angrist, Joshua D., and Alan B. Kreuger. 1994. "Why Do World War II Veterans Earn More Than Non-Veterans?" *Journal of Labor Economics* 21(1): 74-97.

Apel, Robert, and Julie Horney. 2017. "How and Why Does Work Matter? Employment Conditions, Routine Activities, and Crime Among Adult Male Offenders." *Criminology* 55(2): 307-43.

Appy, Christian G. 1993. *Working Class War*. Chapel Hill: University of North Carolina Press.

Asch, Beth J., James R. Hosek, and John T. Warner. 2001. *An Analysis of Pay for Enlisted Personnel*. Santa Monica, Calif.: RAND Corporation.

Asch, Beth J., Trey Miller, and Alessandro Malchiodi. 2012. *A New Look at Gender and Minority Differences in Officer Career Progression in the Military*. Santa Monica, Calif.: RAND Corporation.

Autor, David H., and Mark G. Duggan. 2003. "The Rise in Disability Rolls and the Decline in Unemployment." *Quarterly Journal of Economics* 118(1): 157-206.

Bachman, Jerald G., Peter Freedman-Doan, and Patrick M. O'Malley. 2001. "Should U.S. Military Recruiters Write Off the College-Bound?" *Armed Forces & Society* 27(3): 461-76.

Bailey, Amy Kate, and Bryan L. Sykes. 2018. "Veteran Status, Income, and Intergenerational Mobility Across Three Generations of American Men." *Population Research and Policy Review* 37(4): 539-68.

Barley, Stephen R. 1998. "Military Downsizing and the Career Prospects of Youth." *Annals of the American Academy of Political and Social Science* 559(1): 141-57.

Bellair, Paul E., and Vincent J. Roscigno. 2000. "Local Labor-Market Opportunity and Adolescent Delinquency." *Social Forces* 78(4): 1509-538.

Boesel, David. 1992. "Cutting Recruits: A Profile of the Newly Unqualified." In *Military Cutbacks and the Expanding Role of Education*, edited by Nevzer Stacey. Washington: U.S. Department of Education.

Bouffard, Leana Allen. 2005. "The Military as a Bridging Environment in Criminal Careers: Differential Outcomes of the Military Experience." *Armed Forces & Society* 31(2): 273-95.

———. 2014. "Period Effects in the Impact of Vietnam-Era Military Service on Crime over the Life Course." *Crime & Delinquency* 60(6): 859-83.

Bourdieu, Pierre. 1994. "Rethinking the State: Genesis and Structure of the Bureaucratic Field." *Sociological Theory* 12(1): 1-18.

Cantor, David, and Kenneth C. Land. 1985. "Unemployment and Crime Rates in the Post-World War II United States: A Theoretical and Empirical Analysis." *American Sociological Review* 50(3): 317-32.

Carnevale, Anthony P., Nicole Smith, and Jeff Strohl. 2010. *Help Wanted: Projections of Jobs and Education Requirements Through 2018*. Washington, D.C.: Georgetown University Center on Education and the Workforce.

Crutchfield, Robert D. 1989. "Labor Stratification and Violent Crime." *Social Forces* 68(2): 489-512.

———. 2014. *Get a Job: Labor Markets, Economic Opportunity, and Crime*. New York: New York University Press.

Crutchfield, Robert D., and Susan R. Pitchford. 1997.

"Work and Crime: The Effects of Labor Stratification." *Social Forces* 76(1): 93–118.

Culp, Richard, Tasha Youstin, Kristin Englander, and James Lynch. 2013. "From War to Prison: Examining the Relationship Between Military Service and Criminal Activity." *Justice Quarterly* 30(4): 651–80.

Day, Jennifer Cheeseman, and Kurt J. Bauman. 2000. "Have We Reached the Top? Educational Attainment Projections of the U.S. Population." *Population Division* working paper no. 43. Washington: U.S. Census Bureau.

Defense Manpower Data Center (DMDC). 2015. "Active Duty Military Personnel by Service by Region/Country, September 30, 2015." DRS #54601. Alexandra, Va.: Defense Manpower Data Center.

Doeringer, Peter B., and Michael J. Piore. 1971. *Internal Labor Markets and Manpower Analysis*. Cambridge, Mass.: Massachusetts Institute of Technology.

Dressler, David. 1946. "Men on Parole as Soldiers in World War II." *Social Service Review* 20: 537–50.

Du Bois, W.E.B. (1935) 1998. *Black Reconstruction in America 1860–1880*. Facsimile of the first edition, with an introduction by Davod Levering Lewis. New York: Free Press.

Elder, Glenn, Jr. 1986. "Military Times and Turning Points in Men's Lives." *Developmental Psychology* 22(2): 233–45.

———. 1987. "War Mobilization and the Life Course: A Cohort of World War II Veterans." *Sociological Forum* 2(3): 449–72.

———. 1999. *Children of the Great Depression: Social Change in Life Experience*. Boulder, Colo.: Westview Press.

Erickson, Steven, Robert Rosenheck, Robert Trestman, Julian Ford, and Rani Desai. 2008. "Risk of Incarceration Between Cohorts of Veterans with and without Mental Illness Discharged from Inpatient Units." *Psychiatric Services* 59(2): 178–83.

Ewert, Stephanie, Bryan Sykes, and Becky Pettit. 2014. "The Degree of Disadvantage: Incarceration and Inequality in Education." *Annals of the American Academy of Political and Social Science* 651(1): 24–43.

Fernandez, Richard L. 1996. "Social Representation in the Military: A Reassessment." In *Professionals on the Front Line*, edited by J. Eric Fredland, Curtis L. Gilroy, Roger D. Little, and W. S. Sellman. Washington, D.C.: Brassey's.

Fredland, J. Eric, Curtis L. Gilroy, Roger D. Little, and W. S. Sellman, eds. 1996. *Professionals on the Front Line: Two Decades of the All Volunteer Force*. Washington, D.C.: Brassey's.

Garland, David. 2001a. "Introduction: The Meaning of Mass Imprisonment." *Punishment and Society* 3(1): 5–7.

———. 2001b. *The Culture of Control: Crime and Social Order in Contemporary Society*. Chicago: University of Chicago Press.

Gifford, Brian. 2005. "Combat Casualties and Race: What Can We Learn from the 2003–2004 Iraq Conflict?" *Armed Forces & Society* 31(2): 201–25.

Glaze, Lauren, and Danielle Kaeble. 2014. "Correctional Populations in the United States, 2013." Bulletin NCJ 248479. Washington: U.S. Department of Justice, Bureau of Justice Statistics. Accessed October 17, 2019. http://www.bjs.gov/content/pub/pdf/cpus13.pdf.

Greenberg, Greg, and Robert Rosenheck. 2007. "Risk of Incarceration among Male Veterans and Nonveterans Are Veterans of the All Volunteer Force at Greater Risk?" *Armed Forces & Society* 33(3): 337–50.

———. 2012. "Incarceration Among Male Veterans Relative Risk of Imprisonment and Differences Between Veteran and Nonveteran Inmates." *International Journal of Offender Therapy and Comparative Criminology* 56(4): 646–67.

Grissmer, David W. 1992. "Impact of the Military Drawdown on Youth Employment, Training, and Educational Opportunity." In *Military Cutbacks and the Expanding Role of Education*, edited by Nevzer Stacey. Washington: U.S. Department of Education.

Gupta, Sanjiv, and Jennifer Hickes Lundquist. 2012. "The Converging Proportions of the U.S. Adult Population in the Military and in Prison, 1960–2010." Paper presented at the Annual Meeting of the Population Association of America. New Orleans (April 11–13, 2012).

Gustafson, Kaaryn. 2011. *Cheating Welfare: Public Assistance and the Criminalization of Poverty*. New York: New York University Press.

Han, JooHee. 2018. "Who Goes to College, Military, Prison, or Long-Term Unemployment? Racialized School-to-Labor Market." *Population Research and Policy Review* 37(4): 615–40.

Harcourt, Bernard. 2006. "From the Asylum to the

Prison: Rethinking the Incarceration Revolution." *Texas Law Review* 84(7): 1751–86.

———. 2011a. "An Institutionalization Effect: The Impact of Mental Hospitalization and Imprisonment on Homicide in the United States, 1934–2001." *Journal of Legal Studies* 40(1): 34–83.

———. 2011b. "Reducing Mass Incarceration: Lessons from the Deinstitutionalization of Mental Hospitals in the 1960s." *Ohio State Journal of Criminal Law* 9(1): 53–88.

Heckman, James, and Paul LaFontaine. 2010. "The American High School Graduation Rate: Trends and Levels." *Review of Economics and Statistics* 92(2): 244–62.

Hinton, Elizabeth. 2016. *From the War on Poverty to the War on Crime: The Making of Mass Incarceration in America*. Cambridge, Mass.: Harvard University Press.

Holzer, Harry J., Paul Offner, and Elaine Sorenson. 2005. "What Explains the Continuing Decline in Labor Force Activity Among Young Black Men?" *Labor History* 46(1): 37–55.

Houle, Jason N. 2013. "Disparities in Debt: Parents' Socioeconomic Resources and Young Adult Student Loan Debt." *Sociology of Education* 87(1): 53–69.

Kilburn, M. Rebecca, Lawrence M. Hanser, and Jacob Alex Klerman. 1998. *Estimating AFQT Scores for National Educational Longitudinal Study (NELS) Respondents*. Santa Monica, Calif.: RAND Corporation.

Kitagawa, Evelyn M. 1955. "Components of a Difference Between Two Rates." *Journal of the American Statistical Association* 50(272): 1168–94.

Krivo, Lauren J., and Ruth D. Peterson. 2004. "Labor Market Conditions and Violent Crime Among Youth and Adults." *Sociological Perspectives* 47(4): 485–505.

Lundquist, Jennifer Hickes, Devah Pager, and Eiko Strader. 2018. "Does a Criminal Past Predict Worker Performance? Evidence from One of American's Largest Employers." *Social Forces* 96(3): 1039–68.

Lytell, Maria C., Kenneth Kuhn, Abigail Haddad, Jefferson P. Marquis, Nelson Lim, Kimberly Curry Hall, Robert Stewart, and Jennie W. Wenger. 2015. *Force Drawdowns and Demographic Diversity: Investigating the Impact of Force Reductions on the Demographic Diversity of the U.S. Military*. Santa Monica, Calif.: RAND Corporation.

MacLean, Alair, and Nicholas L. Parsons. 2010. "Unequal Risk: Combat Occupations in the Volunteer Military." *Sociological Perspectives* 53(3): 347–72.

Mare, Robert D., and Christopher Winship. 1984. "The Paradox of Lessening Racial Inequality and Joblessness Among Black Youth: Enrollment, Enlistment, and Employment, 1964–1981." *American Sociological Review* 49(1): 39–55.

Mattick, Hans. 1960. "Parolees in the Army During World War II." *Federal Probation* 24:49–55.

Mitchell, John. 1971. "The War on Crime: The End of the Beginning." Washington: U.S. Department of Justice. Accessed: September 26, 2019. https://www.justice.gov/sites/default/files/ag/legacy/2011/08/23/09-09-1971.pdf.

Morin, Rich. 2011. "A Profile of the Modern Military." In *War and Sacrifice in the Post-9/11 Era: The Military-Civilian Gap*, edited by Paul Taylor. Washington, D.C.: Pew Research Center.

Moskos, Charles, and John Sibley Butler. 1996. *All That We Can Be: Black Leadership and Racial Integration the Army Way*. New York: Basic Books.

Nalty, Bernard C. 1986. *Strength for the Fight: A History of Black Americans in the Military*. New York: The Free Press.

Neal, Derek, and Armin Rick. 2014. "The Prison Boom and the Lack of Black Progress after Smith and Welch." *NBER* working paper no. 20283. Cambridge, Mass.: National Bureau of Economic Research.

Nixon, Richard. 1970. "January 22, 1970: State of the Union Address." Charlottesville: University of Virginia. Accessed September 26, 2019. https://millercenter.org/the-presidency/presidential-speeches/january-22-1970-state-union-address.

Office of the Deputy Assistant Secretary of Defense, Military Community and Family Policy. 2013. *2013 Demographics: Profile of the Military Community*. Washington: U.S. Department of Defense. Accessed October 17, 2019. https://download.militaryonesource.mil/12038/MOS/Reports/2013-Demographics-Report.pdf.

Office of Justice Programs. 1996. "LEAA/OJP Retrospective: 30 Years of Federal Support to State and Local Criminal Justice." Washington: U.S. Department of Justice. Accessed September 26, 2019. https://www.ncjrs.gov/pdffiles1/nij/164509.pdf.

Office of the Under Secretary of Defense, Personnel and Readiness. 2017. *Population Representation in the Military Services, Fiscal Year 2017*. Washington: U.S. Department of Defense. Accessed

October 17, 2019. https://www.cna.org/pop-rep/2017/summary/summary.pdf.

Office of the Under Secretary for Personnel and Readiness. 2000. Population Representation in the Military Services: Fiscal Year 1999. Washington: U.S. Department of Defense. Accessed October 17, 2019. https://prhome.defense.gov/Portals/52/Documents/MRA_Docs/MPP/AP/poprep/1999/.

Oi, Walter Y. 1996. "Historical Perspectives on the All-Volunteer Force: The Rochester Connection." In *Professionals on the Front Line: Two Decades of the All-Volunteer Force*, edited by J. Eric Frieland, Curtis Gilroy, Roger D. Little, and W. S. Sellman. Washington, D.C.: Brassey's.

Pettit, Becky. 2012. *Invisible Men: Mass Incarceration and the Myth of Black Progress*. New York: Russell Sage Foundation.

Pettit, Becky, and Bryan L. Sykes. 2015. "Civil Rights Legislation and Legalized Exclusion: Mass Incarceration and the Masking of Inequality." *Sociological Forum* 30(S1): 589–611.

Pettit, Becky, Bryan L. Sykes, and Bruce Western. 2009. "Technical Report on Revised Population Estimates and NLSY '79 Analysis Tables for the PEW Public Safety and Mobility Project." Cambridge, Mass.: Harvard University.

Pettit, Becky, and Bruce Western. 2004. "Mass Imprisonment and the Life Course: Race and Class Inequality in U.S. Incarceration." *American Sociological Review* 69(2): 151–69.

Phillips, Julie, and Kenneth C. Land. 2012. "The Link Between Unemployment and Crime Rate Fluctuations: An Analysis at the County, State, and National Levels." *Social Science Research* 41(3): 681–94.

Preston, Samuel, Patrick Heuveline, and Michel Guillot. 2001. *Demography: Measuring and Modeling Population Processes*. Malden, Mass.: Blackwell Publishing.

Roediger, David. 2014. *Seizing Freedom: Slave Emancipation and Liberty for All*. New York: Verso.

Sampson, Robert J., and John H. Laub. 1993. *Crime in the Making: Pathways and Turning Points Through Life*. Cambridge, Mass.: Harvard University Press.

———. 1996. "Socioeconomic Achievement in the Life Course of Disadvantaged Men: Military Service as a Turning Point, Circa 1940–1965." *American Sociological Review* 61(3): 347–67.

Segal David R., and Mady Wechsler Segal. 2004. "America's Military Population." *Population Bulletin* 59(4): 3–40.

Shannon, Sarah, Christopher Uggen, Jason Schnittker, Melissa Thompson, Sara Wakefield, and Michael Massoglia. 2017. "The Growth, Scope, and Spatial Distribution of People with Felony Records in the United States, 1948–2010." *Demography* 54(5):1795–818.

Shattuck, Edward. 1945. "Military Service for Men with Criminal Records." *Federal Probation* 9:12–14.

Simon, Jonathan. 2007. *Governing Through Crime: How the War on Crime Transformed American Democracy and Created a Culture of Fear*. New York: Oxford University Press.

Spitzer, Steven. 1975. "Toward a Marxian Theory of Deviance." *Social Problems* 22(5): 638–51.

Steele, Jennifer L., Nicholas Salcedo, and James Coley. 2010. *Service Members in School: Military Veterans' Experiences Using the Post-9/11 GI Bill and Pursuing Postsecondary Education*. Santa Monica, Calif.: RAND Corporation and the American Council on Education.

Sutton, John R. 2004. "The Political Economy of Imprisonment in Affluent Western Democracies, 1960–1990." *American Sociological Review* 69(2): 170–89.

Sykes, Bryan, and Michele Maroto. 2016. "A Wealth of Inequalities: Mass Incarceration, Employment, and Racial Disparities in U.S. Household Wealth, 1996 to 2011." *RSF: The Russell Sage Foundation Journal of the Social Sciences* 2(6): 129–52. DOI: 10.7758/RSF.2016.2.6.07.

Sykes, Bryan, and Becky Pettit. 2014. "Mass Incarceration, Family Complexity, and the Reproduction of Childhood Disadvantage." *Annals of the American Academy of Political and Social Science* 654(1): 127–49.

Tanielian, Terri, and Lisa H. Jaycox, eds. 2008. *Invisible Wounds of War: Psychological and Cognitive Injuries, Their Consequences, and Services to Assist Recovery*. Santa Monica, Calif.: RAND Corporation.

Teachman, Jay, Vaughan Call, and Mady Wechsler Segal. 1993. "The Selectivity of Military Enlistment." *Journal of Political and Military Sociology* 21(2): 287–309.

Teachman, Jay, and Lucky Tedrow. 2016. "Altering the Life Course: Military Service and Contact with the Criminal Justice System." *Social Science Research* 60(4): 74–87.

Thirtle, Michael R. 2001. *Educational Benefits and Officer-Commissioning Opportunities Available to U.S. Military Servicemembers*. Santa Monica, Calif.: RAND Corporation.

Travis, Jeremy, Bruce Western, and Steve Redburn, eds. 2014. *The Growth of Incarceration in the United States: Exploring Causes and Consequences*. Washington, D.C.: National Academies Press.

Tsai, Jack, Robert Rosenheck, Wesley Kasprow, and James McGuire. 2013. "Risk of Incarceration and Clinical Characteristics of Incarcerated Veterans by Race/Ethnicity." *Social Psychiatry and Psychiatric Epidemiology* 48(11): 1777–86.

Turney, Kristin, and Emma Conner. 2019. "Jail Incarceration: A Common and Consequential Form of Criminal Justice Contact." *Annual Review of Criminology* 2(1): 265–90.

Uggen, Christopher. 1999. "Ex-Offenders and the Conformist Alternative: A Job Quality Model of Work and Crime." *Social Problems* 46(1): 127–51.

———. 2000. "Work as a Turning Point in the Life Course of Criminals: A Duration Model of Age, Employment, and Recidivism." *American Sociological Review* 65(4): 529–46.

U.S. Congress. 1989. *Social Representation in the U.S. Military*. CBO Publication no. 499. Washington: U.S. Government Printing Office.

Van der Geest, Victor R., Catrien C.J.H. Bijleveld, and Arjan A.J. Blokland. 2011. "The Effects of Employment on Longitudinal Trajectories of Offending: A Follow-Up of High-Risk Youth from 18 to 32 Years of Age." *Criminology* 49(4): 1195–234.

Wacquant, Loïc. 2001. "Deadly Symbiosis: When Ghetto and Prison Meet and Mesh." *Punishment and Society* 3(1): 95–134.

———. 2010. "Crafting the Neoliberal State: Workfare, Prisonfare, and Social Insecurity." *Sociological Forum* 25(2): 197–220.

Wadsworth, Tim. 2004. "Industrial Composition, Labor Markets, and Crime." *Sociological Focus* 37(1): 1–24.

———. 2006. "The Meaning of Work: Conceptualizing the Deterrent Effect of Employment on Crime Among Young Adults." *Sociological Perspectives* 49(3): 34–68.

West, Heather C., and William J. Sabol. 2009. "Prison Inmates at Midyear 2008—Statistical Tables." Washington: U.S. Department of Justice, Bureau of Justice Statistics.

Western, Bruce. 2002. "The Impact of Incarceration on Wage Mobility and Inequality." *American Sociological Review* 67(4): 526–46.

———. 2006. *Punishment and Inequality in America*. New York: Russell Sage Foundation.

Western, Bruce, and Katherine Beckett. 1999. "How Unregulated Is the U.S. Labor Market? The Penal System as a Labor Market Institution." *American Journal of Sociology* 104(4): 1030–60.

Western, Bruce, and Becky Pettit. 2000. "Incarceration and Racial Inequality in Men's Employment." *Industrial and Labor Relations Review* 54(1): 3–16.

———. 2005. "Black-White Wage Inequality, Employment, and Incarceration." *American Journal of Sociology* 111(2): 553–78.

Wilson, William Julius. 1987. *The Truly Disadvantaged: The Inner City, the Underclass, and Public Policy*. Chicago: University of Chicago Press.

# Working to Avoid Incarceration: Jail Threat and Labor Market Outcomes for Noncustodial Fathers Facing Child Support Enforcement

NOAH D. ZATZ AND MICHAEL A. STOLL

*Child support enforcement is among several contexts in which work requirements are enforced by incarceration for noncompliance. Rather than creating barriers to employment, such incarceration threats may pressure subjects to work more, under worse conditions. We test for this using Fragile Families and Child Wellbeing Study data on respondents' child support, labor market, and criminal justice experiences in twenty cities. We exploit intercity variation in absolute and relative reliance on different child support enforcement techniques, especially punitive ones, such as incarceration, versus financially extractive ones, such as wage garnishment. As predicted, heavier reliance on incarceration sanctions is associated with more hours of work and lower wages among noncustodial fathers most vulnerable to incarceration.*

**Keywords:** incarceration, child support, labor markets, work requirements, legal financial obligations

This study examines the labor market effects of work requirements enforced by threats of future incarceration. It does so in the context of child support enforcement, long linked to the criminal legal system as an important labor market institution, especially for disadvantaged younger men (Holzer, Offner, and Sorensen 2005). Analysis of that linkage has focused on how child support enforcement and incarceration both impede employment. Child support is modeled as a tax that disincentivizes earnings (Miller and Mincy 2012; Cancian, Heinrich, and Chung 2013), and prior incarceration is a "negative credential" that deters hiring (Pager 2008; Stoll and Bushway 2008). Another linkage, however, implies different labor market consequences: both systems impose work requirements on people who are not currently incarcerated but who face incarceration as a sanction for nonwork (Zatz 2019).

Theoretically, a credible threat of incarceration for too little work unambiguously incentiv-

---

Noah D. Zatz is professor of law at the University of California, Los Angeles. Michael A. Stoll is professor of public policy at the University of California, Los Angeles.

© 2020 Russell Sage Foundation. Zatz, Noah D., and Michael A. Stoll. 2020. "Working to Avoid Incarceration: Jail Threat and Labor Market Outcomes for Noncustodial Fathers Facing Child Support Enforcement." *RSF: The Russell Sage Foundation Journal of the Social Sciences* 6(1): 55–81. DOI: 10.7758/RSF.2020.6.1.03. We gratefully acknowledge financial support from the John Randolph Haynes and Dora Haynes Foundation, the Open Society Foundations, and the UCLA Institute for Research on Labor and Employment. The analyses offered are the authors' own and do not necessarily express the views of any funder. We received helpful feedback from Naomi Sugie and invaluable technical and research assistance from the UCLA School of Law Empirical Research Group, especially from Henry Kim. Direct correspondence to: Noah D. Zatz at zatz@law.ucla.edu, UCLA School of Law, 385 Charles E. Young Dr. East, Law Building 1242, Los Angeles, CA 90095-1476.

Open Access Policy: *RSF: The Russell Sage Foundation Journal of the Social Sciences* is an open access journal. This article is published under a Creative Commons Attribution-NonCommercial-NoDerivs 3.0 Unported License.

izes employment by sharply raising the expected cost of nonwork. At the margin, this threat should pressure those facing it to accept working conditions they otherwise would reject, regardless of any past incarceration. All else equal, work should increase and working conditions should deteriorate.

This mechanism is one of compulsion into work, not exclusion from it, and one grounded in potential future incarceration, not current or past incarceration. This shift also implicates the criminal legal system's relationship to the welfare state. The latter's labor disciplining function (Handler and Hasenfeld 1991), intensified by 1990s welfare reforms (Soss, Fording, and Schram 2011), may be migrating back into the carceral state (Rusche and Kirchheimer 1939), alongside increasing attention to un- and underemployment among men (Mead 2007). That cuts against the notion that today's carceral state primarily "warehouses" the economically excluded (Western and Beckett 1999) as neoliberal restructuring produces more precarious labor markets with weaker safety nets (Simon 1993; Wacquant 2009). Work under carceral threat also raises policy concerns about forced labor, workplace vulnerability, and downward pressure on labor standards (Zatz 2019), concerns not captured by measures of employment levels, debt payments, and actual incarceration.

We test for these threat effects by exploiting geographic variation in child support enforcement techniques indicated through parent reports in the Fragile Families and Child Wellbeing Study (Fragile Families) (Geller, Jaeger, and Pace 2018). We hypothesize that heavier reliance on incarceration sanctions for child support nonpayment will increase hours worked and depress wages for noncustodial fathers (NCFs), relative to custodial fathers (CFs). Our data are inadequate to include mothers. This effect should be strongest and clearest among those most exposed to enforcement action and those with relatively low hours and wages. Furthermore, these jail threat effects should be the opposite of those from financial enforcement actions that "tax" earnings. Our results are largely consistent with these hypotheses.

## INCARCERATION SANCTIONS AS WORK ENFORCEMENT IN CHILD SUPPORT

Work requirements enforced by incarceration are familiar in probation, parole, and other forms of criminal legal supervision where seeking and maintaining employment is a widespread, explicit condition of supervision (Doherty 2015; Travis and Stacey 2010). Recent research finds both nontrivial aggregate levels of enforcement leading to incarceration or reincarceration (Zatz et al. 2016) and also parole or probation officer-supervisee interactions involving substantial pressure to work (Gurusami 2017; Augustine 2019). Earlier research had reported that such work requirements were vanishing in practical significance (Simon 1993).

Work requirements also arise from child support even though the underlying obligation is to pay. As a practical matter, however, most obligors must pay out of earnings, especially at the margin where compliance and enforcement are at issue. Poverty and un- or underemployment are endemic among obligors with significant arrears (Sorensen, Sousa, and Schaner 2007). Here, the primary issue is having the earnings with which to pay, not refusing to pay from existing income or assets. In the latter scenario, financial enforcement actions— principally wage garnishment—detect and acquire those funds, directly imposing the underlying tax. But they miss the point when obligors have limited income, the modal problem among those with arrears.

Work behavior is not fixed, however, and so enforcement also focuses on increasing earnings. If obligor un- or underemployment is considered "voluntary" (Mead 2007), penalizing nonwork should cause obligors to substitute work, generating earnings for capture by the tax and its financial enforcement.

Reflecting this analysis, child support law treats support obligations as creating a duty to earn enough to pay, not just to pay enough of what one earns. For instance, the California Supreme Court upheld incarceration as a contempt sanction for an obligor who "fails or refuses to seek and accept available employment for which the parent is suited by virtue of education, experience, and physical ability."[1] There,

---

1. *Moss v. Superior Court*, 950 P.2d 59, 76 (Cal. 1998).

the persistently unemployed obligor had been jailed because the trial judge concluded that he surely "could get a job flipping hamburgers at McDonald's."[2] The 1996 federal welfare reform law also required state child support enforcement systems to authorize ordering a noncustodial parent into the same range of work-related activities the law required of their custodial counterpart, when their child received cash assistance.[3] Most states already had some form of work requirements in their child support laws, often without any connection to cash assistance. A typical statute in Illinois provides that when any obligor is unemployed, "the court may order the person to seek employment and report periodically to the court with a diary, listing or other memorandum of his or her efforts in accordance with such order."[4] Further institutionalizing such requirements has been widely discussed (Sorensen 2010), and it was a priority of the Obama administration (Turetsky 2012).

Additionally, NCF work requirements emerge from the legal regime that permits incarceration as a general child support enforcement technique. Nonpayment may expose obligors to incarceration through civil or criminal contempt proceedings or through criminal prosecution for nonsupport (Patterson 2008; Cook and Noyes 2011; Brito 2012). However, constitutional law limits incarceration of someone lacking the "ability to pay," both for child support and for criminal fines and fees (Colgan 2018; Hampson 2016). In contrast, "willful" or "voluntary" nonpayment, despite the ability to pay, may be punished.

Willful nonpayment, and therefore exposure to incarceration, may be established through voluntary failure to *acquire* the ability to pay through earnings; that was the issue in the *Moss* case. Vice versa, adequate efforts to seek and maintain employment establish a defense to incarceration, even if one remains unable to pay.[5] The incarceration sanction regime thus imposes work requirements functionally, even when the formal demand is simply to pay.

Unemployment's "voluntariness" implicates the scope and intensity of job search and the working conditions that must be accepted, as is well known for analogous inquiries for public benefits eligibility (Williams 1999). These judgments are obscured by competing portrayals of nonpaying obligors as "deadbeats" versus "deadbrokes" (Cammett 2011). Someone who refuses a job requiring sixty hours per week of dangerous work could be classified either way, depending on whether that refusal is deemed justified. Incarceration for nonwork reflects a judgment that the obligor drew this line in the wrong place. Prospectively, threatening incarceration should move obligors toward accepting and maintaining employment, under worse conditions; that is the premise of affirmative arguments for mandatory work programs (Mead 2007). But such pressures should operate even outside formal work programs. Lynne Haney recently found a typical judge holding child support obligors to the standard of a father who worked four jobs and moonlighted mowing lawns (2018). Similarly, Alexes Harris's research on criminal legal debt found judges insisting that those unable to pay "just needed to work harder" (2016, 138).

Of course, an empty threat cannot drive work behavior, but the jail threat appears real. Systematic prevalence estimates have been lacking, but scattered reports suggest substantial use (Brito 2012; Robles and Dewan 2015). Recent research using Fragile Families data has found that, in large U.S. cities, 14 percent of NCFs with arrears have been jailed by the time their child turns nine (Cozzolino 2018), or 5 percent of all fathers, including 15 percent of all African American fathers (Zatz et al. 2016); the last statistic underlines the racial disparities at this nexus of child support, incarceration, and low-wage work.

2. Ibid., 80n16.

3. 42 U.S.C. § 666(a)(15).

4. 50 Ill. Comp. Stat. Ch. 5/505.1.

5. *Turner v. Rogers*, 131 S.Ct. 2507 (2011).

## JAIL THREAT AS A LABOR MARKET INFLUENCE

Any labor market effects of these jail threats would be significant in several ways. Within the literature on incarceration and work, it would highlight how systems with the power to punish can function as labor market institutions that set the terms on which individuals must work or face jail. Such enforced insertion into work to avoid incarceration would complement the now well-known phenomena of workers' removal from the labor force during incarceration (Western and Beckett 1999) and reduced access to employment after release (Pager 2008; Holzer, Raphael, and Stoll 2004). This emphasis on labor market exclusion also has been extended to criminal legal debt (Cadigan and Kirk 2020).

Although the notion of prior incarceration or conviction as a barrier to employment dominates the field, some findings indicate the complementary mechanism explored here. Some research finds temporarily increased employment immediately following release from incarceration, followed by subsequent declines (Pettit and Lyons 2007; Sabol 2007; Seim and Harding 2020). Beneficial assistance via parole supervision has been suggested as an explanation, but that interpretation is hard to square with the accompanying finding that wages decreased during this period (Pettit and Lyons 2007). Enhanced employment prospects should raise wages. A competing explanation would be that supervision applies pressure that lowers the reservation wage (Seim and Harding 2020). Another recent study found that higher rates of immediate post-release work were associated with greater willingness "to take on poorer quality work" (Sugie 2018), precisely what the threat of incarceration is designed to encourage.

Jail threat is particularly significant amid policy interest in "alternatives to incarceration." These often include expanding criminal legal supervision outside prison walls (Phelps 2016) but backed by the threat of incarceration for violating behavioral conditions, including work (Doherty 2015). Work-related conditions and programs, moreover, often are understood as efforts to obtain the benefits of employment despite the barriers associated with reentry. The question raised, however, is the balance between expanding access to better forms of work versus leaving barriers intact while pressuring people into whatever "bad jobs" (Bumiller 2015) are available to, or created for, people with convictions.

This nexus between work mandates and alternatives to incarceration also arises with criminal fines and fees (Harris 2016). Monetary sanctions may constitute an alternative to incarceration at sentencing, but the resulting payment obligation may later be enforced through incarceration (Colgan 2018). Here, too, mandatory work is put forward as an alternative to incarceration for nonpayment, especially through unpaid "community service" that operates outside conventional employment law and below basic labor standards (Stuart 2011; Zatz 2019).

This active use of state power to enforce and regulate work also contrasts with prevailing accounts of contemporary low-wage and precarious work (Bernhardt et al. 2008; Kalleberg 2011). This literature typically portrays declining government regulation of employers unleashing private market forces. In contrast, we explore here the regulation of workers with punitive techniques characteristic of criminal law. Although child support incarceration often arises through civil contempt (Patterson 2008), this civil application of punitive techniques, often complemented by criminal prosecutions, is itself characteristic of a broader pattern of criminalization seen in welfare (Gustafson 2009) and immigration (Eagly 2010). Likewise, scholarship on the contemporary carceral state cautions against overreliance on formal legal categories of criminal, civil, and the like (Beckett and Murakawa 2012).

Labor market regulation also has been absent from the modest child support literature on incarceration sanctions (Patterson 2008; Brito 2012). The topic rose to prominence with the Supreme Court's 2011 *Turner v. Rogers*[6] decision about the right to counsel in contempt proceedings, and with a police officer's murder of Walter Scott as he fled an arrest warrant for

---

6. 131 S.Ct. 2507.

child support nonpayment (Robles and Dewan 2015). This literature, however, largely has focused on procedural rights and on child support's relationship to income support for custodial parents and children, not on its operation as an institution structuring the bottom of the labor market (but see Chung 2011).

In contrast, a significant empirical policy literature addresses how child support enforcement may affect the labor supply of young, disadvantaged men (Holzer, Offner, and Sorensen 2005; Cancian, Heinrich, and Chung 2013). This literature, however, models child support exclusively as a tax on earnings. The resulting substitution effect should reduce work or shift it off the books (Rich, Garfinkel, and Gao 2007; Miller and Mincy 2012). Any potential to increase work is attributed to an income effect, still within the tax framework. In that framework, more enforcement simply intensifies any substitution or income effects. Incarceration figures only in the rear view, as a driver of arrears accrual while an obligor is removed from the labor market (Pirog and Ziol-Guest 2006; Cammett 2011; but see Haney 2018).

Studying these incarceration-backed work requirements bears directly on policy interest in using criminal justice and child support institutions to target work programs toward men (Mead 2007; Sorensen 2010), complementing welfare-to-work programs for custodial parents (primarily women). This interest overlaps with using work programs as an alternative to incarceration for child support nonpayment (Turetsky 2012), as with criminal legal debt. For instance, the Obama administration contrasted its proposed restrictions on states' ability to incarcerate for failure to pay with its endorsement of states' continued authority to incarcerate for failure to work (Office of Child Support Enforcement 2014, 68557).

Analysis of child support work programs has emphasized how services can enhance job finding and retention (Sorensen 2010), not whether the enforcement threat changes responses to constant work opportunities. The literature on welfare-to-work, however, suggests that its employment effects arose in part from making welfare receipt less attractive, not increasing the returns to work, leading participants to exit welfare sooner and for lower earnings (Cancian et al. 2002). In the classic pairing of "help and hassle" (Mead 2007, 54), incarceration takes "hassle" to the extreme. Some suggestive evidence comes from Texas' Non-Custodial Parent Choices program, which used jail threats to mandate participation in workforce development programs (Schroeder and Doughty 2009). One evaluation found negative effects on earnings levels, despite increased employment, and attributed this combination to job gains concentrated in lower-paying positions. Notably, these earnings and potential wage effects generally go unmentioned in reviews that tout the program's positive employment effects (Turetsky 2012).

## RESEARCH QUESTIONS AND HYPOTHESES

Our research question is whether the threat of incarceration for child support nonpayment alters the labor market behavior of NCFs. We hypothesize that this threat should induce increased work effort—measurable by increased annual hours worked—and on terms less attractive to workers—measurable by depressed wage rates. Although we expect NCFs and CFs to differ systematically in their labor market characteristics, these differences should widen as enforcement intensifies because CFs should face de minimis threat from potential child support enforcement.

The threat effect should be strongest among NCFs at greatest risk of enforcement action, especially those in arrears (Miller and Mincy 2012). NCFs without arrears, because either they are current on payments or no child support order yet exists, also should exhibit some threat response, but we expect this to fall in between those with arrears and CFs. The predicted relative ranking of these intermediate groups is ambiguous because those with orders but not arrears have the legal basis for enforcement in place but are selected for labor market behavior that insulates them from enforcement.

We hypothesize that, because those with few or no hours likely have weaker employment prospects, transitions from nonwork to low-hours work could depress median hours among those working even while raising hours overall. We expect hours increases to be concentrated in the bottom half of the overall hours distribution because the jail threat focuses on those deemed voluntarily un- or underemployed. Similarly, wage effects may concentrate at lower wages (among those working), where those with the least to gain financially from working should be most responsive to the nonfinancial jail threat.

These hypotheses are grounded in the theory that jail threat increases the relative attractiveness of work by penalizing nonwork. However, that nonfinancial penalty operates in tandem with the more familiar tax on earnings. The net effect is ambiguous in theory, even assuming the tax's substitution effect dominates its income effect. Accordingly, we predict that any threat effect from jail sanctioning will be most pronounced after the extent of financial sanctions are controlled for, the two sanction types having opposite effects. Furthermore, because the work requirement is linked to a payment requirement, any jail threat effect should interact with the rigor of financial enforcement. Increased hours and decreased wages driven by the jail threat should be more pronounced at lower levels of financial sanctioning.

## DATA AND EMPIRICAL STRATEGY

We use Fragile Families longitudinal survey data from the parents of 4,898 infants, including a systematic oversample of nonmarital births, born in twenty U.S. cities. The weighted sample represents the families of children with hospital births in each of the cities between 1998 and 2000. Response rates decline over the five survey waves (baseline, then years one, three, five, and nine) but remain high, even for the hardest-to-reach group of unmarried fathers in wave 5 (58 percent) (Geller, Jaeger, and Pace 2018).

Fragile Families contains uniquely detailed data about child support and its enforcement, criminal justice contact, and labor market experience, as well as individual characteristics that may influence labor market outcomes. Under the requisite confidentiality agreement and IRB approval, we use restricted data that contain geographic identifiers, city weights, and city-level data that allow for various controls. This allows us, city by city, to construct policy treatment variables measuring a population's exposure to specific types of child support enforcement, to construct dependent variables measuring labor market outcomes within that population,[7] and to control for other relevant influences.

Our analysis relies on labor market, incarceration, and child support enforcement data from waves 2 through 5 because of compatibility issues with wave 1 regarding the longitudinal questions (Miller and Mincy 2012; Rich, Garfinkel, and Gao 2007), and because any threat effect of child support enforcement with respect to the focal child should only become relevant in the years after birth.

### Policy Treatment and Father Status Variables

We create policy treatment variables that measure local jurisdictions' child support enforcement practices. We rely on data (from fathers or mothers) on 3,218 fathers, after excluding those missing weights. The main policy treatment variable is the percentage of NCFs (N = 2,151) ever jailed as a result of a child support enforcement action.

To identify and categorize NCFs, we use wave-specific data from both mothers and fathers on coresidence among the focal child's parents and the focal child, child support orders, and arrears on those support obligations. We divide fathers into four mutually exclusive categories: fathers with arrears (NCF-arrears); fathers with orders but no arrears (NCF-orders); and fathers without orders or arrears who are defined as NCFs (NCF-only) because they live with the focal child less than 100 percent of the time.[8] The remaining fathers are defined as custodial (CF). Because Fragile Families lacks rich, consistent data on parental relationships to nonfocal children, these definitions will misclassify some fathers who are noncustodial (including with orders or arrears) only with re-

---

7. This approach relies on NCFs remaining subject to the child support enforcement practices and labor markets of the focal child's birth city. Tests of respondents' mobility support this assumption's validity.

8. We rejected a 50 percent threshold because of data limitations and our expectation that coresidence between 50 and 100 percent would be more like the former than the latter.

spect to a nonfocal child, especially one with a different mother. This increases imprecision but should not generate spurious positive results.[9]

We include in the policy variable denominators anyone who is an NCF in any wave. This allows us to assess potential variation in NCF subtype responses to enforcement threat and to avoid sensitivity to how the enforcement environment might affect which NCFs receive orders and end up in arrears. Sensitivity checks indicate that alternate definitions (including CFs in or including NCF-onlys from the denominator) do not fundamentally change the results.

The policy variable numerators rely on the survey questions asking, beginning with wave 3, whether any child support enforcement has been taken to collect arrears, and further distinguishing among types of action. We divide these into tax-like financial sanctions (garnishing wages, seizing tax refunds or other assets, or placing liens on property), jail sanctions (incarceration or probation), driver's license suspensions, and other actions (unspecified, specified as Other, or business license suspensions).

This study's methodological advance is to measure the mix of enforcement methods localities employ. Prior studies have measured child support enforcement intensity as one-dimensional, using variables based mostly on state-level policies and expenditures, actual payments (including at the local level), and rates of establishing child support orders within eligible populations (Holzer, Offner, and Sorensen 2005; Nepomnyaschy and Garfinkel 2010; Miller and Mincy 2012).

We pool within cities and across waves mother and father reports of whether a given father has experienced any enforcement action and what type or types.[10] Pooling across waves generates more reliable measures by increasing the number of observations, but it assumes a constant policy environment over time. Given the noted substantial sample attrition, this approach could introduce bias, but, on examination, the demographic composition of attrition does not vary systematically across cities.

Similarly, pooling data across father self-reports and mother reports increases the number of observations and mitigates attrition bias among fathers. However, bias could be introduced by differential attrition rates across cities in conjunction with systematic mother-father differences in child support enforcement reports.[11] Daniel Miller and Ronald Mincy (2012) performed validity checks on mothers' reports of fathers' child support arrears and found evidence of their reliability. Moreover, the Current Population Survey uses mothers' reports from the biannual Child Support Supplement as the basis for national estimates of child support compliance.

Our measure of jail sanctions also incorporates Fragile Families' criminal justice questions. Beginning with wave 2, this series asks about incarceration or conviction, with specification of the underlying charges that include child support nonpayment as one option.[12] These questions capture some fathers who faced enforcement with respect to a nonfocal child,[13] and they provide some redundancy with the direct child support questions, mitigating underreporting. They also increase the number of father self-reports because, due to a survey administration error, NCFs mostly were not

---

9. Intercity variation in fathers' rate of multipartner fertility could create a risk of bias.

10. One parent's report of an action dominates negative or missing reports from the other.

11. Mother and father reports show incarceration sanctions at similar rates, but mother reports show much lower rates for other actions, which presumably are much less visible than incarceration.

12. This method aggregates incarceration arising from civil contempt and criminal prosecution. We doubt the procedural differences much affect NCFs' experience of incarceration threat. Indeed, survey answers may not distinguish them, given child support questions about probation and mother questions about father incarceration without a conviction predicate (Geller, Jaeger, and Pace 2016). For similar reasons, we include reports of criminal convictions for nonsupport that may not have led to incarceration.

13. Two fathers with reported incarceration for child support nonpayment were otherwise coded as custodial in relation to the focal child in all waves; these were recoded as NCF for policy variable purposes.

**Table 1.** Child-Support Enforcement Action Rates by Type and City, Among Noncustodial Fathers

| | Raw N | Any Action (1) | Jail (2) | (SE) | Financial (3) | (SE) | Driver's License (4) | Other (5) |
|---|---|---|---|---|---|---|---|---|
| Chicago | 53 | 3% | 0% | | 0% | (0%) | 0% | 3% |
| Boston | 59 | 10 | 4 | (0%) | 3 | (3) | 0 | 3 |
| Corpus Christi | 174 | 13 | 3 | (1) | 7 | (2) | 0 | 3 |
| Austin | 137 | 13 | 6 | (4) | 4 | (2) | 0 | 3 |
| New York | 104 | 15 | 0 | | 10 | (6) | 5 | 2 |
| Indianapolis | 167 | 16 | 8 | (2) | 5 | (0) | 0 | 4 |
| San Antonio | 47 | 16 | 2 | (2) | 1 | (1) | 0 | 14 |
| Oakland | 139 | 16 | 1 | (0) | 5 | (1) | 4 | 8 |
| San Jose | 110 | 20 | 8 | (7) | 8 | (8) | 2 | 3 |
| Newark | 162 | 20 | 10 | (2) | 6 | (2) | 2 | 6 |
| Detroit | 150 | 21 | 6 | (1) | 7 | (2) | 1 | 8 |
| Philadelphia | 146 | 23 | 4 | (1) | 10 | (2) | 2 | 8 |
| Milwaukee | 184 | 27 | 11 | (2) | 10 | (2) | 4 | 7 |
| Baltimore | 166 | 27 | 6 | (2) | 5 | (1) | 7 | 11 |
| Nashville | 54 | 28 | 17 | (8) | 7 | (3) | 0 | 8 |
| Norfolk | 49 | 29 | 17 | (3) | 10 | (0) | 9 | 1 |
| Jacksonville | 61 | 30 | 5 | (1) | 19 | (11) | 3 | 6 |
| Toledo | 59 | 31 | 9 | (2) | 11 | (3) | 6 | 13 |
| Richmond | 173 | 33 | 16 | (6) | 12 | (3) | 2 | 10 |
| Pittsburgh | 51 | 58 | 41 | (7) | 15 | (4) | 9 | 5 |

*Source:* Authors' calculations from the Fragile Families and Child Wellbeing Survey.
*Note:* Wave 2 weights.

asked the child support questions in waves 3 and 4. This provides another reason to include mother reports of incarceration sanctions through both the criminal justice and child support series, which also mitigates the father underreporting known to occur in the former (Dwyer Emory et al. 2020; Geller, Jaeger, and Pace 2016).[14]

Table 1 presents intercity variation in child support enforcement actions taken as a percentage of all NCFs and using Fragile Families wave 2 weights. Throughout, cities vary within the same state. Column 1 represents the extensive margin of all actions taken within a city. Our analysis relies on the significant variation by city in column 2, showing the rate of incarceration as an enforcement action. Localities also make extensive use of financial sanctions and driver's license suspensions, shown in columns 3 and 4. The data show variation across locales in these enforcement actions as well. Column 5 presents residual reports of some action other than jail, financial, or driver's license sanctions.

Our measures of jail, financial, and driver's license sanctions are not mutually exclusive, either within a city or even for one individual, who may report more than one action. Although jail and financial sanctions correlate positively (as driver's license suspensions do, too), they do not operate in lockstep. Correlation coefficients between these policy variables are about 48 percent and weakly statistically significant, indicating significant heterogeneity. We use this heterogeneity to isolate the impact of jail enforcement from fi-

14. When nonsupport involves a child in common, mothers may have better information about resulting incarceration, and less incentive to suppress it, than they do for most other offenses, though this may be less true where support is assigned to and retained by the state (Dwyer Emory et al. 2020).

nancial enforcement in the regression analysis that follows.

We acknowledge and have attempted to mitigate potential bias relating to self-reports, counterpart reports, and differential attrition, as well as sample size limitations. Ultimately, these are endemic to the large research literature relying on Fragile Families and other surveys, including their use to specify child support-related independent variables (Miller and Mincy 2012). We report standard errors for our main jail and financial sanction policy variables in columns 2 and 3,[15] suppressing them in the other columns to conserve space. They indicate considerable uncertainty about the rank ordering of cities, especially in the middle of the distribution, but also clear differentiation between the low and high ends.[16] In a further test of robustness, we ran twenty variations on our main models, each one dropping one city from the analysis. In no case was the change in main results substantial.

With respect to external validity, respondent reports of enforcement actions taken against themselves or their counterparts are an imperfect proxy for the actual rate of enforcement actions representing the policy environment. Nonetheless, the two should be systematically related, and there is no reason to expect intercity variation in the relationship that would introduce bias. These remain the best available sources. Rich, reliable administrative data have proven difficult to obtain (Cook and Noyes 2011). Federal child support performance indicators are reported by state and do not measure sanctions against individual obligors, let alone their type. However, our measures are broadly consistent with the available data. Pittsburgh, our highest enforcement city, sits within Pennsylvania, which consistently ranked at the top of national child support enforcement intensity during the relevant period (Solomon-Fears 2007). Pittsburgh's county (Allegheny) claims to be a top enforcer among urban areas (Family Division 2017). It regularly conducts highly publicized arrests of obligors in arrears, pursuant to a local policy change in 1999 (at the beginning of Fragile Families data collection) emphasizing jail sanctions (*Pittsburgh Post-Gazette* 1999; Roebuck 2007). Vice versa, Chicago, our lowest enforcement city, sits within Illinois, which consistently ranked toward the bottom of federal measures (Solomon-Fears 2007), and its county (Cook) was cited for lax enforcement during the relevant period (Smith 2002).

In general, relying on Fragile Families reports for our policy treatment variables likely distorts our absolute estimates of individual cities' sanction rates. We have no reason, however, to expect these limitations to substantially distort what our analysis relies on, which is cities' relative reliance on particular sanctions, especially incarceration. In most scenarios, these limitations should simply introduce noise that biases us toward null results. Furthermore, because Fragile Families data do not capture the entire population potentially subject to child support enforcement in each city—primarily by sampling based on one birth cohort—even accurate rates for the surveyed population likely differ from what a more inclusive measure would capture. Nonetheless, there is no apparent reason why this limitation would produce spurious positive results, and it represents the enforcement environment for those most similar to the fathers whose labor market behavior we measure. We also test multiple outcomes to mitigate the influence of spurious results in any one domain.

Of course, our policy treatment variables measure an enforcement environment that is not randomly assigned. Although the procedures and standards governing the establishment and enforcement of child support orders are set at the state level with substantial federal influence, implementation occurs at the local level. Accordingly, even within states, localities can and do exercise discretion to use different intensities and different methods of enforcement (Cook and Noyes 2011), and so there are

---

15. Because the policy variables use Fragile Families weights, the standard errors do not strictly track the raw N also displayed in table 1.

16. For instance, there is no overlap between the upper bound of the 90 percent confidence interval (not shown) of the eight cities with the lowest jail sanction rate and the lower bound of the 90 percent confidence interval of the six cities with the highest jail sanction rate.

sound reasons to believe these actions are independent across enforcement areas.

Nonetheless, the rate of incarceration sanctions could be endogenous to the labor market characteristics of those facing sanctions. For example, obligors' labor market characteristics should influence the presence, level, and duration of arrears, which may in turn trigger an incarceration sanction.[17] We tested for such endogeneity by running a regression predicting individual child support incarceration sanctions as a function of any arrears amounts and indicator variables for cities. The city coefficients were large relative to those for arrears and highly correlated (0.78) with our jail threat policy variable (detailed results available on request). This is inconsistent with variations in city incarceration rates being an artifact of varying arrears levels and instead supports the assumption of policy independence. Furthermore, for wages, any endogeneity should dampen, not exaggerate, any positive results. As among those with similar arrears, we would expect enforcement to target those with a higher earnings capacity, leading incarceration rates to correlate with higher wages, the opposite of our predicted threat effect.

## Dependent Variables

To construct our dependent variables, we pool observations on fathers' labor market outcomes and other relevant variables across waves 2 through 5 to increase sample size and statistical power, resulting in 8,930 father-wave observations.[18] Our final sample consists of 8,362 father-wave observations. We eliminate as outliers 230 father-wave observations reporting hourly wage rates equal to or less than $1 or greater than $50, or reporting annual hours worked equal to or greater than three thousand. We also eliminate 338 father-wave observations where the father has been identified as experiencing a child support jail sanction in that or any prior wave. This ensures that we measure only the general deterrence effect of the general risk of future sanction, not the specific deterrence effect of having previously experienced the sanction; the latter is of related interest but should not vary with city threat level. This makes ours a conservative test for a jail threat effect because the behavior of those previously sanctioned (but removed from our sample) could reflect both mechanisms (Stafford and Warr 1993); having been previously sanctioned may well select for those most likely to be responsive to the prospective threat even absent prior sanction.[19]

The labor market outcome variables are annual hours worked and wage rates. Annual hours worked is measured by taking the average hours per week the respondents report working in most recent formal employment and multiplying by the number (including zero) of weeks worked in formal employment over the past year. This continuous measure allows more precise measurement of work levels, capturing transitions from nonwork to work and increased hours among those already working.

We use wage rates to measure how jail threat may induce NCFs to accept lower job quality. This captures both entry into employment at a wage that, absent the threat, would have been below the reservation wage, and also deterioration of wages within employment due to reduced bargaining power when job loss may trigger incarceration. Earnings cannot capture this because we predict its components of wages and hours to move in opposite directions. Fragile Families did not systematically ask about wage rates but instead elicited earnings over one of several periods; a substantial minority answered with hourly earnings (wages), but other units included days, weeks, or year. Thus, where necessary, we measured wage rates by

---

17. We found no statistically significant relationship between the incarceration sanction rate and possible enforcement triggers such as the percentage of fathers (or specifically those in arrears) who were African American, high school nongraduates, or who had incomes below the poverty line at the focal child's birth.

18. We focus exclusively on fathers because of the small population and lack of analogous data on noncustodial mothers.

19. We also analyzed an alternative sample including these 338 observations, but this produced no material difference in the results. This also mitigates the concern that underreporting of jail sanctions would lead to inclusion in our main sample of some observations that would have been excluded with full information.

**Table 2.** Differences in Hours and Wages Between Father Categories, by Jail Threat Level

| Father Category | Low Threat | Medium Threat | High Threat | High-Low |
|---|---|---|---|---|
| **Annual hours worked** | | | | |
| NCF-only versus CF | −486 | −492 | −521 | −35 |
| NCF-orders versus CF | −191 | −307 | −213 | −22 |
| NCF-arrears versus CF | −531 | −567 | −614 | −84 |
| **Wage rates** | | | | |
| NCF-only versus CF | −4.11 | −6.22 | −6.57 | −2.47*** |
| NCF-orders versus CF | −2.78 | −4.32 | −5.51 | −2.73*** |
| NCF-arrears versus CF | −4.12 | −6.48 | −8.17 | −4.05*** |

*Source:* Authors' calculations from the Fragile Families and Child Wellbeing Survey.
*Note:* Threat levels are defined by jail action rates of <= 7 percent (low); > 7 percent, <= 11 percent (medium); > 11 percent (high). All father category differences within threat level are statistically significant at 1 percent level. NCF = noncustodial fathers; CF = custodial fathers.
*$p < .1$; **$p < .05$; ***$p < .01$

constructing weekly earnings and dividing by weekly hours.[20]

### Initial Results (Unadjusted)

We first explore at the unadjusted mean level initial evidence with respect to the expected jail threat's relationship to wage rates and annual hours worked. Table 2 provides differences in hours worked and in wages between NCFs and CFs within cities grouped by low, medium, or high jail threat, as specified in the table. Not surprisingly, all of these differences are statistically significant, as would be expected if CF versus NCF status selected for labor market characteristics.

Of greater interest is how the difference between CFs and NCFs itself varies with the level of jail threat. In regard to hours worked, we do not find significant differences between high and low threat cities in NCF-CF differences in hours worked. This is unsurprising because these unadjusted results take no account of the concurrent operation of other sanctions, as well as a host of other individual- and city-level factors. To address these considerations, regression analysis is needed.

Even without regression analysis, however, the wage rate results are consistent with our hypotheses. The NCF-CF gap in wage rates is largest in high jail threat cities, significantly higher than in low threat cities across each subtype of NCF. Moreover, this high-low difference is largest for the NCFs in arrears who are most vulnerable to jail threat.

### Analytic Strategy

Based on equation (1), we regress individual wages and hours on our policy variables measuring city-level enforcement methods:

$$LF_i = \alpha + Incar_{ci}\beta_1 + \beta'_2 CEI_{ci} + \beta'_3 FS_i + Incar_{ci} * \beta'_4 FS_i + \beta'_5 X_i + \beta_6 Wave_i + \beta'_7 Z_{ci} + e_{ci}. \quad (1)$$

$LF$ refers to annual hours worked and wage rates. *Incar* indicates the citywide jail sanction rate; *CEI* refers to the vector of the other policy variables measuring financial, driver's license, and other sanctions; and *FS* indicates categorical variables for the father's custodial status, CFs being the reference category. *X* refers to the vector of individual-level control variables that includes father's race, age, nativity, educational attainment, prior conviction or incarceration (regardless of offense type), as well as current absence from the labor market due to current school, disability, or incarceration. *Z* indicates citywide control variables that include racial-

---

20. Because the survey contains data on neither days per week nor hours per day, when daily earnings were reported, we assumed five days of work per week, which helped motivate our relatively aggressive outlier cutoff of $50 per hour. We found little sensitivity to an alternate measure assuming eight hours per day.

**Table 3.** Annual Hours Worked Regressions, Jail and Financial Action Rate Results

| | Jail Action Rate | | | Financial Action Rate | | |
|---|---|---|---|---|---|---|
| | | Quantile Regressions | | | Quantile Regressions | |
| Father Category | OLS (1) | 25th (2) | 50th (3) | OLS (4) | 25th (5) | 50th (6) |
| NCF-only versus CF | 116.58 | 1,244.52 | 633.55* | 758.29 | −318.74 | 235.03 |
| | (0.46) | (1.50) | (1.90) | (1.26) | (−0.19) | (0.36) |
| NCF-orders versus CF | 10.73 | 254.57 | 308.37 | 106.21 | 584.71 | −650.48 |
| | (0.05) | (0.34) | (1.02) | (0.20) | (0.39) | (−1.07) |
| NCF-arrears versus CF | 19.50 | 880.00 | 378.27 | 200.80 | −1,060.39 | −1,171.45 |
| | (0.03) | (0.90) | (0.96) | (0.25) | (−0.57) | (−1.56) |

*Source:* Authors' calculations from the Fragile Families and Child Wellbeing Survey.
*Note:* Based on table A2. T-stats in parentheses. NCF = noncustodial fathers; CF = custodial fathers.
*$p < .1$; **$p < .05$; ***$p < .01$

ethnic representation, unemployment and poverty rate, region, and the mean household income. Because the data are clustered by survey wave, we controlled for wave fixed effects as indicated by *Wave*. Variable means (standard deviation) are presented in table A1, both for the overall sample and by father's custodial status. Unless otherwise noted, OLS methods are used to estimate models for both wages rates and annual hours worked. Because the data are clustered by city, we use standard errors clustered on cities.[21]

The policy treatment variables are interacted with father's custodial status to allow differential slope estimates of the influences of enforcement actions by vulnerability to child support enforcement. CFs, who theoretically should be unresponsive to the child support enforcement policy environment, serve as the reference category. Measuring the change in labor market outcomes relative to CFs (Miller and Mincy 2012) also mitigates the risk that observed correlations between policy variables and NCF labor market outcomes are driven by unobserved differences in cities' general labor market characteristics rather than by the influence of policy variation.

## MAIN (ADJUSTED) RESULTS

We present results for annual hours worked followed by those for wages.

### Annual Hours Worked

Table 3 presents summary regression results for annual hours worked, highlighting the interactions between custodial status and jail or financial sanction rates. Full results for all policy and father status variables are reported in table A2. All regression models also include the complete set of individual and citywide controls described, but their coefficient estimates are suppressed to conserve space; results are consistent with conventional expectations.

Column 1 presents coefficient estimates for the sample as a whole. Recall, the key identifying coefficient estimate of the threat of jail is the interaction between father custodial status, in particular NCFs with arrears, and the percentage of all NCFs who faced a jail enforcement action. Columns 2 and 3 examine potential heterogeneity in the threat effect of jail by presenting quantile regression estimates at the 25th and 50th percentiles of the hours distribution, respectively. Analysis of the data not shown here indicates that annual hours for NCFs in arrears

---

21. Including city fixed effects was not possible due to multicollinearity, including, unavoidably, with the policy variables. Models that included those city indicator variables not excluded by collinearity produced results comparable to the main model. We also tested a hierarchical linear modeling approach using city levels and robust standard errors. Results (available on request) were similar to our main model with clustered standard errors; we report the latter for ease of interpretation of the magnitude of effects.

**Table 4.** Annual Hours Worked Regressions, Marginal Effects with Jail-Financial Interactions

| | Jail Action Rate | | | Financial Action Rate | | |
|---|---|---|---|---|---|---|
| | | Quantile Regressions | | | Quantile Regressions | |
| Father Category | OLS (1) | 25th (2) | 50th (3) | OLS (4) | 25th (5) | 50th (6) |
| NCF-only versus CF | 127.94 | 2,262.04* | 719.93 | 744.30 | -828.54 | 241.56 |
| | (0.24) | (1.91) | (1.44) | (1.12) | (0.47) | (0.33) |
| NCF-orders versus CF | 399.03 | 1,108.53 | 271.94 | -163.21 | -321.49 | -614.91 |
| | (0.96) | (1.00) | (0.58) | (0.32) | (0.20) | (0.91) |
| NCF-arrears versus CF | 1,291.78** | 3,497.67** | 886.44 | -534.01 | -2,507.32 | -1,714.65* |
| | (2.36) | (2.30) | (1.38) | (0.62) | (1.27) | (2.06) |

*Source:* Authors' calculations from the Fragile Families and Child Wellbeing Survey.
*Note:* Based on table A3. Jail coefficients calculated at mean level of financial sanctions, and financial coefficients calculated at mean level of jail sanctions. T-stats in parentheses. NCF = noncustodial fathers; CF = custodial fathers.
*$p < .1$; **$p < .05$; ***$p < .01$

(and also NCF-onlys) are disproportionately located in the bottom quartile and bottom half of the overall hours distribution. Thus, these regressions examine the part of the hours distribution where the threat may be greatest for those most vulnerable to that threat and where responsiveness to threat may be greatest as well, a point to which we will return.

The expected positive effect of jail on hours (relative to CFs) is nontrivial only at the 25th and 50th percentiles, and there it is marginally statistically significant (10 percent) only for NCF-onlys in column 3's quantile regression at median hours. Similarly, the expected effect of financial sanctions in the opposite direction, that is, a tax effect reducing hours worked, is present at the 25th and 50th percentiles for NCFs in arrears (columns 5 and 6); however, it is neither statistically significant there nor consistently present across other measures.

These models assume independence among the policy variables. However, localities can and do use multiple enforcement methods concurrently. Moreover, even the jail sanction alone aims both to increase work effort and to tax back the resulting earnings. Thus, the jail threat coefficient is likely to include competing and countervailing influences of other actions such as financial sanctions, even while controlling for these actions. To mitigate this problem, we further interact the main jail and financial enforcement action variables with one another, as well as with fathers' custodial status, as before.[22] This triple interaction increases independence in the estimates of the jail enforcement variable by netting out the influence of financial sanctions. However, this comes at the cost of losing statistical power.

Table 4 presents summary results with jail and financial sanction rates interacted.[23] Summing the main and interacted effects is particularly informative (Brambor, Clark, and Golder 2006). Accordingly, we report here the marginal effects of an increase in the jail sanction rate at the mean level of financial sanctioning and, vice versa, the marginal effect coefficients for financial sanction rates (jail sanctioning at mean level). These are generated from postestimation simulations of hours worked, holding the means and marginal effects of all control variables constant while allowing the values of the jail (or financial) enforcement variable to vary by its distribution at its estimated effect (coefficient).

22. To avoid excess complexity, we do not interact either jail or financial sanctions with driver's license or other sanctions.

23. Full results for all policy and father status variables are reported in table A3.

In this interacted model, we find coefficients of the marginal effect of jail sanctioning on annual hours of NCFs with arrears (relative to CFs, the reference group) to increase across the board, relative to the model that is not interacted. In the OLS model (column 1), these marginal effects coefficients are of substantial magnitude (1,291.78 hours) in the predicted positive direction and statistically significant (5 percent). Given that the policy variable scale is between 0 and 1, we can interpret the magnitude of this influence as a 10 percentage point increase in jail threat (at mean financial sanctions) predicting an increase in annual hours worked of 129 hours (several weeks' worth of full-time work) for NCFs in arrears.

The effect is dramatically larger (3,497.67 hours) and similarly significant in the 25th percentile regression shown in column 2. Substantively, this implies that a 10 percent increase in the jail sanction rate corresponds (at mean financial sanctions) to increased annual hours worked of 46 percent (350/768) at the 25th percentile versus 5 percent (89/1,748) at median hours (column 3), and 9 percent (129/1,498) at the mean, relative to hours worked at 0 percent jail sanctioning. Table A3 also shows that, across all three interacted regression models, the main jail coefficient is large and significant for NCFs in arrears, the most dramatic results being in the 25th percentile regression.

The concentration of positive effects on annual hours worked at the bottom of the hours distribution appears to reflect a combination of increased hours among those working and nonwork-work transitions.[24] Because fewer than 10 percent of all observations reflect zero hours, peaking at 15 percent for both NCF-only and NCF-arrears, even substantial nonwork-work transitions would not necessarily affect the 25th percentile. To the extent that nonwork-work transitions do drive increased annual hours worked, they do so primarily through work at relatively low annual hours, driving up the 25th percentile much more than the median; a transition from zero hours to below-median hours will not affect the median. Indeed, we would expect nonwork-work transitions to result in work at the low end of the hours distribution among those working, which should drag down 25th percentile and median hours within this population. To probe this, and in contrast to our main results that include zero-hour reports, we also ran the same regression models on annual hours worked among those reporting nonzero hours. These results (not shown but available on request) show marginal effects of jail sanctioning on hours worked (among those working at all) that are small in magnitude, inconsistent in sign, and not even marginally statistically significant; this holds across all NCF categories, with and without jail-financial interactions, and across mean, 25th percentile, and median hours. As we will discuss further, this suggests, but does not establish, that our main results reflect both nonwork-work transitions and within-work hours increases.

The interacted model can be used to further disentangle the influence of the jail and financial sanctions by conducting simulations at different levels of financial sanctions. The large, negative, statistically significant jail-financial interaction coefficients (table A3, columns 1 through 3) indicate that the positive effect of jail sanctioning upon annual hours worked declines with increased financial sanctioning, as expected. Figure 1 illustrates this with the postestimation simulation of the marginal effects of jail sanctioning for all father types at low (25th percentile), medium (50th percentile), and high (75th percentile) levels of financial sanctioning, showing 95 percent confidence intervals. The simulations support the expectation that jail threat influence on hours, especially for NCFs in arrears, is more pronounced at lower levels of financial sanctioning. The coefficients (not shown separately) for the marginal effect of the jail sanction rates on hours

---

24. We also ran regressions with an indicator variable for any hours worked substituting for annual hours worked. The results (not shown) indicate substantial, statistically significant increases in employment for NCF-only and NCF-arrears, but not for NCF-orders, associated with increased jail sanctioning. This implies that some of the observed increase in hours among NCF-arrears is attributable to nonwork-work transitions, though we interpret these results with caution because the employment results do not track the hours results for NCF-only, which were small and insignificant in the interacted OLS model.

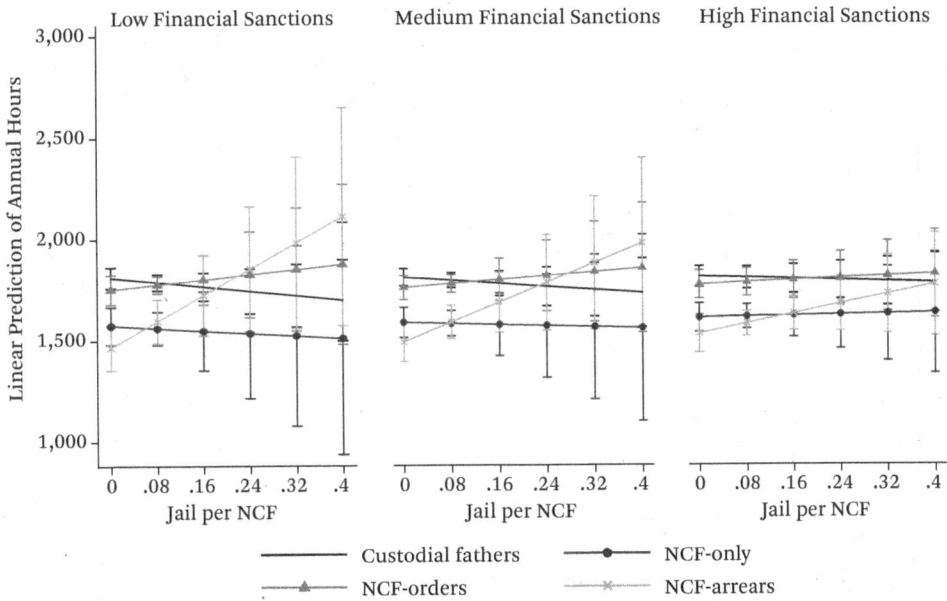

**Figure 1.** Response of Hours Worked to Jail Sanctions, by Financial Sanction Level

*Source:* Authors' calculations from the Fragile Families and Child Wellbeing Survey.
*Note:* Based on jail-financial interacted OLS regressions, table A3. NCF = noncustodial fathers.

for the arrears group are 1,890 (low), 1,412 (medium), and 630 (high), the first two statistically significant at the 5 percent level.

More generally, figure 1 shows graphically how the jail threat influence on hours worked operates across the father type categories in the interacted model. Across all levels of financial sanctions, we see slopes of the jail threat influence on hours for NCFs-orders and NCF-onlys that are between those for NCFs-arrears and for CFs. This pattern follows the hypothesis that the jail threat influence on NCFs should be ordered by the vulnerability to that threat.

Not only are increasing rates of jail sanctioning associated with increasing hours worked for NCFs, especially those in arrears, but also the opposite is true for financial sanctioning. Figure 2 illustrates graphically (95 percent confidence intervals) the predicted margins of the jail versus financial sanction influences on hours worked for NCFs in arrears based on interacted regression results in table 4, columns 1 and 4. The figure demonstrates clearly that the marginal influences of jail or financial sanctions on hours worked move in opposite directions, consistent with expectations.

**Wage Rates**

The presentation of results for wage rates follows closely that for annual hours worked. Table 5 first presents summary regression results for wage rates, without jail-financial interactions, for mean, 25th percentile, and median hours in columns 1 through 3, respectively. Column 1 shows the coefficient estimate for NCFs in arrears is negative as expected and highly statistically significant (1 percent level). Furthermore, the magnitude of the influence is substantial. A 10 percentage point increase in jail enforcement threat predicts a wage rate decline of $1.27 for NCFs in arrears (relative to CFs). We also find evidence of a substantial and statistically significant (5 percent level) tax impact of financial sanctions operating in the opposite direction for NCFs in arrears (column 4).

As with hours worked, analysis of data not shown here indicates that NCFs in arrears are concentrated in the bottom quartile and bottom half of the overall wage rate distribution. Columns 2 and 3 examine potential heterogeneity in the threat effect of jail with quantile regression estimates at the 25th and 50th percentiles of the wage distribution, respectively.

**Figure 2.** Response of Hours Worked to Jail Versus Financial Sanctions, for NCFs with Arrears

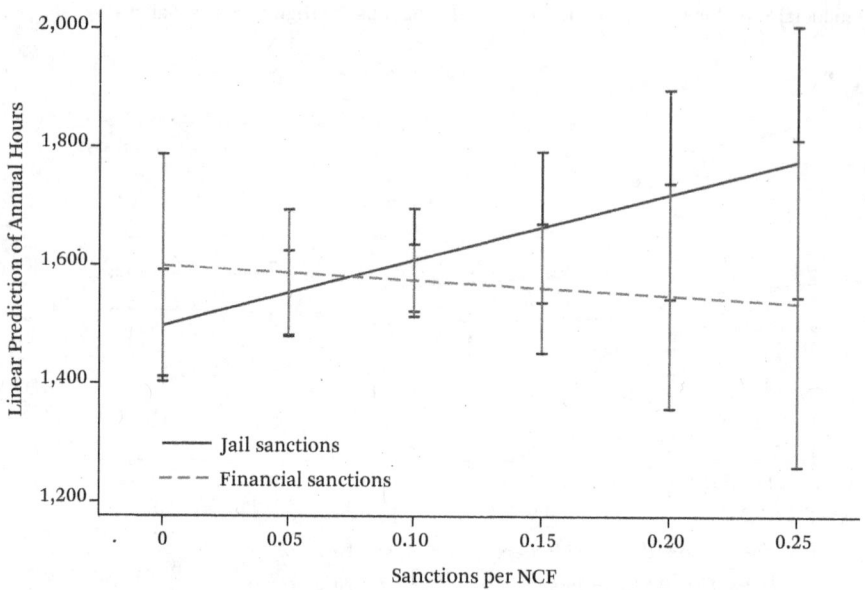

*Source:* Authors' calculations from the Fragile Families and Child Wellbeing Survey.
*Note:* Based on jail-financial interacted OLS regressions, table A3. Jail coefficients calculated at mean level of financial sanctions, and financial coefficients calculated at mean level of jail sanctions. NCF = noncustodial fathers.

**Table 5.** Wage Rate Regressions, Jail and Financial Action Rate Results

| | Jail Action Rate | | | Financial Action Rate | | |
| | | Quantile Regressions | | | Quantile Regressions | |
| Father Category | OLS (1) | 25th (2) | 50th (3) | OLS (4) | 25th (5) | 50th (6) |
|---|---|---|---|---|---|---|
| NCF-only versus CF | -6.38** | -5.86* | -10.30*** | 10.35** | 1.23 | 1.97 |
| | (-2.32) | (-1.89) | (-2.61) | (2.65) | (0.20) | (0.25) |
| NCF-orders versus CF | -5.98 | -1.30 | -4.21 | 5.01 | -4.14 | -0.43 |
| | (-1.66) | (-0.47) | (-1.18) | (0.69) | (-0.73) | (-0.06) |
| NCF-arrears versus CF | -12.68*** | -6.47* | -8.54* | 16.92** | 9.75 | 9.25 |
| | (-4.41) | (-1.77) | (-1.83) | (2.87) | (1.40) | (1.04) |

*Source:* Authors' calculations from the Fragile Families and Child Wellbeing Survey.
*Note:* Based on table A2. T-stats in parentheses. NCF = noncustodial fathers; CF = custodial fathers.
*p < .1; **p < .05; ***p < .01

These results are again negative, statistically significant (10 percent levels), and substantial for NCFs in arrears. Although, in absolute terms, the magnitude of the influence is much smaller than that for the sample as a whole, the wage distribution is highly asymmetrical above and below median. For those at the 25th percentile, for instance, the roughly $0.65 wage decrease for NCFs with arrears associated with a 10 percent point increase in jail sanctioning corresponds to a 6.8 percent decline in wage rates (from $9.53 at 0 percent jail), relative to (again) a 6.8 percent ($0.85/$12.59) decrease at median wages and a 9.1 percent decrease at mean wages ($1.27/$14.00).

Table 6 presents summary results from re-

**Table 6.** Wage Rate Regressions, Marginal Effects with Jail-Financial Interactions

| | Jail Action Rate | | | Financial Action Rate | | |
|---|---|---|---|---|---|---|
| | OLS | Quantile Regressions | | OLS | Quantile Regressions | |
| | | 25th | 50th | | 25th | 50th |
| Father Category | (1) | (2) | (3) | (4) | (5) | (6) |
| NCF-only versus CF | −0.81 | −2.08 | −4.47 | 6.17 | −1.50 | −1.36 |
| | (0.23) | (0.47) | (0.79) | (1.62) | (0.23) | (0.16) |
| NCF-orders versus CF | −6.62 | −1.22 | −4.53 | 5.34 | −4.45 | −0.57 |
| | (0.76) | (0.29) | (0.86) | (0.57) | (0.74) | (0.07) |
| NCF-arrears versus CF | −12.25** | −5.71 | −9.67 | 16.77** | 9.74 | 9.39 |
| | (2.16) | (1.00) | (1.33) | (2.49) | (1.31) | (1.00) |

*Source:* Authors' calculations from the Fragile Families and Child Wellbeing Survey.
*Note:* Based on table A3. Jail coefficients calculated at mean level of financial sanctions, and financial coefficients calculated at mean level of jail sanctions. T-stats in parentheses. NCF = noncustodial fathers; CF = custodial fathers.
*$p < .1$; **$p < .05$; ***$p < .01$

gression models that interact jail and financial sanctioning rates, showing the marginal effect coefficients for jail sanction rates (with financial sanctioning at mean level) and for financial sanction rates (with jail sanctioning at mean level). For NCFs in arrears, magnitudes change little but statistical significance declines somewhat across the board, as expected with the enlarged standard errors associated with the interacted model. Nonetheless, the similarly substantial in magnitude but opposite in sign effects for jail versus financial actions both remain significant at the 5 percent level in the OLS interacted model (columns 1 and 4). In contrast, all the significant results for NCF-onlys disappear as we move from the noninteracted to interacted models.

Figure 3 again shows post-estimation simulations of the jail threat influence on mean wages for all father types at the 25th (low), 50th (medium), and 75th (high) percentiles of financial sanctions. Here, variation across levels of financial sanctioning for NCFs in arrears is not substantial. Again, the slopes for NCFs with orders and NCF-onlys largely fall between those for NCFs with arrears and CFs, except for NCF-onlys at low levels of financial sanctioning.

Again comparing jail and financial sanctioning, figure 4 shows the predicted margins of their influences on wages for NCFs in arrears based on interacted regression results in columns 1 and 4 of table 6. These are nearly mirror images, moving in opposite directions, as expected.

## DISCUSSION

Overall, the reported results are largely consistent with our hypothesized labor market effects of jail threat for failure to work to pay child support. We observe the distinctive combination of declining wages and increasing hours as jail threat rises. This differentiates the posited threat effect from a barrier to employment, such as past incarceration, which should depress both wages and hours. Indeed, though we have treated it mainly as a control rather than a primary object of analysis, a city's rate of suspending driver's licenses to enforce child support obligations does produce this contrasting barriers pattern (Cadigan and Kirk 2020), with consistently large, statistically significant negative effects on both hours worked and wages (tables A2, A3).

Furthermore, this pattern of more work at lower wages appears specifically in the differential response to jail rates of NCFs in arrears (relative to CFs), consistent with their greater vulnerability to jail threat relative not only to CFs but also to other NCFs. The response is particularly strong among those with lower hours, consistent both with where the threat would be concentrated and where it would most likely produce the strongest response. This jail threat response also interacts with the intensity of fi-

**Figure 3.** Response of Wages to Jail Sanctions, by Financial Sanction Level

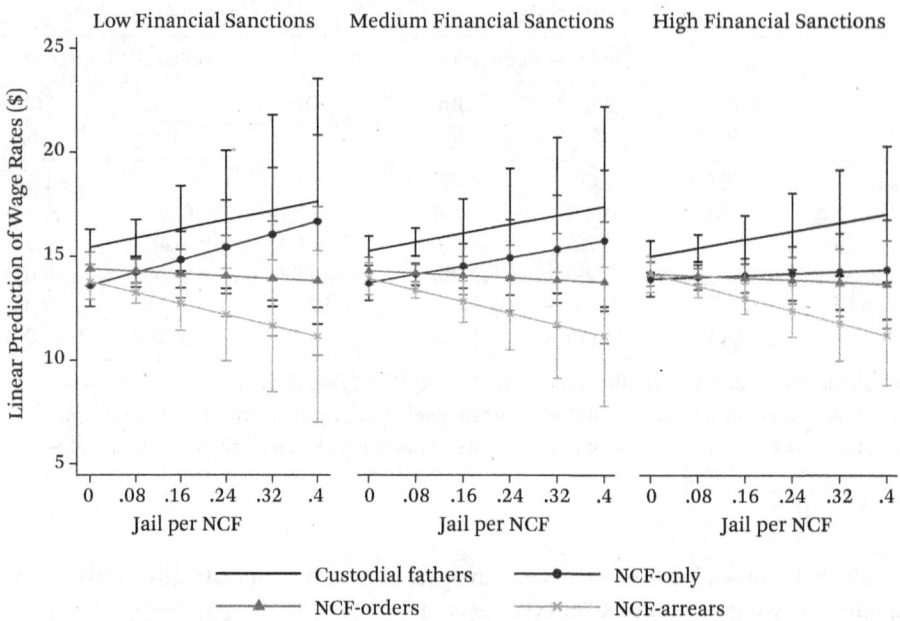

*Source:* Authors' calculations from the Fragile Families and Child Wellbeing Survey.
*Note:* Based on jail-financial interacted OLS regressions, table A3. NCF = noncustodial fathers.

**Figure 4.** Response of Wages to Jail Versus Financial Sanctions, for NCFs with Arrears

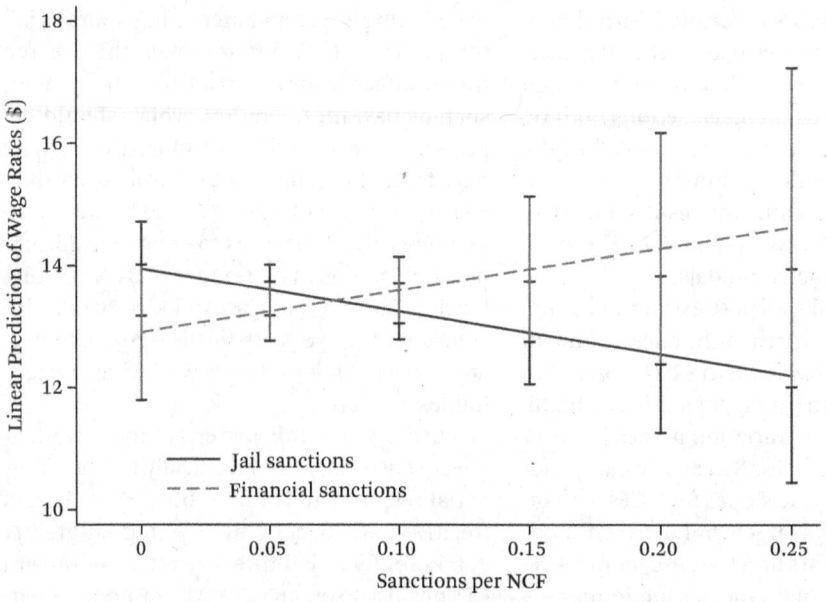

*Source:* Authors' calculations from the Fragile Families and Child Wellbeing Survey.
*Note:* Based on jail-financial interacted OLS regressions, table A3. Jail coefficients calculated at mean level of financial sanctions, and financial coefficients calculated at mean level of jail sanctions. NCF = noncustodial fathers.

nancial sanctioning, operating most strongly where payment collection efforts are weakest.

Relatedly, jail and financial sanctioning consistently exhibit effects that operate in opposite directions, for both hours and wages. Again, this is theoretically consistent with competing threat and tax mechanisms of influence. Indeed, this may help explain the heretofore surprisingly weak evidence (Miller and Mincy 2012) of the expected work disincentives in analyses that model child support enforcement exclusively as a tax. Such offsetting effects are consistent with how work requirements are sometimes thought to enable policymakers to counteract work disincentives associated with a tax, but variation in the relative intensity of jail versus financial sanctioning highlights the difficulty of calibrating such offsetting, including the risk that jail threats might substantially overcorrect.

This confluence of several distinct, albeit related, theoretically predicted results—the effects of jail threat on both hours and wages, their concentration among NCFs in arrears and particularly those with the lowest hours, and the interaction with levels of financial sanctioning that operate in the opposite direction—enhances our confidence in their validity. That said, not all our results clearly support the predicted effects of jail threat. None of our measures show any statistically significant effect on NCFs with orders but not arrears. The NCF-only group responds to jail threat in ways broadly similar to NCF-arrears in the models without jail-financial interactions, but with that interaction added, this similarity persists only for the hours response among those with relatively low hours. Although they suggest some jail threat effect, it is unclear how to interpret the results for NCFs without arrears. NCF-only may be a particularly heterogeneous group. Some could be quite unresponsive to the sanction regime because they have stable earnings and pay regularly (weakening incentives to establish an order through the formal child support system). Others with marginal employment prospects may lack orders because of disconnection from custodial mothers and state systems or the limited prospect of collecting support, and these fathers might be more responsive to intensified enforcement.

Some ambiguity in how to interpret our results arises from our measurement of hours and wages specifically in formal employment. The National Research Council has suggested that findings of increased hours of work under parole supervision (Pettit and Lyons 2007; Sabol 2007; Seim and Harding 2020) might reflect work requirements pushing parolees to substitute formal (measured) for informal (unmeasured) work (Travis, Western, and Redburn 2014). Such informal-formal transitions do not intrinsically explain the additional association between increased formal hours and decreased wages that Becky Pettit and Christopher Lyons found for parolees (2007) and that we find here for NCFs with arrears. The theory could, however, be extended to posit that such transitions also sacrifice a wage premium for informality.

We doubt that informal-formal shifts explain our results. This mechanism requires pressure toward formality to a degree that outweighs the hypothesized diminished ability to pay support associated with a lost wage premium. This is less plausible in the child support context where payments provide an independent way to satisfy work obligations, whereas documentation of work may be more independently important in the parole context. Addressing the issue empirically is challenging because Fragile Families data does not include a single, consistent measure of total annual informal hours, and its data on hours in subtypes of informal work cannot reliably be aggregated. Nonetheless, we did run our regressions on individuals' largest annual hours worked in any one subtype of informal work, which provides a reasonable proxy for overall informal hours. Differences in informal hours between CF and NCF-arrears as a function of jail rate were trivial in size and not remotely statistically significant. This is difficult to square with substitution away from informality driving the observed effects on formal hours.

Our results also leave open some questions about the mechanisms by which jail threat influences hours and wages, with potentially important implications both empirically and in policy significance. As noted, transitions from nonwork to low-hours work clearly play a significant role. In theory, these transitions could explain the entire increase in annual hours worked. If those entries are into lower-wage work, they could explain the wage effects as well. However, we doubt that is the case for two reasons.

First, as noted, jail threat's association with increased annual hours worked among the entire population coexists with having no effect on the distribution of hours among those reporting at least some work. The latter is inconsistent with the hypothesis that the former is driven exclusively by nonwork-work transitions. That is because such transitions concentrated in the bottom of the entire hours distribution should cause the 25th and 50th percentiles of hours to fall among the subset of those working, even though hours increase among the entire population. We anticipate that effect empirically because the NCF-only and NCF-arrears groups are overrepresented in the bottom of the hours distribution among those working; so, too, are those with relatively low wages. In addition, we would expect un- and underemployment to correlate with weaker employment prospects. Thus, those transitioning into work in response to jail threat would be more likely to move into less steady jobs with relatively low hours. But no such downward shift in hours among the working population is observed in association with the jail threat that drives these NCFs into work.

Instead, stasis in the hours distribution among those working is more consistent with a combination of nonwork-work transitions and within-work hours increases. Both would drive overall increases in hours worked. The latter, however, necessarily would also shift the hours distribution upward among those working. This, in turn, would offset the former's tendency to shift that distribution downward. Such a combination, then, would reconcile our findings with regard to hours worked among both the entire population and the working population.

Second, a mix of nonwork-work transitions and within-work hours increases is more plausible in theory. Recall that our hours indicator is measured over a year. It would be surprising if people with zero annual weeks of work responded strongly to jail threat by adding hundreds of additional work hours, but those with, say, five or six annual weeks of work were unmoved.

Ultimately, with Fragile Families data we cannot decompose those working into those who would not have worked absent jail threat and those who would have worked regardless. Accordingly, we cannot directly measure the relative contributions of these two mechanisms to increasing hours.

Similarly, we cannot determine the extent to which wage declines are driven by hours increases. Lower wages could be associated with added hours, if workers are driven by the jail threat to accept less attractive jobs they otherwise would have declined. But wages also could decline within hours that would have been worked even absent the jail threat, because workers' ability to bargain for or switch jobs for higher wages is undermined by their increased vulnerability to sanctions for periods of un- or underemployment.

Future research addressing these empirical questions about nonwork-work transitions versus within-work changes could affect our findings' policy implications. Entry into employment, or increased hours up to a point, might be considered an unalloyed good. In contrast, within-individual wage losses at constant hours are more unambiguously troubling. In the context of child support enforcement specifically, such losses would suggest that efforts to increase some noncustodial parents' hours worked as a way to increase their ability to pay also could, through downward wage pressure, have the perverse effect of undermining other noncustodial parents' ability to earn and pay. Indeed, the availability of new entrants at low wages would be expected to put downward wage pressure on those who would be working regardless.

More generally, the "right to quit" provides an important self-help mechanism, aside from direct legal regulation, in combating abusive or exploitative working conditions (Pope 2010). Accordingly, forced entry into employment at rock bottom wages might be viewed as independently concerning, even though increased work and earnings have their upsides.

Insofar as increased hours are seen as a policy gain, all else equal, different policy tools might achieve that gain. Using the threat of jail to counteract un- and underemployment by lowering reservation wages (and other dimensions of job quality) brings potential costs in downward pressure on labor standards at the bottom of the labor market, exposure to the risk of incarceration, and diminished autonomy at work (Zatz 2019). Employment increases might also be achieved by raising the returns to work rather than intensifying the costs of nonwork (Sorensen 2010).

For these reasons, the potential for increased work to enable greater support payments (Dwyer Emory et al. 2020) does not settle the question, especially when increased work is linked to lower wages rather than enhanced earnings capacity. Furthermore, although increased support payments can enhance the well-being of low-income households with children of noncustodial parents, private intrafamily transfers are not the only way to do so (Brito 2012). Nor do increased payments necessarily deliver such benefits, given that they often are captured by the state to offset expenditures on public assistance.

## LIMITATIONS

One may worry that our results could be an artifact of the mechanical problem that enforcement actions can only be taken against NCFs in arrears. This concern is tempered by further analysis of the data regarding enforcement actions by type cross-tabbed by fathers' custodial type categories (table A1). City-based threat levels are uniformly experienced across father category. We also observe some statistically significant results for NCF-only, in the same direction as NCF-arrears, which suggests the operation of some threat effect against those who have not directly experienced any formal enforcement action.

The NCF-only group, with no orders established, also raises the possibility that NCFs could respond to jail threat with intensified efforts to avoid enforcement, not with increased compliance. This could manifest in differential survey attrition. If such attrition correlated with difficulty complying, it could inflate hours of work among those responding. However, this mechanism would also predict an association between greater jail threat and increased reported wages, the opposite of what we find.[25]

More generally, Fragile Families data are limited by substantial survey attrition. Any bias this introduces, however, should be toward null results. That bias would result from attrition concentrated among those with weaker labor market prospects, where we expect stronger response to jail threat, and among later waves, where enforcement threat likely increases with focal child age. This is in addition to other potential sources of statistical noise already noted. The attrition limitations of Fragile Families also mean our results are most persuasive in regard to the existence of the jail threat influence on hours and wages, and less so in regard to its precise magnitude.

Finally, as a study of work requirements enforced by jail threat, this study is limited by contextual features of child support enforcement. Because the underlying obligation is to pay, the work requirements are sometimes less direct and are intertwined with the financial disincentives of a tax. If anything, this should dampen our results, as our jail-financial interactions suggest, relative to a pure work requirement. This conjunction of work and payment obligations, however, is itself an important policy phenomenon, not only in child support but also in criminal fines and fees, as well as in probation and parole requirements to pay both child support and criminal legal debt (Zatz 2019).

## CONCLUSION

Our findings suggest how criminal legal institutions can drive people (deeper) into the labor market under deteriorating conditions. A similar mechanism may also operate outside the child support enforcement context, in other domains with work requirements enforced by potential incarceration, including criminal legal supervision generally and court debt specifically. This phenomenon implies that empirical and policy focus on how incarceration erects barriers to employment is importantly incomplete, and it highlights the value of analyzing the quality of work, not only its quantity.

---

25. As noted separately, we also find little evidence of such differential attrition. Enforcement avoidance also might lead to differential out-migration among those still responding. This would seem only to introduce noise, however; such relocations also are relatively rare.

**Table A1.** Summary Statistics

|  | Overall Mean (SD) | CF Mean (SD) | NCF-Only Mean (SD) | NCF-Orders Mean (SD) | NCF-Arrears Mean (SD) |
|---|---|---|---|---|---|
| Proportion of sample | 100% | 44.01% | 17.48% | 23.75% | 12.76% |
| **Individual-level variables** | | | | | |
| Wage rate | 14.7 (8.9) | 17.1 (10.1) | 12.0 (6.9) | 13.5 (7.3) | 11.7 (6.7) |
| Annual hours | 1,728 (846) | 1,936 (713) | 1,445 (918) | 1,709 (867) | 1,397 (921) |
| African American | 46% (50%) | 28% (45%) | 60% (49%) | 61% (49%) | 65% (48%) |
| Hispanic | 28% (45%) | 36% (48%) | 23% (42%) | 22% (42%) | 20% (40%) |
| Other | 4% (20%) | 5% (21%) | 4% (20%) | 4% (20%) | 4% (19%) |
| Father age | 28 (7) | 29 (7) | 26 (7) | 29 (7) | 26 (7) |
| U.S. born | 83% (38%) | 74% (44%) | 87% (33%) | 90% (30%) | 96% (19%) |
| High school grad | 35% (48%) | 26% (44%) | 41% (49%) | 44% (50%) | 42% (49%) |
| Some college | 23% (42%) | 26% (44%) | 17% (38%) | 23% (42%) | 19% (40%) |
| College grad | 11% (31%) | 19% (39%) | 4% (20%) | 4% (19%) | 2% (13%) |
| Not working: jail | 2% (15%) | 0% (2%) | 7% (25%) | 2% (14%) | 5% (21%) |
| Not working: school | 0% (6%) | 0% (6%) | 1% (7%) | 0% (6%) | 0% (6%) |
| Not working: disabled | 2% (15%) | 2% (13%) | 2% (16%) | 3% (18%) | 3% (16%) |
| Ever convicted | 26% (44%) | 16% (36%) | 38% (49%) | 29% (45%) | 44% (49%) |
| Ever incarcerated | 41% (49%) | 25% (43%) | 55% (50%) | 49% (50%) | 69% (46%) |
| **City-level variables** | | | | | |
| Jail action rate | 7% (7%) | 7% (7%) | 7% (7%) | 8% (7%) | 8% (7%) |
| Financial action rate | 8% (4%) | 7% (4%) | 7% (4%) | 8% (4%) | 8% (4%) |
| Driver's license action rate | 3% (2%) | 3% (2%) | 2% (2%) | 3% (3%) | 3% (2%) |
| Other actions rate | 6% (3%) | 6% (3%) | 6% (3%) | 7% (3%) | 7% (3%) |
| Foreign-born | 13% (11%) | 15% (12%) | 13% (10%) | 13% (10%) | 11% (9%) |
| African American | 16% (9%) | 15% (8%) | 16% (8%) | 17% (9%) | 17% (9%) |
| Hispanic | 16% (18%) | 18% (19%) | 15% (17%) | 16% (19%) | 14% (18%) |
| Mean income | 75,513 (14,475) | 75,476 (15,038) | 75,621 (13,603) | 75,765 (14,471) | 75,033 (13,555) |
| Metro population | 2,862,211 (3,519,790) | 2,883,260 (3,575,541) | 3,052,477 (3,510,689) | 3,006,180 (3,683,314) | 2,257,652 (2,904,356) |
| Unemployment rate | 5.6% (1.9%) | 5.5% (1.9%) | 5.2% (1.6%) | 5.8% (1.9%) | 6.0% (1.9%) |

*Source:* Authors' calculations from the Fragile Families and Child Wellbeing Survey and the Current Population Survey.
*Note:* City level controls based on CPS metropolitan area data, 1998 through 2010, averaged across individual wave years, except metro population ages eighteen through sixty-four and unemployment rate based on Fragile Families data by sample city MSA, averaged across month of interview. CF = custodial fathers; NCF = noncustodial fathers.

**Table A2.** Annual Hours Worked and Wage Rate Regressions, Without Jail-Financial Interactions

| Enforcement Action Rates and Father Categories | Annual Hours Worked | | | Wages | | |
|---|---|---|---|---|---|---|
| | | Quantile Regressions | | | Quantile Regressions | |
| | OLS (1) | 25th (2) | 50th (3) | OLS (4) | 25th (5) | 50th (6) |
| NCF-only | -250.64*** | -417.49*** | -191.16*** | -2.41*** | -0.50 | -0.99 |
| | (-5.61) | (-2.95) | (-3.35) | (-6.02) | (-0.95) | (-1.47) |
| NCF-orders | -49.76 | -122.47 | -3.41 | -1.36* | 0.16 | -0.47 |
| | (-0.76) | (-0.90) | (-0.06) | (-2.00) | (0.32) | (-0.72) |
| NCF-arrears | -185.36* | -478.71** | -130.95* | -1.98*** | -1.02 | -1.39 |
| | (-1.91) | (-2.39) | (-1.78) | (-3.18) | (-1.50) | (-1.60) |
| **Jail** | 32.93 | 201.54 | -276.86 | 4.71 | 0.60 | 3.66 |
| | (.17) | (0.42) | (-1.44) | (1.62) | (0.34) | (1.61) |
| × NCF-only | 116.58 | 1,244.52 | 633.55* | -6.38** | -5.86* | -10.30*** |
| | (0.46) | (1.50) | (1.90) | (-2.32) | (-1.89) | (-2.61) |
| × NCF-orders | 10.73 | 254.57 | 308.37 | -5.98 | -1.30 | -4.21 |
| | (0.05) | (0.34) | (1.02) | (-1.66) | (-0.47) | (-1.18) |
| × NCF-arrears | 19.50 | 880.00 | 378.27 | -12.68*** | -6.47* | -8.54* |
| | (0.03) | (0.90) | (0.96) | (-4.41) | (-1.77) | (-1.83) |
| **Financial** | 113.58 | 434.46 | 901.91* | -9.99 | -1.26 | -2.89 |
| | (.20) | (0.36) | (1.86) | (-1.24) | (-0.28) | (-0.50) |
| × NCF-only | 758.29 | -318.74 | 235.03 | 10.35** | 1.23 | 1.97 |
| | (1.26) | (-0.19) | (0.36) | (2.65) | (0.20) | (0.25) |
| × NCF-orders | 106.21 | 584.71 | -650.48 | 5.01 | -4.14 | -0.43 |
| | (0.20) | (0.39) | (-1.07) | (0.69) | (-0.73) | (-0.06) |
| × NCF-arrears | 200.80 | -1,060.39 | -1,171.45 | 16.92** | 9.75 | 9.25 |
| | (0.25) | (-0.57) | (-1.56) | (2.87) | (1.40) | (1.04) |
| **Driver's license** | -1,137.90* | -1,561.82 | -1,195.62** | 8.12 | -6.15 | 2.53 |
| | (-2.10) | (-1.19) | (-2.25) | (0.86) | (-1.25) | (0.40) |
| × NCF-only | 750.92 | 622.18 | 1,165.48 | -6.14 | 4.95 | 1.88 |
| | (1.04) | (0.28) | (1.30) | (-0.88) | (0.59) | (0.18) |
| × NCF-orders | 705.53 | 920.88 | 1,100.54 | -7.65 | 2.99 | -4.77 |
| | (0.94) | (0.46) | (1.37) | (-0.81) | (0.40) | (-0.50) |
| × NCF-arrears | -3,780.82** | -5,951.37** | -885.43 | -23.88** | -7.52 | -25.82** |
| | (-2.30) | (-2.33) | (-0.86) | (-3.28) | (0.79) | (-2.12) |
| **Other actions** | 226.87 | 742.80 | 121.59 | -6.20 | 4.89 | -1.37 |
| | (0.60) | (0.81) | (0.33) | (-1.07) | (1.43) | (-0.32) |
| × NCF-only | -718.65 | -515.64 | -673.49 | 8.93* | -4.41 | 3.32 |
| | (-1.13) | (-0.32) | (-1.04) | (2.07) | (-0.73) | (0.43) |
| × NCF-orders | -96.43 | -649.71 | -19.58 | 2.95 | 7.35 | -1.28 |
| | (-0.15) | (-0.46) | (-0.03) | (0.41) | (-1.39) | (-0.19) |
| × NCF-arrears | 423.58 | 1,599.41 | -586.49 | 1.05 | -7.88 | 1.94 |
| | (0.43) | (0.87) | (0.79) | (0.20) | (-1.15) | (0.22) |
| $R^2$/pseudo-$R^2$ | 0.256 | 0.230 | 0.132 | 0.356 | 0.144 | 0.211 |

*Source:* Authors' calculations from the Fragile Families and Child Wellbeing Survey.
*Note:* N = 8,362. T-stats in parentheses. NCF = noncustodial fathers. Reference group is custodial fathers.
*$p < .1$; **$p < .05$; ***$p < .01$

**Table A3.** Annual Hours Worked and Wage Rate Regressions, with Jail-Financial Interactions

| Enforcement Action Rates and Father Categories | Annual Hours Worked | | | Wages | | |
|---|---|---|---|---|---|---|
| | | Quantile Regressions | | | Quantile Regressions | |
| | OLS (1) | 25th (2) | 50th (3) | OLS (4) | 25th (5) | 50th (6) |
| NCF-only | -250.13*** | -564.69*** | -214.55*** | -3.10*** | -0.86 | -1.81** |
| | (-4.20) | (-3.22) | (-2.89) | (-6.00) | (-1.31) | (-2.16) |
| NCF-orders | -97.25 | -225.95 | -3.74 | -1.30* | -0.19 | -0.39 |
| | (-1.25) | (-1.34) | (-1.05) | (-1.75) | (0.30) | (-0.48) |
| NCF-arrears | -349.15*** | -754.23*** | -334.20*** | -2.07** | -1.19 | -1.17 |
| | (-3.91) | (-3.19) | (-3.35) | (-2.63) | (-1.34) | (-1.04) |
| **Jail** | -495.15 | -383.57 | -179.42 | 5.97 | -0.16 | 5.18 |
| | (-1.19) | (-0.25) | (-0.28) | (0.51) | (-0.03) | (0.71) |
| × NCF-only | 100.82 | 4,195.34* | 851.86 | 8.86 | 3.64 | 5.83 |
| | (0.10) | (1.72) | (0.83) | (1.22) | (0.40) | (0.50) |
| × NCF-orders | 1,008.04 | 2,669.37 | 252.60 | -7.61 | -1.79 | -5.05 |
| | (1.20) | (1.19) | (0.27) | (-0.44) | (-0.21) | (-0.47) |
| × NCF-arrears | 3,200.70*** | 6,949.58** | 3,086.97** | -11.57 | -4.59 | -10.89 |
| | (2.90) | (2.25) | (2.37) | (-1.02) | (-0.40) | (-0.74) |
| **Financial** | -29.06 | -36.78 | 912.03 | -9.17 | -1.49 | -2.23 |
| | (-0.05) | (-0.03) | (1.63) | (-1.08) | (-0.30) | (-0.35) |
| × NCF-only | 717.71 | 1,067.06 | 370.91 | 15.64*** | 4.11 | 8.73 |
| | (1.10) | (0.59) | (0.49) | (4.28) | (0.61) | (1.02) |
| × NCF-orders | 433.93 | 1,208.91 | -633.87 | 4.37 | -5.01 | -1.08 |
| | (0.75) | (0.73) | (0.49) | (0.60) | (-0.80) | (-0.14) |
| × NCF-arrears | 1,337.69 | 877.27 | 442.96 | 17.43** | 10.84 | 8.19 |
| | (1.60) | (0.41) | (0.49) | (2.69) | (1.36) | (0.81) |
| **Jail × financial** | 4,163.15 | 4,947.45 | -715.84 | -9.30 | 4.48 | -12.76 |
| | (1.36) | (0.43) | (-0.15) | (-0.12) | (0.10) | (-0.23) |
| × NCF-only | 357.97 | -25,519.38 | -1,741.37 | -127.59** | -75.54 | -135.85 |
| | (0.05) | (-1.34) | (-0.22) | (-2.57) | (-1.06) | (-1.50) |
| × NCF-orders | -8,038.92 | -20,602.95 | 255.21 | 13.09 | 7.58 | 6.84 |
| | (-1.39) | (-1.20) | (0.04) | (0.11) | (0.12) | (0.08) |
| × NCF-arrears | -25,197.61** | -45,564.80* | -29,046.71** | -8.98 | -14.74 | 16.10 |
| | (-3.11) | (-1.96) | (-2.96) | (-0.11) | (-0.17) | (0.15) |
| **Driver's license** | -1,248.65** | -1,303.82 | -1,116.60* | 8.30 | -6.36 | 2.21 |
| | (-2.13) | (-0.96) | (-1.95) | (0.89) | (-1.25) | (0.34) |
| × NCF-only | 757.19 | 1,678.45 | 1,222.81 | -2.67 | 7.84 | 4.10 |
| | (1.06) | (0.74) | (1.27) | (-0.54) | (0.92) | (0.38) |
| × NCF-orders | 900.34 | 1,426.99 | 1,103.86 | -7.51 | 3.19 | -4.07 |
| | (1.18) | (0.71) | (1.30) | (-0.87) | (0.42) | (-0.42) |
| × NCF-arrears | -3,345.50* | -4,373.76* | -649.93 | -23.43*** | -7.18 | -25.79** |
| | (-2.05) | (-1.70) | (-0.60) | (-3.20) | (-0.74) | (-2.10) |
| **Other actions** | 243.23 | 706.91 | 100.99 | -6.33 | 4.65 | -1.04 |
| | (0.65) | (0.78) | (0.26) | (-1.09) | (1.37) | (-0.24) |
| × NCF-only | -691.77 | -1,347.95 | -529.79 | 8.06** | -5.99 | 2.34 |
| | (-1.08) | (-0.84) | (-0.78) | (2.23) | (-0.99) | (0.31) |
| × NCF-orders | -129.39 | -724.89 | 25.79 | 3.27 | -6.71 | -1.96 |
| | (-0.20) | (-0.52) | (0.04) | (0.46) | (-1.27) | (-0.29) |
| × NCF-arrears | 359.89 | 1,293.52 | 1,422.71* | 1.33 | -7.21 | 1.39 |
| | (0.39) | (0.71) | (1.85) | (0.26) | (-1.05) | (0.16) |
| $R^2$/pseudo-$R^2$ | 0.256 | 0.231 | 0.133 | 0.356 | 0.144 | 0.211 |

*Source:* Authors' calculations from the Fragile Families and Child Wellbeing Survey.
*Note:* N = 8,362. T-stats in parentheses. NCF = noncustodial fathers. Reference group is custodial fathers.
*$p < .1$; **$p < .05$; ***$p < .01$

# REFERENCES

Augustine, Dallas. 2019. "Working Around the Law: Navigating Legal Barriers to Good Work During Reentry." *Law & Social Inquiry* 44(3): 726–51.

Beckett, Katherine, and Naomi Murakawa. 2012. "Mapping the Shadow Carceral State: Toward an Institutionally Capacious Approach to Punishment." *Theoretical Criminology* 16(2): 221–44.

Bernhardt, Annette, Heather Boushey, Laura Dresser, and Chris Tilly. 2008. Introduction to *The Gloves-Off Economy: Workplace Standards at the Bottom of America's Labor Market*, edited by Annette Bernhardt, Heather Boushey, Laura Dresser, and Chris Tilly. Ithaca, NY: Cornell University Press.

Brambor, Thomas, William Roberts Clark, and Matt Golder. 2006. "Understanding Interaction Models: Improving Empirical Analyses." *Political Analysis* 14(1): 63–82.

Brito, Tonya. 2012. "Fathers Behind Bars: Rethinking Child Support Policy Toward Low-Income Fathers and Their Families." *Journal of Gender, Race & Justice* 15(3): 617–73.

Bumiller, Kristin. 2015. "Bad Jobs and Good Workers: The Hiring of Ex-Prisoners in a Segmented Economy." *Theoretical Criminology* 19(3): 336–54.

Cadigan, Michele, and Gabriela Kirk. 2020. "On Thin Ice: Bureaucratic Processes of Monetary Sanctions and Job Insecurity." *RSF: The Russell Sage Foundation Journal of the Social Sciences* 6(1): 113–31. DOI: 10.7758/RSF.2020.6.1.05.

Cammett, Ann. 2011. "Deadbeats, Deadbrokes, and Prisoners." *Georgetown Journal on Poverty Law & Policy* 18(2): 127–68.

Cancian, Maria, Robert H. Haveman, Daniel R. Meyer, and Barbara Wolfe. 2002. "Before and After TANF: The Economic Well-Being of Women Leaving Welfare." *Social Service Review* 76(4): 603–41.

Cancian, Maria, Carolyn J. Heinrich, and Yiyoon Chung. 2013. "Discouraging Disadvantaged Fathers' Employment: An Unintended Consequence of Policies Designed to Support Families." *Journal of Policy Analysis and Management* 32(4): 758–84.

Chung, Yiyoon. 2011. "Child Support as Labor Regulation." *Journal of Sociology & Social Welfare* 38(3): 73–99.

Colgan, Beth A. 2018. "The Excessive Fines Clause: Challenging the Modern Debtors' Prison." *UCLA Law Review* 65(2): 2–77.

Cook, Steven, and Jennifer L. Noyes. 2011. "The Use of Civil Contempt and Criminal Nonsupport as Child Support Enforcement Tools: A Report on Local Perspectives and the Availability of Data." Madison: University of Wisconsin–Madison Institute for Research on Poverty.

Cozzolino, Elizabeth. 2018. "Public Assistance, Relationship Context, and Jail for Child Support Debt." *Socius* 4(1): 1–25.

Doherty, Fiona. 2015. "Obey All Laws and Be Good: Probation and the Meaning of Recidivism." *Georgetown Law Journal* 104(2): 291–354.

Dwyer Emory, Allison, Lenna Nepomnyaschy, Maureen R. Waller, Daniel P. Miller, and Alexandra Haralampoudis. 2020. "Providing After Prison: Nonresident Fathers' Formal and Informal Contributions to Children." *RSF: The Russell Sage Foundation Journal of the Social Sciences* 6(1): 84–112. DOI: 10.7758/RSF.2020.6.1.04.

Eagly, Ingrid V. 2010. "Prosecuting Immigration." *Northwestern University Law Review* 104(4): 1281–359.

Family Division. 2017. "Family Division Bench Warrant Amnesty Program." Press release (August). Pittsburgh: Fifth Judicial District of Pennsylvania, County of Allegheny.

Geller, Amanda, Kate Jaeger, and Garrett T. Pace. 2016. "Surveys, Records, and the Study of Incarceration in Families." *Annals of the American Academy of Political and Social Science* 665(1): 22–43.

———. 2018. "Using the Fragile Families and Child Wellbeing Study (FFCWS) in Life Course Health Development Research." In *Handbook of Life Course Health Development*, edited by Neal Halfon, Christopher B. Forrest, Richard M. Lerner, and Elaine M. Faustman. Cham, CH: Springer International Publishing.

Gurusami, Susila. 2017. "Working for Redemption: Formerly Incarcerated Black Women and Punishment in the Labor Market." *Gender & Society* 31(4): 433–56.

Gustafson, Kaaryn. 2009. "The Criminalization of Poverty." *Journal of Criminal Law and Criminology* 99(3): 643–716.

Hampson, Christopher D. 2016. "The New American Debtors' Prisons." *American Journal of Criminal Law* 44(1): 1–48.

Handler, Joel F., and Yeheskel Hasenfeld. 1991. *The Moral Construction of Poverty: Welfare Reform in America*. Newbury Park, Calif.: Sage Publications.

Haney, Lynne. 2018. "Incarcerated Fatherhood: The Entanglements of Child Support Debt and Mass Imprisonment." *American Journal of Sociology* 124(1): 1–48.

Harris, Alexes. 2016. *A Pound of Flesh: Monetary Sanctions as Punishment for the Poor*. New York: Russell Sage Foundation.

Holzer, Harry J., Paul Offner, and Elaine Sorensen. 2005. "Declining Employment Among Young Black Less-Educated Men: The Role of Incarceration and Child Support." *Journal of Policy Analysis and Management* 24(2): 329–50.

Holzer, Harry J., Steven Raphael, and Michael A. Stoll. 2004. "Will Employers Hire Ex-Offenders? Employer Preferences, Background Checks and Their Determinants." In *Imprisoning America: The Social Effects of Mass Incarceration*, edited by Mary Pattillo, David Weiman, and Bruce Western. New York: Russell Sage Foundation.

Kalleberg, Arne L. 2011. *Good Jobs, Bad Jobs: The Rise of Polarized and Precarious Employment Systems in the United States, 1970s–2000s*. New York: Russell Sage Foundation.

Mead, Lawrence M. 2007. "Toward a Mandatory Work Policy for Men." *The Future of Children* 17(2): 43–72.

Miller, Daniel P., and Ronald B. Mincy. 2012. "Falling Further Behind? Child Support Arrears and Fathers' Labor Force Participation." *Social Service Review* 86(4): 604–35.

Nepomnyaschy, Lenna, and Irwin Garfinkel. 2010. "Child Support Enforcement and Fathers' Contributions to Their Nonmarital Children." *Social Service Review* 84(3): 341–80.

Office of Child Support Enforcement. 2014. "Flexibility, Efficiency, and Modernization in Child Support Enforcement Programs." *Federal Register* 79(221): 68548–87. Accessed October 14, 2019. https://www.govinfo.gov/content/pkg/FR-2014-11-17/pdf/2014-26822.pdf.

Pager, Devah. 2008. *Marked: Race, Crime, and Finding Work in an Era of Mass Incarceration*. Chicago: University of Chicago Press.

Patterson, Elizabeth G. 2008. "Civil Contempt and the Indigent Child Support Obligor: The Silent Return of Debtor's Prison." *Cornell Journal of Law & Public Policy* 18(1): 95–141.

Pettit, Becky, and Christopher Lyons. 2007. "Status and the Stigma of Incarceration: The Labor Market Effects of Incarceration by Race, Class, and Criminal Involvement." In *Barriers to Reentry?: The Labor Market for Released Prisoners in Post-Industrial America*, edited by Shawn D. Bushway, David F. Weiman, and Michael A. Stoll. New York: Russell Sage Foundation.

Phelps, Michelle S. 2016. "Mass Probation: Toward a More Robust Theory of State Variation in Punishment." *Punishment & Society* 19(1): 53–73.

Pirog, Maureen A., and Kathleen M. Ziol-Guest. 2006. "Child Support Enforcement: Programs and Policies, Impacts and Questions." *Journal of Policy Analysis and Management* 25(4): 943–90.

*Pittsburgh Post-Gazette*. 1999. "Crackdown Nets Support." April 19, 1999, C-2.

Pope, James Gray. 2010. "Contract, Race, and Freedom of Labor in the Constitutional Law of 'Involuntary Servitude.'" *Yale Law Journal* 119: 1474–567.

Rich, Lauren M., Irwin Garfinkel, and Qin Gao. 2007. "Child Support Enforcement Policy and Unmarried Fathers' Employment in the Underground and Regular Economies." *Journal of Policy Analysis and Management* 26(4): 791–810.

Robles, Frances, and Shaila Dewan. 2015. "Skip Child Support. Go to Jail. Lose Job. Repeat." *New York Times*, April 20, 2015.

Roebuck, Karen. 2007. "Deadbeat Allegheny County Parents Offered Amnesty." *Pittsburgh Tribune Review*, October 26.

Rusche, Georg, and Otto Kirchheimer. 1939. *Punishment and Social Structure*. New Brunswick, N.J.: Transaction Publishers.

Sabol, William. 2007. "Local Labor Market Conditions and Post-Prison Employment Experiences of Offenders Released from Ohio State Prisons." In *Barriers to Reentry?: The Labor Market for Released Prisoners in Post-Industrial America*, edited by Shawn D. Bushway, David F. Weiman, and Michael A. Stoll. New York: Russell Sage Foundation.

Schroeder, Daniel, and Nicholas Doughty. 2009. "Texas Non-Custodial Parent Choices: Program Impact Analysis." Austin, Tex.: Lyndon B. Johnson School of Public Affairs.

Seim, Josh, and David J. Harding. 2020. "Parolefare: Post-prison Supervision and Low-Wage Work." *RSF: The Russell Sage Foundation Journal of the Social Sciences* 6(1): 173–95. DOI: 10.7758/RSF.2020.6.1.08.

Simon, Jonathan. 1993. *Poor Discipline: Parole and*

the *Social Control of the Underclass, 1890–1990.* Chicago: University of Chicago Press.

Smith, Kristina E. 2002. "The Complicated Game of Child Support in Illinois: Does Anyone Really Win?" *Public Interest Law Reporter* 7(2): 1–7.

Solomon-Fears, Carmen. 2007. "Child Support Enforcement Program Incentive Payments: Background and Policy Issues." *CRS* report no. RL34203. Washington, D.C.: Congressional Research Service.

Sorensen, Elaine. 2010. "Rethinking Public Policy Toward Low-Income Fathers in the Child Support Program." *Journal of Policy Analysis and Management* 29(3): 604–10.

Sorensen, Elaine, Liliana Sousa, and Simon Schaner. 2007. "Assessing Child Support Arrears in Nine Large States and the Nation." Washington, D.C.: Urban Institute.

Soss, Joe, Richard C. Fording, and Sanford Schram. 2011. *Disciplining the Poor: Neoliberal Paternalism and the Persistent Power of Race.* Chicago: University of Chicago Press.

Stafford, Mark C., and Mark Warr. 1993. "A Reconceptualization of General and Specific Deterrence." *Journal of Research in Crime and Delinquency* 30(2): 123–35.

Stoll, Michael A., and Shawn Bushway. 2008. "The Effect of Criminal Background Checks on Hiring Ex-Offenders." *Criminology and Public Policy* 7(3): 371–404.

Stuart, Forrest. 2011. "Race, Space, and the Regulation of Surplus Labor. Policing African Americans in Los Angeles's Skid Row." *Souls: A Critical Journal of Black Politics, Culture, and Society* 13(2): 197–212.

Sugie, Naomi F. 2018. "Work as Foraging: A Smartphone Study of Job Search and Employment After Prison." *American Journal of Sociology* 123(5): 1453–91.

Travis, Jeremy, Bruce Western, and Steven Redburn, eds. 2014. *The Growth of Incarceration in the United States: Exploring Causes and Consequences.* Washington, D.C.: The National Academies Press, National Research Council.

Travis, Lawrence F., and James Stacey. 2010. "A Half Century of Parole Rules: Conditions of Parole in the United States, 2008." *Journal of Criminal Justice* 38(4): 604–08.

Turetsky, Vicki. 2012. "Alternatives to Incarceration." Information Memorandum IM-12-01. Washington: U.S. Department of Health and Human Services, Office of Child Support Enforcement.

Wacquant, Loïc. 2009. *Punishing the Poor: The Neoliberal Government of Social Insecurity.* Durham, N.C.: Duke University Press.

Western, Bruce, and Katherine Beckett. 1999. "How Unregulated Is the U.S. Labor Market? The Penal System as a Labor Market Institution." *American Journal of Sociology* 104(4): 1030–60.

Williams, Lucy A. 1999. "Unemployment Insurance and Low Wage Work." In *Hard Labor: Women and Work in the Post-Welfare Era*, edited by Joel F. Handler and Lucie White. Armonk, N.Y.: M. E. Sharpe.

Zatz, Noah D. 2019. "Get to Work or Go to Jail: State Violence and the Racialized Production of Precarious Work." *Law & Social Inquiry.* Published online December 12. DOI: 10.1017/lsi.2019.56.

Zatz, Noah D., Tia Koonse, Theresa Zhen, Lucero Herrera, Han Lu, Steven Shafer, and Blake Valenta. 2016. "Get to Work or Go to Jail: Workplace Rights Under Threat." Los Angeles: UCLA Labor Center.

# PART II

# Criminal Justice Policies as Structural Barriers to Employment

# Providing After Prison: Nonresident Fathers' Formal and Informal Contributions to Children

ALLISON DWYER EMORY, LENNA NEPOMNYASCHY, MAUREEN R. WALLER, DANIEL P. MILLER, AND ALEXANDRA HARALAMPOUDIS

*Incarceration among young, minority, economically disadvantaged men is pervasive in the United States and can impair their employment prospects. Because many of these men are fathers, incarceration also has serious implications for their ability to support their children. This article investigates the associations between incarceration and nonresident fathers' cash and in-kind contributions to their children's household economy. It then examines whether policies intended to protect employment opportunities mitigate the potential costs of incarceration for nonresident fathers' economic support of their children. Using longitudinal data from the Fragile Families and Child Wellbeing Study and new state policy data, we find that paternal incarceration reduces formal and informal support and that some policies offset the incarceration penalty, but clear differences by fathers' race emerge.*

**Keywords:** nonresident fathers, public policy, child support, informal support, incarceration

---

**Allison Dwyer Emory** is assistant professor in the Department of Sociology at the University at Buffalo. **Lenna Nepomnyaschy** is associate professor at the Rutgers School of Social Work. **Maureen R. Waller** is associate professor in the Department of Policy Analysis and Management at Cornell University. **Daniel P. Miller** is associate professor at the Boston University School of Social Work. **Alexandra Haralampoudis** is a PhD candidate at the Rutgers School of Social Work.

© 2020 Russell Sage Foundation. Dwyer Emory, Allison, Lenna Nepomnyaschy, Maureen R. Waller, Daniel P. Miller, and Alexandra Haralampoudis. 2020. "Providing After Prison: Nonresident Fathers' Formal and Informal Contributions to Children." *RSF: The Russell Sage Foundation Journal of the Social Sciences* 6(1): 84–112. DOI: 10.7758/RSF.2020.6.1.04. This research was supported by generous funding from the William T. Grant Foundation, the Fatherhood Research and Practice Network, and the Cornell Institute for the Social Sciences. We are also grateful for the Fragile Families and Child Wellbeing Study Data Workshop, which is supported by the Eunice Kennedy Shriver National Institute of Child Health & Human Development (R25HD074544 and R01HD036916). We appreciate the data collection efforts of Loren Greene, Shreya Reddy, and Margaret Thomas. The content is solely the responsibility of the authors and does not necessarily represent the official views of our funders. Direct correspondence to: Allison Dwyer Emory at ademory@buffalo.edu, Department of Sociology, University at Buffalo, 430 Park Hall, Buffalo, New York 14260; Lenna Nepomnyaschy at lennan@ssw.rutgers.edu; Maureen R. Waller at waller@cornell.edu; Daniel P. Miller at dpmiller@bu.edu; and Alexandra Haralampoudis at alexandra.haralampoudis@rutgers.edu.

Open Access Policy: *RSF: The Russell Sage Foundation Journal of the Social Sciences* is an open access journal. This article is published under a Creative Commons Attribution-NonCommercial-NoDerivs 3.0 Unported License.

Criminal justice contact among young, minority, economically disadvantaged men is pervasive in the United States and has enduring collateral consequences. A criminal record, even for low-level offenses, has lasting repercussions for the economic opportunities available to these men (Pager 2003; Uggen et al. 2014; Western 2001). Because many men who have been incarcerated are fathers (Glaze and Maruschak 2010), criminal justice contact also has serious consequences for their ability to contribute to their children's household economy by hindering accumulation of economic, human, and social capital. Policies that make it more difficult for employers to screen out individuals with criminal records may mitigate these problems and make it easier for former offenders to access stable employment which, in turn, is associated with greater financial support of children and desistance from crime (Apel and Horney 2017; Denver, Siwach, and Buschway 2017). It is less clear, however, whether these policies operate as expected for fathers with histories of incarceration.

Building on a growing body of work that investigates how criminal justice contact influences father involvement (Turney and Wildeman 2013; Waller and Swisher 2006; Geller, Garfinkel, and Western 2011), this study begins by examining the association between having an incarceration history and fathers' cash and in-kind contributions to their children's household economy. We focus specifically on contributions from fathers who live apart from their biological children because nonresidence is the most prevalent living arrangement among fathers who have had contact with the criminal justice system (Glaze and Maruschak 2010). We extend previous research by examining a wider array of economic contributions that nonresident fathers may provide in addition to formal child support, such as informal cash and in-kind support. We also extend research that has focused on economic support provided in early childhood by using longitudinal data to observe the contributions of nonresident fathers from the time of the child's birth through age fifteen. By linking longitudinal survey data from the Fragile Families and Child Wellbeing Study to a new database of state policies, this study is also uniquely able to examine whether policies intended to protect employment opportunities for individuals with criminal records can mitigate the potential harmful consequences of incarceration for nonresident fathers' provision of economic resources to their children.

## INCARCERATION AND FATHERS' CONTRIBUTIONS TO CHILDREN

In 2007, more than 2.7 million children in the United States had a parent in jail or prison (Pew Charitable Trusts 2010), an experience that has lasting implications for the resources available to these children and their households. Children of incarcerated fathers are more likely to face economic hardship and require help from government assistance programs (DeFina and Hannon 2010; Sugie 2012; Sykes and Pettit 2015; Schwartz-Soicher, Geller, and Garfinkel 2011). These disadvantages may reflect fathers' diminished ability to contribute to their children's households. The collateral consequences of incarceration fall most heavily on black families, given that black men are eight times more likely to be incarcerated than white men, and black children are at least four times more likely to experience a father's incarceration than white children (Pew Charitable Trusts 2010; Wildeman 2009; Western and Wildeman 2009).

Qualitative research suggests that economically disadvantaged fathers often prioritize their emotional relationships and time with children over their performance as breadwinners (Edin and Nelson 2013; Hamer 2001; Roy 2004; Waller 2002, 2009). Ethnographic studies of low-income African American families have described the importance of kin-based networks in which family members exchange goods and services to meet immediate family needs. Nonresident fathers and their relatives can play key roles by contributing resources like childcare (Edin and Lein 1997; Roy and Burton 2007; Stack 1975). Although many economically disadvantaged fathers, including those with histories of incarceration, are highly involved in their children's lives (Waller 2009), evidence suggests that paternal incarceration diminishes involvement and contact with children even after release (Geller 2013; Swisher and Waller 2008; Turney and Wildeman 2013). Some studies find much of this reduction in contact is driven by decreases in the probability that fathers reside with their children (Geller 2013; Turney and Wildeman 2013), though incarceration also reduces father-child contact among nonresident fathers both during and after incarceration (Geller 2013; Swisher and Waller 2008; Western and Smith 2018).

It is less clear, however, whether there are similar reductions in fathers' financial contributions to children post-incarceration. Fathers' provision of formal child support (as mandated by legal child support orders) is the most commonly measured type of financial contribution to their child's household in large-scale surveys and is typically the focus of policies designed to increase nonresident fathers' economic support of their children. However, nonresident fathers may also provide monetary support informally to their children, either instead of or in concert with formal child support payments. Fathers may also provide in-kind (noncash) contributions for their children, such as clothes, diapers, entertainment items, food, medicine, or school supplies. Previous research indicates that in-kind and informal support is viewed differently than formal child support in economically disadvantaged families because of its greater symbolic and emotional significance (Hamer 2001; Kane, Nelson, and Edin 2015; Pate 2002; Roy and Dyson 2010; Waller 2002; Waller and Plotnick 2001). It also contributes more to fathers' and children's feelings of closeness in their relationship than formal child support does (Waller, Dwyer Emory, and Paul 2018). Recent studies also point to the benefits of in-kind support to children over and above formal child support (Nepomnyaschy et al. 2014).

Economic theory suggests that fathers' time and money may be complementary or reciprocal: when fathers contribute, they may also visit in order to monitor that their contributions are being appropriately spent (Weiss and Willis 1985). Fathers may also contribute more support because they are more aware of children's needs and have more opportunities to contribute when they visit (Nepomnyaschy 2007). On the other hand, fathers' time with children may substitute for financial contributions to children, consistent with ideas about family adaptation and familism documented in some ethnographic studies of African American and Latino communities (Coltrane, Parke, and Adams 2004; Jarrett and Burton 1999).

Empirical studies find that fathers with a history of incarceration are less likely to provide any economic support to young children (Washington, Juan, and Haskins 2018; Geller, Garfinkel, and Western 2011), and those who do contribute provide a lesser amount (Geller, Garfinkel, and Western 2011). Similarly, fathers with a history of incarceration are more likely to have accrued child support arrears—debt associated with nonpayment or underpayment of formal child support (Turner and Waller 2017; McLeod and Gottlieb 2018; Katzenstein and Waller 2015). A portion of this debt may be owed to the state to reimburse welfare costs, and may include Medicaid birthing costs, interest, and other fines and fees. Fathers' accumulation of arrears leads to less engagement in the formal labor force (Miller and Mincy 2012; Cancian, Heinrich, and Chung 2013), further reducing their formal child support contributions (Cancian, Heinrich, and Chung 2013). Fathers who accumulate arrears can be incarcerated for child support noncompliance and continue to accrue arrears during incarceration (Cozzolino 2018; Zatz and Stoll 2020), suggesting the potential for long-term and compounding negative impacts of incarceration for formal child support and arrears.

Among previously incarcerated fathers, informal cash and in-kind contributions are also apt to be lower because fathers maintain fewer informal support arrangements post-incarceration (Swisher and Waller 2008), and informal support is closely linked to the time they spend with their children (Nepomnyaschy 2007; Turner and Waller 2017; Waller, Dwyer Emory, and Paul 2018). Indeed, one study finds that formerly incarcerated fathers provided goods such as clothes, school supplies, and other material items for their children less frequently than their never-incarcerated counterparts (Washington, Juan, and Haskins 2018). Further, research suggests that formal and informal cash child support are substitutes in that fathers' informal contributions can stop if and when mothers obtain a child support order and formal support begins to be withheld from their wages (Nepomnyaschy and Garfinkel 2010; Sariscsany, Garfinkel, and Nepomnyaschy 2019).

Two mechanisms have been identified that may link fathers' history of incarceration with lower economic contributions to their children's households. First, as described earlier, previously incarcerated fathers are more likely to live apart from their children (Geller, Garfinkel, and Western 2011; Geller 2013). A large body of work documents lower household resources among children living apart from their fathers (McLanahan, Tach, and Schneider 2013; McLanahan 2004; Carlson and Berger 2013). A much higher prevalence of nonresidence among fathers with incarceration histories may therefore explain lower average financial contributions for this group (Geller, Garfinkel, and Western 2011). Consistent with these findings, the negative association between incarceration and fathers' provision of economic support is strongest for fathers who were previously resident with their children, though it is also observed for children with never-resident fathers (Washington, Juan, and Haskins 2018).

A second mechanism points to the lower earnings of fathers with a history of incarceration to explain their smaller financial contributions (Geller, Garfinkel, and Western 2011). This association reflects the economic vulnerability of these fathers and their precarious place in the formal economy, as demonstrated by many of the articles in this issue. Incarcerated fathers lose wages and employment opportunities and often accrue arrears during their incarceration (Western and Pettit 2005; McLeod and Gottlieb 2018). This economic impairment continues well after release. Formerly incarcerated men face wage penalties lasting up to seven years after release and are less able to find secure employment (Pettit and Lyons 2009; Western 2001). Men with criminal records face pervasive employment discrimination, which is particularly stark for black applicants, for whom race and a criminal record are compounding disadvantages (Pager 2007, 2003; Pager, Western, and Sugie 2009; Pettit and Lyons 2007). Regardless of race, men with criminal records receive callbacks for job interviews half as often as those without records, but because all black men are called back at a lower rate, this disadvantage is compounded for black men with records (Pager 2003).

It is also possible that men with records may choose not to apply to better jobs because they anticipate discrimination. This process, referred to as identity threat or rejection sensitivity (Naft and Downey 2019), could also lead to worse employment outcomes and fewer resources for the children of men with criminal records. Such fathers may also have less access to, or even withdraw from, social networks that can provide instrumental assistance during the job search process (Lageson 2016b; Smith 2005). Because black men are more likely to experience incarceration than their white counterparts (Pew Charitable Trusts 2010; Western and Wildeman 2009), the economic impairment of a criminal record is particularly relevant to their ability to contribute to their children's households.

## POLICY PROTECTIONS FOR FORMERLY INCARCERATED FATHERS

States have adopted multiple strategies to address the disadvantages of formerly incarcerated individuals in the labor market. The most direct approach has been to regulate employer behavior during the hiring process, which can take two forms: regulating the use of records as a basis for hiring decisions or explicitly banning questions about criminal records on applications as in the more recent ban-the-box policies. These regulations, which govern the legal use of records by public and public contract employers, private employers, or licensing agencies (Doleac and Hasen 2016; Legal Action Center 2004), encourage employers to consider individuals with records on a case-by-case basis. Qualitative studies of hiring managers suggest that such personal consideration may increase the likelihood of their employment (Lageson, Vuolo, and Uggen 2015; Pager, Western, and Sugie 2009).

Policies that rely on employers to follow laws regulating the use of records during hiring have a longer history and are more widespread than the more recent ban-the-box policies that explicitly prohibit employers from asking about records (Legal Action Center 2004, 2009; D'Alessio, Stolzenberg, and Flexon 2015). Regulations that rely on employer compliance, however, may be vulnerable to limited enforcement and familiarity among employers and applicants alike. For example, Wisconsin has some of the oldest and most comprehensive state policies incorporating criminal records into employment discrimination laws.[1] Nevertheless, studies conducted within the state have documented record-based hiring discrimination well after the passage of these laws (Pager 2003; Hlavka, Wheelock, and Cossyleon 2015), suggesting that laws may be unknown or disregarded. This is not entirely unexpected, given that enforcing employment discrimination laws may require expensive legal action (Jacobs 2015).

More recent ban-the box-policies have received a great deal of attention from policy advocates and the popular press (Avery 2019; Rodriquez 2017). A few studies examine the consequences of these policies, providing insight into the mechanisms that may be operating in our analysis. In particular, some research suggests such policies may reduce stereotype avoidance by encouraging job seekers to apply for better-paid and more stable jobs. Indeed, evaluations of local ban-the-box policies in Washington, D.C., and Durham, North Carolina, attribute greater rates of hiring to increases in applications from individuals with records (Atkinson and Lockwood 2014; Berracasa et al. 2016). Despite widespread support for these policies, evidence for their efficacy in improving economic opportunity is mixed. In fact, recent evaluations of ban-the-box policies using more rigorous study designs indicate these policies may fail to improve the employment prospects of black men due to increased racial discrimination (Doleac and Hasen 2016; Vuolo, Lageson, and Uggen 2017; Agan and Starr 2018). One theory advanced to explain this phenomenon is statistical discrimination, the idea that employers may be using race as a stand-in for criminal records to avoid hiring men they believe are more likely to have a record (Doleac and Hasen 2016; Vuolo, Lageson, and Uggen 2017). Although some employers may do so consciously, others may default to implicit stereotypes of black men's criminality, perceiving these applicants less favorably when evaluating their suitability as employees (Agan and Starr 2018). Consistent with these studies, recent work also links policies regulating the legal use of records to lower employment among black fathers (Dwyer Emory 2019).

A second set of policies limits the degree to which information on criminal records is available to employers rather than regulating the ability to use that information. If criminal records are easily available to employers, state laws prohibiting employers from using them may not be enough to protect applicants from discrimination or encourage applicants with records to apply (Hlavka, Wheelock, and Cossyleon 2015; Spaulding et al. 2015; Jacobs 2015). Policies targeting the accessibility of criminal records are thus also potentially important tools for protecting the employment opportunities of individuals with histories of incarceration. State-level variation is substantial in the degree to which official criminal records are readily accessible (Legal Action Center 2004). In states that do not make records easily available, individuals with criminal records may also be less hesitant about applying for positions (Naft and Downey 2019), more engaged with informal networks critical to job-finding (Smith 2005; Lageson 2016b), or given crucial individualized employer assessments (Lageson, Vuolo, and Uggen 2015). Indeed, one study links restricted access to criminal records to greater probability of hiring formerly incarcerated individuals, though potentially to the detriment of individuals without records (Finlay 2008). These policies may also be susceptible to the same racial discrimination seen in studies of ban-the-box and employment policies, given that they also limit employer access to information about records (Doleac and Hasen 2016; Vuolo, Lageson, and Uggen 2017; Agan and Starr 2018).

---

1. Wisconsin prohibits blanket bans against hiring individuals with criminal records and considering arrests that never led to conviction, and the law clearly defines such uses of records as a violation of state employment discrimination laws outside a small list of excepted professions (Legal Action Center 2004). These policies have been in place since at least 1990.

## POLICY PROTECTIONS AND FATHERS' ECONOMIC CONTRIBUTIONS

Considering their implications for fathers' economic opportunities, policies that attempt to mitigate the negative impacts of a criminal justice record on labor market experiences are also likely to have implications for nonresident fathers' contributions to children. The direction of these associations may differ by the type of contribution, however. Fathers involved in the criminal justice system may be incentivized to find formal employment in response to pressure from child support enforcement (Zatz and Stoll 2020) and probation requirements (Seim and Harding 2020). Unlike voluntary forms of support, formal child support is collected primarily through automatic withholding of wages earned in formal employment and thus mechanically related to fathers' employment and earnings (ACF 2016). Thus policies that improve access to stable employment in the formal sector should unambiguously increase fathers' formal child support payments and slow the accrual of arrears, though perhaps not entirely mitigate the cost of a criminal record, given the other structural barriers fathers face to finding high-quality employment (Warner, Kaiser, and Houle 2020).

The implications of these policies are more ambiguous for fathers' provision of informal and in-kind support because these types of support are less directly related to their employment opportunities. Research generally confirms that formal child support and informal cash support are substitutes, and that in-kind support is often provided alongside formal support (Sariscsany, Garfinkel, and Nepomnyaschy 2019; Nepomnyaschy and Garfinkel 2010). Therefore, if policies improve fathers' ability to pay formal support, they may have an inverse association with provision of informal or voluntary cash support and a complementary association with in-kind support. Formerly incarcerated men whose access to the formal labor market is restricted may still be able to work informally, in either off-the-books or underground employment (Sykes and Geller 2017). To the extent that policies restrict formal economic opportunities, fathers may either pay little support of any kind or substitute informal and in-kind contributions to their children's household if unable to meet formal support obligations paid through withholdings. These alternative employment strategies, however, may increase illegal activity and the risk for reincarceration (Apel and Horney 2017; Denver, Siwach, and Buschway 2017; Uggen 2000), which would reduce fathers' ability to make either formal or informal contributions in the long term. As is true of formal support, however, these relationships with incarceration have largely not been the focus of research.

## PRESENT STUDY

This study is the first to consider both the extent of the incarceration penalty for nonresident fathers' provision of multiple types of support and the degree to which protective policies moderate the association between fathers' incarceration histories and their contributions to children. Taking advantage of rich longitudinal survey data from the Fragile Families and Child Wellbeing Study, we examine associations between incarceration and nonresident fathers' contributions to their children's household economy from early childhood (age one) until adolescence (age fifteen). We examine multiple forms of economic support, including nonresident fathers' provision of formal child support, accrual of arrears, informal cash support, and in-kind (noncash) contributions. Although arrears are not direct measures of fathers' contributions, they are of great concern to policymakers because they are disproportionately owed by low-income fathers and are negatively associated with employment, child support payments, and relationships with coparents and children (Cancian, Heinrich, and Chung 2013; Sorensen, Sousa, and Schaner 2007; Miller and Mincy 2012; Turner and Waller 2017).

In addition, using a new dataset of state-by-year policies relating to fathers' reentry into the labor force following criminal justice involvement, we explore whether state policies designed to protect the employment opportunities of individuals with histories of incarceration moderate the association between paternal incarceration and economically disadvantaged men's contributions to their children's household economy. On the basis of research showing potentially harmful effects of such policies for black men's employment, we also expect that black fathers may benefit less from these policies and may even face additional racial discrimination in states with ostensibly protective policy landscapes.

## METHODS

The data for this study come from the Fragile Families and Child Wellbeing Study (FF). The FF interviewed mothers and fathers of approximately five thousand children born in twenty large cities in fifteen states between 1998 and 2000 (baseline) and conducted follow-up interviews when children were one, three, five, nine, and fifteen years old.[2] Because parents with nonmarital births were oversampled (a 3:1 ratio), these data are ideal for the study of economically disadvantaged nonresident fathers (Reichman et al. 2001). The FF provides extensive longitudinal data on nonresident fathers' contributions of material goods to their children, parent and child characteristics, and family processes that allow us to estimate the association between incarceration and fathers' contributions over and above other predictors of father involvement. Crucially, both father residence and history of incarceration are measured at each follow-up wave, allowing us to identify the population of interest for the present study.

We merge the longitudinal FF survey data (covering the years from 1998 through 2015) with a state-level policy database we collected for this study through an extensive review of state laws and amendment history. These data document employment protection policies for those with histories of criminal justice involvement across these years. Despite the many other areas in which policies could support or impede formerly incarcerated fathers' access to the formal economy, we focus on those relevant for employment, given its salience for fathers' provision of support (Geller, Garfinkel, and Western 2011). Building on the work of the Legal Action Center's Barriers to Reentry Project (2004, 2009), we collected data on eight state policies related to the employment of individuals with criminal records (all U.S. states) and ease of access to those records (fifteen states in the FF data) for the years from 1998 through 2014. We describe these policies in detail in the following section. Merging these sources of data enables us to identify the legal employment protections fathers may have received given their state of residence and incarceration history at the time of each follow-up interview. Data are merged using the state in which the father resides because the policies and employment context of these states are most relevant for fathers' ability to provide support for children. Fathers' state is the same as that in which the mother and child reside for the vast majority of families where both parents' states are available, and results are thus nearly identical when data are merged on mothers' state of residence.

### Sample

We pool data from five follow-up waves of the FF study based on mother and father core surveys (years one, three, five, and nine) and the primary caregiver survey (year fifteen). Our analytic sample is restricted to observations for which we have valid information on the key dependent (mother-reported formal support, informal support, in-kind support, or arrears) and key independent (combined mother-father reports of paternal incarceration) variables and policies of interest at a given wave (N = 7,888).[3] As our outcome of interest is nonresident fathers' economic contributions to the household, we exclude observations in which the mother did not live with the focal child at least half the time or reported that the focal child's biological father was no longer alive (N = 759). To ensure that fathers were capable of participation in the formal economy, we further exclude observations in which fathers are incarcerated at the time of the survey (N = 288). Finally, given the importance of correctly matching fathers to their state of residence, and thus the policy regime of that state in the year of the interview, observations are excluded in two instances. One is if the father's state

---

2. At age fifteen, only the primary caregiver was interviewed. These respondents were overwhelmingly mothers.

3. Policy data were not available after 2014, so year fifteen interviews conducted in 2016 and 2017 were excluded.

could not be identified (N = 1,753).[4] Another is if he did not live in a U.S. state (N = 69) at the time of the mother's interview.[5]

The final analytic sample is an unbalanced panel of 4,890 observations, incorporating 2,254 unique families observed one (834), two (632), three (445), four (257), or five (86) times within the panel. The sample varies between models because observations were included in the panel if they were nonmissing for at least one dependent variable. Data on state policies dealing with criminal records were available only for fathers living in the original fifteen FF states (approximately 95 percent of all cases). Thus sample sizes are slightly smaller for models using this policy variable. With this sample, we used multiple imputation with chained equations to impute missing values for control variables. Most variables were not missing information, and typically fewer than 10 percent of observations were missing, father-reported variables such as impulsivity, nativity, poverty, and employment (approximately 15 to 30 percent missing) excepted. We create twenty imputed datasets, which we use for all analyses.

## Measures

Measures of father attributes and contributions are drawn from FF data, while policy data are constructed from our data collection based on variables identified by the Legal Action Center (2004).

### Nonresident Fathers' Economic Contributions

This study examines four measures that help us understand nonresident fathers' contributions to children's household economy as reported by mothers at each follow-up wave of the study: formal child support, informal cash support, in-kind support, and child support arrears. At each wave of the FF, mothers who report having a formal child support order are asked how much fathers are obligated to pay under these orders and how much of this amount they actually did pay in the past year. We calculate an annual amount of child support received based on these reports; all monetary values are adjusted for inflation to 2017 dollars. Formal support for mothers who do not have a child support order is coded 0.

Mothers are also asked at each wave about informal cash support that nonresident fathers provide either in addition to or instead of formal child support. We create a measure of informal cash provided in the previous year, given that this is the amount reported in the one-, nine-, and fifteen-year waves. At the three- and five-year waves, the amount is reported over the previous two years. We therefore divide the reported amount by two to create a comparable measure.

In-kind support is measured as the frequency with which the nonresident father buys items the child needs, as reported by the mother. When the child was one, three, five, and nine years old, mothers report how often the father provided age-appropriate items, such as toys, medicine, clothes, food, childcare items (such as diapers at age one), or camp-school tuition (at age nine). Mothers were asked about a list of five to nine items, varying by survey wave. After recoding, responses ranged from 0 (never) to 3 (often), and were averaged across the items to create an index at each survey wave (Cronbach's α = .91, .90, .90, and .94 respectively). At age fifteen, mothers are asked one question: "Fathers may provide all sorts of items that children need, such as food, clothes, school supplies, camp or school tuition, gifts or other personal items. How often does the father buy or pay for any of these items for the child?" We rescale the responses to be consis-

---

4. Father's state of residence was drawn from the father interview for 76 percent of the observations. For the remaining 24 percent, observations in which fathers were not interviewed, it was determined by mother reports of how far the father lived from the mother. Fathers who were reported to live fewer than thirty miles away were placed in the mothers' state of residence. Although the baseline FF data collection encompassed only fifteen states, over the five follow-up survey waves, fathers have moved and the geographic distribution includes forty-six states.

5. This restriction excludes fathers living in U.S. territories and Washington, D.C., because policy data and state-level control variables were not consistently available for jurisdictions.

tent with previous survey waves (0 = never, 2 = sometimes, and 3 = often). At some waves, this question is skipped if fathers had not seen the child in the past year; these fathers are coded as never providing in-kind support.

Finally, we consider the amount of child support arrears that fathers have accrued. Mothers with a child support order in place are asked at each wave whether the father has any arrears on that child support order owed to either her or the state and, if yes, the amount owed. We create a total amount of arrears at each survey wave, coding fathers as having no arrears if they have no debt or do not have a child support order. Because arrears may not be owed directly to the mother, mothers may be unaware of obligations to the state. Thus we consider the amounts recorded for this variable to be lower bounds of how much fathers actually owe.

*Fathers' Incarceration*
Fathers' incarceration history is the main predictor variable in these analyses. To address underreporting of incarceration, we follow previous studies using the FF in creating a combined dichotomous measure of fathers' incarceration history (see, for example, Geller et al. 2012; Wildeman, Turney, and Yi 2016). At each survey wave, fathers are considered to have a history of incarceration if either the mother or father report that the father ever spent time in jail or prison. This variable therefore measures whether the father has ever been incarcerated by the time of the survey, not necessarily new or recent incarceration experiences or other kinds of contact with the criminal justice system.

*State Policy Indices*
Drawing on the categorizations created by the Legal Action Center (2004) as well as on research on the barriers that formerly incarcerated men face on entering the formal economy, we create two policy indices: an employment policy index and a criminal records index. These capture the distinction between policies that regulate the use of records (employment policy index), and the ease with which employers can access that information regardless of legality (records policy index). This distinction is particularly important given the challenges associated with enforcing employment laws (Jacobs 2015) because the records policies measure availability of official information as implemented by the state rather than rely on assumptions of employer behavior. To ensure that the policy is relevant for the fathers' economic activity and provision of support, state policies are measured in the year prior to the interview year. The component policies for each index are summarized in table A1.

The employment policy index includes six policies regulating employers' use of criminal records during the hiring process. This six-item index captures whether state law prohibits private employers, public employers, or licensing agencies from having blanket restrictions against hiring individuals with records, and whether these same three entities are prohibited from considering arrests that did not lead to convictions.[6] The index is constructed as the proportion (0 = none to 1 = all) of these six employment protection policies enacted by a state in a given year. On this index, a score of 0 indicates that the father lives in a state with no restrictions on the legal use of criminal records during hiring (ostensibly least protective); a score of 1 indicates that all six protections are in place (most protective). On average, throughout the study period, states had implemented 30 percent (approximately two of six) of protective policies related to employment, and showed relatively little variation within states over time.

The records policy index captures whether the state maintains a searchable online database of all criminal records or only cases under current criminal justice supervision (probation, parole, corrections). A score of 0 (least protective) indicates that the state makes all criminal records available online, a score of 0.5 indicates that only those under current supervision can be identified, and a score of 1 (most protective) indicates these official records are

---

6. These policies do not include the more recent ban-the-box policies, which were primarily adopted at the state level in the late 2010s (Avery 2019) and are thus not measured in our policy data or relevant for most of the Fragile Families data time frame.

not easily accessible. On average, states had half of their protective policies related to criminal records access in place; seven states changed their policies over the study period (for state-level descriptive statistics, see table A2).

*Control Variables*

We include a rich set of controls, based on research on risks for both criminal justice involvement and participation in the formal economy (Sykes and Geller 2017; Washington, Juan, and Haskins 2018), that may confound the relationship between incarceration and fathers' contributions to their children's household. We are careful not to include variables that may be on the causal pathway between incarceration and economic support, such as fathers' work status or earnings, because we are interested in estimating the direct effect of this association. Results were robust, however, to including controls for other relevant but nonconfounding variables such as multipartner fertility and whether parents shared multiple biological children (findings available on request). We also include a number of geographic and state-level controls to account for factors that could confound associations between fathers' incarceration, state policies, and provision of support.

To measure fathers' criminogenic risk, we control for Year 1 measures of previous incarceration, substance use, and fathers' self-reported impulsivity. Fathers' impulsivity is a FF modification of Scott Dickman's (1990) dysfunctional impulsivity scale. Fathers report the extent to which they agree with six statements such as "I often don't think before I act" or "I often say/do things without considering consequences," creating a scale (Cronbach's α = .84) ranging from 0 (least impulsive) to 3 (most impulsive). To account for variation in criminogenic risk by age (Farrington 1986), we also control for father age as a time-varying measure. We also include baseline controls for father's education level (less than high school, high school or GED, some college or more), employment, poverty level (deep poverty, poverty, near poverty, and nonpoor), nativity, and race-ethnicity to capture factors that contribute to both criminal justice involvement risk and fathers' participation in the formal economy. Given the salience of racial perception by employers, we classify fathers as being black if they report being either non-Hispanic black or Hispanic black, excepting those who had ever taken the survey in Spanish, because these fathers may face an additional language barrier in the formal economy. Other race-ethnicity categories include non-Hispanic white, Hispanic of any other race, and another racial category. We also control for whether mothers report the same racial-ethnic background as fathers, parents' marital status at the time of the focal child's birth, and a time-varying measure of whether the father was ever coresident with his child. Finally, we control for an indicator of survey wave to adjust for wave-specific variation.

In each state-year, we include one-year lagged measures of the percentage of the state population in poverty (University of Kentucky Center for Poverty Research 2017), percent of the state population unemployed (BLS 2018), imprisonment rate per hundred thousand residents (Carson and Mulako-Wangota 2018), violent and property crime rates per hundred thousand residents (FBI 2018), state-level minimum wages (University of Kentucky Center for Poverty Research 2017), per capita child support expenditures (Mincy, Miller, and De la Cruz Toledo 2016), and census region. All dollar values are adjusted for inflation. To account for the possibility that fathers are responding to policy regimes or economic conditions by moving, we also include a control for whether fathers were living in a different state than the mother at the time of their child's birth. In supplemental analyses, however, we found no evidence that fathers with records move opportunistically to states with more favorable policies.

**Analytic Strategy**

Our analyses proceed in three stages using our unbalanced family-year panel. First, we estimate the relationship between incarceration and the four measures of fathers' economic contributions to their children's households using random-effects models. Next, we test whether state-level policies moderate the associations between incarceration and economic contributions. Based on the literature discussed earlier, we expect that the associations between incarceration and fathers' contributions and the degree to which policies moderate this association will differ by fathers' racial-ethnic background. Thus, as a final step, we also estimate models stratified by race, looking separately at fathers who are black (of any ethnicity) versus nonblack. All models are estimated with robust standard errors, which are equivalent to clustering on individuals in a panel model. Sensitivity tests are also conducted to test the robustness of our findings to alternative sample specifications. Findings (available on request) were robust to excluding fathers incarcerated for child support noncompliance and never-incarcerated fathers with histories of conviction or arrest. Because the 2008 recession occurs in the middle of our panel and may have hit the economically vulnerable particularly hard, we omit observations occurring after 2008 as a sensitivity check; results are consistent and thus not driven by the recession. Results are also consistent in multilevel models that nest data at the state level. Finally, to account for the possibility of underlying differences between states that are otherwise unobserved, we include state indicator variables to estimate associations only within states (see table A3). Results are mostly consistent in these state fixed-effects models.

## RESULTS

Table 1 presents descriptive statistics for the individual and family-level variables in our analyses for the full sample and by nonresident fathers' incarceration history; it also indicates significant differences between fathers with and without prior incarceration. On average, nonresident fathers contributed approximately $1,100 of formal and $930 of informal cash child support per year to their children's households across the panel. They provided low levels (1 = rarely) of in-kind (noncash) support over the period and accrued approximately $2,700 in arrears. Notably, more than half (55 percent) of the observations were contributed by fathers who had a history of incarceration. As expected, these fathers contributed far less formal and informal cash child support, contributed in-kind support less frequently, and had much higher arrears (nearly three times

higher) than fathers without incarceration histories.

The characteristics of fathers in this sample reflect both the FF oversample of children born to unmarried parents in large cities and the current study's focus on nonresident fathers. Thus fathers in the sample are overwhelmingly nonwhite and have both low levels of education and high baseline poverty levels. In the full sample, approximately 80 percent of fathers were working at the child's birth, 10 percent reported a drug or alcohol problem, and nearly 40 percent had been incarcerated before the focal child reached age one. In general, fathers with incarceration histories were more disadvantaged on all these indicators.

## Incarceration and Fathers' Economic Contributions

Table 2 presents results from random-effects regression models of the associations of fathers' incarceration history with their contributions to children's households. These models include all previously discussed individual and state-level controls, other than the employment and records policy index measures, which are included in models shown in tables 3 through 5. The tables report linear coefficients and the absolute value of robust standard errors. Fathers who have been incarcerated provide less formal ($427) and informal ($402) cash child support and less frequent (0.31, or one-third of a standard deviation) in-kind support relative to fathers who have not had such an experience. Additionally, fathers who have been incarcerated have on average just over $2,130 more child support debt (arrears) than those who have not. These associations are consistent with the descriptive results and remain robust to the inclusion of a rich set of individual- and state-level controls.

The associations between fathers' characteristics and their contributions differ across outcomes. Fathers who are older, white (relative to black), and those with some college or higher education (relative to no high school degree) provide more formal support. Fathers who were older ($p < .1$), ever resided with their children, were married at birth, and were nonpoor (relative to deep poverty) provided more informal support. Older fathers ($p < .1$) and those who

**Table 1.** Descriptive Statistics of Father Attributes

|  | Full Sample (N=4,890) Mean (SD) or % | Never Incarcerated (N=2,218) Mean (SD) or % | Ever Incarcerated (N=2,672) Mean (SD) or % | Sig Diff |
|---|---|---|---|---|
| **Father contributions (time varying)** | | | | |
| Formal child support ($) | 1,104.44 (2,439.97) | 1,405.47 (2,867.58) | 856.08 (1,986.67) | *** |
| Informal cash support ($) | 927.45 (2,415.81) | 1,306.91 (3,012.10) | 619.52 (1,732.21) | *** |
| In-kind support (0–3) | 1.07 (0.97) | 1.26 (0.98) | 0.91 (0.93) | *** |
| Arrears ($) | 2,696.51 (7,907.30) | 1,370.68 (5,269.30) | 3,818.85 (9,445.87) | *** |
| **Father attributes (time varying)** | | | | |
| Age | 32.86 (8.39) | 33.22 (9.27) | 32.56 (7.55) | ** |
| Ever coresident with child (%) | 58.26 | 58.61 | 57.97 | |
| Living in different state than baseline (%) | 5.36 | 5.00 | 5.65 | |
| **Father attributes (baseline)** | | | | |
| Race (%) | | | | |
| White, non-Hispanic | 12.33 | 13.39 | 11.45 | * |
| Black | 66.40 | 64.25 | 68.19 | ** |
| Hispanic | 18.04 | 19.16 | 17.10 | + |
| Other, non-Hispanic | 3.23 | 3.20 | 3.26 | |
| Race different from child's mother (%) | 16.03 | 15.42 | 16.54 | |
| Born in the United States (%) | 91.72 | 88.19 | 94.66 | *** |
| Married at birth (%) | 9.59 | 13.62 | 6.25 | *** |
| Education level at child's birth (%) | | | | |
| Less than high school | 31.62 | 24.84 | 37.25 | *** |
| High school or GED | 43.66 | 43.00 | 44.22 | |
| Some college or more | 24.72 | 32.16 | 18.54 | *** |
| Baseline poverty level (%) | | | | |
| Deep poverty (<.5x FPL) | 14.00 | 10.92 | 16.55 | *** |
| Poverty (<1x FPL) | 15.13 | 13.39 | 16.58 | * |
| Near poor (<2x FPL) | 24.63 | 22.65 | 26.27 | * |
| Nonpoor (>2x FPL) | 46.24 | 53.04 | 40.60 | *** |
| Employment at child's birth (%) | 79.3 | 87.3 | 72.6 | *** |
| Drug-alcohol use at child's birth (%) | 10.36 | 5.59 | 14.31 | *** |
| Incarcerated before year 1 (%) | 37.39 | 0.00 | 68.42 | *** |
| Impulsivity one-year (range 0–3) | 1.07 (1.11) | 0.98 (0.90) | 1.14 (1.11) | *** |

*Source:* Authors' calculations based on data from the Fragile Families and Child Wellbeing Study.
*Note:* Bivariate regressions used to test significance of difference between fathers with and without incarceration histories, significance level of this difference indicated in the final column. SD = standard deviation. FPL = federal poverty level.
$^+p < .1$; $^*p < .05$; $^{**}p < .01$; $^{***}p < .001$

**Table 2.** Random-Effects Models of Associations Between Incarceration and Fathers' Contributions to Children

|  | Formal Child Support | | Informal Cash Support | | In-Kind Support | | Arrears | |
| --- | --- | --- | --- | --- | --- | --- | --- | --- |
|  | B | (SE) | B | (SE) | B | (SE) | B | (SE) |
| Paternal incarceration | -426.95*** | (125.24) | -401.91*** | (115.07) | -0.31*** | (0.05) | 2,130.24*** | (493.91) |
| **Time-varying father attributes** | | | | | | | | |
| Age | 13.25* | (6.45) | 11.27 | (7.21) | 0.00+ | (0.00) | -29.14+ | (16.36) |
| Ever coresident with child | -146.81+ | (87.10) | 478.87*** | (85.60) | 0.35*** | (0.04) | -363.46 | (296.81) |
| Moved states since baseline | 161.88 | (210.72) | 57.78 | (179.61) | -0.25*** | (0.06) | -92.08 | (636.46) |
| **Baseline father attributes** | | | | | | | | |
| Father race-ethnicity | | | | | | | | |
| Black | -680.53*** | (172.27) | -20.13 | (151.30) | 0.09+ | (0.05) | 527.16 | (373.53) |
| Hispanic | -245.98 | (197.76) | 19.51 | (184.25) | -0.01 | (0.07) | 448.67 | (477.26) |
| Other, non-Hispanic | -511.45+ | (306.73) | 265.85 | (412.62) | 0.20+ | (0.12) | 469.42 | (1,050.61) |
| Race different from child's mother | 18.39 | (128.27) | -137.57 | (132.10) | -0.11* | (0.05) | 93.21 | (336.49) |
| Born in the United States | 183.11 | (186.55) | -181.88 | (218.58) | 0.09 | (0.07) | 348.35 | (565.46) |
| Married at birth | 32.23 | (189.66) | 396.39+ | (210.58) | -0.09 | (0.06) | 65.07 | (515.14) |
| Education | | | | | | | | |
| High school or GED | 189.35* | (85.78) | 166.68 | (90.46) | -0.01 | (0.04) | -459.57 | (355.27) |
| Some college or more | 482.48*** | (121.09) | 251.60* | (120.18) | 0.05 | (0.05) | -195.25 | (463.31) |
| Household poverty level | | | | | | | | |
| Poverty | -46.83 | (137.10) | 201.00 | (134.04) | 0.07 | (0.07) | -469.77 | (573.29) |
| Near poor | -18.05 | (118.33) | 222.24+ | (118.78) | 0.04 | (0.06) | -493.70 | (537.86) |
| Nonpoor | 242.74* | (119.51) | 417.24*** | (122.21) | 0.04 | (0.06) | -406.24 | (521.99) |
| Employed | 190.56* | (93.58) | -109.31 | (103.07) | -0.04 | (0.05) | -10.14 | (449.45) |
| Drug-alcohol use | -11.78 | (115.61) | -20.90 | (113.29) | -0.11* | (0.05) | 53.23 | (442.17) |
| Early incarceration | -41.69 | (111.81) | -92.99 | (100.89) | -0.01 | (0.05) | -305.18 | (564.41) |
| Impulsivity | 1.61 | (67.43) | 1.27 | (62.99) | -0.01 | (0.03) | -151.15 | (225.77) |

**State characteristics (lagged)**

| | Model 1 | | Model 2 | | Model 3 | | Model 4 | |
|---|---|---|---|---|---|---|---|---|
| Poverty rate | -23.06 | (25.84) | -5.82 | (26.90) | -0.01 | (0.01) | 190.85* | (89.23) |
| Unemployment rate | 44.22 | (54.37) | 19.83 | (47.38) | -0.01 | (0.02) | -38.05 | (160.19) |
| Imprisonment rate | 0.63 | (0.59) | 0.10 | (0.61) | 0.00 | (0.00) | -1.95 | (2.24) |
| Violent crime rate | -0.69 | (0.44) | 1.01* | (0.46) | -0.00 | (0.00) | 0.62 | (1.40) |
| Property crime rate | 0.03 | (0.14) | -0.02 | (0.14) | 0.00 | (0.00) | -0.59 | (0.41) |
| State minimum wage | 153.85** | (52.51) | -57.62 | (61.11) | 0.02 | (0.02) | 295.28* | (137.56) |
| Per capita child support expenditures | 3.49 | (6.48) | -5.11 | (7.41) | -0.00 | (0.00) | 49.61* | (20.60) |
| Census region | | | | | | | | |
| Midwest | -6.79 | (153.87) | -266.05+ | (154.91) | -0.06 | (0.06) | 1,732.57*** | (492.57) |
| South | 239.84 | (198.13) | -416.50* | (178.95) | -0.09 | (0.08) | 1,871.01** | (570.85) |
| West | -261.69 | (195.83) | -196.33 | (204.92) | 0.03 | (0.08) | 368.25 | (716.94) |
| Observations | 4,704 | | 4,447 | | 4,779 | | 4,613 | |
| Unique observations | 2,233 | | 2,158 | | 2,233 | | 2,218 | |

*Source*: Authors' calculations based on data from the Fragile Families and Child Wellbeing Study.

*Note*: Figures are linear coefficients. Robust standard errors (SE) in parentheses. Models control for wave, father-year random effects.

+ $p < .1$; * $p < .05$; ** $p < .01$; *** $p < .001$

were ever coresident, did not move, and were of the same race as their child's mother provided in-kind support more frequently. Notably, none of the individual-level characteristics considered here were associated with accrual of arrears over and above incarceration; however, fathers who lived in the Midwest or the South had higher arrears than those in the Northeast, as did those in states with higher poverty rates and states that spent more per capita on child support. Fathers who lived in the South also provided less informal support than those living in the Northeast.

## Moderation Effects of Policies

Analyses in table 3 explore whether protective policies related to employment and records access for individuals with criminal justice involvement moderate the negative associations between incarceration and fathers' contributions to children's households. The first panel shows the unmoderated incarceration models from table 2 for comparison. The second examines interactions between incarceration and protective employment policies, and the third examines interactions between incarceration and records policies.

With respect to employment policies, we find no significant interactions between such policies and incarceration for the provision of formal, informal, or in-kind support, suggesting that these policies do not reduce the incarceration penalty for these outcomes. We do find a significant and positive interaction with incarceration for fathers' accrual of child support arrears, indicating that these types of policies may actually exacerbate the link between incarceration and greater accrual of arrears. Specifically, in states that have no protective employment policies in place, the incarceration penalty (that is, the difference between the arrears accrued by ever- and never-incarcerated fathers) is $1,503, but the incarceration penalty in states with all six protective policies is $1,824 greater.

The findings related to records policies in the third panel are mixed. In particular, we find that the hypothesis that protective policies reduce the penalty associated with incarceration is only supported for some types of contributions. In states that have the most limited access to criminal records, the incarceration penalty is reduced by $2,969 for arrears accrual and $610 for formal support. The incarceration penalty for informal support, however, is $438 larger in states that have more protective criminal record policies. At the same time, the incarceration penalties associated with in-kind support are not sensitive to the accessibility of records. Another important series of findings emerge from the third panel. For informal support, formal support, and arrears, the coefficients for the records policy index are also significant, and in what might appear to be unexpected directions. The inclusion of the interaction term between incarceration and the records policy index means that the coefficients for the policy index describe the expected difference in contributions and arrears for fathers with no history of incarceration. This result indicates that these policies have implications for fathers who do and do not have histories of incarceration, an unexpected finding we address in greater detail in the discussion. These findings remain robust in the fixed-effects model as well (table A3), though the policy coefficient does not reach statistical significance in the model of informal support due to large standard errors.

To facilitate interpretation, we also present the results from the bottom panel of table 3 graphically. Based on the interaction models, figure 1 shows the predicted values of formal support, informal support, and arrears by fathers' incarceration history and presence of protective access to records policies. Holding all controls constant, our models indicate that never-incarcerated fathers provide more informal support ($1,437 versus $943) but less formal support ($1,051 versus $1,551) and thus accrue more arrears ($2,146 versus $3,668) when living in more protective states. Fathers with a history of incarceration fare better with respect to arrears, and are predicted to owe less in more protective states ($2,821 versus $4,310). Despite the larger incarceration penalty, the higher level of informal support provided by fathers without incarceration histories living in the most protective states means that those with incarceration histories end up paying similar amounts ($791 versus $735) in the most and least protective states. Similarly, the amount of

**Table 3.** Interaction Effects of Incarceration with Policies on Contributions for All Fathers

|  | Formal Child Support | Informal Cash Support | In-Kind Support | Arrears |
|---|---|---|---|---|
| **Incarceration main-effects models (table 2)** | | | | |
| Incarceration | -426.95*** | -401.91*** | -0.31*** | 2,130.24*** |
|  | (106.74) | (114.14) | (0.04) | (372.85) |
| Observations | 4,704 | 4,447 | 4,779 | 4,613 |
| Unique observations | 2,233 | 2,158 | 2,233 | 2,218 |
| **Employment policy index interactions** | | | | |
| Incarceration | -413.27** | -473.33*** | -0.29*** | 1,503.30*** |
|  | (151.75) | (156.97) | (0.06) | (548.06) |
| Policy | -5.57 | -288.64 | 0.13 | 8.88 |
|  | (255.46) | (243.00) | (0.10) | (750.00) |
| Incarceration x policy | -38.64 | 209.38 | -0.06 | 1,823.29* |
|  | (240.43) | (246.48) | (0.09) | (888.90) |
| Observations | 4,704 | 4,447 | 4,779 | 4,613 |
| Unique individuals | 2,233 | 2,158 | 2,233 | 2,218 |
| **Records policy index interactions** | | | | |
| Incarceration | -703.85*** | -207.82+ | -0.32*** | 3,682.04*** |
|  | (167.94) | (123.67) | (0.06) | (632.83) |
| Policy | -500.06** | 493.62** | -0.01 | 1,481.84*** |
|  | (168.99) | (183.87) | (0.06) | (420.30) |
| Incarceration x policy | 610.04*** | -437.70* | -0.01 | -2,968.79*** |
|  | (179.54) | (200.58) | (0.07) | (591.09) |
| Observations | 4,558 | 4,314 | 4,637 | 4,470 |
| Unique individuals | 2,177 | 2,102 | 2,177 | 2,160 |

*Source:* Authors' calculations based on data from the Fragile Families and Child Wellbeing Study.
*Note:* Robust standard errors in parentheses. Models include controls for all variables from table 3.
+$p < .1$; *$p < .05$; **$p < .01$; ***$p < .001$

formal support paid by fathers with histories of incarceration is more consistent across states with different policies ($957 versus $847) than one might expect given the large incarceration penalty for formal support (-$704). In short, the results indicate that protective records policies are associated with some disadvantages for never-incarcerated fathers and small gains for their ever-incarcerated counterparts.

## Differences by Race

It is difficult to account for these patterns without a closer examination of race, particularly given the salience of race as a compounding disadvantage for formerly incarcerated men seeking employment (Pager 2003, 2007). Although our sample is majority black (66.4 percent), stratifying the sample by race demonstrates stark differences by race that are masked in the full model. Models estimated for black and nonblack fathers separately (tables 4 and 5), show that records policy associations are concentrated among black fathers.

Black fathers with a history of incarceration provide significantly less formal and informal support, less frequent in-kind support, and accrue more arrears than black fathers who have not been incarcerated (table 4, first panel). As in the full sample, protective employment policies only moderate the association between incarceration and child support arrears (table 4, second panel). This sole significant interaction coefficient indicates that protective em-

**Figure 1.** Predicted Levels of Father Contributions and Arrears by Incarceration History and Records Policy Regime

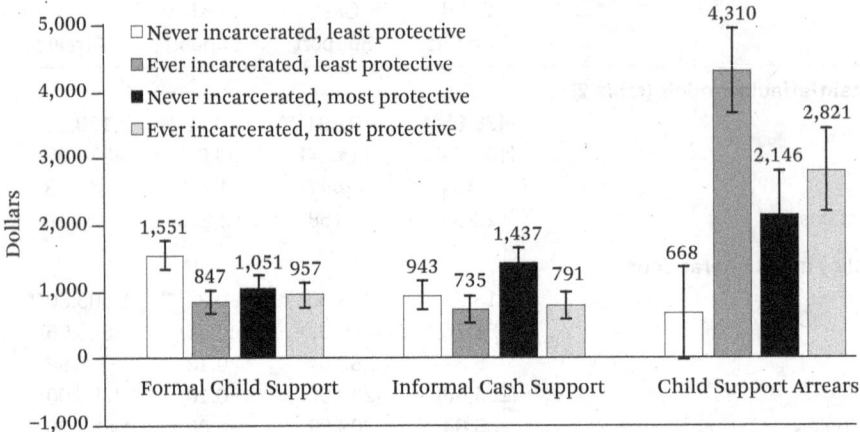

*Source:* Authors' calculations based on data from the Fragile Families and Child Wellbeing Study and data on state policies collected by authors. Error bars indicate 95% confidence interval around the predicted levels.

ployment policies may exacerbate the negative association between incarceration and support for black fathers. Living in a state that offers only limited official access to criminal records (table 4, third panel) has significant implications for black fathers both with and without histories of incarceration. More restrictive access to criminal record databases is associated with reduced incarceration penalties for formal child support and child support arrears, but a relatively larger incarceration penalty for informal child support. The associations presented in table 4 are robust to including state fixed effects (table A3).

As illustrated by the predicted values in figure 2, policies restricting access to criminal records databases are relevant for all black fathers living in more protective states, which

**Figure 2.** Predicted Levels of Black Father Contributions and Arrears by Incarceration History and Records Policy Regime

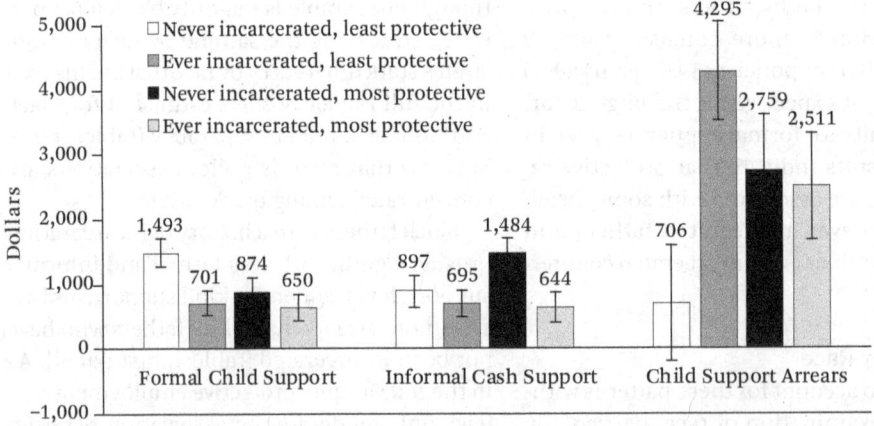

*Source:* Authors' calculations based on data from the Fragile Families and Child Wellbeing Study and data on state policies collected by authors. Error bars indicate 95% confidence interval around the predicted levels.

**Table 4.** Interaction Effects of Incarceration with Policies on Contributions for Black Fathers

|  | Formal Child Support | Informal Cash Support | In-Kind Support | Arrears |
|---|---|---|---|---|
| **Incarceration main-effects models** | | | | |
| Incarceration | −553.03*** | −462.32*** | −0.27*** | 1,662.39** |
|  | (131.33) | (112.08) | (0.06) | (606.67) |
| Observations | 3,116 | 2,962 | 3,178 | 3,031 |
| Unique observations | 1,414 | 1,373 | 1,421 | 1,398 |
| **Employment policy index interactions** | | | | |
| Incarceration | −532.48*** | −446.75** | −0.22** | 763.04 |
|  | (155.17) | (148.80) | (0.07) | (742.32) |
| Policy | 404.61 | −100.82 | 0.18 | 635.36 |
|  | (275.03) | (252.31) | (0.13) | (964.92) |
| Incarceration x policy | −66.21 | −39.63 | −0.15 | 2,488.69* |
|  | (275.55) | (252.40) | (0.12) | (1,097.28) |
| Observations | 3,116 | 2,962 | 3,178 | 3,031 |
| Unique individuals | 1,414 | 1,373 | 1,421 | 1,398 |
| **Records policy index interactions** | | | | |
| Incarceration | −791.18*** | −201.92 | −0.32*** | 3,588.96*** |
|  | (187.53) | (142.97) | (0.07) | (797.38) |
| Policy | −618.86** | 586.94*** | −0.12+ | 2,052.79** |
|  | (205.96) | (215.53) | (0.07) | (534.04) |
| Incarceration x policy | 567.59** | −638.25** | 0.06 | −3,837.09*** |
|  | (216.73) | (236.34) | (0.08) | (754.03) |
| Observations | 3,011 | 2,866 | 3,077 | 2,929 |
| Unique individuals | 1,379 | 1,338 | 1,386 | 1,360 |

*Source:* Authors' calculations based on data from the Fragile Families and Child Wellbeing Study and data on state policies collected by authors.
*Note:* Robust standard errors in parentheses. Models include controls for all variables from table 3 except paternal race-ethnicity.
+$p < .1$; *$p < .05$; **$p < .01$; ***$p < .001$

means that the reduced incarceration penalty may not translate into marked improvements for formerly imprisoned black fathers. Relative to fathers living in states that provide access to a criminal record database, never-incarcerated black fathers living in states that have more limited access to criminal records pay less formal child support ($874 versus $1,495), accrue greater child support arrears ($2,759 versus $706), and provide more informal child support ($1,484 versus $897). In this context, black fathers with a history of incarceration are ultimately predicted to provide statistically similar amounts of formal and informal support across policy regimes, though accrue slightly less in arrears, despite significant differences in the incarceration penalty across states.

Notably, the interaction models for the non-black sample (table 5) yield quite different results. Unlike in the models for black fathers (table 4), policies do not moderate incarceration penalties, nor are they significantly associated with the contributions of never-incarcerated fathers.

## DISCUSSION

In this study, we sought to understand the implications of incarceration for nonresident

**Table 5.** Interaction Effects of Incarceration with Policies on Contributions, Nonblack fathers

|  | Formal Child Support | Informal Cash Support | In-Kind Support | Arrears |
|---|---|---|---|---|
| **Incarceration main-effects models** | | | | |
| Incarceration | -189.70 | -350.87 | -0.38*** | 3,082.20*** |
|  | (262.72) | (275.12) | (0.08) | (878.61) |
| Observations | 1,588 | 1,485 | 1,601 | 1,582 |
| Unique observations | 819 | 785 | 812 | 820 |
| **Employment policy index interactions** | | | | |
| Incarceration | -177.64 | -575.21 | -0.40*** | 2,775.27*** |
|  | (311.47) | (368.51) | (0.10) | (807.93) |
| Policy | -775.41 | -905.91⁺ | 0.02 | -1,236.80 |
|  | (560.18) | (545.23) | (0.15) | (1,009.80) |
| Incarceration x policy | -35.83 | 712.16 | 0.08 | 975.67 |
|  | (445.91) | (533.57) | (0.15) | (1,500.76) |
| Observations | 1,588 | 1,485 | 1,601 | 1,582 |
| Unique individuals | 819 | 785 | 812 | 820 |
| **Records policy index interactions** | | | | |
| Incarceration | -435.36 | -387.59 | -0.30** | 3,901.12*** |
|  | (357.97) | (240.33) | (0.10) | (1,040.01) |
| Policy | 31.41 | 0.60 | 0.14 | 760.84 |
|  | (320.87) | (326.21) | (0.10) | (729.58) |
| Incarceration x policy | 450.99 | 50.67 | -0.12 | -1,617.02⁺ |
|  | (333.72) | (344.13) | (0.12) | (950.48) |
| Observations | 1,547 | 1,448 | 1,560 | 1,541 |
| Unique individuals | 798 | 764 | 791 | 800 |

*Source:* Authors' calculations based on data from the Fragile Families and Child Wellbeing Study and data on state policies collected by authors.
*Note:* Robust standard errors in parentheses. Models include controls for all variables from table 3.
⁺$p < .1$; *$p < .05$; **$p < .01$; ***$p < .001$

fathers' economic contributions to their children's households and the degree to which employment-related policies might mitigate such incarceration penalties. Consistent with prior work and our first hypothesis, we find strong evidence that incarceration reduces nonresident fathers' formal cash, informal cash, and in-kind (noncash) contributions, and increases their accrual of child support arrears. On a population level, this overall finding is particularly concerning for the intergenerational transmission of racial disparities given that black children and their fathers are most likely to experience paternal incarceration (Western and Wildeman 2009; Wildeman 2009).

Our results are more nuanced in regard to how some policies can mitigate some collateral consequences of incarceration, reflecting competing hypotheses about how these policies might operate. On the one hand, policies that limit employers' ability to access or use criminal records in the hiring process may reduce the costs of incarceration for such fathers' contributions to their children's households. On the other hand, these policies may create opportunities for racial discrimination against black men if some employers use racial heuristics to guess about applicants' propensity for incarceration or default to racial stereotypes about criminality. In these cases, the presence of such policies could negatively affect black fathers, even if they have never been incarcerated.

Our results suggest that both of these things may be occurring simultaneously, depending on the type of policy and outcome examined. First, employment policies that regulate employers' use of criminal records during hiring are associated with a larger incarceration penalty for nonresident fathers' accrual of child support arrears (but not other outcomes). This is particularly evident for black fathers with incarceration histories, for whom living in states where the use of criminal records during the employment process is highly regulated is associated with the accrual of nearly $2,500 more in arrears relative to those in states in which the use of records is left to employer discretion. To the extent that increased arrears are a signal of fathers' inability to find high-quality jobs in the formal economy, these findings could indicate that employers are either unintentionally or deliberately substituting racial discrimination for criminal record discrimination. This interpretation is consistent with one study looking at these same policies that finds such negative associations with employment among black, but not white, fathers (Dwyer Emory 2019). We do not find evidence that such policies moderate the associations between incarceration and provision of either formal or informal support, nor that these policies increase the arrears of black fathers without records. Together, these patterns suggest that these policies do not improve the economic opportunities available to fathers with incarceration histories. These null findings may also reflect limited awareness or enforcement of these kinds of policies, or successful strategies to offset the costs passed on to children.

Second, policies that limit employers' ability to access official records seem to open up opportunities for racial discrimination despite reducing some discrimination on the basis of criminal history. The incarceration penalty for all fathers' and, in particular, black fathers' provision of formal support and the accrual of arrears is lower in states that have more limited record access than in those that make official records accessible. At the same time, our results suggest that the benefit from these protective policies to formerly incarcerated fathers was offset by lower levels of formal support and greater accrual of arrears by never-incarcerated fathers living in the same states. Thus, though protective records policies appear to mitigate the incarceration penalty, the broader consequence of these policies is that fathers in protective states pay roughly the same formal support and accrue approximately the same arrears, independent of their incarceration. These findings are evident among our subsample of black fathers but are entirely absent for nonblack fathers. Unlike for the employment policies, the implementation of the access policies we consider is unambiguous because they measure what data the state makes available online rather than laws that must be enforced. Thus differences in findings between the two types of protective policies may reflect the differential implementation of employment and access policies rather than different underlying effects of these policies.

Several potential theories explain the different pattern of results we observe for black fathers, though due to data limitations this article cannot directly evaluate potential mechanisms like employment quality, unemployment, earnings, or indirect pathways through family relationships or contact. Previous scholars have linked ban-the-box policies (Doleac and Hasen 2016; Vuolo, Lageson, and Uggen 2017) and employment policies (Dwyer Emory 2019) that restrict the use of records to statistical discrimination, wherein employers use race as a proxy for criminal justice involvement when they are unable to access prospective employees' criminal records. Our findings are also consistent with a subtler form of racial bias, in which employers may not intentionally use race as a marker but instead default to racial stereotypes about criminality when evaluating black applicants in the absence of other information (Agan and Starr 2018). Because this discrimination plausibly affects access to high-quality jobs for black fathers, it is less likely that formal cash support is withheld from their paychecks and more likely that they accumulate arrears. Thus, never-incarcerated black fathers' provision of formal support and arrears accrual is more similar to that of fathers with prior incarcerations and worse than those living in states that provide easier access to records.

Our hypotheses for how policies should influence fathers' provision of informal cash and in-kind support were ambiguous, given that research indicates that these voluntary types of provisions can be substitutes for the provision of formal support (Nepomnyaschy and Garfinkel 2010; Sariscsany, Garfinkel, and Nepomnyaschy 2019). Fathers working in the formal economy—whose formal child support is likely to be automatically withdrawn from their paycheck—may be less likely to also make informal cash contributions, though they still may provide in-kind support. Alternatively, fathers who cannot find jobs in the formal economy and thus contribute less formal support and accumulate greater arrears may be able to generate income in the informal or underground economy, allowing them to make informal cash contributions.

Our results indeed point to this type of substitution among black fathers. Although policies that protect access to records are associated with reductions in the incarceration penalty for the provision of formal child support, they are actually associated with increases in this penalty for the provision of informal support. And although they are associated with reduced formal support for black fathers with no incarceration history, they are also associated with increases in informal cash support contributions for this group. This substitution means that children receive comparable cash support from their fathers across policy regimes, but the implications for the fathers themselves are real. Notably, the accrual of arrears and potential substitution of informal or riskier illegal work for formal employment may put fathers at greater risk of future incarceration (Zatz and Stoll 2020). The provision of in-kind support is consistently lower for formerly incarcerated fathers, but neither the size of that difference nor the frequency of provision is sensitive to the policies tested in this study.

Our results should be considered in light of several potential limitations. First, although we include a strong set of state-level controls, we cannot completely control for all possible state-level differences that could be associated with states' enactment of protective policies and fathers' provision of child support. To address this potential source of bias, we specify fixed-effects models in supplementary analyses that control for unobserved characteristics of states and produce comparable results. Second, we cannot observe how employers actually implement these policies. As mentioned, some evidence suggests that both individuals and employers may not be aware of the existence of these policies. Further, even if employers knowingly violate policies related to asking about criminal records, pursuing employment discrimination cases is costly, timely, and difficult; it is also highly unlikely that employers will be sanctioned (Jacobs 2015). Finally, even when official criminal justice records are not legally available, much information on criminal justice involvement is publicly available via internet searches (Lageson 2016a). These limitations prevent a strong causal interpretation of our findings, and thus we rely on theory and consistency with previous causal studies to interpret our results. We suggest that this is a fertile area for future research.

Second, given data limitations, we can only measure fathers' involvement with the criminal justice system using a variable capturing whether the father had ever been incarcerated by the time of the survey interview. This is a blunt measure of incarceration because it cannot identify important differences in the type of facility, length of incarceration, or conditions of confinement that themselves have important implications for fathers' ability to find work after release. Moreover, this measure also fails to capture the many fathers who have relevant criminal records but not histories of incarceration. As many as half of the fathers in the comparison group of never-incarcerated fathers may have such records (Dwyer Emory 2019). Practically, because policies should also affect these fathers' economic prospects, the comparisons between the two groups may be substantially attenuated, though findings were robust to excluding never-incarcerated fathers with known records from the analysis and using alternative definitions of incarceration. Finally, measurement error is likely in mothers' reports of both formal child support and arrears. Unlike other kinds of support, these forms of formal support are often automatically withheld or owed to the state rather than the mother (ACF 2016). Mothers, particularly those who have limited interactions with their child's father, may not know the extent to which the father has paid or owes child support. Our measure of arrears and analytic approach also cannot fully capture the bidirectional association between arrears and incarceration, though findings were robust to excluding fathers for whom nonpayment of child support was the primary reason for incarceration. Specifically, child support nonpayment and the resultant arrears can lead to incarceration (Zatz and Stoll 2020), but arrears often accrue during incarceration due to the difficulty of modifying child support orders as well as after release due to men's impaired economic prospects. Although likely measured with some error, these indicators of fathers' contributions to their children's households are the best available and are consistently measured across waves in the survey data.

Incarceration is pervasive in the United States, affecting millions of families every year and generating enduring collateral consequences. Research emphasizes that this experience makes it more likely that fathers live apart from their children (Geller 2013; Geller, Garfinkel, and Western 2011; Western and Smith 2018; Western, Lopoo, and McLanahan 2004), and our findings make it clear that this experience has serious implications for nonresident fathers' ability to provide for their children. Moreover, both incarceration and its negative consequences for fathers' contributions to their children's household economies are concentrated among black families. Policies aimed at addressing the economic opportunities available to these fathers, however, may have more complex implications for fathers' support than previously considered due to the inseparability of race- and criminal record–based discrimination in the United States. If we are to better understand the mechanisms through which these associations operate to determine how policies could better support fathers' ability to provide for their children, additional research is needed.

**Table A1.** Components of State Policy Indices

| Index | State Policy |
|---|---|
| Employment policy | Private employers cannot ask about or consider arrests that did not lead to convictions when making hiring decisions (yes/limited/no) |
| | Public employers cannot ask about or consider arrests that did not lead to convictions when making hiring decisions (yes/limited/no) |
| | Licensing agencies cannot ask about or consider arrests that did not lead to convictions when making hiring decisions (yes/limited/no) |
| | Private employers cannot issue blanket bans against the hiring of individuals with criminal records (yes/limited/no) |
| | Public employers cannot issue blanket bans against the hiring of individuals with criminal records (yes/limited/no) |
| | Licensing agencies cannot issue blanket bans against the licensing of individuals with criminal records (yes/limited/no) |
| Criminal records policy | State maintains searchable criminal records database (yes/no) |
| | State maintains searchable supervision records database (yes/no) |

*Source:* Authors' compilation.

**Table A2.** Attributes of States in Sample, Lagged by One Year (N=246 Unique State Years)

| | Mean or % | SD | Minimum | Maximum |
|---|---|---|---|---|
| **State policy scores** | | | | |
| Employment policies | 0.33 | 0.33 | 0.00 | 1.00 |
| Criminal records policies[a] | 0.55 | 0.55 | 0.00 | 1.00 |
| **State attributes, lagged by one year** | | | | |
| Unemployment (%) | 5.30 | 1.50 | 2.40 | 10.50 |
| Minimum wage ($) | 7.40 | 0.98 | 3.35 | 9.39 |
| Poverty (%) | 12.38 | 3.10 | 4.50 | 21.70 |
| Imprisonment rate (per 100,000 residents) | 451.47 | 149.27 | 126.00 | 862.00 |
| Violent crime rate (per 100,000 residents) | 463.79 | 162.29 | 103.70 | 903.20 |
| Property crime rate (per 100,000 residents) | 3,371.91 | 846.25 | 1,718.20 | 5,849.80 |
| Child support expenditures (per capita) | 21.12 | 7.58 | 8.50 | 43.83 |
| Census region (%) | | | | |
| Northeast | 19.9 | | | |
| Midwest | 25.2 | | | |
| South | 41.1 | | | |
| West | 13.8 | | | |

*Source*: Authors' calculations based on state policies data collected by authors for states in the analytic sample.
*Note*: The primary sample includes thirty-nine unique states due to fathers' residential mobility.
[a]N=150 because access policies have been collected for only a subset of states, including the fifteen original Fragile Families states.

Table A3. Interaction Effects of Incarceration with Policies on Contributions for All Fathers, State Fixed Effects

| | All Fathers | | | | Black Fathers | | | |
|---|---|---|---|---|---|---|---|---|
| | Formal Child Support | Informal Cash Support | In-Kind Support | Arrears | Formal Child Support | Informal Cash Support | In-Kind Support | Arrears |
| **Incarceration main-effects model** | | | | | | | | |
| Incarceration | −416.29*** | −403.88*** | −0.32*** | 2,118.90*** | −559.43*** | −444.33*** | −0.28*** | 1,636.50*** |
| | (126.73) | (115.25) | (0.05) | (493.58) | (135.95) | (112.38) | (0.06) | (600.75) |
| Observations | 4,704 | 4,447 | 4,779 | 4,613 | 3,116 | 2,962 | 3,178 | 3,031 |
| Unique observations | 2,233 | 2,158 | 2,233 | 2,218 | 1,414 | 1,373 | 1,421 | 1,398 |
| **Employment policy index interactions** | | | | | | | | |
| Incarceration | −380.26* | −494.83** | −0.29*** | 1,524.35*** | −507.06** | −470.99** | −0.23*** | 818.07 |
| | (152.84) | (156.97) | (0.06) | (542.92) | (154.41) | (150.31) | (0.07) | (730.98) |
| Policy | 475.91 | 352.78 | 0.20 | 1,619.96 | 774.48 | 779.74+ | 0.35 | 1,777.55 |
| | (540.75) | (558.69) | (0.19) | (1,687.45) | (544.36) | (426.84) | (0.27) | (2,731.00) |
| Incarceration x policy | −105.73 | 260.82 | −0.09 | 1,740.02* | −135.06 | 63.24 | −0.14 | 2,292.56* |
| | (254.44) | (244.01) | (0.10) | (878.71) | (299.59) | (246.03) | (0.13) | (1,030.69) |
| Observations | 4,704 | 4,447 | 4,779 | 4,613 | 3,116 | 2,962 | 3,178 | 3,031 |
| Unique individuals | 2,233 | 2,158 | 2,233 | 2,218 | 1,414 | 1,373 | 1,421 | 1,398 |
| **Records policy index interactions** | | | | | | | | |
| Incarceration | −693.10*** | −212.10+ | −0.32*** | 3,615.09*** | −806.90*** | −195.15 | −0.33*** | 3,405.16*** |
| | (169.50) | (122.44) | (0.06) | (621.07) | (189.76) | (141.44) | (0.07) | (769.86) |
| Policy | −443.81* | 229.76 | −0.05 | 1,794.52** | −455.52* | 408.99 | −0.15 | 2,884.12*** |
| | (188.50) | (214.27) | (0.07) | (610.16) | (226.43) | (256.25) | (0.08) | (810.62) |
| Incarceration x policy | 593.08*** | −412.36* | 0.00 | −2,912.69*** | 589.89** | −615.50** | 0.07+ | −3,629.93*** |
| | (181.03) | (201.18) | (0.07) | (575.91) | (215.51) | (236.37) | (0.09) | (724.59) |
| Observations | 4,558 | 4,314 | 4,637 | 4,470 | 3,011 | 2,866 | 3,077 | 2,929 |
| Unique individuals | 2,177 | 2,102 | 2,177 | 2,160 | 1,379 | 1,338 | 1,386 | 1,360 |

*Source:* Authors' calculations based on data from the Fragile Families and Child Wellbeing Study and data on state policies collected by authors.
*Note:* Robust standard errors in parentheses. Models include controls for all variables from table 3 and state fixed effects.
+ $p < .1$; * $p < .05$; ** $p < .01$; *** $p < .001$

## REFERENCES

Administration for Children and Families (ACF). 2016. *Office of Child Support Enforcement Annual Report to Congress*. Washington: U.S. Department of Health and Human Services. Accessed October 2, 2019. https://www.acf.hhs.gov/sites/default/files/programs/css/fy_2016_annual_report.pdf.

Agan, Amanda, and Sonja Starr. 2018. "Ban the Box, Criminal Records, and Racial Discrimination: A Field Experiment." *Quarterly Journal of Economics* 133(1): 191–235.

Apel, Robert, and Julie Horney. 2017. "How and Why Does Work Matter? Employment Conditions, Routine Activities, and Crime Among Adult Male Offenders." *Criminology* 55(2): 307–43.

Atkinson, Daryl V., and Kathleen Lockwood. 2014. "The Benefits of Ban the Box." Durham, N.C.: Southern Coalition for Social Justice. Accessed October 2, 2019. https://www.southerncoalition.org/wp-content/uploads/2018/11/BantheBox_WhitePaper-2.pdf.

Avery, Beth. 2019. "Ban the Box: U.S. Cities, Counties, and States Adopt Fair Hiring Policies." Washington, D.C.: National Employment Law Project. Accessed October 2, 2019. https://www.nelp.org/publication/ban-the-box-fair-chance-hiring-state-and-local-guide.

Berracasa, Colenn, Alexis Estevez, Charlotte Nugent, Kelly Roesing, and Jerry Wei. 2016. "The Impact of 'Ban the Box' in the District of Columbia." Washington: Office of the District of Columbia Auditor.

Bureau of Labor Statistics (BLS 2018). "State Unemployment Rate." Federal Reserve Economic Data (FRED). Washington: U.S. Bureau of Labor Statistics. Data downloaded from https://fred.stlouisfed.org (accessed October 18, 2019)..

Cancian, Maria, Carolyn J. Heinrich, and Yiyoon Chung. 2013. "Discouraging Disadvantaged Fathers' Employment: An Unintended Consequence of Policies Designed to Support Families." *Journal of Policy Analysis and Management* 32(4): 758–84.

Carlson, Marcia, and Lawrence M. Berger. 2013. "What Kids Get from Parents: Packages of Parental Involvement across Complex Family Forms." *Social Service Review* 87(2): 213–49.

Carson, E. Ann, and Joseph Mulako-Wangota. 2018. "Imprisonment Rates of Total Jurisdiction Population." Corrections Statistical Analysis Tool (CSAT)–Prisoners. Washington: U.S. Bureau of Justice Statistics. Accessed October 2, 2019. https://www.bjs.gov/nps.

Coltrane, Scott, Ross D. Parke, and Michele Adams. 2004. "Complexity of Father Involvement in Low-Income Mexican American Families." *Family Relations* 53(2): 179–89.

Cozzolino, Elizabeth. 2018. "Public Assistance, Relationship Context, and Jail for Child Support Debt." *Socius* 4 (January): 2378023118757124.

D'Alessio, Stewart J., Lisa Stolzenberg, and Jamie L. Flexon. 2015. "The Effect of Hawaii's Ban the Box Law on Repeat Offending." *American Journal of Criminal Justice* 40(2): 336–52.

DeFina, Robert H., and Lance Hannon. 2010. "The Impact of Adult Incarceration on Child Poverty: A County-Level Analysis, 1995–2007." *Prison Journal* 90(4): 377–96.

Denver, Megan, Garima Siwach, and Shawn Buschway. 2017. "A New Look at the Employment and Recidivism Relationship Through the Lens of a Criminal Background Check." *Criminology* 55(1): 174–204.

Dickman, Scott J. 1990. "Functional and Dysfunctional Impulsivity: Personality and Cognitive Correlates." *Journal of Personality and Social Psychology* 58(1): 95–102.

Doleac, Jennifer L., and Benjamin Hasen. 2016. "Does 'Ban the Box' Help or Hurt Low-Skilled Workers? Statistical Discrimination and Employment Outcomes When Criminal Histories Are Hidden." *NBER* working paper no. 22469. Cambridge, Mass.: National Bureau of Economic Research.

Dwyer Emory, Allison. 2019. "Unintended Consequences: Protective State Policies and the Employment of Fathers with Criminal Records." *Fragile Families* working paper no. WP19-04-FF. Princeton, N.J.: Princeton University. Accessed October 2, 2019. https://fragilefamilies.princeton.edu/sites/fragilefamilies/files/wp19-04-ff.pdf.

Edin, Kathryn, and Laura Lein. 1997. "Work, Welfare, and Single Mothers' Economic Survival Strategies." *American Sociological Review* 62(2): 253–66.

Edin, Kathryn, and Timothy J. Nelson. 2013. *Doing the Best I Can: Fatherhood in the Inner City*. Berkeley: University of California Press.

Farrington, David P. 1986. "Age and Crime." *Crime and Justice* 7 (January): 189–250.

Federal Bureau of Investigation (FBI). 2018. "Uniform

Crime Reporting Statistics." UCR Data Online. Washington: U.S. Department of Justice. Accessed October 2, 2019. http://www.ucrdatatool.gov.

Finlay, Keith. 2008. "Effect of Employer Access to Criminal History Data on the Labor Market Outcomes of Ex-Offenders and Non-Offenders." *NBER* working paper no. 13935. Cambridge, Mass.: National Bureau of Economic Research.

Geller, Amanda. 2013. "Paternal Incarceration and Father-Child Contact in Fragile Families." *Journal of Marriage and Family* 75(5): 1288–303. DOI: 10.1111/jomf.12056.

Geller, Amanda, Carey E. Cooper, Irwin Garfinkel, Ofira Schwartz-Soicher, and Ronald B. Mincy. 2012. "Beyond Absenteeism: Father Incarceration and Child Development." *Demography* 49(1): 49–76.

Geller, Amanda, Irwin Garfinkel, and Bruce Western. 2011. "Paternal Incarceration and Support for Children in Fragile Families." *Demography* 48(1): 25–47.

Glaze, Laren E., and Laura M. Maruschak. 2010. "Parents in Prison and Their Minor Children." *Bureau of Justice Statistics* special report no. NCJ 222894. Washington: U.S. Department of Justice. Accessed October 2, 2019. https://www.bjs.gov/content/pub/pdf/pptmc.pdf.

Hamer, Jennifer. 2001. *What It Means to Be Daddy: Fatherhood for Black Men Living Away from Their Children*. New York: Columbia University Press.

Hlavka, Heather R., Darren Wheelock, and Jennifer E. Cossyleon. 2015. "Narratives of Commitment: Looking for Work with a Criminal Record." *Sociological Quarterly* 56(2): 213–36.

Jacobs, James B. 2015. *The Eternal Criminal Record*. Cambridge, Mass.: Harvard University Press.

Jarrett, Robin L., and Linda M. Burton. 1999. "Dynamic Dimensions of Family Structure in Low-Income African American Families: Emergent Themes in Qualitative Research." *Journal of Comparative Family Studies* 30(2): 177–87.

Kane, Jennifer B., Timothy J. Nelson, and Kathryn Edin. 2015. "How Much In-Kind Support Do Low-Income Nonresident Fathers Provide? A Mixed-Method Analysis." *Journal of Marriage and Family* 77(3): 591–611.

Katzenstein, Mary Fainsod, and Maureen R. Waller. 2015. "Taxing the Poor: Incarceration, Poverty Governance, and the Seizure of Family Resources." *Perspectives on Politics* 13(3): 638–56. DOI: 10.1017/S153759271500122X.

Lageson, Sarah Esther. 2016a. "Digital Punishment's Tangled Web." *Contexts* 15(1): 22–27.

———. 2016b. "Found Out and Opting Out: The Consequences of Online Criminal Records for Families." *Annals of the American Academy of Political and Social Science* 665(1): 127–41.

Lageson, Sarah Esther, Mike Vuolo, and Christopher Uggen. 2015. "Legal Ambiguity in Managerial Assessments of Criminal Records." *Law & Social Inquiry* 40(1): 175–204.

Legal Action Center. 2004. "After Prison: Roadblocks to Reentry. A Report on State Legal Barriers Facing People with Criminal Records." Washington, D.C.: Legal Action Center. Accessed October 2, 2019. https://lac.org/roadblocks-to-reentry/index.php.

———. 2009. "After Prison: Roadblocks to Reentry 2009 Update." Washington, D.C.: Legal Action Center.

McLanahan, Sara. 2004. "Diverging Destinies: How Children Are Faring Under the Second Demographic Transition." *Demography* 41(4): 607–27.

McLanahan, Sara, Laura Tach, and Daniel Schneider. 2013. "The Causal Effects of Father Absence." *Annual Review of Sociology* 39: 399–427.

McLeod, Branden A., and Aaron Gottlieb. 2018. "Examining the Relationship Between Incarceration and Child Support Arrears Among Low-Income Fathers." *Children and Youth Services Review* 94 (November): 1–9.

Miller, Daniel P., and Ronald B. Mincy. 2012. "Falling Further Behind? Child Support Arrears and Fathers' Labor Force Participation." *Social Service Review* 86(4): 604–35.

Mincy, Ronald B., Daniel P. Miller, and Elia De la Cruz Toledo. 2016. "Child Support Compliance During Economic Downturns." *Children and Youth Services Review* 65(June): 127–39.

Naft, Michael, and Geraldine Downey. 2019. "Rejection Sensitivity as a Determinant of Well-Being During Reentry." In *Current Directions in Ostracism, Social Exclusion and Rejection Research*, edited by Selma C. Rudert, Rainer Greifeneder, and Kipling Williams. New York: Routledge.

Nepomnyaschy, Lenna. 2007. "Child Support and Father-Child Contact: Testing Reciprocal Pathways." *Demography* 44(1): 93–112.

Nepomnyaschy, Lenna, and Irwin Garfinkel. 2010. "Child Support Enforcement and Fathers' Contributions to Their Nonmarital Children." *Social Service Review* 84(3): 341–80.

Nepomnyaschy, Lenna, Daniel P. Miller, Steven Garasky, and Neha Nanda. 2014. "Nonresident Fathers and Child Food Insecurity: Evidence from Longitudinal Data." *Social Service Review* 88(1): 92–133.

Pager, Devah. 2003. "The Mark of a Criminal Record." *American Journal of Sociology* 108(5): 937–75.

———. 2007. "Two Strikes and You're Out: The Intensification of Racial and Criminal Stigma." In *Barriers to Reentry? The Labor Market for Released Prisoners in Post-Industrial America*, edited by Shawn Bushway, Michael A. Stoll, and David F. Weiman. New York: Russell Sage Foundation.

Pager, Devah, Bruce Western, and Naomi Sugie. 2009. "Sequencing Disadvantage: Barriers to Employment Facing Young Black and White Men with Criminal Records." *Annals of the American Academy of Political and Social Science* 623(1): 195–213.

Pate, David J. 2002. "An Ethnographic Inquiry into the Life and Expectations of African American Fathers with Children on W-2." In *Fathers of Children in W-2 Families*. Vol. 2. W-2 Child Support Demonstration Evaluation: Report on Nonexperimental Analyses. Institute for Research on Poverty, University of Wisconsin-Madison.

Pettit, Becky, and Christopher J. Lyons. 2007. "Status and the Stigma of Incarceration: The Labor Market Effects of Incarceration, by Race, Class, and Criminal Involvement." In *Barriers to Reentry? The Labor Market for Released Prisoners in Post-Industrial America*, edited by Shawn Bushway, Michael A. Stoll, and David F. Weiman. New York: Russell Sage Foundation.

———. 2009. "Incarceration and the Legitimate Labor Market: Examining Age-Graded Effects on Employment and Wages." *Law & Society Review* 43(4): 725–56.

Pew Charitable Trusts. 2010. "Collateral Costs: Incarceration's Effect on Economic Mobility." Washington, D.C.: The Pew Charitable Trusts. Accessed October 2, 2019. https://www.pewtrusts.org/~/media/legacy/uploadedfiles/pcs_assets/2010/collateralcosts1pdf.pdf.

Reichman, Nancy E., Julien O. Teitler, Irwin Garfinkel, and Sara S. McLanahan. 2001. "Fragile Families: Sample and Design." *Children and Youth Services Review* 23(4-5): 303–26.

Rodriquez, Michelle Natividad. 2017. ""Ban the Box" Is a Fair Chance For Workers With Records." Fact Sheet. New York: National Employment Law Project. Accessed October 2, 2019. https://s27147.pcdn.co/wp-content/uploads/Ban-the-Box-Fair-Chance-Fact-Sheet.pdf.

Roy, Kevin. 2004. "Three-Block Fathers: Spatial Perceptions and Kin-Work in Low-Income African American Neighborhoods." *Social Problems* 51(4): 528–48.

Roy, Kevin, and Linda Burton. 2007. "Mothering Through Recruitment: Kinscription of Nonresidential Fathers and Father Figures in Low-Income Families." *Family Relations* 56(1): 24–39.

Roy, Kevin, and Omari Dyson. 2010. "Making Daddies into Fathers: Community-Based Fatherhood Programs and the Construction of Masculinities for Low-Income African American Men." *American Journal of Community Psychology* 45(1-2): 139–54.

Sariscsany, Laurel, Irwin Garfinkel, and Lenna Nepomnyaschy. 2019. "Describing and Understanding Child Support Trajectories." *Social Service Review* 93(2): 143–82.

Schwartz-Soicher, Ofira, Amanda Geller, and Irwin Garfinkel. 2011. "The Effect of Paternal Incarceration on Material Hardship." *Social Service Review* 85(3): 447–73.

Seim, Josh, and David J. Harding. 2020. "Parolefare: Post-prison Supervision and Low-Wage Work." *RSF: The Russell Sage Foundation Journal of the Social Sciences* 6(1): 173–95. DOI: 10.7758/RSF.2020.6.1.08.

Smith, Sandra Susan. 2005. "'Don't Put My Name on It': Social Capital Activation and Job-Finding Assistance among the Black Urban Poor." *American Journal of Sociology* 111(1): 1–57.

Sorensen, Elaine, Liliana Sousa, and Simone Schaner. 2007. "Assessing Child Support Arrears in Nine Large States and the Nation." Washington, D.C.: The Urban Institute.

Spaulding, Shayne, Robert I. Lerman, Harry J. Holzer, and Lauren Eyster. 2015. *Expanding Economic Opportunity for Young Men and Boys of Color through Employment and Training*. Washington, D.C.: The Urban Institute.

Stack, Carol B. 1975. *All Our Kin: Strategies for Survival in a Black Community*. New York: Basic Books.

Sugie, Naomi F. 2012. "Punishment and Welfare: Paternal Incarceration and Families' Receipt of Public Assistance." *Social Forces* 90(4): 1403–27.

Swisher, Raymond R., and Maureen R. Waller. 2008. "Confining Fatherhood: Incarceration and Paternal Involvement Among Nonresident White, African American, and Latino Fathers." *Journal of Family Issues* 29(8): 1067–88.

Sykes, Bryan L., and Amanda Geller. 2017. "Mass Incarceration and the Underground Economy in America." *Fragile Families* working paper no. 17-03-FF. Princeton, N.J.: Princeton University. Accessed October 2, 2019. https://fragilefamilies.princeton.edu/sites/fragilefamilies/files/wp17-03-ff.pdf.

Sykes, Bryan L., and Becky Pettit. 2015. "Severe Deprivation and System Inclusion Among Children of Incarcerated Parents in the United States After the Great Recession." *RSF: The Russell Sage Foundation Journal of the Social Sciences* 1(2): 108–32. DOI: 10.7758/RSF.2015.1.2.06.

Turner, Kimberly J., and Maureen R. Waller. 2017. "Indebted Relationships: Child Support Arrears and Nonresident Fathers' Involvement With Children." *Journal of Marriage and Family* 79(1): 24–43.

Turney, Kristin, and Christopher Wildeman. 2013. "Redefining Relationships: Explaining the Countervailing Consequences of Paternal Incarceration for Parenting." *American Sociological Review* 78(6): 949–79.

Uggen, Christopher. 2000. "Work as a Turning Point in the Life Course of Criminals: A Duration Model of Age, Employment, and Recidivism." *American Sociological Review* 65(4): 529–46.

Uggen, Christopher, Mike Vuolo, Sarah Lageson, Ebony Ruhland, and Hilary K. Whitham. 2014. "The Edge of Stigma: An Experimental Audit of the Effects of Low-Level Criminal Records on Employment." *Criminology* 52(4): 627–54.

University of Kentucky Center for Poverty Research. 2017. "UKCPR National Welfare Data, 1980–2016." Lexington: University of Kentucky. Accessed October 2, 2019. http://www.ukcpr.org/national-welfare-data

Vuolo, Mike, Sarah Lageson, and Christopher Uggen. 2017. "Criminal Record Questions in the Era of 'Ban the Box.'" *Criminology & Public Policy* 16(1): 139–65.

Waller, Maureen R. 2002. *My Baby's Father: Unmarried Parents and Paternal Responsibility*. Ithaca, N.Y.: Cornell University Press.

———. 2009. "Family Man in the Other America: New Opportunities, Motivations, and Supports for Paternal Caregiving." *Annals of the American Academy of Political and Social Science* 624(1): 156–76.

Waller, Maureen R., Allison Dwyer Emory, and Elise Paul. 2018. "Money, Time, or Something Else? Measuring Nonresident Fathers' Informal and In-Kind Contributions." *Journal of Family Issues* 39(3): 3612–40.

Waller, Maureen R., and Robert Plotnick. 2001. "Effective Child Support Policy for Low-Income Families: Evidence from Street Level Research." *Journal of Policy Analysis and Management* 20(1): 89–110.

Waller, Maureen R., and Raymond Swisher. 2006. "Fathers' Risk Factors in Fragile Families: Implications for 'Healthy' Relationships and Father Involvement." *Social Problems* 53(3): 392–420.

Warner, Cody, Joshua Kaiser, and Jason N. Houle. 2020. "Locked Out of the Labor Market? State-Level Hidden Sentences and the Labor-Market Outcomes of Recently Incarcerated Young Adults." *RSF: The Russell Sage Foundation Journal of the Social Sciences* 6(1): 132–51. DOI: 10.7758/RSF.2020.6.1.06

Washington, Heather M., Shao-Chiu Juan, and Anna R. Haskins. 2018. "Incapacitated Involvement: Incarceration and Fatherhood in Fragile Families at Age 9." *Journal of Family Issues* 39(13): 3463–86.

Weiss, Yoram, and Robert J. Willis. 1985. "Children as Collective Goods and Divorce Settlements." *Journal of Labor Economics* 3(3): 268–92.

Western, Bruce. 2001. "Incarceration, Unemployment, and Inequality." *Focus* 21(1): 32–36.

Western, Bruce, Leonard M. Lopoo, and Sara McLanahan. 2004. "Incarceration and the Bonds Between Parents in Fragile Families." In *Imprisoning America: The Social Effects of Mass Incarceration*, edited by Mary E. Pattillo, David F. Weiman, and Bruce Western. New York: Russell Sage Foundation.

Western, Bruce, and Becky Pettit. 2005. "Black-White Wage Inequality, Employment Rates, and Incarceration." *American Journal of Sociology* 111(2): 553–78.

Western, Bruce, and Natalie Smith. 2018. "Formerly Incarcerated Parents and Their Children." *Demography* 55(3): 823–47.

Western, Bruce, and Christopher Wildeman. 2009. "The Black Family and Mass Incarceration." *Annals of the American Academy of Political and Social Science 621(1): 221–42.

Wildeman, Christopher. 2009. "Parental Imprisonment, the Prison Boom, and the Concentration of Childhood Disadvantage." *Demography* 46(2): 265–80.

Wildeman, Christopher, Kristin Turney, and Youngmin Yi. 2016. "Paternal Incarceration and Family Functioning Variation across Federal, State, and Local Facilities." *ANNALS of the American Academy of Political and Social Science* 665(1): 80–97.

Zatz, Noah D., and Michael A. Stoll. 2020. "Working to Avoid Incarceration: Jail Threat and Labor Market Outcomes for Noncustodial Fathers Facing Child Support Enforcement." *RSF: The Russell Sage Foundation Journal of the Social Sciences* 6(1): 55–81. DOI: 10.7758/RSF.2020.6.1.03.

# On Thin Ice: Bureaucratic Processes of Monetary Sanctions and Job Insecurity

MICHELE CADIGAN AND GABRIELA KIRK

*Research on court-imposed monetary sanctions has not yet fully examined the impact that processes used to manage court debt have on individuals' lives. Drawing from both interviews and ethnographic data in Illinois and Washington State, we examine how the court's management of justice-related debt affect labor market experiences. We conceptualize these managerial practices as procedural pressure points or mechanisms embedded within these processes that strain individuals' ability to access and maintain stable employment. We find that, as a result, courts undermine their own goal of recouping costs and trap individuals in a cycle of court surveillance.*

**Keywords:** monetary sanctions, procedural hassle, court surveillance, poverty, employment

Research investigating monetary sanctions—the fines, fees, restitution, costs, and surcharges that court systems impose—has revealed the ways these legal financial obligations (LFOs) create precarious conditions for the justice-involved (Harris 2016; Harris, Evans, and Beckett 2010; Edelman 2017). Within a burgeoning literature examining how LFOs shape the lives of those who incur these debts, researchers highlight racial and ethnic differences in amounts imposed (Harris, Evans, and Beckett 2011), sanctions for nonpayment (Bannon, Diller, and Nagrecha 2010; Harris 2016; Friedman and Pattillo 2019), and the financial strain LFO payments can place on poor debtors (Colgan 2018; Beckett and Harris 2011). Researchers also find that the discretion in imposing and collecting monetary sanctions by clerks, judges, and community supervision officers has led to inconsistent and inequitable practices (Alexander et al. 1998; Ruback and Shaffer 2005; Olson and Ramker 2001; Beckett and Harris 2011).

Scholars have yet to examine, however, the

---

**Michele Cadigan** is a PhD candidate in sociology at the University of Washington. **Gabriela Kirk** is a PhD candidate in sociology at Northwestern University.

© 2020 Russell Sage Foundation. Cadigan, Michele, and Gabriela Kirk. 2020. "On Thin Ice: Bureaucratic Processes of Monetary Sanctions and Job Insecurity." *RSF: The Russell Sage Foundation Journal of the Social Sciences* 6(1): 113–31. DOI: 10.7758/RSF.2020.6.1.05. The authors contributed equally to this article and are listed alphabetically. This research was funded by a grant from Arnold Ventures. The PI is Alexes Harris at the University of Washington. We thank Alexes Harris, Charles Camic, Sarah Quinn, and Mary Pattillo for feedback on earlier drafts; and the Multi-State Study of Monetary Sanctions research team, who contributed to the data collection process. Direct correspondence to: Michele Cadigan at mlcadig@uw.edu, 211 Savery Hall, Box 353340, Seattle, WA 98195; and Gabriela Kirk at gabrielakirk2022@u.northwestern.edu, Northwestern University, Department of Sociology, 1810 Chicago Ave., Evanston, IL 60208.

Open Access Policy: *RSF: The Russell Sage Foundation Journal of the Social Sciences* is an open access journal. This article is published under a Creative Commons Attribution-NonCommercial-NoDerivs 3.0 Unported License.

possible destabilizing effects of court processes used for managing payments on those burdened with this debt. Previous work has demonstrated the punishing nature of the court process itself prior to conviction (Feeley 1979; Kohler-Hausmann 2018) and the ways that court surveillance profoundly shapes the lives of the justice-involved (Goffman 2014; Cozzolino 2018; Brayne 2014; Vanhaelemeesch, Vander Beken, and Vandevelde 2014), but it has not discussed the management of court debt as part of this surveillance of individuals over time. Monetary sanctions are a particularly important context in which to examine this process because they can be more enduring and pervasive than other forms of justice system supervision. Focusing on impacts on employment, this study examines how court bureaucratic processes for monitoring and incentivizing payment toward LFOs place pressure and strain on the lives of individuals outside the formal punishment of the debt. For financially strained individuals, access to stable employment is vital to paying off court debt and exiting the criminal justice system (Harris 2016). Thus, when courts use a system for managing payments that strains labor market participation, they undermine their goal of recouping costs and trap individuals in an endless cycle of court surveillance.

Work on the pre-sentencing process has defined procedural hassle as the "burdens and opportunity costs attendant to complying with the legal proceedings" (Kohler-Hausmann 2013, 353). In the case of monetary sanctions, respondents in this study identified particular practices within the court that extracted time and resources beyond the debt itself that constrained their ability to access and maintain stable employment. Drawing from interview data and ethnographic court observations, we conceptualize these particular practices as *procedural pressure points* to pinpoint the mechanisms embedded in the court's process for managing payment that strained labor market experiences and led to this counterproductive system. This concept allows for a more detailed analysis of the specific practices that contribute to procedural hassle, particularly in the post-sentencing process, and enables examination of the unique consequences associated with each practice. Further, by looking at each point within the process separately, we describe how these practices related to each other and affected individuals differently depending on their access to resources such as stable housing and reliable transportation. Three practices emerged as procedural pressure points with unique transaction costs in the courts' debt management process: compliance review hearings, failure to appear (FTA) warrants, and driver's license suspensions for unpaid LFOs. These practices led to missed days of work, made it difficult to get to work on time, and strained individuals' time and resources needed to seek employment.

This article expands the literature that examines the ways criminal justice involvement impedes full and consistent labor market participation—adding a new focus on court administrative processes for debt collection. In addition to adding empirical findings to scholarship on monetary sanctions, the article adds to our understanding of the court system as an institution of surveillance, management, and particularly enduring social control. Even more, these court processes for managing and punishing individuals with court-related debt suggest that this is truly a story of managing and punishing poverty given that we find procedural pressure points disproportionately affect the poor. Criminal justice involvement is both a cause of economic insecurity and a consequence (Wacquant 2001; Western 2002). The imposition of monetary sanctions and the particular processes through which courts attempt to collect them highlight another important mechanism by which penal expansion contributes to inequality for a wide range of individuals.

## COURT MANAGEMENT OF MONETARY SANCTIONS

Monetary sanctions encompass a range of financial penalties the court system imposes. Fines serve as economic sanctions tied directly to particular offenses; restitution is a calculated debt owed to victims for damage or harm inflicted; and fees, assessments, and surcharges are imposed to compensate the state for a defendant's "use" of the court system (Friedman and Pattillo 2019). Initially, LFOs were seen as an alternative and less punitive sanction to incarceration and probation for lower-level offenses (Gordon and Glaser 1991; Hillsman 1990; Ruback and Bergstrom 2006). Today, they are frequently imposed in addition to other sanctions, such as incarceration, community supervision, or mandated treatment (Bannon, Diller, and Nagrecha 2010). This change is in part a result of the rapidly increasing expense of an expanding criminal justice system that has led courts to shift costs onto those arrested and convicted in the form of fees and surcharges (Friedman and Pattillo 2019; Appleman 2016). Although court actors conceptualize discretionary fines and restitution as part of the formal punishment, the various fees, assessments, and surcharges operate often as "hidden sentences" in that court actors view them as falling outside judge-imposed punishment (Kaiser 2016; Martin 2018). Because monetary sanctions often fall on the indignant and those least able to pay, these practices have led to significant unpaid court debt—approximately ten million people in the United States owing more than $50 billion (National Center for Victims of Crime 2011).

Previous scholarship on monetary sanctions centers on the inequalities in imposing these costs and sanctioning noncompliance. We look instead at the inequalities that the systems used to manage payments produce. This focus is in line with another strand of sociological criminal justice research on procedural punishment. Research on court processes has shown simply making court contact, regardless of conviction as the final outcome, instigates procedural obligations that often lead to a loss of time and money for defendants (Kohler-Hausmann 2018; Feeley 1979). Issa Kohler-Hausmann (2018) finds that continued pretrial court appearances for low-level offenses serve as a form of social control and use a managerial model to supervise people over time. These appearances function as performances in which defendants show court actors that they are "governable" and responsible individuals capable of complying with court orders. This procedural hassle and performance are court techniques that operate in lieu of formal punishment, particularly confinement and conviction. Just as social control of misdemeanor justice is unique to its context (Kohler-Hausmann 2013), the forms of social control in monetary sanctions follow their own logics and operate within their own constraints. Although the consequences to employment are similar, this work highlights a different intention of the court in managing individuals over time, in this case, debt collection (Martin 2018).

Previous studies of procedural hassle focus primarily on pre-sentencing processes, but the strain caused by surveillance and sanctions related to community supervision post-sentencing can have similar impacts on people's lives. To varying degrees, probation and parole can extract significant time and resources from individuals by monitoring their compliance with court orders through mandatory check-ins, drug testing, and electronic monitoring (Simon 1993; Petersilia 2003; Werth 2011; Travis 2005). These forms of supervision often claim to help people gain stability, but instead destabilize lives and make finding stable housing and high-quality employment more difficult (Young and Petersilia 2016; Seim and Harding 2020). Those who fail to comply are at risk of violation and additional punishment, including incarceration (Petersilia 2003). Similarly, failing to pay monetary sanctions can trigger an escalation of consequences, including repeated court hearings, sanctions such as jail time, and fines, fees, and interest in addition to the original sentence (Harris 2016; Martin et al. 2018; Friedman and Pattillo 2019).

Interrogating the court processes that manage LFO payment compliance is an important missing piece of this conversation on procedural hassle and managerial justice because it often co-occurs with other forms of punishment and supervision and operates at multiple levels of offenses. Moreover, payment monitoring can persist long after other sanctions, such as parole or probation, have ended (Harris 2016). This study marries the scholarship on procedural punishment and formal sanctioning because monetary sanctions present a case where both operate simultaneously. Just as Michelle Phelps (2013) conceptualizes "back-end net widening" to describe the policies around probation that exacerbate mass incarceration. We demonstrate how court practices used to monitor payment compliance contribute to back-end procedural hassle that does not end with a case disposition and that strains labor market participation of the justice-involved.

Furthermore, examining court management of LFO debt as a process of court surveillance and management of people over time, particularly the poor, highlights the court's role in poverty governance. Poverty governance has been most commonly studied within welfare and social services bureaucracies that work to directly monitor and surveil the poor (Seim 2017; Elliott and Bowen 2018; Soss, Fording, and Schram 2011; Eubanks 2018; Gilliom 2001). Within the criminal legal system, similar arguments of poverty governance have been made regarding the monitoring and enforcement of child support (Cozzolino 2018) and of parole supervision (Seim and Harding 2020; Simon 1993; Werth 2011). Thinking about the court as a bureaucratic institution that manages individuals over time rather than as solely an arbiter of justice changes the way we conceptualize the relationships and interactions between court actors and individuals with LFOs. Current U.S. social control and its form of poverty governance have turned toward "paternalist and custodial approaches to poverty" (Schram, Fording, and Soss 2008, 18) that favor direct administrative oversight and punitive enforcement. In the case of monetary sanctions, we highlight the ongoing monitoring of LFOs as another example of a poverty governance characterized by direct, ongoing surveillance and governance of those who cannot afford to pay their court debts.

## MONETARY SANCTIONS AND EMPLOYMENT

Given that access to financial resources is critical to paying off LFO debt and exiting the court system, the ability of individuals of low socioeconomic status to repay court debts depends on job stability (Harris 2016). The relationship between employment precarity and criminal justice contact has been widely found to contribute to accumulated disadvantage and inequality, particularly among poor and marginalized communities (Travis 2005; Clear 2009; Wakefield and Uggen 2010; National Research Council 2014). Work examining this relationship provides powerful evidence demonstrating that contact with the justice system limits job prospects (Pager 2009; Uggen et al. 2014), lowers long-term earnings (Harding et al. 2017; Western 2002), and shapes labor market participation (Seim and Harding 2020; Harding et al. 2018). Moreover, these effects are disproportionately concentrated and exacerbated among African American and Hispanic communities (Western 2006; Western and Pettit 2005).

Monetary sanctions have an impact on a much wider population of individuals than these previous studies of employment and criminal justice contact have conceptualized. Monetary sanctions are imposed in nearly all cases, including felonies, traffic infractions, and those that include a suspended sentence without formal conviction (Bannon, Diller, and Nagrecha 2010; Harris 2016). In 2011, 26.4 million adults reported being pulled over in a traffic stop; half of them received a citation (Langton and Durose 2013). Combined with the roughly 4.5 million individuals under probation and parole each year and the 2.2 million incarcerated, monetary sanctions reflect a much larger reach of the system given that people in all three groups have likely been sentenced to monetary sanctions (Harris et al. 2017; Kaeble et al. 2016). Scholars have shown that this debt affects employment prospects in various ways—poor credit, wage garnishment, and the prevention of expungement among them (Harris 2016; Harris, Evans, and Beckett 2010). In addition, unpaid LFOs lead to limits on occupational licensing and driver's license suspension, creating additional barriers to accessing a range of employment possibilities (Warner, Kaiser, and Houle 2020). This work has not, however, focused on identifying the specific mechanisms within the court's collection process that reinforce poverty through employment strain. Thus, if LFO management impinges on people's ability to access and maintain stable employment, then this system may be trapping individuals in a cycle of poverty, court surveillance, and direct social control.

## METHODOLOGY

The data for this article were collected as part of the Multi-State Study of Monetary Sanctions.[1] The purpose of the larger project is to deeply examine the process of assessing, monitoring, and recouping criminal justice–related debt and understand the experiences of those burdened with this debt across eight U.S. states. In the collection of these data, strained labor market participation and procedural hassle emerged as salient themes. In this analysis, we draw from data collected in Illinois and Washington State using jurisdictions across each as comparative cases, leveraging differences and similarities to identify nuances and build on existing theories of labor market participation and criminal justice contact (Luker 2008).

Between January 2017 and February 2018, the research team conducted 126 in-depth interviews with residents of Illinois and Washington State who had been sentenced to pay court costs, fines, fees, and restitution resulting from a misdemeanor or felony case (both traffic and criminal charges).[2] In each state, respondents were recruited in multiple counties that varied in size, population density, political affiliation, socioeconomic status, and racial composition. Given differences in court structures and county size, the final sample included seven counties in Illinois and three in Washington State.[3] We recruited this convenience sample of respondents using a range of methods. We hung flyers in courthouses, attorney offices, libraries, local businesses, legal clinics, and nonprofit service organizations in addition to posting advertisements on Craigslist. We also approached individuals in courthouses, community supervision offices, food banks, and reentry programs. A number of respondents were recruited through referrals from other interviewees. We used a standardized screening form with potential respondents to confirm that they had been sentenced to monetary sanctions and to ensure that we recruited individuals with a range of offense types, such as traffic infractions and drug cases, at both the misdemeanor and the felony level. Although we aimed to interview those who were still paying LFOs, we did not exclude those who had completed their payments.

Once recruited, a member of the research team either scheduled a time and location for the interview or conducted the interview at the time of recruitment if the respondent was available. Researchers conducted interviews in private rooms in courthouses or local libraries, in coffee shops and fast food restaurants, in respondents' homes, outside food banks and gas stations, and at local parks. Interviews lasted on average forty-five minutes; participants were compensated for their time with $15 in cash. The interviews were audio recorded and transcribed by a private transcription company. To ensure anonymity, we have changed the names of the respondents and have not named the counties studied. Table 1 presents a breakdown of the demographic information of the final sample of respondents. The two samples were quite similar in terms of gender, income, and employment. The samples differed somewhat by race and ethnicity. The sample was not intended to be representative of individuals sentenced to LFOs because reliable statewide data on the distribution of monetary sanctions were not available (see Martin et al. 2018).

We used a uniform interview protocol that included both survey and open-ended ques-

---

1. The Multi-State Study of Monetary Sanctions is housed at the University of Washington Sociology Department, funded by Arnold Ventures and led by PI Alexes Harris. Illinois and Washington data used here were collected with the approval and support of The Institutional Review Boards of Northwestern University and the University of Washington.

2. Interviews were conducted by the coauthors and Mary Pattillo, Brian Sargent, Frank Edwards, Emmi Obarra, Brandon Alston, Erica Banks, Niamba Baskerville, Brittany Friedman, and Austin Jenkins.

3. Illinois has a unified court system, meaning that only one level of court deals with all cases per county. Our Washington State data include three levels of court: municipal, district, and superior. In two counties, municipal courts manage misdemeanors and gross misdemeanors, district courts handle both misdemeanor and felony cases, and superior courts handle felony and some gross misdemeanor charges. In the third county, a district court handles the misdemeanor and gross misdemeanor cases and a superior court handles felonies. Throughout this article, we refer to the different court systems in Washington as jurisdictions (n = 8) and in Illinois as counties (n = 7).

**Table 1.** Respondent Demographics

|  | IL<br>N = 67<br>Percent | WA<br>N = 59<br>Percent | Total<br>N = 126<br>Percent |
|---|---|---|---|
| **Gender** | | | |
| Female | 58 | 59 | 59 |
| Male | 40 | 37 | 39 |
| Transgender | 1 | 2 | 1 |
| Declined | 0 | 2 | 1 |
| **Race** | | | |
| Black | 55 | 12 | 35 |
| White | 37 | 58 | 48 |
| Asian or Pacific Islander | 1 | 3 | 1 |
| Native American | 0 | 8 | 4 |
| Multiracial or other | 4 | 17 | 10 |
| Declined | 1 | 2 | 2 |
| Latino or Hispanic | 12 | 22 | 16 |
| Income less than $1,500/month | 60 | 68 | 63 |
| **Employment (at time of interview)** | | | |
| Employed | 49 | 49 | 49 |
| Unemployed, but looking | 27 | 27 | 27 |
| Unemployed, not looking | 24 | 24 | 24 |
| **Ever experienced homelessness** | | | |
| Yes | 48 | 64 | 56 |
| Don't know | 10 | 2 | 6 |
| **Criminal case** | | | |
| Felony case | 31 | 15 | 24 |
| Misdemeanor case | 22 | 31 | 26 |
| Both felony and misdemeanor | 46 | 53 | 49 |
| Don't know | 0 | 2 | 1 |

*Source:* Author's calculations.

tions about individuals' current and past experiences with the court system. We asked respondents to report the amount of LFOs they were assessed across their cases, whether they received payment notices, and whether they knew how their LFOs were broken down across fines, fees, interest, restitution, and other costs. Respondents were rarely aware of the breakdown, particularly in instances when they had multiple cases or where they also paid private attorney fees. In Illinois, 78 percent of respondents reported being assessed more than $1,000 in LFOs; of those, 17 percent reported owing more than $10,000. In Washington State, at least 85 percent of respondents reported owing more than $1,000 in LFOs; 48 percent of those individuals reported owing more than $10,000 over the course of their lives.

We asked respondents a series of questions about the impact monetary sanctions had had on their lives financially, materially, and emotionally, including "How have your LFOs affected your ability to get your life in order?," "How much do you worry about your LFOs?," and "How do you make payments?" Particularly in regard to employment, we asked about the respondents' occupation, numbers of hours worked per week, periods of unemployment, and how their criminal record, as well as LFOs in particular, shaped their ability to find a job.

At the time of the interview, 49 percent of respondents were currently employed, 27 percent were unemployed but looking, and 24 percent were unemployed and not looking. Although individuals' current employment statuses were recorded, the focus of the broader research project was on both the present and past impact of monetary sanctions on the lives of individuals with felony and misdemeanor convictions. Thus, the accounts of respondents reflected any impacts to employment rather than solely those on employment at the time of the interview. Many respondents described precarious employment situations, having started new jobs within a few days of their interview, or were recently unemployed.

In addition, we conducted a combined three hundred hours of courtroom observations across the same jurisdictions we recruited respondents. We observed traffic, misdemeanor, and felony proceedings as well as LFO assessment and payment review hearings. We recorded handwritten field notes while observing due to restrictions on recording devices and then later typed these observations. In the field notes, we documented conversations among and between court personnel and individuals with LFOs, case information, general descriptions of the courtrooms, and local court practices. Because discussions regarding ability to pay, sources of income, payment amounts, compliance with LFOs, and payment schedules occur in open court in Illinois and Washington State, we observed a range of cases involving individuals with differential access to financial resources. For example, in Illinois we saw a young woman make a one-time payment of $4,700 on the day of her sentencing and others who struggled to make a $10 payment over multiple visits. These observations also provided insight into the practices used when individuals fail to comply or appear for court.

To analyze the interview data, we identified themes in the transcripts regarding labor market participation and court processes. From there, we constructed a codebook and coded interview transcripts using NVivo 11. Key codes used to analyze our interview data include conversations of employment history, stated struggles with accessing and maintaining employment, experiences attending court, consequences for failure to pay LFOs, discussions about failing to appear at hearings, employer reactions to criminal justice system involvement, access to financial resources, and transportation. Using this coding scheme, we identified both barriers to accessing employment previously captured in the literature as well as several less explored processes related to the court bureaucratic system used to manage LFOs.

Once we had identified these themes among the interview data, we examined the field notes for interactions that reflected similar themes including mentions of employment, requirements for appearance, failure to appear, and consequences for nonpayment. We then wrote analytic memos to describe the similarities and differences in court proceedings within each jurisdiction and summarized the coded data. Although criminal justice systems in Illinois and Washington State operate differently in terms of structure and laws, we came to identify a broadly defined conceptual understanding of procedural pressure points that incorporated the variation within and between states. This concept aims to provide a common vocabulary in which to discuss elements of these processes and the consequences they produce.

## FINDINGS

Across Illinois and Washington State, courts relied on various bureaucratic processes in an effort to manage and monitor collection of LFOs. Fines, fees, restitution, and interest were often but not always managed as a lump sum, blurring the distinction between punishment and administrative costs related to the use of the system. In the post-sentencing process, individuals either paid their LFOs in full or set up a payment plan. If they failed to pay or were inconsistently paying, individuals were notified via mail or in person during hearings that they needed to come back to court to make a payment or explain why they could not do so.[4] Missing payments also triggered driver's li-

---

4. A number of counties and jurisdictions in Illinois and Washington State utilize private collection agencies to collect unpaid LFOs. Based on our knowledge of court processes, debt that has been sent to collections some-

cense suspensions, which for many respondents who choose to drive anyway led to a misdemeanor charge for driving while a license is suspended. Failing to appear at court hearings often led to a failure to appear warrant. Once a warrant was issued, individuals could be arrested, placed in jail, or in Washington State, could file a motion and appear before a judge to have their warrant be quashed for a fee.

Conceptualizing each step of the LFO management process as a procedural point that can be scrutinized allows us to narrow in on the consequences and transaction costs of each decision rather than the process as a whole. Moreover, this concept helps identify particular points in the system of managing payments that are particularly burdensome and counterproductive and thus helps improve court practices and increase people's capacity to be successful postconviction. We focus our discussion here on three procedures intended to enforce and monitor payment: payment review hearings, failing to appear at these hearings, and driver's license suspensions. These procedures and their consequences disrupted labor market participation, particularly for low-income individuals, making it more difficult to pay off debt and further embedding them in systems of justice.

## "It Takes Forever to Get Up Out of There": In-Person Review Hearings

As mentioned, monetary sanctions are a part of nearly every sentence imposed in the jurisdictions studied. Judges in Illinois and Washington State often stated the range of fines that could be imposed for a particular offense prior to the agreed-upon sentence, but rarely specified the amounts of all of the additional court costs and fees out loud. One judge in a rural county in Illinois read, "A class C misdemeanor is punishable by up to thirty days in jail, up to $1,500 fine." Once the negotiated sentence was agreed to, the judge read that the actual sentence was a "$200 fine plus costs and six months of supervision." In this particular county, these costs ranged from an additional $500 to more than $2,000, depending on the offense. In Washington State, although most judges specified some fees during sentencing such as a public defender fee, criminal conviction fee, and a Victim Penalty Assessment fee, additional costs such as interest, community supervision fees, and mandatory drug testing were rarely if ever mentioned. Although fines in both states can be negotiated or waived, some fees and costs are considered mandatory. Evident in the language used in the court, these "costs" are not considered part of the punishment itself, but instead as part of the cost of participating in the system. As Alexes Harris (2016) writes, they reflect a "pay to play" mentality of the court.

Because the amounts of monetary sanctions were often not highlighted as the most notable part of the sentence or plea, many respondents reported not knowing that they had agreed to such a large amount. Janet, a woman interviewed in Illinois, discussed not fully realizing what she was agreeing to before pleading to a sentence that included $3,000 in monetary sanctions. She said at the time her focus was on avoiding jail and exiting the court process as quickly as possible and not on the costs sentenced. "I think it's unfair because when you're in that [situation], you're not thinking logically. You're thinking freedom. And so I'm gonna tell you whatever you want to hear. You want money? All right, as long as you ain't taking me. And then once we're out of the courthouse and I moved on with my life, and you think you granted [sic] this for me without a job, and then want to know why I'm in your courthouse three months later, because you want to know where my money's at." Consistent with work on the pretrial experience (see Feeley 1979), several respondents mentioned quickly pleading to their original cases to avoid having to return to court. Much to their dismay, they soon realized this plea deal did not necessarily mean the end of their court appearances if they were not able to pay their LFOs in a timely manner.

---

times triggers similar court appearances described here, sometimes becomes a civil judgment, and other times does not require any further interactions with the court. The use of these agencies likely creates a different set of obstacles for those unable to pay. A few respondents reported interactions with collection agencies. The processes involved for those who may be paying collection agencies are beyond the scope of these data.

All seven counties studied in Illinois and at least two of eight jurisdictions in Washington State mandated in-person review hearings when the payment of LFOs was not completed in a timely manner. These hearings created an additional and often separate time commitment to other types of court-related appearances, such as probation check-ins, drug treatment appointments, or anger management classes. The frequency of the hearings varied by court, ranging from each week to every few months. The primary purpose of these hearings in Washington State was for judges to gather information to assess when it appeared nonpayment was willful (*Bearden v. Georgia*, 1983).[5] Judges would then use their discretion to decide whether to impose additional punishments for noncompliance. In contrast, judges in Illinois were largely unconcerned with willfulness. Instead, individuals with outstanding LFOs were required to appear before the judge with either some amount of payment or a reason for why they were not making a payment that day. Although judges sometimes threatened to sanction individuals with jail time for missing payments, we rarely observed an individual not already in custody actually sanctioned in either state. Rather, respondents reported they would simply tell the judge that they did not have the money and were given more time and another court date. As a result, these hearings for some individuals went on indefinitely following the case.

Respondents in these jurisdictions aired concerns regarding the strain these hearings placed on their work commitments. Across both states, these payment compliance hearings frequently required individuals to appear at court on time only to wait, sometimes for hours, for their case to be called. Respondents in Illinois commonly complained about judges appearing an hour after the time they had been notified to appear or mentioned needing to wait for the entire court session only to spend a few minutes, or even seconds, dealing with their case. As one respondent in a rural Illinois county lamented, "I don't like this because you have to be here at 8:30 a.m., and he [the judge] don't start calling people until 10:30 a.m., sometimes. It's ridiculous because I've missed a whole day's work for this." These hearings were not scheduled for a specific time on the day's court docket and were mixed in with all of the cases for the day. A respondent in a suburban county in Illinois expressed frustration that other cases were prioritized before her own. "What I don't understand is, you've got people like me that has a job, but yet, I may have done wrong. I own that. But, why is you taking the people sitting in jail, before me? They're not going anywhere. If you release them, they've got all day to be released. Let me get back to work." Although both the frequency of these hearings and the motivation for them varied between and within states, the outcomes were similar in that these additional court appearances directly strained individuals' ability to work.

Respondents in jurisdictions with regularly held review hearings expressed frustration at how repeated court appearances had a direct impact on their earnings and, as a result, their ability to pay off their court debt. Teddy, a man from Illinois who owed around $2,300 across multiple jurisdictions at the time of our interview, reported that taking the day off work affected his ability to make payments toward his monetary sanctions. As he explained, "That's a whole $60 right there that's being taken out of my paycheck because I had to take a day off. That's $160 that could be toward my bills or toward that file they want. It's affecting me." The missed wages as a result of taking time off work ($60) on top of the cost of the LFO payment ($100) impinged on his ability to meet other needs. Previous research notes how court debt itself infringes on individuals' lives. This procedural hassle added another dimension of strain on time, finances, and employment. By way of contrast, Jim from Illinois was able to use a paid vacation day to deal with his payment hearings. He thus characterized these hearings as a mere inconvenience rather than a heavy burden, saying, "I took a paid vacation day to come here and mess with this bull crap. I got ten of them left. I'm good. I'm still getting paid while I'm sitting here talking to you." The level of strain on employment varied by the

---

5. *Bearden v. Georgia*, 461 U.S. 660, 103 S. Ct. 2064, 76 L. Ed.2d 221 (1983).

type of employment and how accommodating that employment could be to these interruptions. For those with paid time off, flexible scheduling, and salaried income, the procedural hassle of these hearings was less disruptive.

Regardless of the flexibility granted by paid time off, several respondents noted that their employers were suspicious as to why they had to continue taking time off to attend court, leading to a strained relationship with employers who might have already accommodated a stigmatizing criminal record. This was the case for Larry, who had been charged with more than $14,000 in fines, fees, restitution, and costs related to a domestic dispute charge. Following a recent job loss, he had fallen behind on his monthly payments of $75 toward his LFOs. This prompted the judge to increase the frequency of his hearings to every two weeks until he caught up, threatening to revoke his conditional discharge and resentence the case with jail or prison time. At the time of the interview, he had caught up enough with his payments that the hearings were scheduled once a month. When asked how his court debt had affected his life, Larry responded, "The employment, not so much really except for when I have to go keep on telling them I have to go to court. That's the big one because they want to know why. What have you done?" These frequent hearings led to attendance issues for him at work that drew suspicion from both his boss and coworkers. He also remarked, "It's the worst thing you have to tell your employer. Well, you're going to court again? Everybody wants to know why you're going to court and I never tell them anything. I go, It's none of your business. It's personal." Not only does missing work because of these hearings carry an opportunity cost, but the frequency of these short payment hearings also strained Larry's relationship with his employer.

The procedural pressure on employment also varied by an individual's financial means and how quickly and easily LFOs could be paid off. Those who could not pay their debts off quickly were often required to attend these hearings over much longer periods or with more frequency than those who could afford regular payments. Respondents who could make only small payments reported needing several years to pay off the debt. In Illinois, the scheduling of these hearings was further complicated by a lack of consideration for ability to pay. Conversations between the judge and the individual with LFOs surrounding payment typically structured expectations for the timing of the next court date rather than any real measurement of financial ability. Al, a forty-four-year-old man in Illinois, described how courtroom interactions typically played out in one small, rural Illinois jurisdiction. "I just hear [the judge], 'Hey, where do you work? You ain't got no money?' [defendant], 'I'll get you next month.' [Judge], 'When [do] you get paid?' [Defendant], 'Oh, I get paid Friday.' [Judge], 'Oh, okay. You owe $200, have it paid off by next Friday.' They have you on a weekly schedule. It's all about money. You know, and it's crazy. You ain't asked that lady if she has five kids to feed." Al's observations of courtroom practices captures the different level of pressure those who struggle to make payments face relative to more financially stable defendants. Chen, a man in Washington State who lived rent free with his wealthy sister and had a flexible work schedule, reported that making payments was never an issue. "I worked more just to get that done faster. I could've worked less and I could still be paying on it now and have it impact my life less in that sense, financially or time wise, but I was just like, you know what, this is a priority. Just get it done and get it out of the way." Chen would typically pay double or triple the minimum payment amount toward his LFOs as he had few other financial responsibilities. Thus he never had to attend a compliance hearing and was debt free within two years of his release from prison. Payment review hearings are then disproportionately straining the employment of those who are most in need of income to pay off their debt and exit the court system.

Payment review hearings functioned as procedural pressure points because they were key moments of bureaucratic procedural hassle in the monetary sanctions system. Although beneficial for avoiding jail and supervision violations and for spreading the payments over time, the constant rescheduling of payment review hearings strained employment, which further perpetuated the cycle of criminal justice contact by decreasing available income to pay off these debts. This pressure was more intense for low-income individuals who could not afford to make regular or large payments toward their LFOs and for those who were paid hourly or who were less able to take time off of work. Additionally, the perpetual nature of these review hearings opened up the possibility for ongoing surveillance and monitoring of those with debt as it often extended their supervision or probation.

## "I Didn't Miss a Payment, I Missed Court": Failing to Appear and Warrants

While payment compliance review hearings shaped employment experiences, failing to appear was even more consequential. Throughout our observations, failure to appear at these hearings often resulted in a bench warrant, which granted the state the authority to arrest and hold an individual in jail either until paying a bond amount or fee determined by a judge or until the next hearing. Imposing such a financial penalty to a warrant is a common practice in other states as well (see Cahill 2012; Flannery and Kretschmar 2012; Diller 2010). These warrants often turned routine traffic stops or other law enforcement interactions into arrests. In some jurisdictions, amounts for FTA bench warrants were set to the amount of outstanding LFOs, or, in one Washington jurisdiction, just the restitution. For some, this meant tens of thousands of dollars—the highest observed bond set for an FTA being $167,882.37 in Washington State. Terrence from Illinois explained the process: "If you owe $2,000, you got a warrant for that. You know what I'm saying? But if you come to court and get, I don't care how much it is, $50, $30, reschedule." Terrence stresses the benefits of coming to court no matter the payment, but respondents missed hearings for a variety of reasons. Research on FTA warrants has found that low-income individuals are at particular risk for receiving these warrants given their limited access to transportation, incomplete information, and competing work or childcare responsibilities (Zettler and Morris 2015; Rosenbaum et al. 2012). By setting bond amounts equal to the outstanding debt, courts attempted to recoup the entirety of what is owed regardless of the financial strain on individuals' lives by forcing them to either pay their LFO balance or stay in jail.

For low-income individuals who could not or did not show up to their compliance review hearings and could not afford to pay the set bond or fee, these warrants resulted in arrests and short stints in jail. These warrants were particularly consequential to employment, as in the case of Darius, a thirty-six-year-old man in Washington State who owed LFOs for a felony conviction and was issued a FTA warrant after missing a payment compliance review hearing. The warrant then resulted in a short stint in jail. He described it this way:

> [This particular county's] LFOs hit me the worst because they have reviews concerning their LFOs. During these reviews, if I'm not able to get notice of the court date, the review date, they immediately put an NCIC [National Crime Information Center] nationwide warrant on you. . . . I was just stopped on a random stop. . . . they arrested me and held me in their county jail for two days. Then I was transported to [the county where I missed my review hearing] and held until my court date for another two days only for the judge to say, "You haven't been making payments." I lost my job. It was very important for me at the time because I had no source of income.

Like many people with felony convictions, Darius had a precarious housing situation. As a result, he missed his summons for court in the mail and subsequently missed his court date. After a warrant was issued and he was arrested and jailed for four days, he lost his job. Being incarcerated, if only for a few days, is shown to have a negative impact on labor market participation (Harding et al. 2018). In Darius's case, being arrested for a FTA cost him his employment and shaped his future ability to make payments toward his court debt. In Illinois, even when these warrants only resulted in being booked for an arrest and avoiding jail, they still led to unexplained absences from work. A few respondents reported driving to work when they were pulled over for a more routine traffic stop only to be taken to jail immediately until they were able to post bond later that day. Overall, FTA warrants for compliance review hearings not only strained labor market participation, but made it more difficult for low-income individuals to make the payments necessary to comply with payment orders.

While some respondents reported they were unable to physically get to hearings, fear over being sanctioned with jail time for nonpayment kept them from coming to court. Scholars find that the threat of incarceration can lead to system avoidance, or purposefully avoiding institutional contact to avoid surveillance and further criminal justice contact (Goffman 2014; Brayne 2014). Chris, a thirty-six-year-old man in Illinois who owed $1,300 at the time of our interview, said he avoided court when he did not have enough money to make payments toward his LFOs. When asked the reason for his most recent warrant, he said, "Not going to court. I'm not going to lie to you, bro. If I don't have at least $15 to $200 in my pocket to give him, I don't go." This system avoidance only increased the likelihood of being served an FTA warrant and jailed as a result. In one jurisdiction in Washington State, multiple respondents reported that the court did not jail people solely for failing to pay their LFOs. However, Angelique, a woman we spoke to at a soup kitchen, told us that she refuses to go to court out of fear of being thrown in jail, despite being summoned multiple times related to nonpayment of her LFOs from a charge of riding public transit without a ticket. The stress of possible jail time, even when it was not likely to occur, was a frequent fear among those unable to pay and those with outstanding debt.

Although not appearing in court often led to the imposition of a warrant, we observed instances when defense attorneys in Washington State successfully made a case that their clients should be given another chance to appear. During one observation, a man who was not present in court had his attorney request to reschedule the hearing rather than issue a warrant: "I have every reason to believe he would come to court," the defense attorney told the judge. "I have always been in good contact with him and his family. I ask that you hold the warrant today and allow him to come back tomorrow. He can come in 10:30 a.m." The 10:30 a.m. docket for the dates the defense attorney proposed were all full, so the judge pushed the attorney to accept a 3:00 p.m. docket. The defense attorney continued, "He is employed between noon and 8:00 p.m. and I'm trying not to interrupt employment if possible." Discussion went on between the judge and attorneys. Then the defense attorney caved: "Okay, we ask that this be set over to the 3:00 p.m. docket tomorrow so he can give his employer enough notice."

Consistent contact with attorneys, checking in with the court, payment history, and a person's record of FTAs often came up in conversations during hearings when attorneys advocated to issue or not issue a bench warrant. Those with unpaid LFOs who were able to stay in contact with their attorneys demonstrated their compliance to the court and then had an advocate who could avoid the issuance of the warrant. However, in multiple Illinois courts, hearings did not require attorneys and thus no one was present to advocate against a warrant if the individual failed to appear. We observed judges at the end of each docket go through the list of no-shows with the prosecutor, setting bond amounts and warrants for those with misdemeanor and felony cases. The presence of defense attorneys is thus important within the process of imposing bench warrants for failing to appear at review hearings, a practice not present across court systems.

## "I'm Already on Thin Ice": Driver's License Suspensions

Courts often use suspending or revoking driver licenses as both a punishment for nonpayment and a mechanism for enforcing the collection of monetary sanctions on a variety of both criminal and traffic cases (Carnegie and Eger 2009). Although this practice has changed rapidly in the past few years because of new legislation and civil suits, millions have had their licenses suspended for failure to pay monetary sanctions (Marsh 2017; Fernandes et al. 2019). These suspensions made it more difficult to get to court and comply with court orders, particularly in rural areas, and led to additional convictions. Conceptualizing driver's license suspensions as a procedural pressure point highlights the ways they affect employment indirectly by exacerbating the procedural hassle of the payment management system.

Research on driver's license suspensions as a result of monetary sanctions notes that this practice has direct impacts on labor market participation by making it difficult to get to work and seek new employment (Carnegie 2007; ACLU 2017). Tammy, a white woman in Washington first became involved in the criminal justice system after she was stopped for speeding and had her license suspended for her inability to pay the traffic fine. As she explained, "[Having a license means] more job opportunities because I could get somewhere where they're paying more or [giving] more hours. Even looking for a job in this area because why would I look for a job across town when that's gonna be a good hour, hour-and-a-half walk every day to and from work." Respondents like Tammy similarly noted that not having a valid license made it more difficult to pay off their monetary sanctions given their diminished employment opportunities. Particularly in rural and suburban communities, the ability to drive was essential to employment. A respondent in rural Illinois remarked, "No public transportation down here. Ain't no buses down here like it is in the city up north. You don't have a car down here, you're basically stuck." Taken together, these respondents point to the difficult choice individuals sanctioned with driver's license suspensions needed to make: drive on a suspended license to get to work or find employment and risk incurring additional misdemeanor charges; or do not drive and constrain their ability to access employment opportunities.

Many of the respondents whose licenses had been suspended chose to drive anyway, some explicitly citing a need to get to work or court as outweighing the risk of incurring new charges. For Rob, a man living in a rural area of Washington State who had a suspended license and about $2,000 in court debt at the time of our interview, driving was a necessity if he was to be able to pay off his LFOs. When asked how not having a driver's license affected him, he responded, "Caused a lot of stress in my life. Worrying about if there's a cop behind me at every corner, every turn, and if I'm going to get pulled over on the way to work and lose my job because I'm not at work because I'm being hauled off to jail or they're towing my car or what not." Individuals in rural areas often spent more time driving, drove farther distances for work, and found themselves on faster interstate highways, increasing the likelihood of being pulled over. In both Illinois and Washington State, driving on a suspended license is a misdemeanor. Thus individuals with unpaid debt related to relatively small traffic tickets could find themselves with new misdemeanor charges on their records if they chose to drive. One individual in the same Washington county estimated that he had about forty convictions for driving while his license was suspended but no other criminal charges in the previous twenty years. These new charges were often accompanied by substantial monetary sanctions and additional fees imposed by the state to reinstate licenses. Respondents in Illinois reported paying between $500 and $3,500 in fines and costs plus an additional $250 reinstatement fee to get their licenses back.

These charges for driver's license suspensions in both states not only came with new LFOs, adding more debt to already delinquent accounts, but also meant more time in court and further exposure to procedural hassle that impinged on employment. Daniel, a thirty-six-year-old African American man in Washington State, owed more than $6,000 in LFOs at the time of our interview and best exemplifies this relationship. After getting pulled over during a routine traffic stop in a rural county, Daniel was charged with driving with a suspended license. Because he lived five hours away from the courthouse, however, without a license he was unable to make his initial court appearance. As a result, a warrant was issued for his arrest and he was picked up in the town where he was living. He was subsequently held for a week and half as he was transported to the jurisdiction that summoned him, missing a significant amount of work. After being released, he was given a new court date. We spoke with him outside of the courthouse right before his new court date, to which his fiancée had driven him.

> I tried to reschedule, but I guess you can't reschedule court dates out there. So they tell me if I couldn't come out here, then basically

I'm going to have a warrant for my arrest. I'm just like, "What the fuck?" I had to call off work and I'm already on thin ice. So I'm pretty sure when I get back to [my job] I might either get suspended for my attendance issue, or fucking fired. But most likely fired, so I'm just like . . . [I live] five hours away. I don't have a license, like you said on top of that I work a full-time job. I'm not going to be able to come out here.

This preconviction procedural hassle mirrors what previous scholars have identified (Feeley 1979; Kohler-Hausmann 2018). However, this particular type of charge is the direct result of the practices courts use to monitor and enforce payments toward LFOs. Driver's license suspensions as a court practice thus increase the strain the court places on employment.

License suspensions can trigger additional court hearings, more opportunities to miss these hearings, and potentially new criminal convictions. Moreover, these hearings occur in addition to payment compliance review hearings and these convictions add more debt to already significant LFOs. This process creates an endless cycle of court appearances, charges, and potential short stints in jail for those who cannot afford to pay off their original LFOs. To pay, these individuals may need to violate the law to maintain their jobs.

Moreover, some employers require a valid driver's license for employment. These jobs are inaccessible to those attempting to earn income to pay off court debts and either exit the system or minimize the number of court appearances required of them. Tim, a self-employed rancher in his thirties in Washington State once convicted of driving under the influence when he was eighteen, explained that, although he understood the difficulty poor individuals face when their licenses are suspended, he could not hire anyone without a valid license. He said, "I'm a business owner, and the first question I ask is do you have your own transportation? [If they don't] then, you're probably not gonna hire that person, because the job still needs to get done. Whenever I don't show up, my horses still have to get fed." Thus, even when individuals chose to drive on a suspended license, our respondents suggested that employers may screen out applicants who cannot produce a valid one.

Although driving license suspensions can facilitate more strain on labor market participation, variation in how jurisdictions handle driving on a suspended license either increased or alleviated some of this strain. For example, Tony in Illinois explained during an interview that after repeatedly driving with a suspended license, his license was revoked. He remarked, "So therefore I was suspended, go to court, fined, didn't have the money, didn't pay the fine. But of course I wanted to keep driving. And I'm driving on the fine so, get another one, then they make it a revoke. A revoke, they make it a felony, there it just adds up and adds up. And before you know it you owe $3,000." Tony didn't know about the very first suspension for a missing emissions sticker. After he was unable to pay the fines for the first misdemeanor charge of driving on a suspended license, the suspensions spiraled. For Tony, the simple act of driving turned into a felony conviction that came with more fines, fees, and procedural hassle. In contrast, a few Washington State courts have recently stopped actively pursuing cases of driving while a license is suspended when the suspension is for unpaid LFOs (ACLU 2017). Although individuals in those locations may still struggle to pay off the initial debt, this prosecutorial practice prevents the cumulative and additive nature of these convictions and LFO debt.

## DISCUSSION AND CONCLUSION

Focusing on procedural pressure points in the justice system's management of monetary sanctions illuminates how different post-sentencing practices work to further surveil and disadvantage the poor. Although the location of these points and the strain on individuals' employment status varied depending on the practices of court systems and individuals' access to resources, the way these pressure points destabilized the employment of those burdened with debt was largely the same. Hearings to review payment compliance were seen as helpful in avoiding additional sanctioning and punishment, but ultimately strained the ability of wage-workers and those with traditional work schedules to maintain steady employment and earnings essential to paying off LFOs. Failing to appear at these hearings was even more consequential for employment because it often resulted in bench warrants, subsequent arrest, and brief incarceration. Suspended driver licenses for failure to pay only exacerbated this strain given that it made attending court hearings and accessing labor markets more difficult. These mechanisms of compliance ultimately undermined the system's stated goals, in this case debt collection, and ensnared low-income individuals in a perpetual system of court surveillance.

Conceptualizing these procedural pressure points embedded in these court surveillance systems may have important implications for other outcomes of interest to criminal justice scholars and policymakers. The pressure to pay off LFOs to escape court surveillance or elude jail time coupled with the multitude of barriers straining access to formal labor markets may push some to illicit markets. Warrants have been shown to motivate some to exit the formal labor market, where risks of detection are heightened, and toward illegal forms of income (Goffman 2014; Brayne 2014). In addition, the frustrating and transactional nature of these hearings may speak to a perceived lack of procedural justice and undermine desistance from crime (Lind and Tyler 1988; Thibaut and Walker 1975). Finally, the strain of procedural pressure points may vary in important ways by race, ethnicity, gender, and family status. Further research is therefore needed to explore such variation in experiences with monetary sanctions.

Some scholars have argued that monetary sanctions can be a useful tool as an alternative to more severe sanctions such as incarceration or community supervision when LFO amounts are kept to a manageable level for indigent individuals (Brett and Nagrecha 2019; Colgan 2019). Using graduated sanctions or day fines, fines calculated based on an individual's income are one way, advocates argue, that courts can assess manageable LFO amounts that enable individuals to exit the court system in a reasonable amount of time (Colgan 2018, 2019; Brett and Nagrecha 2019). Further, when used appropriately, restitution in particular allows individuals to repair harm done to victims or their communities. Researchers have found a link between restitution completion and lower recidivism rates for both adults and juveniles, but only when the payment amounts were financially feasible (Outlaw and Ruback 1999; Colgan 2019; Ervin and Schneider 1990; Jacobs and Moore 1994). Additionally, scholars have called for the elimination of court fees that raise revenue for both the government and the court, instead funding the courts through taxes (Brett and Nagrecha 2019).

Broadly and locally, the landscape of the system of monetary sanctions is rapidly changing. In 2018, Illinois's state legislature passed the Criminal and Traffic Assessment Act to create a sliding scale waiver for individuals whose income is up to 400 percent of the poverty line to limit the burden of court costs and fees from criminal offenses. This waiver eliminates court costs for those below the poverty line. Within Washington State, as a result of the judicial outcomes in the *State of Washington v. Blazina* (2013) and *State of Washington v. Ramirez* (2018), courts are mandated to consider present and future ability to pay when assessing LFOs.[6] In June 2018, the Washington State legislature implemented a new law barring courts from imposing any nonmandatory financial obligations on indigent defendants and discontinued the use of a 12 percent interest rate added to all delinquent fines and fees. These changes indicate a growing concern over the disproportionate burden monetary sanctions places on the poor, but these laws do not automatically apply to those holding outstanding debt prior to these changes. Even more, these efforts to more seriously consider ability to pay when imposing LFOs do not apply to restitution in either state, to punitive fines in Illinois, and mandatory fees in Washington State. Finally, such discussions and reform efforts rarely consider how the pro-

---

6. *State of Washington v. Blazina*, 182 Wn.2d at 839 (May 2013); *State of Washington v. Ramirez*, No. 95249-3 (September 2018).

cess of managing court debt itself can strain labor market participation and thus further impede individuals' ability to pay.

Although some may argue that holding more frequent payment review hearings enables courts to provide individuals with ample opportunity to make a case for their inability to pay and escape formal sanctioning, we find that these practices are counterproductive and affect people's future ability to pay by straining labor market participation. Advocates recently called for ending the practice of issuing warrants for those who fail to appear at nonpayment review hearings and even eliminating court summons for payment notices and nonpayment review hearings overall (Brett and Nagrecha 2019). Having an informal process or mechanism that allows individuals to check in about their payment compliance and request waivers when financial circumstances change could considerably lessen the strain on individuals who work during the court's operating hours or cannot get to court for other reasons. Further, providing access to attorneys to explain payment compliance can help individuals understand their legal options and advocate on their behalf. Finally, decoupling driver's license suspensions from unpaid LFOs could greatly reduce the cyclical and enduring nature of court debt (Fernandes et al. 2019).

This article highlights the important way courts manage people over time and create a cycle of criminal justice embeddedness. Moving forward, research examining how shifting policies around the system of monetary sanctions shapes the lives of individuals, particularly the poor, needs to pay particular attention to not just the amounts imposed, but also the method used to manage payments. This article also contributes to a larger conversation on court surveillance and labor market experiences of the justice-involved. Through the conceptualization of procedural pressure points, we suggest that there are a multitude of ways the justice system shapes the labor market experience of those entrenched in it; these can often be additive. Even with efforts to decarcerate and to destigmatize criminal records, embedment in inefficient systems laden with procedural pressure points would continue to strain the justice-involved.

## REFERENCES

ACLU. 2017. "Driven to Fail: The High Cost of Washington's Most Ineffective Crime—DWLS III." Seattle: American Civil Liberties Union of Washington.

Alexander, David, Jan Montgomery, Geoff Hamilton, Darryl Dutton, and Richard Griswold. 1998. "Fines and Restitution: Improvement Needed in How Offenders' Payment Schedules Are Determined: Report to the Chairman, Senate Committee on the Judiciary, and the Chairman, Subcommittee on Crime, House Committee on the Judiciary." GAO/GGD-98-89. Washington: U.S. Government Accountability Office.

Appleman, Laura I. 2016. "Nickel and Dimed into Incarceration: Cash Register Justice in the Criminal System." *Boston College Law Review* 57(5): 1483.

Bannon, Alicia, Rebekah Diller, and Mitali Nagrecha. 2010. "Criminal Justice Debt: A Barrier to Reentry." New York: Brennan Center for Justice.

Beckett, Katherine, and Alexes Harris. 2011. "On Cash and Conviction." *Criminology & Public Policy* 10(3): 509–37.

Brayne, Sarah. 2014. "Surveillance and System Avoidance: Criminal Justice Contact and Institutional Attachment." *American Sociological Review* 79(3): 367–91.

Brett, Sharon, and Mitali Nagrecha. 2019. "Proportionate Financial Sanctions: Policy Prescriptions for Judicial Reform." Cambridge, Mass.: Harvard Law School, Criminal Justice Policy Program.

Cahill, Meagan. 2012. "Focusing on the Individual in Warrant-Clearing Efforts." *Criminology & Public Policy* 11(3): 473–82.

Carnegie, Jon. 2007. "Driver's License Suspensions, Impacts and Fairness Study." FHWA NJ-2007-020. New Brunswick: New Jersey Department of Transportation.

Carnegie, Jon, and Robert Eger III. 2009. "Reasons for Drivers License Suspension, Recidivism and Crash Involvement Among Suspended/Revoked Drivers." Washington, D.C.: American Association of Motor Vehicle Administrators.

Clear, Todd R. 2009. *Imprisoning Communities: How Mass Incarceration Makes Disadvantaged Neighborhoods Worse.* Oxford: Oxford University Press.

Colgan, Beth A. 2018. "The Excessive Fines Clause: Challenging the Modern Debtors' Prison." *UCLA Law Review* 65(1): 2.

———. 2019. "Addressing Modern Debtors' Prisons with Graduated Economic Sanctions That Depend on Ability to Pay." The Hamilton Project. Washington, D.C.: Brookings Institution.

Cozzolino, Elizabeth. 2018. "Public Assistance, Relationship Context, and Jail for Child Support Debt." *Socius* 4(1): 1–25.

Diller, Rebekah. 2010. "The Hidden Costs of Florida's Criminal Justice Fees." New York: Brennan Center for Justice.

Edelman, Peter. 2017. *Not a Crime to Be Poor: The Criminalization of Poverty in America*. New York: The New Press.

Elliott, Sinikka, and Sarah Bowen. 2018. "Defending Motherhood: Morality, Responsibility, and Double Binds in Feeding Children." *Journal of Marriage and Family* 80(2): 499–520.

Ervin, Laurie, and Anne Schneider. 1990. "Explaining the Effects of Restitution on Offenders: Results from a National Experiment in Juvenile Courts." In *Criminal Justice, Restitution, and Reconciliation*, edited by Joe Hudson and Burt Galaway. Monsey, N.Y.: Criminal Justice Press/Willow Tree Press.

Eubanks, Virginia. 2018. *Automating Inequality: How High-Tech Tools Profile, Police, and Punish the Poor*. New York: St. Martin's Press.

Feeley, Malcolm. 1979. *The Process Is the Punishment: Handling Cases in a Lower Criminal Court*. New York: Russell Sage Foundation.

Fernandes, April, Michele Cadigan, Frank Edwards, and Alexes Harris. 2019. "Monetary Sanctions: A Review of Revenue Generation, Legal Challenges, and Reform." *Law & Social Sciences Review* 15(1): 397–413.

Flannery, Daniel, and Jeff Kretschmar. 2012. "Fugitive Safe Surrender: Program Description, Initial Findings, and Policy Implications." *Criminology & Public Policy* 11(3): 437–59.

Friedman, Brittany, and Mary Pattillo. 2019. "Statutory Inequality: The Logics of Monetary Sanctions in State Law." *RSF: The Russell Sage Foundation Journal of the Social Sciences* 5(1): 174–96. DOI: 10.7758/RSF.2019.5.1.08.

Gilliom, John. 2001. *Overseers of the Poor*. Chicago: University of Chicago Press.

Goffman, Alice. 2014. *On the Run: Fugitive Life in an American City*. Chicago: University of Chicago Press.

Gordon, Margaret A., and Daniel Glaser. 1991. "The Use and Effects of Financial Penalties in Municipal Courts." *Criminology* 29(4): 651–76.

Harding, David J., Jeffrey D. Morenoff, Anh P. Nguyen, and Shawn D. Bushway. 2017. "Short- and Long-Term Effects of Imprisonment on Future Felony Convictions and Prison Admissions." *Proceedings of the National Academy of Sciences* 114(42): 11103–108.

———. 2018. "Imprisonment and Labor Market Outcomes: Evidence from a Natural Experiment." *American Journal of Sociology* 124(1): 49–110.

Harris, Alexes. 2016. *A Pound of Flesh: Monetary Sanctions as Punishment for the Poor*. New York: Russell Sage Foundation.

Harris, Alexes, Heather Evans, and Katherine Beckett. 2010. "Drawing Blood from Stones: Legal Debt and Social Inequality in the Contemporary United States." *American Journal of Sociology* 115(6): 1753–99.

———. 2011. "Courtesy Stigma and Monetary Sanctions: Toward a Socio-Cultural Theory of Punishment." *American Sociological Review* 76(2): 234–64.

Harris, Alexes, Beth M. Huebner, Karin D. Martin, Mary Pattillo, Becky Pettit, Sarah Shannon, Bryan L. Sykes, Christopher Uggen, and April Fernandes. 2017. "Monetary Sanctions in the Criminal Justice System." New York: Laura and John Arnold Foundation.

Hillsman, Sally T. 1990. "Fines and Day Fines." *Crime and Justice* 12 (January): 49–98.

Jacobs, Susan, and David C. Moore. 1994. "Successful Restitution as a Predictor of Juvenile Recidivism." *Juvenile and Family Court Journal* 45(1): 3–14.

Kaeble, Danielle, Lauren Glaze, Anastasios Tsoutis, and Todd Minton. 2016. "Correctional Populations in the United States, 2014." NCJ 249513. Washington: U.S. Department of Justice.

Kaiser, Joshua. 2016. "Revealing the Hidden Sentence: How to Add Transparency, Legitimacy, and Purpose to Collateral Punishment Policy." *Harvard Law & Policy Review* 10(1): 123–84.

Kohler-Hausmann, Issa. 2013. "Misdemeanor Justice: Control Without Conviction." *American Journal of Sociology* 119(2): 351–93.

———. 2018. *Misdemeanorland: Criminal Courts and Social Control in an Age of Broken Windows Policing*. Princeton, N.J.: Princeton University Press.

Langton, Lynn, and Matthew Durose. 2013. "Police Behavior During Traffic and Street Stops, 2011." NCJ 242937. Washington: U.S. Department of Justice.

Lind, E. Allan, and Tom R. Tyler. 1988. *The Social*

Psychology of Procedural Justice. New York: Plenum Press.

Luker, Kristin. 2008. *Salsa Dancing into the Social Sciences: Research in an Age of Info-Glut*. Cambridge, Mass: Harvard University Press.

Marsh, Andrea. 2017. "Rethinking Driver's License Suspensions for Nonpayment of Fines and Fees." Williamsburg, Va.: National Center for State Courts.

Martin, Karin D. 2018. "Monetary Myopia: An Examination of Institutional Response to Revenue from Monetary Sanctions for Misdemeanors." *Criminal Justice Policy Review* 29(6-7): 630-62.

Martin, Karin D., Bryan L. Sykes, Sarah Shannon, Frank Edwards, and Alexes Harris. 2018. "Monetary Sanctions: Legal Financial Obligations in US Systems of Justice." *Annual Review of Criminology* 1(1): 471-95.

National Center for Victims of Crime. 2011. "Making Restitution Real: Five Case Studies on Improving Restitution Collection." Washington, D.C.: National Center for Victims of Crime.

National Research Council. 2014. *The Growth of Incarceration in the United States: Exploring Causes and Consequences*. Washington, D.C.: National Academies Press.

Olson, David E., and Gerard F. Ramker. 2001. "Crime Does Not Pay, But Criminals May: Factors Influencing the Imposition and Collection of Probation Fees." *Justice System Journal* 22(1): 29-46.

Outlaw, Maureen C., and R. Barry Ruback. 1999. "Predictors and Outcomes of Victim Restitution Orders." *Justice Quarterly* 16(4): 847-69.

Pager, Devah. 2009. *Marked: Race, Crime, and Finding Work in an Era of Mass Incarceration*, reprint ed. Chicago: University of Chicago Press.

Petersilia, Joan. 2003. *When Prisoners Come Home: Parole and Prisoner Reentry*. Oxford: Oxford University Press.

Phelps, Michelle S. 2013. "The Paradox of Probation: Community Supervision in the Age of Mass Incarceration." *Law & Policy* 35(1-2): 51-80.

Rosenbaum, David, Nicole Hutsell, Alan Tomkins, Brian Bornstein, Mitchel Herian, and Elizabeth Neeley. 2012. "Court Date Reminder Postcards: A Benefit-Cost Analysis of Using Reminder Cards to Reduce Failure to Appear Rates." *Judicature* 95(4): 177-87.

Ruback, R. Barry, and Mark H. Bergstrom. 2006. "Economic Sanctions in Criminal Justice: Purposes, Effects, and Implications." *Criminal Justice and Behavior* 33(2): 242-73.

Ruback, R. Barry, and Jennifer N. Shaffer. 2005. "The Role of Victim-Related Factors in Victim Restitution: A Multi-Method Analysis of Restitution in Pennsylvania." *Law and Human Behavior* 29(6): 657-81.

Schram, Sanford F., Richard C. Fording, and Joe Soss. 2008. "Neo-Liberal Poverty Governance: Race, Place and the Punitive Turn in US Welfare Policy." *Cambridge Journal of Regions, Economy and Society* 1(1): 17-36.

Seim, Josh. 2017. "The Ambulance: Toward a Labor Theory of Poverty Governance." *American Sociological Review* 82(3): 451-75.

Seim, Josh, and David J. Harding. 2020. "Parolefare: Post-prison Supervision and Low-Wage Work." *RSF: The Russell Sage Foundation Journal of the Social Sciences* 6(1): 173-95. DOI: 10.7758/RSF.2020.6.1.08.

Simon, Jonathan. 1993. *Poor Discipline: Parole and the Social Control of the Underclass, 1890-1990*. Chicago: University of Chicago.

Soss, Joe, Richard C. Fording, and Sanford F. Schram. 2011. *Disciplining the Poor: Neoliberal Paternalism and the Persistent Power of Race*. Chicago: University of Chicago Press.

Thibaut, John W., and Laurens Walker. 1975. *Procedural Justice: A Psychological Analysis*. Hillsdale, N.J.: Lawrence Erlbaum.

Travis, Jeremy. 2005. *But They All Come Back: Facing the Challenges of Prisoner Reentry*. Washington, D.C.: The Urban Institute.

Uggen, Christopher, Mike Vuolo, Sarah Lageson, Ebony Ruhland, and Hilary K. Whitham. 2014. "The Edge of Stigma: An Experimental Audit of the Effects of Low-Level Criminal Records on Employment." *Criminology* 52(4): 627-54.

Vanhaelemeesch, Delphine, Tom Vander Beken, and Stijn Vandevelde. 2014. "Punishment at Home: Offenders' Experiences with Electronic Monitoring." *European Journal of Criminology* 11(3): 273-87.

Wacquant, Loïc. 2001. "The Penalisation of Poverty and the Rise of Neo-Liberalism." *European Journal on Criminal Policy and Research* 9(4): 401-12.

Wakefield, Sara, and Christopher Uggen. 2010. "Incarceration and Stratification." *Annual Review of Sociology* 36(1): 387-406.

Warner, Cody, Joshua Kaiser, and Jason N. Houle.

2020. "Locked Out of the Labor Market? State-Level Hidden Sentences and the Labor-Market Outcomes of Recently Incarcerated Young Adults." *RSF: The Russell Sage Foundation Journal of the Social Sciences* 6(1): 132–51. DOI: 10.7758/RSF.2020.6.1.06

Werth, Robert. 2011. "I Do What I'm Told, Sort of: Reformed Subjects, Unruly Citizens, and Parole." *Theoretical Criminology* 16(3): 329–46.

Western, Bruce. 2002. "The Impact of Incarceration on Wage Mobility and Inequality." *American Sociological Review* 67(4): 526–46.

———. 2006. *Punishment and Inequality in America*. New York: Russell Sage Foundation.

Western, Bruce, and Becky Pettit. 2005. "Black-White Wage Inequality, Employment Rates, and Incarceration." *American Journal of Sociology* 111(2): 553–78.

Young, Kathryne M., and Joan Petersilia. 2016. "Keeping Track: Surveillance, Control, and the Expansion of the Carceral State." *Harvard Law Review* 129(5): 1318–60.

Zettler, Haley R., and Robert G. Morris. 2015. "An Exploratory Assessment of Race and Gender-Specific Predictors of Failure to Appear in Court Among Defendants Released via a Pretrial Services Agency." *Criminal Justice Review* 40(4): 417–30.

# Locked Out of the Labor Market? State-Level Hidden Sentences and the Labor Market Outcomes of Recently Incarcerated Young Adults

CODY WARNER, JOSHUA KAISER, AND JASON N. HOULE

A long literature attests to labor market penalties for having a criminal record. No research, however, has explored whether state-level policies that restrict social participation of the justice-involved contribute to these labor market consequences. Such policies, or hidden sentences, have clear implications for labor market outcomes but are difficult to measure. In this article, we leverage a combination of nationally representative individual data and state-level data on hidden sentences to ask whether the labor market penalties of incarceration are contingent on a state's hidden sentence regime in young adulthood. Our results demonstrate that living in a state with moderate and high hidden sentences exacerbates the labor market consequences of incarceration, and that this pattern may contribute to racial disparities in labor market outcomes following incarceration.

**Keywords:** incarceration, employment, earnings, hidden sentences

An extensive body of research focuses on whether contact with the penal system, and incarceration in particular, is a barrier to the labor market. Results of this work have shown that incarceration restricts employment (Pager 2003, 2007), reduces earnings (Lyons and Pettit 2011; Western 2002), and increases the risk of dropping out of the labor force (Apel and Sweeten 2010; Western and Pettit 2005). Given the concentration of incarceration among young men of color, research is increasingly considering heterogeneity in the labor market consequences of incarceration by race and ethnicity (Apel and Powell 2019; Lyons and Pettit 2011; Pager 2007; Western and Sirois 2018). Less research, however, has considered the relevance of state-level laws and social policies that may amplify or dampen the labor market consequences of criminal justice contact.

Our study advances this literature in two ways. First, we ask whether an often-discussed but rarely measured feature of state punishment regimes contributes to disparities in labor market outcomes by criminal justice contact among young adults. In particular, scholars frequently argue that federal and state policies

**Cody Warner** is associate professor in the Department of Sociology and Anthropology at Montana State University. **Joshua Kaiser** is resident scholar in sociology at Dartmouth College. **Jason N. Houle** is associate professor in sociology at Dartmouth College.

© 2020 Russell Sage Foundation. Warner, Cody, Joshua Kaiser, and Jason N. Houle. 2020. "Locked Out of the Labor Market? State-Level Hidden Sentences and the Labor Market Outcomes of Recently Incarcerated Young Adults." *RSF: The Russell Sage Foundation Journal of the Social Sciences* 6(1): 132–51. DOI: 10.7758/RSF .2020.6.1.06. Direct correspondence to: Cody Warner at cody.warner@montana.edu, Montana State University, Department of Sociology and Anthropology, 2-128 Wilson Hall, Bozeman, MT 59717.

Open Access Policy: *RSF: The Russell Sage Foundation Journal of the Social Sciences* is an open access journal. This article is published under a Creative Commons Attribution-NonCommercial-NoDerivs 3.0 Unported License.

restricting occupational licensing and employment options for the justice-involved are mechanisms linking incarceration to labor market disparities (see, for example, Western 2002, 528). These penalties (what we call hidden sentences) apply largely outside of or in addition to the judge-issued, criminal law sanctions (such as probation or imprisonment) tied to criminal convictions (Kaiser 2016). Some of the more well-known hidden sentences are those that restrict voting rights, restrict access to public or subsidized housing, restrict access to welfare benefits, or create legal financial obligations through fines and fees (ABA 2013; Geller and Curtis 2011; Harris 2016; Uggen and Manza 2002). These policies and restrictions have the potential to restrict labor market participation, but the relationship between hidden sentences and the labor market outcomes of the justice-involved has not been examined.

Second, we focus specifically on the relevance of incarceration and hidden sentences during the young adult years (twenty-five to thirty), for a cohort who came of age during the era of mass incarceration. This is an important time frame for both labor market outcomes and risk of criminal justice contact and incarceration. In young adulthood, early career experiences lay the foundation for future employment and earnings trajectories, and set the stage for advantage or disadvantage to accumulate across the life course (Blau and Duncan 1967; Cheng 2014; DiPrete and Eirich 2006). Young people transitioning to adulthood are also prime targets for incarceration and other forms of criminal justice contact, especially young men of color; and this contact has the potential to create lasting consequences for a range of outcomes, including labor market participation (Steinberg, Chung, and Little 2004; Wakefield and Apel 2016).

Thus, we ask whether hidden sentences are linked with labor market outcomes (employment and earnings), whether hidden sentences exacerbate the consequences of incarceration during young adulthood, and whether the association between hidden sentences and labor market outcomes varies by race-ethnicity. Our core results are based on a combination of individual data from the 1997 cohort of the National Longitudinal Survey of Youth (NLSY97) and state-level data on hidden sentences derived from the National Inventory of Collateral Consequences of Conviction (NICCC). Taken together, our findings advance existing research by bridging the literatures on the effects of incarceration on inequality (Wakefield and Uggen 2010) and on state policies that create and sustain collateral consequences (Harris 2016; Kaiser 2016; Uggen and Manza 2002).

## INCARCERATION, RACE, AND LABOR MARKET OUTCOMES IN YOUNG ADULTHOOD

The labor market consequences of criminal justice contact have received a great deal of scrutiny. The bulk of this evidence shows that individuals struggle in the labor market following incarceration.[1] For example, audit studies show that callback rates for individuals with a criminal record are substantially lower than for individuals with no record (Pager 2003). Studies based on survey data have found an incarceration penalty on employment ranging from 10 to 30 percent, and a wage penalty of 10 to 40 percent (Apel and Sweeten 2010; Western 2002, 2006; Raphael 2007). Evidence also indicates that the labor market consequences of incarceration are not uniform, with several studies exploring heterogeneity by race-ethnicity. Devah Pager (2007) argues that a criminal record reinforces racial stereotypes, especially among black males, and intensifies the stigma of incarceration. For example, relative to formerly incarcerated whites, blacks have lower rates of labor market participation after prison and experience slower post-prison wage growth that extends well beyond the period of incarceration (Apel and Powell 2019; Lyons and Pettit 2011; Western and Sirois 2018).

Incarceration is conceptualized as a turning point in the life course that disrupts adult development, the effects of which reverberate and accumulate as people age (Pettit and Western

---

1. Studies based on matching administrative data on incarceration with data from unemployment insurance systems do not always find negative effects of incarceration, and some have found short-term positive effects (Travis and Western 2014).

2004; Sampson and Laub 1992; Western 2002). After decades of growth, incarceration has become an increasingly common feature of the transition to adulthood among disadvantaged segments of the population (Pettit and Western 2004). It is important to examine the labor market consequences of criminal justice contact during the transition to adulthood because it is a period when risk of incarceration peaks and labor market inequalities start to emerge (Cheng 2014; Pettit and Western 2004). Incarceration during this critical stage can therefore contribute to a pattern of cumulative disadvantage in the worlds of education, work, and interpersonal relationships (Steinberg, Chung, and Little 2004; Western 2002).

Three primary mechanisms have been proposed to account for the labor market consequences of incarceration: selection, incapacitation, and stigma. According to the selection explanation, incarceration has no independent effect on labor market outcomes, but rather the criminal justice system disproportionately "selects" individuals who are not willing or able to hold down work (Pager 2007). Evidence is clear that formerly incarcerated individuals—even in the absence of incarceration—would struggle to be competitive in the labor market (Western 2006). But it is also the case that exposure to incarceration (that is, incapacitation) can fundamentally alter an individual's employability through gaps in work history, loss of job skills, and the loss of the informal social networks often pivotal for landing employment. Finally, a criminal record works as a negative credential that prohibits labor market participation through social stigma and formal exclusion. Pager (2003) refers to a criminal record as a "status mark of dishonor," impacting how employers view the reputation, reliability, and trustworthiness of those with a criminal record, black males in particular. In support of this, large shares of employers, when prompted, report that they would not knowingly hire someone with a criminal record (Holzer 1996). Thus, even though the criminal justice system disproportionally selects those who may struggle in the labor market, the evidence is clear that going to prison contributes to larger patterns of labor market disadvantage.

A criminal record is disqualifying not only because of incapacitation or informal exclusion through social stigma, but also for the formal, state-imposed sanctions that create barriers to full societal participation. This kind of exclusion, outlined in the following section, is often discussed but rarely directly measured, either as direct exclusion in the labor market or as a broader collection of policies that alter and limit participation in other social and economic spheres (Miller and Stuart 2017; Petersilia 2003; Travis 2002).

## HIDDEN SENTENCES AS LABOR MARKET BARRIERS

As of 2015, more than thirty-five thousand laws across the United States impose more than forty thousand penalties on the justice-involved beyond visible forms of punishment like imprisonment and probation (Kaiser 2016). These policies restrict those with a criminal record from working certain types of jobs entirely or obtaining necessary certifications, from holding a driver's license or voting, from receiving financial aid or government benefits, and from numerous other social and economic activities (Petersilia 2003; Travis 2002). Researchers refer to such policies using varying definitions and terms, including collateral consequences, collateral sanctions, civil disabilities, and invisible punishments (Chin 2011; Travis 2002; Uggen and Stewart 2014; Whittle 2018). Following Joshua Kaiser (2016), we adopt the terminology of *hidden sentences* to emphasize first, that these policies are state-imposed punishments based on a variety of criminal labels, such as conviction, indictment, or an arrest record (Chin 2011; Whittle 2018), and, second, that they are distinct from visible sentences largely because legal processes keep them obscured to different degrees throughout public and private spheres (Kaiser 2016; Travis 2002). Hidden sentences have the potential to affect individual labor market outcomes in three ways: direct restrictions on employment-related rights and privileges; indirect restrictions on employment through limits on other kinds of citizenship rights and social participation; and informal filters on the labor market due to overwhelming experiences of administrative burden, uncertainty, and stigmatization.

First, hidden sentences can limit access either to certain kinds of employment directly or to the occupational and business licenses necessary to them (Pager 2007; Petersilia 2003; Travis 2002). For example, felony convictions automatically exclude individuals from licenses in various medical occupations, barbering and beautician services, independent contracting, and other fields, and several kinds of convictions can create bans from public office, law enforcement, and segments of the civil service. In addition, many employers and certifiers, such as state bars or accounting boards, are empowered to exclude based on indictments, arrests, or other kinds of criminal justice contact. Second, hidden sentences that limit other citizenship rights and restrict societal participation can create barriers in the labor market. For instance, hidden sentences that curtail driver's licenses can both prohibit the justice-involved from delivery services, commercial trucking, and other employment that requires driving, and restrict where and when individuals can work. Indeed, Michele Cadigan and Gabriela Kirk (2020) document how driver's license suspensions, as a postconviction mechanism used to collect legal fines and fees, can affect labor market participation because of subsequent difficulties traveling to court hearings or places of employment. Hidden sentences that impose residence restrictions or prohibit even the ability to be present in certain locations (such as schools or day cares) also limit employment options (Beckett and Herbert 2010). Restrictions on firearms can prevent even nonviolent offenders from serving in private investigations and security, and disfranchisement can make the justice-involved unqualified to serve in some public employment even when other hidden sentences do not (Stavsky 2002; Uggen and Manza 2002).

Hidden sentences also enable employers and occupational gatekeepers (along with landlords, lenders, and other private parties) to run background checks and empower them to use arrest and conviction histories as factors in hiring, firing, and other employment decisions—thereby enabling the social stigma that puts the justice-involved at a disadvantage in the labor market (Pager 2003, 2007; Uggen et al. 2014). These more comprehensive employment barriers are often based on the broadest criminal labels. Such background checks and general criminal offense registries frequently include misdemeanors, drug and public order offenses, and arrests or indictments that never lead to convictions.

Third, state hidden sentences can affect how individuals approach and experience the labor market through administrative burden. As a policy regime increases in sheer size and complexity, so do the learning costs, compliance costs, and psychological costs of participating in the relevant programs or activities (Herd and Moynihan 2019). The result is a system of barriers that often cause avoidance, noncompliance, or participation in ways that are not predicted by a straightforward reading of the policies themselves. Research on the welfare state and economic regulation shows that the administrative burden of a particular policy regime can have negative impacts on participation in educational applications and financial aid (Hoxby and Turner 2015), immigration and nationalization (Heinrich 2018), voting and voter registration (Burden et al. 2014), medical insurance (Moynihan, Herd, and Ribgy 2016), and other social and economic activities.

Hidden sentence regimes can create similar experiences of administrative burden and therefore alter labor market participation in ways beyond formal restrictions themselves. Unlike the civil death laws of the past that excluded felons from society with a single law, hidden sentence regimes impact employment and citizenship status through a myriad of restrictions that vary by state and offense type, that apply under different circumstances and for different lengths of time, that encompass activities that are very narrow (for example, wool dealing or particular educational loans) or extremely broad (for example, all public employment in a state), and that depend on various employers' and other decision-makers' discretion (Ewald 2012; Kaiser 2016). As a result, these restrictions may "pile on" to create a hopelessly tangled policy of restrictions that take their toll one after another and can carry extreme compliance costs and offer very little benefit (Uggen and Stewart 2014). As a result, we expect the size and complexity of a state's hidden sentence regime alone to amplify its impact on labor market outcomes.

Hidden sentences as a form of state surveillance may also create stigma and result in avoidance of formal institutions. Research shows that surveillance and coercion policies are so pervasive that individuals often avoid public institutions altogether, often in fear that interacting with institutions such as hospitals or banks can increase surveillance and lead to apprehension by authorities (Brayne 2014; Remster and Kramer 2018). Indeed, surveillance policies themselves are frequently associated with increasing levels of administrative burden (Waldo, Lin, and Millett 2007).

Finally, hidden sentence policies have the potential to play a role in larger patterns of racial inequality. Government policies can either narrow or widen gaps in broad outcomes, including the labor market. Affirmative action programs, for example, contributed to a narrowing of wage inequality between whites and blacks (see Lyons and Pettit 2011, 258). On the other hand, the expansion of the criminal justice system is often conceptualized as a broader policy approach that has widened racial inequality. Given how common criminal justice contact is in the lives of minority citizens, and thus the accompanying hidden sentences, it is thus plausible that any exclusion created by hidden sentences could contribute to racial inequalities.

In sum, in this article we contribute to the large and growing literature on the labor market consequences of incarceration during young adulthood and consider whether and how state-level hidden sentence regimes are implicated in this relationship. Specifically, we ask how and to what extent state-level hidden sentences are responsible for producing inequalities in labor market outcomes between those with and without a history of incarceration. We ask three key research questions. First, are state-level hidden sentences associated with labor market outcomes among justice-involved young adults, net of other individual and state-level characteristics? Second, are disparities in labor market outcomes by incarceration status larger in states with more punitive hidden sentences? And, third, is there evidence that state-level hidden sentences are more consequential for justice-involved young adults of color than white young adults?

## DATA AND APPROACH

To answer these questions, we draw data from several sources. Individual-level data are drawn from the 1997 cohort of the National Longitudinal Survey of Youth (NLSY97), a nationally representative longitudinal dataset that has regularly surveyed a cohort of American young adults born between 1980 and 1984. Respondents have been interviewed a maximum of seventeen times since the first interview in 1997, and were age thirty to thirty-six at the most recent round of data collection. The data have been used to examine the impact of incarceration and other forms of criminal justice contact on a variety of outcomes, including earnings and labor market participation (Apel and Powell 2019; Apel and Sweeten 2010). To capture state-level hidden sentences, we use data from the National Inventory of the Collateral Consequence of Conviction (NICCC), a collaborative effort of the American Bar Association and the National Institute of Justice that identifies all postconviction hidden sentences in all U.S. jurisdictions. The database covers a range of hidden sentences, including those related to employment, occupational licensing, housing, voting, and education (for more information on the NICCC, see Kaiser 2016, 129).[2] Finally, we capture other potentially relevant state-level characteristics (see below) by drawing on data from the U.S. Census, American Community Survey, Bureau of Justice Statistics, and the University of Kentucky Center for Poverty Research. These state-level data are linked to a restricted version of the NLSY97 that includes state of residence identifiers for respondents.

For all individual-level dependent and independent variables, we standardize the data by age to focus on a specific period of young adulthood, from age twenty-five to age thirty. We focus on this range for two reasons: first, because most young adults in this age range have completed their education, begun their transition to adulthood, entered the workforce, and attempted to begin their adult careers (Danziger and Ratner 2010); and, second, to be consistent

2. See also the NICCC website, https://niccc.csgjusticecenter.org (accessed September 27, 2019).

with research on labor market outcomes in the transition to adulthood, which also focuses on young adults within this age range (Danziger and Ratner 2010; Silva 2012; Sironi 2018; Swartz, McLaughlin, and Mortimer 2017). By 2015, the last round of data collection, all NLSY97 respondents are at least thirty years old; research has established that the period of young adulthood is pivotal is establishing earnings trajectories and inequalities (Rindfuss 1991). Employment information is available for 7,599 respondents at or around the age thirty interview, and earnings are available for 7,505 respondents. We use listwise deletion on dependent and independent variables to omit a total of 1,818 respondents from the analyses, leaving us with a sample of 7,166.

## Labor Market Outcomes

Our focal dependent variables are labor market indicators of any employment, full-time employment, and earnings at age thirty. Given that much employment after prison is fleeting and informal (Western and Sirois 2018), our first dependent variable is a dichotomous variable coded 1 if respondents reported, at the age thirty interview, that they were employed in any month since the previous interview. Full-time employment is a dichotomous variable coded 1 if respondents reported working an average of thirty-five hours or more per week for at least half of the preceding year at the age thirty interview. Respondents reported wages from salary, commissions, and tips at the age thirty interview. We adjust wages for inflation and report in constant 2010 dollars and log transform wages to reduce heteroskedasticity.

## Criminal Justice Contact

At each wave of data collection, NLSY97 respondents provide detailed information on criminal justice contact and subsequent processing since the previous interview. Respondents are first asked whether they have been arrested since the last interview, and, if applicable, follow-up questions about charges, convictions, and periods of incarceration. Additional spells of incarceration are captured via a residence item, taken at each interview, indicating that a respondent's current dwelling is jail, prison, or a work release facility. Our focal independent variable is the experience of incarceration during young adulthood in the period leading up to the measurement of our labor market indicators at age thirty. This dichotomous measure is coded 1 if a respondent reported a spell of incarceration between ages twenty-five and thirty and zero otherwise. Further, in supplementary models, we examine variation across indicators of criminal justice contact with a mutually exclusive categorical measure of no criminal justice contact (referent), arrested only, arrested and convicted with no incarceration, and incarcerated.

## Hidden Sentences

The NICCC is an impressive documentation of the laws and policies that create the systems of hidden sentences operating across U.S. jurisdictions. For each state, plus the federal government, the NICCC provides a thorough list of all current hidden sentences that could apply to someone with a criminal record. To capture the administrative burden of hidden sentences, we focus on the total number of hidden sentences identified for each state in the NICCC. However, not all hidden sentences are automatically enforced, making it impossible to tell exactly which hidden sentences apply to a given person at a given time. To help deal with this uncertainty, we restrict our total measure to capture only those hidden sentences that are automatically put in place on arrest, conviction, or other criminalizing statuses (that is, that require no discretionary action to activate). Furthermore, we take advantage of state-to-state variation in hidden sentences to create a three-category measure of mandatory hidden sentences based on the overall percentile distribution: low-hidden sentences (less than 25th percentile; referent), mid-hidden sentences (25th to 75th percentile), and high-hidden sentences (greater than 75th percentile).

To combine the individual-level data with the hidden sentences data, we use state identifiers available at each wave of the NLSY97 data collection. For respondents who report an arrest, conviction, or incarceration, we match hidden sentences based on the state of residence at the time of the arrest. For those respondents who are not arrested between the ages of twenty-five and thirty, we take the hidden sentences category in the state of residence at age thirty.

## Control Variables

The criminal justice system disproportionately selects from disadvantaged segments of the population (Western 2006). We follow research by accounting for a range of individual and state-level characteristics that may confound our association of interest (Apel and Powell 2019; Apel and Sweeten 2010; Western 2002). At the individual level, we leverage the NLSY97 data to control for gender (female = referent), race (white [referent], black, Hispanic, other), as well as a series of young adult life-course characteristics taken at age twenty-five (prior to the measure of incarceration and the dependent variables). This includes corresponding employment and earnings variables, as described, as well as a lagged measure of criminal justice contact (coded 1 if a respondent was ever arrested leading up to the age twenty-five interview). We control for educational attainment with a categorical variable capturing highest degree earned at age twenty-five: less than high school degree (referent), high school degree, two-year college with no degree, two-year college with degree, four-year college with no degree, and four-year college with degree. We also account for young adult relationship status: unmarried (referent), cohabitating, married, and divorced-separated. Parenthood is a dichotomous variable coded 1 if the household roster includes a resident child, and zero otherwise. Similarly, homeownership is a dichotomous indicator coded 1 if the respondent reports owning or making payments on a home. Finally, we account for parent-child coresidence with a dichotomous variable coded 1 if one or more parents is listed on the household roster.

Furthermore, and because hidden sentences have been cast as the result of social exclusionary policies and a shrinking social safety net (Plassmeyer and Sliva 2018), we also account for relevant state-level characteristics that may confound our association of interest. These measures are based on annual state-level data, averaged from 2005 through 2014.

State sociodemographic characteristics are from the U.S. Census Bureau decennial census and American Community Survey, and include the percentage of the state that is non-Hispanic black, the percentage of residents with a four-year degree or higher, and the unemployment rate. Drawing from data compiled by the University of Kentucky Center for Poverty Research, we also control for the gross state product (in millions of dollars) and the maximum Temporary Assistance for Needy Families and Supplemental Nutrition Assistance Program benefits for a family of four between 2004 and 2015. Finally, using data from the Bureau of Justice Statistics, we control for the incarceration rate. These measures are based on the state of residence at the time of the age thirty interview.

## Analytic Strategy

We predict any employment and full-time employment among those employed using linear probability models and logged wages using linear regression. Given our interest in state-level hidden sentences, we cluster all standard errors by state of residence. For any employment and wages, we start with an estimate of the incarceration penalty net of individual control variables, including the lagged dependent variable. We add hidden sentences in model 2 to examine whether hidden sentences are a mechanism linking incarceration to labor market struggles. In model 3, we account for additional state-level characteristics that could drive any relationship between hidden sentences and labor market outcomes. To determine whether hidden sentences exacerbate the consequences of incarceration for employment or earnings, we model an interaction between incarceration and hidden sentences in the full model 4. In the final models, we predict full-time employment among those who report some employment (n = 6,022), and wages among those who report nonzero wages (n = 5,812). We also present results stratified by race. To conserve space, and to maintain the focus on the key variables of interest, we omit the coefficients and standard errors for all control variables.[3]

---

3. For full tables of all dependent variables, see the online appendix (https://www.rsfjournal.org/content/6/1/132/tab-supplemental).

**Figure 1.** Mandatory Hidden Sentences in the United States

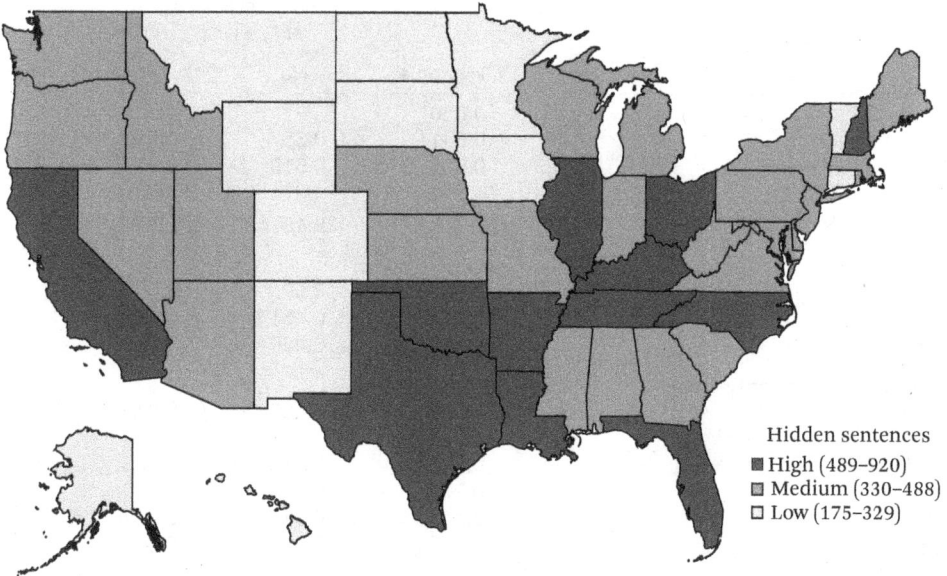

*Source:* Authors' compilation of NICCC (American Bar Association 2013).

## RESULTS

We start by noting that that hidden sentences are ubiquitous across U.S. states, averaging more than eight hundred hidden sentences that may apply following a criminal conviction or other criminal status (mean = 868.27, SD = 312.73). In addition, states have an average of more than four hundred hidden sentences that are categorized as mandatory (mean = 441.29, SD = 173.94). We show state variation in hidden sentences, based on the levels of mandatory hidden sentences described, in figure 1. This map indicates that states with high levels of mandatory hidden sentences tend to be concentrated in the southern United States, although both high- and low-level states are observed in nearly every region.

Table 1 shows descriptive statistics for the full sample and by incarceration status. Between the ages of twenty-five and thirty, 5.6 percent (n = 405) of the NLSY97 respondents experienced a spell of incarceration and these individuals were disadvantaged in the labor market. Relative to their never-incarcerated counterparts, recently incarcerated individuals are less likely to report that they worked (either at all or full-time) leading up to the age thirty interview, and reported approximately $20,000 lower annual earnings.

Table 1 also shows that that most NLSY97 respondents live in states classified as either mid- or high-hidden sentences (low = 9.2 percent, mid = 45.3 percent, high = 45.5 percent). There are no differences in exposure to hidden sentences based on a history of recent incarceration. That is, the table shows that the levels of hidden sentences in the states where respondents with or without a recent incarceration live are not significantly different.

Hidden sentences do not appear to play an independent role in young adult employment outcomes, given that the results in table 2 show that a recent incarceration decreases the probability of employment at age thirty, and this relationship is not explained by exposure to hidden sentences.

After accounting for a host of individual-level potential sources of spuriousness and pre-incarceration employment, and consistent with existing work (see Apel and Ramakers 2019), we find in model 1 of table 2 that young adults with a recent incarceration are 16.6 percentage points less likely to report having been employed in any month in the prior year. This

**Table 1.** Descriptive Statistics for All Variables

|  | Full Sample | Incarcerated Ages Twenty-Five to Thirty | | t-Test |
|---|---|---|---|---|
|  |  | No | Yes |  |
| Incarceration (1=yes) | 0.056 | — | — |  |
| Any employment (1=yes) | 0.841 | 0.857 | 0.590 | *** |
| Full-time employment (1=yes) | 0.601 | 0.619 | 0.301 | *** |
| Wages[a] | 28,104.1 | 29,221.2 | 9,456.2 | *** |
|  | (28,025.3) | (28,187.2) | (16,296.8) |  |
| **Hidden sentences (HS)** |  |  |  |  |
| Low HS state (referent) | 0.092 | 0.093 | 0.077 |  |
| Mid HS state | 0.453 | 0.451 | 0.489 |  |
| High HS state | 0.455 | 0.456 | 0.435 |  |
| **Control variables (at age twenty-five)** |  |  |  |  |
| Gender (male=1) | 0.501 | 0.482 | 0.815 | *** |
| Race |  |  |  |  |
|   White (referent) | 0.506 | 0.514 | 0.363 | *** |
|   Black | 0.274 | 0.266 | 0.412 | *** |
|   Hispanic | 0.213 | 0.212 | 0.217 |  |
|   Other race | 0.007 | 0.007 | 0.007 |  |
| Education |  |  |  |  |
|   Less than high school degree (referent) | 0.122 | 0.108 | 0.343 | *** |
|   High school degree | 0.280 | 0.272 | 0.412 | *** |
|   Two-year college (no degree) | 0.172 | 0.176 | 0.106 | *** |
|   Two-year college (degree) | 0.059 | 0.062 | 0.022 | ** |
|   Four-year college (no degree) | 0.152 | 0.155 | 0.109 | * |
|   Four-year college (degree) | 0.214 | 0.226 | 0.007 | *** |
| Relationship status |  |  |  |  |
|   Unmarried (referent) | 0.524 | 0.519 | 0.612 | *** |
|   Cohabitating | 0.179 | 0.179 | 0.168 |  |
|   Married | 0.250 | 0.257 | 0.136 | *** |
|   Divorced-separated | 0.047 | 0.045 | 0.084 | *** |
| Parent (1=yes) | 0.434 | 0.422 | 0.630 | *** |
| Homeownership (1=yes) | 0.164 | 0.169 | 0.079 | *** |
| Coresidence with parents (1=yes) | 0.288 | 0.285 | 0.331 | * |
| Arrested before age twenty-five (1=yes) | 0.326 | 0.294 | 0.859 | *** |
| Full-time employment (age twenty-five) | 0.572 | 0.584 | 0.369 | *** |
| Wages[a] (age twenty-five; thousands of dollars) | 21.01 | 21.61 | 10.95 | *** |
|  | (18.82) | (18.66) | (18.66) |  |
| State % non-Hispanic black | 12.70 | 12.63 | 13.85 | ** |
|  | (8.196) | (8.154) | (8.801) |  |
| State % with four-year degree | 27.79 | 27.83 | 27.17 | ** |
|  | (4.446) | (4.449) | (4.350) |  |
| State unemployment rate | 6.824 | 6.829 | 6.740 |  |
|  | (1.061) | (1.063) | (1.026) |  |
| State maximum allowable welfare | 1079.4 | 1081.8 | 1038.3 | *** |
|  | (188.9) | (189.2) | (176.3) |  |
| Gross state product in millions | 669,803.1 | 673,608.3 | 606,279.5 | * |
|  | (608,615.4) | (611,915.6) | (547,395.2) |  |
| State incarceration rate | 462.0 | 460.1 | 492.6 | *** |
|  | (135.7) | (135.6) | (133.7) |  |
| Observations | 7,166 | 6,761 | 405 |  |

*Source:* Authors' compilation based on NLSY97 (U.S. Bureau of Labor Statistics 2015), NICCC (American Bar Association 2013), U.S. Census (2000, 2010), NPS (U.S. Bureau of Justice Statistics 2017), and National Welfare Data (University of Kentucky Center for Poverty Research 2019).
*Note:* Standard deviations for continuous variables only (in parentheses).
[a] Wages reported in 2010 dollars.
+$p < .1$; *$p < .05$; **$p < .01$; ***$p < .001$

**Table 2.** Linear Probability Models Predicting Young Adult Employment

|  | Any | | | | Full-Time[a] |
|---|---|---|---|---|---|
|  | Model 1 | Model 2 | Model 3 | Model 4 | Model 4 |
| Young adult incarceration | −0.166*** | −0.166*** | −0.167*** | −0.022 | −0.174 |
|  | (0.026) | (0.026) | (0.026) | (0.062) | (0.106) |
| Low hidden sentences (HS) (referent) | — | — | — | — | — |
| Mid hidden sentences |  | −0.018 | −0.006 | 0.001 | 0.045[+] |
|  |  | (0.017) | (0.017) | (0.017) | (0.025) |
| High hidden sentences |  | −0.019 | 0.003 | 0.009 | 0.071* |
|  |  | (0.016) | (0.020) | (0.021) | (0.030) |
| **Interactions** |  |  |  |  |  |
| Incarceration x mid HS |  |  |  | −0.158* | −0.004 |
|  |  |  |  | (0.073) | (0.119) |
| Incarceration x high HS |  |  |  | −0.158* | 0.077 |
|  |  |  |  | (0.074) | (0.113) |
| Constant | 0.471*** | 0.487*** | 0.566*** | 0.568*** | 0.368*** |
|  | (0.021) | (0.029) | (0.068) | (0.068) | (0.102) |
| **Control variables** |  |  |  |  |  |
| Individual | Yes | Yes | Yes | Yes | Yes |
| State | No | No | Yes | Yes | Yes |
| N | 7,166 | 7,166 | 7,166 | 7,166 | 6,022 |
| $R^2$ | 0.178 | 0.178 | 0.179 | 0.180 | 0.114 |

*Source:* Authors' compilation based on NLSY97 (U.S. Bureau of Labor Statistics 2015), NICCC (American Bar Association 2013), U.S. Census (2000, 2010), NPS (U.S. Bureau of Justice Statistics 2017), and National Welfare Data (University of Kentucky Center for Poverty Research 2019).
*Note:* Standard errors in parentheses (all standard errors clustered at state-level); coefficients and standard errors for individual- and state-level controls omitted.
[a] Full-time employment predicted for those who report any employment in past year.
$^+p < .1$; $^*p < .05$; $^{**}p < .01$; $^{***}p < .001$

association is robust to the addition of the hidden sentences in model 2, and hidden sentences themselves are not directly associated with employment in the full sample. The results change little with the inclusion of other state-level variables in model 3. However, the results in model 4 indicate that hidden sentences exacerbate the consequences of a recent incarceration for young-adult employment. Recently incarcerated respondents living in states with low-levels of hidden sentences are not significantly less likely than their nonincarcerated peers to have worked at some point in the year leading up to their age thirty interview. Instead, the decreased probability of employment in young adulthood is concentrated among respondents living in states with middle and high levels of hidden sentences.

If hidden sentences work in combination with a recent incarceration to restrict any involvement in the labor market, they appear to be less consequential for full-time employment. The final model of table 2 (labeled also as model 4 to reflect that the only change is the outcome measure) shows that, among those who reported any employment in the year leading up to the age thirty interview, the association between incarceration and full-time employment is not significantly moderated by state-level hidden sentences.

In table 3, we predict any (panel A) and full-

**Table 3.** Linear Probability Models Predicting Young Adult Employment

|  | Whites[a] | | Blacks[a] | | Hispanics[a] | |
|---|---|---|---|---|---|---|
|  | Model 1 | Model 2 | Model 1 | Model 2 | Model 1 | Model 2 |
| **Panel A. Any employment** | | | | | | |
| Young adult incarceration | -0.099* | -0.023 | -0.196*** | 0.220 | -0.201*** | -0.112 |
|  | (0.035) | (0.098) | (0.048) | (0.141) | (0.048) | (0.082) |
| Low hidden sentences (HS) (referent) | — | — | — | — | — | — |
| Mid hidden sentences | 0.021 | 0.024 | -0.098+ | -0.077 | 0.005 | 0.013 |
|  | (0.017) | (0.018) | (0.055) | (0.058) | (0.032) | (0.034) |
| High hidden sentences | 0.023 | 0.027 | -0.094+ | -0.076 | 0.057 | 0.063 |
|  | (0.026) | (0.026) | (0.055) | (0.059) | (0.050) | (0.051) |
| Interactions | | | | | | |
|   Incarceration x mid HS |  | -0.072 |  | -0.432** |  | -0.096 |
|  |  | (0.110) |  | (0.143) |  | (0.148) |
|   Incarceration x high HS |  | -0.103 |  | -0.407** |  | -0.105 |
|  |  | (0.109) |  | (0.166) |  | (0.100) |
| Constant | 0.468*** | 0.469*** | 0.878*** | 0.848*** | 0.548** | 0.562** |
|  | (0.077) | (0.076) | (0.212) | (0.220) | (0.151) | (0.152) |
| **Panel B. Full-time employment** | | | | | | |
| Young adult incarceration | -0.126* | -0.084 | -0.170** | 0.093 | -0.109+ | -0.357** |
|  | (0.047) | (0.138) | (0.050) | (0.259) | (0.056) | (0.106) |
| Low hidden sentences (referent) | — | — | — | — | — | — |
| Mid hidden sentences | 0.071* | 0.073* | 0.016 | 0.031 | -0.089 | -0.102 |
|  | (0.025) | (0.025) | (0.054) | (0.049) | (0.056) | (0.056) |
| High hidden sentences | 0.103** | 0.103** | 0.069 | 0.083 | -0.135 | -0.152+ |
|  | (0.031) | (0.031) | (0.063) | (0.058) | (0.070) | (0.072) |
| Interactions | | | | | | |
|   Incarceration x mid HS |  | -0.072 |  | -0.267 |  | 0.162 |
|  |  | (0.150) |  | (0.268) |  | (0.151) |
|   Incarceration x high HS |  | -0.016 |  | -0.274 |  | 0.347* |
|  |  | (0.157) |  | (0.265) |  | (0.119) |
| Constant | 0.418** | 0.418** | 0.534* | 0.509* | 0.581+ | 0.557+ |
|  | (0.125) | (0.125) | (0.207) | (0.192) | (0.311) | (0.331) |
| **Controls** | | | | | | |
| Individual | Yes | Yes | Yes | Yes | Yes | Yes |
| State | Yes | Yes | Yes | Yes | Yes | Yes |

*Source:* Authors' compilation based on NLSY97 (U.S. Bureau of Labor Statistics 2015), NICCC (American Bar Association 2013), U.S. Census (2000, 2010), NPS (U.S. Bureau of Justice Statistics 2017), and National Welfare Data (University of Kentucky Center for Poverty Research 2019).

*Note:* Standard errors in parentheses (all standard errors clustered at state-level); Coefficients and standard errors for individual- and state-level controls omitted.

[a] Sample sizes: whites (panel A 3,625, panel B 3,151), blacks (panel A 1,967, panel B 1,549), Hispanics (panel A 1,523, panel B 1,278).

+$p < .1$; *$p < .05$; **$p < .01$; ***$p < .001$

time employment (panel B) separately for white, black, and Hispanic young adults, and find evidence that hidden sentences are more strongly associated with adverse labor market outcomes for blacks than whites.

Looking first at model 1, which accounts for all covariates, incarceration is negatively associated with employment for all groups, but the association is stronger for blacks and Hispanics than it is for whites. When we include the interaction between hidden sentences and incarceration in model 2, we find that the employment penalty associated with incarceration is strongest in states that have more hidden sentences among blacks, but not among whites and Hispanics.[4] This is consistent with the notion that hidden sentences may have more deleterious consequences for formerly incarcerated black young adults than for white young adults.

We find less evidence that hidden sentences moderate the association between incarceration and full-time employment by race (panel B), similar to our results for the full sample. In panel B, recently incarcerated blacks residing in states with middle and high levels of hidden sentences are still less likely than their nonincarcerated peers to be employed full time, but these coefficients do not reach conventional levels of statistical significance.

We estimate the association between incarceration, hidden sentences, and logged earnings in table 4. Across all models, we find evidence that the negative association between incarceration and earnings is stronger in states that have more hidden sentences. After adjusting for state- and individual-level controls in model 3, we replicate research and find that young adults with a recent incarceration report significantly lower earnings than their counterparts. In model 4, we find that this association is stronger in states with moderate and high levels of hidden sentences. In states with low hidden sentences, formerly incarcerated young adults report 38 percent lower wages than those who were not incarcerated, but this difference is not statistically significant. Both interaction terms, however, are negative and significant. This suggests that the incarceration wage disparity is substantially larger and statistically significant in states with more hidden sentences. And that, in our sample, the incarceration wage penalty is primarily driven by those who live in states with a more robust hidden sentence policy regime.

However, one question is whether this association is driven by non-earners, or whether we also observe disparities among wage earners. When we restrict our analyses to earners only (final column of table 4), we find less evidence that state hidden sentences moderate the association between incarceration and wages. When we restrict the dependent variable to those respondents who report some wages, the coefficients for the interaction terms—though consistent in direction with those in model 4—mostly fail to reach conventional levels of statistical significance. This implies that to the extent that state hidden sentence policies exacerbate disparities in wages by incarceration status, they do so by preventing access to employment, not by creating disparities among wage earners.

Finally, in table 5 we ask whether incarceration wage disparities across states vary by race-ethnicity. We find some evidence that incarceration wage disparities are largest in states with moderate and high levels of hidden sentences, and that these disparities are larger for blacks than they are for whites and Hispanics.

The results in panel A show that recently incarcerated whites and blacks who live in states with higher levels of hidden sentences earn significantly less than their nonincarcerated counterparts. Although the interaction terms are larger for formerly incarcerated black young adults, the difference between the interaction terms for whites and blacks is not statistically

---

4. The difference between the interaction coefficients for whites and blacks is statistically significant in states with moderate levels of hidden sentences ($z = 2.00$) and nears statistical significance in states with high levels ($z = 1.53$) (using Paternoster et al. 1998). Furthermore, we note that it is only among blacks that an interaction between incarceration and a *continuous* measure of hidden sentences is significant. Thus, for blacks, but not others, the probability of any employment declines as hidden sentences rise.

**Table 4.** Linear Regression Models Predicting Young Adult Earnings

|  | All Respondents | | | | Earners Only[a] |
|---|---|---|---|---|---|
|  | Model 1 | Model 2 | Model 3 | Model 4 | Model 4 |
| Young adult incarceration | −2.454*** | −2.451*** | −2.462*** | −0.379 | −0.251 |
|  | (0.227) | (0.225) | (0.223) | (0.615) | (0.207) |
| Low hidden sentences (HS) (referent) | — | — | — | — | — |
| Mid hidden sentences |  | −0.369* | −0.071 | 0.034 | 0.006 |
|  |  | (0.145) | (0.203) | (0.200) | (0.064) |
| High hidden sentences |  | −0.341* | 0.160 | 0.250 | 0.140[+] |
|  |  | (0.151) | (0.231) | (0.231) | (0.070) |
| **Interactions** |  |  |  |  |  |
| Incarceration x mid HS |  |  |  | −2.340** | −0.488 |
|  |  |  |  | (0.691) | (0.300) |
| Incarceration x high HS |  |  |  | −2.176** | −0.304 |
|  |  |  |  | (0.687) | (0.292) |
| Constant | 5.470*** | 5.785*** | 5.181*** | 5.194*** | 8.691*** |
|  | (0.204) | (0.251) | (0.624) | (0.617) | (0.328) |
| **Control variables** |  |  |  |  |  |
| Individual | Yes | Yes | Yes | Yes | Yes |
| State | No | No | Yes | Yes | Yes |
| N | 7,166 | 7,166 | 7,166 | 7,166 | 5,812 |
| $R^2$ | 0.224 | 0.224 | 0.226 | 0.228 | 0.218 |

*Source:* Authors' compilation based on NLSY97 (U.S. Bureau of Labor Statistics 2015), NICCC (American Bar Association 2013), U.S. Census (2000, 2010), NPS (U.S. Bureau of Justice Statistics 2017), and National Welfare Data (University of Kentucky Center for Poverty Research 2019).
*Note:* Standard errors in parentheses (all standard errors clustered at state-level); coefficients and standard errors for individual- and state-level controls omitted.
[a] This model restricts the sample to only those respondents who report nonzero earnings.
[+]$p < .1$; *$p < .05$; **$p < .01$; ***$p < .001$

significant. When the outcome is restricted to earners, in panel B, some evidence indicates that formerly incarcerated blacks and Hispanics earn less if they live in states with higher levels of hidden sentences, but the coefficients mostly fail to reach conventional levels of statistical significance.

## Supplementary Models for Criminal Justice Contact

The models focus on how hidden sentences moderate the association between incarceration and labor market outcomes in young adulthood. However, recent research shows that the deleterious outcomes attributed to incarceration are also documented for individuals who experience other forms of criminal justice contact, such as arrests or convictions that do not lead to incarceration (Sugie and Turney 2017; Uggen et al. 2014). Many hidden sentences, too, apply to those who are arrested or are convicted but not incarcerated (Kaiser 2016). Thus in supplementary models we examine whether hidden sentences moderate the association between criminal justice contact, broadly defined, and labor market outcomes. To do so, we created a four-category mutually exclusive measure of criminal justice contact. We estimated models identical to those in tables 2 and 4, for employment, full-time employment, and earn-

**Table 5.** Linear Regression Models Predicting Young Adult Earnings by Race-Ethnicity

|  | Whites[a] | | Blacks[a] | | Hispanics[a] | |
| --- | --- | --- | --- | --- | --- | --- |
|  | Model 1 | Model 2 | Model 1 | Model 2 | Model 1 | Model 2 |
| **Panel A. Ln wages (all respondents)** | | | | | | |
| Young adult incarceration | −2.039*** | 0.073 | −2.612*** | 1.512 | −2.347*** | −1.653[+] |
|  | (0.393) | (0.809) | (0.396) | (1.191) | (0.385) | (0.851) |
| Low hidden sentences (HS) (referent) | — | — | — | — | — | — |
| Mid hidden sentences | 0.092 | 0.169 | −0.191 | 0.099 | 0.061 | 0.138 |
|  | (0.252) | (0.253) | (0.528) | (0.464) | (0.333) | (0.342) |
| High hidden sentences | 0.232 | 0.307 | −0.697 | −0.300 | 0.483 | 0.525 |
|  | (0.314) | (0.318) | (0.554) | (0.495) | (0.611) | (0.616) |
| Interactions | | | | | | |
| Incarceration x mid HS |  | −2.368* |  | −3.773* |  | −1.065 |
|  |  | (0.980) |  | (1.315) |  | (1.267) |
| Incarceration x high HS |  | −2.383* |  | −4.888** |  | −0.684 |
|  |  | (0.994) |  | (1.278) |  | (0.993) |
| Constant | 4.447*** | 4.472*** | 5.050* | 4.432* | 8.741*** | 8.797*** |
|  | (0.821) | (0.827) | (2.079) | (2.003) | (1.927) | (1.903) |
| **Panel B. Ln wages (earners)** | | | | | | |
| Young adult incarceration | −0.337** | −0.325 | −0.678** | 0.191 | −0.841** | −0.096 |
|  | (0.123) | (0.305) | (0.239) | (0.637) | (0.278) | (0.356) |
| Low hidden sentences (referent) | — | — | — | — | — | — |
| Mid hidden sentences | −0.022 | −0.021 | −0.151 | −0.091 | 0.044 | 0.125 |
|  | (0.072) | (0.075) | (0.185) | (0.179) | (0.140) | (0.137) |
| High hidden sentences | 0.158[+] | 0.158[+] | −0.136 | −0.068 | 0.219 | 0.219 |
|  | (0.089) | (0.093) | (0.173) | (0.171) | (0.204) | (0.205) |
| Interactions | | | | | | |
| Incarceration x mid HS |  | −0.030 |  | −0.839 |  | −1.848* |
|  |  | (0.359) |  | (0.659) |  | (0.925) |
| Incarceration x high HS |  | 0.006 |  | −1.047 |  | −0.388 |
|  |  | (0.347) |  | (0.814) |  | (0.408) |
| Constant | 8.883*** | 8.882*** | 8.871*** | 8.768*** | 8.157*** | 8.068*** |
|  | (0.338) | (0.338) | (0.708) | (0.701) | (0.661) | (0.670) |
| **Controls** | | | | | | |
| Individual | Yes | Yes | Yes | Yes | Yes | Yes |
| State | Yes | Yes | Yes | Yes | Yes | Yes |

*Source:* Authors' compilation based on NLSY97 (U.S. Bureau of Labor Statistics 2015), NICCC (American Bar Association 2013), U.S. Census (2000, 2010), NPS (U.S. Bureau of Justice Statistics 2017), and National Welfare Data (University of Kentucky Center for Poverty Research 2019).
*Note:* Standard errors in parentheses (all standard errors clustered at state-level); coefficients and standard errors for individual- and state-level controls omitted.
[a] Sample sizes: whites (panel A 3,625, panel B 3,071), blacks (panel A 1,967, panel B 1,468), Hispanics (panel A 1,523, panel B 1,232).
[+]$p < .1$; *$p < .05$; **$p < .01$; ***$p < .001$

ings.[5] Broadly, we find that the association between criminal justice contact—including conviction and arrest—and labor market outcomes is stronger in states that have higher levels of hidden sentences. We also find some evidence that the labor market penalties associated with hidden sentences are stronger for blacks than whites across levels of criminal justice contact. This suggests that hidden sentences have the potential to exacerbate labor market disparities by race and criminal justice contact, even among those who are not formally incarcerated.

## DISCUSSION

According to recent estimates, between seventy and one hundred million Americans have a criminal record (Vallas and Dietrich 2014), 7.3 million adults have been incarcerated (Shannon et al. 2017), and more than six hundred thousand are released from prison every year (Carson 2018). Incarceration—and criminal justice contact more broadly—has therefore become an increasingly common turning point in the life course for millions of people, especially young men of color. Research shows that these young people experience long and lasting consequences in the labor market that accumulate over time, one of the many ways that the criminal justice system creates and reinforces existing social inequality (Kirk and Wakefield 2017; Wakefield and Uggen 2010). The informal social stigma attached to a criminal label is often implicated in the labor market struggles of formerly incarcerated individuals (Pager 2003). In this study, we advance research by examining the role that formal stigma, operating through state-level laws and policies that limit social participation (Travis 2002), plays in the relationship between incarceration and labor market outcomes.

Our primary conclusion is that state-level hidden sentences appear to exacerbate the consequences of multiple kinds of criminal justice contact for labor market outcomes. Young adults with a recent incarceration, in particular, are less likely to find employment if they live in states that have higher levels of hidden sentences, and the earnings penalty of incarceration is larger in states with more hidden sentence laws and policies. In other words, the association between incarceration and labor market outcomes appears to depend in part on the state in which one lives and the overall burden that results from high levels of hidden sentences that accompany criminal justice processing. Individuals with recent incarceration spells in states with low levels of hidden sentences pay a smaller penalty than their peers in other states. Moreover, our supplemental analyses shows that the association between recent arrests or convictions and employment is larger in states with higher levels of hidden sentences. These findings align with those of Cadigan and Kirk (2020), who show how the management of monetary sanctions by courts can shape labor market experiences. Through the scheduling of compliance hearings or imposition of additional sanctions (such as suspension of a driver's license, bench warrants, short period of incarcerations), courts create pressure points that make it difficult to find and maintain employment. Combined, these studies show that consequences of incarceration and other forms of criminal justice contact emerge as a result of postconviction policies, laws, and mechanisms of compliance.

We find that the moderating role of hidden sentences is a stronger predictor of entry into employment than it is of disparities among those who are employed (including wages among earners and full-time employment among the employed). This suggests that hidden sentences may limit initial access to the labor market, but if justice-involved individuals are able to get a job, these policies may play a smaller role in labor market inequalities. Future research should consider whether hidden sentences amplify firm-level discrimination that prevents the formerly incarcerated from gaining access to employment (Pager 2007). That is, the question remains whether hidden sentences limit access to the labor market, broadly, or only to certain sectors of the labor market that the justice-involved are likely to enter. Additional research should therefore exam-

---

5. For the full results of these models, see the online appendix (https://www.rsfjournal.org/content/6/1/132/tab-supplemental).

ine how hidden sentences are linked to entry into specific occupations. In particular, it would be useful to better understand how individuals interact with the labor market in the face of hidden sentences, including segments of the labor market that are entirely blocked off, and whether shifts are discernable in occupational sectors of the justice-involved before and after incarceration via hidden sentence policies.

Our findings also raise concerns that hidden sentences may exacerbate racial disparities in socioeconomic outcomes, at least among the justice-involved. We find that hidden sentences are more strongly associated with access to employment for black formerly incarcerated respondents than for whites or Hispanics. This finding is in line with, and supports, recent research that shows evidence for a "racialized reentry" (Western and Sirois 2018), where the labor market penalties of incarceration are stronger for blacks than for whites (Apel and Powell 2019; Lyons and Pettit 2011). One interpretation of these findings is that hidden sentences institutionalize discrimination and make it easier for employers to discriminate against people of color. Pager (2003) argues that a criminal record works in combination with minority status to intensify stigma for blacks relative to whites; our findings show that this may work formally through state-level policies in combination with the informal stigma accompanying a conviction. Furthermore, even in the absence of discrimination or race-specific effects, hidden sentences may exacerbate racial disparities in employment outcomes given that blacks are far more likely to be subject to the pernicious consequences of hidden sentences than whites are (see Sugie and Turney 2017).

To our knowledge, this is the first attempt at quantifying the link between hidden sentences and labor market outcomes of justice-involved young adults, and we show that hidden sentences compound a history of incarceration, especially in states where such policies are more pervasive. However, our study is not without limitations. First, we are unable to directly measure the mechanisms linking hidden sentences with labor market outcomes. Although we argue that hidden sentences may limit access to the labor market directly through occupational restrictions and licensing, indirectly through social exclusion and limiting full citizenship, and more broadly through administrative burden, we are unable to directly measure these mechanisms. We do, however, find indirect support for them. In supplementary models, our findings were strongest for mandatory (relative to discretionary) hidden sentences, suggesting that hidden sentences are more consequential when they are more likely to be enforced or implemented. Our results were also similar for both employment-related hidden sentences and hidden sentences that are not directly related to employment (such as those that affect drivers' licenses, welfare access, or residence locations). This constitutes suggestive evidence that hidden sentences—even those that do not restrict specific occupations—may play a role in labor market outcomes. That said, a careful examination of exactly how hidden sentences contribute to labor market struggles after incarceration is warranted.

Second, looming over any of the mechanisms we suggest is the broader issue of enforcement. Some hidden sentences are automatically triggered, such as those that automatically disseminate criminal records to various state and nonstate employers, impose mandatory civil fines and forfeitures, or make the justice-involved completely ineligible for public employment in many states. Others require discretionary action to be activated, such as when statutes grant medical, barbering, and other professional boards the power to consider arrests and convictions in the granting or renewal of occupational licenses. We focus here on those hidden sentences that are categorized as automatic, but it is clearly difficult to know exactly how or when hidden sentences become activated. In Wisconsin, for instance, barbering and cosmetology boards are required to deny, restrict, or suspend the licenses of those who are convicted of a felony, but it is unknown how often the boards actually comply with such a mandate. Such questions are more relevant with "mandatory" laws that involve more interpretation. In Delaware, for instance, anyone convicted of a crime "substantially related" to the practice of barbering or beautician services is ineligible for a license, but no legal guidelines list such crimes. One suggested avenue for future research, then, would be to follow a cohort of individuals as they progress though the system, examining what hidden sentences become activated at various stages and what actors drive those decisions. It would also be useful to examine whether hidden sentences are context dependent, given that larger views on crime and crime control across jurisdictions could affect the activation of hidden sentences.

Third, further research is needed to more clearly examine how a state's labor force is affected by hidden sentences. The current framework of the NICCC database prohibits connecting specific hidden sentences to specific occupational domains, but this issue clearly warrants additional attention. Fourth, although we are interested in the effect of these policies on labor market outcomes for the justice-involved, our study is only correlational. Although we control for an array of characteristics that may confound our association of interest, we cannot speak to causality with this study design, and it would be useful to test our conclusions using methodologies that can more fully account for observed and unobserved sources of spuriousness. Finally, our measure of hidden sentences is time stable, and thus we cannot determine whether changes in hidden sentences change labor market outcomes. This is an important area for future research, especially in light of recent attempts to remove postconviction barriers and ease reintegration (Love and Schlussel 2019).

Additional research should also consider whether hidden sentences affect other outcomes associated with incarceration. Restrictions on access to financial aid, for example, could play an important role in the link between incarceration and educational attainment. More broadly, hidden sentences may drive larger patterns of socioeconomic inequality through differential access to credit and opportunities to accumulate wealth (Sykes and Maroto 2016). Given that states have increasingly been charged with and granted power to implement social and economic policies, future research might also consider how additional aspects of the state social policy regime are associated with outcomes among the justice-involved. For example, state-level policies regarding child support could be useful in understanding the relationship between parental incarceration and child outcomes. This is especially important given that Noah Zatz and Michael Stoll (2020) show that the threat of incarceration to enforce court-mandated work requirements can push noncustodial fathers into low-wage employment. Thus, more research is needed to determine how hidden sentences affect individual, family, and community outcomes following arrests, convictions, and periods of incarceration.

Taken together, our findings provide important insights on the relationship between criminal justice contact and socioeconomic inequality through labor market participation. In response to recent calls to push beyond average effects of incarceration (Apel and Ramakers 2019; Kirk and Wakefield 2017), our findings show how state-level policies of social exclusion interact with criminal justice contact to put justice-involved individuals at a distinct disadvantage in the labor market. This provides important insights on how the overall consequences of criminalization play out in jurisdictions across the country.

## REFERENCES

American Bar Association (ABA). 2013. "National Inventory of the Collateral Consequences of Conviction." Chicago: American Bar Association. Accessed January 23, 2020. https://niccc.csgjustice center.org.

Apel, Robert, and Kathleen Powell. 2019. "Level of Criminal Justice Contact and Early Adult Wage Inequality." *RSF: The Russell Sage Foundation Journal of the Social Sciences* 5(1): 198–222. DOI: 10.7758/RSF.2019.5.1.09.

Apel, Robert, and Anke Ramakers. 2019. "Impact of Incarceration on Employment Prospects." In *Handbook of the Consequences of Sentencing and Punishment Decisions*, edited by Beth M. Huebner and Natasha A. Frost. New York: Routledge.

Apel, Robert, and Gary Sweeten. 2010. "The Impact of Incarceration on Employment during the Transition to Adulthood." *Social Problems* 57(3): 448–79.

Beckett, Katherine, and Steve Herbert. 2010. *Banished: The New Social Control in Urban America*. New York: Oxford University Press.

Blau, Peter M., and Otis Dudley Duncan. 1967. *The American Occupational Structure*. New York: Free Press.

Brayne, Sarah. 2014. "Surveillance and System Avoidance: Criminal Justice Contact and Institutional Attachment." *American Sociological Review* 79(3): 367–91. DOI: 10.1177/0003122414530398.

Burden, Barry C., David T. Canon, Kenneth R. Mayer, and Donald P. Moynihan. 2014. "Election Laws, Mobilization, and Turnout: The Unanticipated Consequences of Election Reform." *American Journal of Political Science* 58(1): 95–109. DOI: 10.1111/ajps.12063.

Cadigan, Michele, and Gabriela Kirk. 2020. "On Thin Ice: Bureaucratic Processes of Monetary Sanctions and Job Insecurity." *RSF: The Russell Sage Foundation Journal of the Social Sciences* 6(1): 113–31. DOI: 10.7758/RSF.2020.6.1.05.

Carson, E. Ann. 2018. "Prisoners in 2016." CNJ 251149. Washington, D.C.: Bureau of Justice Statistics.

Cheng, Siwei. 2014. "A Life Course Trajectory Framework for Understanding the Intracohort Pattern of Wage Inequality." *American Journal of Sociology* 120(3): 633–700. DOI: 10.1086/679103.

Chin, Gabriel J. 2011. "The New Civil Death: Rethinking Punishment in the Era of Mass Conviction." *University of Pennsylvania Law Review* 160(6): 1789–833.

Danziger, Sheldon, and David Ratner. 2010. "Labor Market Outcomes and the Transition to Adulthood." *The Future of Children* 20(1): 133–58.

DiPrete, Thomas A., and Gregory M. Eirich. 2006. "Cumulative Advantage as a Mechanism for Inequality: A Review of Theoretical and Empirical Developments." *Annual Review of Sociology* 32(1): 271–97.

Ewald, Alec C. 2012. "Collateral Consequences in the American States." *Social Science Quarterly* 93(1): 211–47. DOI: 10.1111/j.1540-6237.2011.00831.x.

Geller, Amanda, and Marah A. Curtis. 2011. "A Sort of Homecoming: Incarceration and the Housing Security of Urban Men." *Social Science Research* 40(4): 1196–1213. DOI: 10.1016/j.ssresearch.2011.03.008.

Harris, Alexes. 2016. *A Pound of Flesh: Monetary Sanctions as Punishment for the Poor*. New York: Russell Sage Foundation.

Heinrich, Carolyn J. 2018. "Presidential Address: 'A Thousand Petty Fortresses': Administrative Burden in U.S. Immigration Policies and Its Consequences." *Journal of Policy Analysis and Management* 37(2): 211–39. DOI: 10.1002/pam.22046.

Herd, Pamela, and Donald P. Moynihan. 2019. *Administrative Burden: Policymaking by Other Means*. New York: Russell Sage Foundation.

Holzer, Harry J. 1996. *What Employers Want: Job Prospects for Less-Educated Workers*. New York: Russell Sage Foundation.

Hoxby, Caroline M., and Sarah Turner. 2015. "What High-Achieving Low-Income Students Know about College." *American Economic Review* 105(5): 514–17. DOI: 10.1257/aer.p20151027.

Kaiser, Joshua H. 2016. "Revealing the Hidden Sentence: How to Add Transparency, Legitimacy, and Purpose to Collateral Punishment Policy." *Harvard Law & Policy Review* 10(1): 123–84.

Kirk, David S., and Sara Wakefield. 2017. "Collateral Consequences of Punishment: A Critical Review and Path Forward." *Annual Review of Criminology* 1:171–94. DOI: 10.1146/annurev-criminol-032317-092045.

Love, Margaret, and David Schlussel. 2019. "Reducing Barriers to Reintegration: Fair Chance and Expungement Reforms in 2018." Washington, D.C.: Collateral Consequences Resource Center.

Lyons, Christopher J., and Becky Pettit. 2011. "Compounded Disadvantage: Race, Incarceration, and Wage Growth." *Social Problems* 58(2): 257–80. DOI: 10.1525/sp.2011.58.2.257.

Miller, Reuben Jonathan, and Forrest Stuart. 2017. "Carceral Citizenship: Race, Rights and Responsibility in the Age of Mass Supervision." *Theoretical Criminology* 21(4): 532–48.

Moynihan, Donald P., Pamela Herd, and Elizabeth Ribgy. 2016. "Policymaking by Other Means: Do States Use Administrative Barriers to Limit Access to Medicaid?" *Administration & Society* 48(4): 497–524. DOI: 10.1177/0095399713503540.

Pager, Devah. 2003. "The Mark of a Criminal Record." *American Journal of Sociology* 108(5): 937–75.

———. 2007. *Marked: Race, Crime, and Finding Work in an Era of Mass Incarceration*. Chicago: University of Chicago Press.

Paternoster, Raymond, Robert Brame, Paul Mazerolle, and Alex Piquero. 1998. "Using the Correct Statistical Test for the Equality of Regression

Coefficients." *Criminology* 36(4): 859–66. DOI: 10.1111/j.1745-9125.1998.tb01268.x.

Petersilia, Joan. 2003. *When Prisoners Come Home: Parole and Prisoner Reentry*. New York: Oxford University Press.

Pettit, Becky, and Bruce Western. 2004. "Mass Imprisonment and the Life Course: Race and Class Inequality in U.S. Incarceration." *American Sociological Review* 69(2): 151–69. DOI: 10.1177/000312240406900201.

Plassmeyer, Mark, and Shannon Sliva. 2018. "Social Exclusion as a State-Level Predictor of Changes in Collateral Sanctions." *Criminal Justice Review* 43(2): 236–51. DOI: 10.1177/0734016817721292.

Raphael, Steven. 2007. "Early Incarceration Spells and the Transition to Adulthood." In *The Price of Independence: The Economies of Early Adulthood*, edited by Sheldon Danziger and Cecilia E. Rouse. New York: Russell Sage Foundation.

Remster, Brianna, and Rory Kramer. 2018. "Race, Space, and Surveillance: Understanding the Relationship Between Criminal Justice Contact and Institutional Involvement." *Socius* 4(January): 2378023118761434. DOI: 10.1177/2378023118761434.

Rindfuss, Ronald R. 1991. "The Young Adult Years: Diversity, Structural Change, and Fertility." *Demography* 28(4): 493–512.

Sampson, Robert J., and John H. Laub. 1992. "Crime and Deviance in the Life Course." *Annual Review of Sociology* 18: 63–84.

Shannon, Sarah K.S., Christopher Uggen, Jason Schnittker, Melissa Thompson, Sara Wakefield, and Michael Massoglia. 2017. "The Growth, Scope, and Spatial Distribution of People with Felony Records in the United States, 1948–2010." *Demography*, September, 1–24. DOI: 10.1007/s13524-017-0611-1.

Silva, Jennifer M. 2012. "Constructing Adulthood in an Age of Uncertainty." *American Sociological Review* 77(4): 505–22. DOI: 10.1177/0003122412449014.

Sironi, Maria. 2018. "Economic Conditions of Young Adults Before and After the Great Recession." *Journal of Family and Economic Issues* 39(1): 103–16. DOI: 10.1007/s10834-017-9554-3.

Stavsky, Mark M. 2002. "No Guns or Butter for Thomas Bean: Firearms Disabilities and Their Occupational Consequences." *Fordham Urban Law Review* 30(5): 1759–813.

Steinberg, Laurence, He Len Chung, and Michelle Little. 2004. "Reentry of Young Offenders from the Justice System: A Developmental Perspective." *Youth Violence and Juvenile Justice* 2(1): 21–38. DOI: 10.1177/1541204003260045.

Sugie, Naomi F., and Kristin Turney. 2017. "Beyond Incarceration: Criminal Justice Contact and Mental Health." *American Sociological Review* 82(4): 719–43. DOI: 10.1177/0003122417713188.

Swartz, Teresa Toguchi, Heather McLaughlin, and Jeylan T. Mortimer. 2017. "Parental Assistance, Negative Life Events, and Attainment During the Transition to Adulthood." *Sociological Quarterly* 58(1): 91–110. DOI: 10.1080/00380253.2016.1246898.

Sykes, Bryan L., and Michelle Maroto. 2016. "A Wealth of Inequalities: Mass Incarceration, Employment, and Racial Disparities in U.S. Household Wealth, 1996 to 2011." *RSF: The Russell Sage Foundation Journal of the Social Sciences* 2(6): 129–52. DOI: 10.7758/RSF.2016.2.6.07.

Travis, Jeremy. 2002. "Invisible Punishment: An Instrument of Social Exclusion." In *Invisible Punishment: The Collateral Consequences of Mass Imprisonment*, edited by Marc Mauer and Meda Chesney-Lind. New York: New Press.

Travis, Jeremy, and Bruce Western. 2014. "The Growth of Incarceration in the United States: Exploring Causes and Consequences." Washington, D.C.: National Academies Press. http://johnjay.jjay.cuny.edu/nrc/nas_report_on_incarceration.pdf.

Uggen, Christopher, and Jeff Manza. 2002. "Democratic Contraction? Political Consequences of Felon Disenfranchisement in the United States." *American Sociological Review* 67(6): 777–803.

Uggen, Christopher, and Robert Stewart. 2014. "Piling on: Collateral Consequences and Community Supervision." *Minnesota Law Review* 99(5): 1871–910.

Uggen, Christopher, Mike Vuolo, Sarah Lageson, Ebony Ruhland, and Hilary K. Whitham. 2014. "The Edge of Stigma: An Experimental Audit of the Effects of Low-Level Criminal Records on Employment." *Criminology* 52(4): 627–54. DOI: 10.1111/1745-9125.12051.

University of Kentucky Center for Poverty Research (UKCPR). 2019. "UKCPR National Welfare Data, 1980–2017." Lexington, Ky. Accessed October 7, 2019. http://ukcpr.org/resources/national-welfare-data.

U.S. Bureau of Justice Statistics. 2017. *National Prisoner Statistics Program (NPS)*. Washington: Office of Justice Programs.

U.S. Bureau of Labor Statistics, Department of Labor. 2015. *National Longitudinal Survey of Youth 1997 Cohort, 1997–2015*. Columbus, Ohio: Center for Human Resource Research, Ohio State University.

U.S. Census Bureau. 2000. "Census 2000 Summary File 1." Retrieved from https://www.socialexplorer.com/ (accessed October 7, 2019).

———. 2010. "Census 2010 Summary File 1." Retrieved from https://www.socialexplorer.com/ (accessed October 7, 2019).

———. 2017. "2005–2015 American Community Survey 1-Year State-Level Estimates." Retrieved from https://www.socialexplorer.com/ (accessed October 7, 2019).

Vallas, Rebecca, and Sharon Dietrich. 2014. *One Strike and You're Out: How We Can Eliminate Barriers to Economic Security and Mobility for People with Criminal Records*. Washington, D.C.: Center for American Progress. Accessed September 27, 2019. https://cdn.americanprogress.org/wp-content/uploads/2014/12/Vallas CriminalRecordsReport.pdf.

Wakefield, Sara, and Robert Apel. 2016. "Criminal Justice and the Life Course." In *Handbook of the Life Course*, vol. II, edited by Michael J. Shanahan, Jeylan T. Mortimer, and Monica Kirkpatrick Johnson. Cham: Springer International. DOI: 10.1007/978-3-319-20880-0_13.

Wakefield, Sara, and Christopher Uggen. 2010. "Incarceration and Stratification." *Annual Review of Sociology* 36(1): 387–406. DOI: 10.1146/annurev.soc.012809.102551.

Waldo, James, Herbert S. Lin, and Lynette I. Millett, eds. 2007. *Engaging Privacy and Information Technology in a Digital Age*. Washington, D.C.: National Academies Press.

Western, Bruce. 2002. "The Impact of Incarceration on Wage Mobility and Inequality." *American Sociological Review* 67(4): 526–46.

———. 2006. *Punishment and Inequality in America*. New York: Russell Sage Foundation.

Western, Bruce, and Becky Pettit. 2005. "Black-White Wage Inequality, Employment Rates, and Incarceration." *American Journal of Sociology* 111(2): 553–78. DOI: 10.1086/432780.

Western, Bruce, and Catherine Sirois. 2018. "Racialized Re-Entry: Labor Market Inequality After Incarceration." *Social Forces* 97(4): 1–26. DOI: 10.1093/sf/soy096.

Whittle, Tanya N. 2018. "Felony Collateral Sanctions Effects on Recidivism: A Literature Review." *Criminal Justice Policy Review* 29(5): 505–24. DOI: 10.1177/0887403415623328.

Zatz, Noah D., and Michael A. Stoll. 2020. "Working to Avoid Incarceration: Jail Threat and Labor Market Outcomes for Noncustodial Fathers Facing Child Support Enforcement." *RSF: The Russell Sage Foundation Journal of the Social Sciences* 6(1): 55–81. DOI: 10.7758/RSF.2020.6.1.03.

# PART III

# The Effects of Post-prison Employment on Future Criminal Justice Involvement

# Post-prison Employment Quality and Future Criminal Justice Contact

JOE LABRIOLA

*Several theories linking post-prison employment to recidivism suggest that the quality of employment has a causal effect on future criminal justice contact. However, previous work testing these theories has not accounted for differential selection into high-quality employment. Using six years of post-release employment records, I document how post-prison job quality varies by industry. Then, I use inverse propensity score weighting to estimate the effect of job quality on future arrests and prison spells. Some evidence indicates that parolees who find high-quality employment experience fewer arrests or returns to prison than otherwise similar parolees who find low-quality employment, with the effects most evident when comparing employment in the highest- and lowest-quality industries. Low-quality employment does not appear to reduce future criminal justice contact relative to unemployment.*

**Keywords:** employment, job quality, recidivism

More than 625,000 prisoners were released from state and federal prisons in the United States in 2016 (Carson 2018). A large majority of such released prisoners experience criminal justice contact in the years after release (Alper, Durose, and Markman 2018). Given that extended contact with the criminal justice system is associated with negative effects on employ-

---

**Joe LaBriola** is a PhD candidate in sociology at the University of California, Berkeley.

© 2020 Russell Sage Foundation. LaBriola, Joe. 2020. "Post-prison Employment Quality and Future Criminal Justice Contact." *RSF: The Russell Sage Foundation Journal of the Social Sciences* 6(1): 154–72. DOI: 10.7758/RSF.2020.6.1.07. Collection of the data used in this research was funded by the Russell Sage Foundation, the University of Michigan Center for Local, State, and Urban Policy, the National Poverty Center at the University of Michigan, the National Institute of Justice (2008-IJ-CX-0018), the National Science Foundation (SES-1061018, SES-1060708), and the Eunice Kennedy Shriver National Institute of Child Health and Human Development (1R21HD060160 01A1), and by center grants from the Eunice Kennedy Shriver National Institute of Child Health and Human Development to the Population Studies Centers at the University of Michigan (R24 HD041028) and at the University of California, Berkeley (R24 HD073964). The author acknowledges additional support from the National Science Foundation Graduate Research Fellowship Program (1752814), the NICHD (T32-HD007275), and a Student Award from the University of California, Berkeley, Institute for Research on Labor and Employment. This work has benefited from feedback from those working on *The Transition to Adulthood After Prison* book project, as well as from those attending presentations on this project given to the University of California, Berkeley, MAX-Soc Working Group and the Russell Sage Foundation's Criminal Justice System as a Labor Market Institution conference. Direct correspondence to: Joe LaBriola at joelabriola@berkeley.edu, 410 Barrows Hall, University of California, Berkeley, CA, 94720.

Open Access Policy: *RSF: The Russell Sage Foundation Journal of the Social Sciences* is an open access journal. This article is published under a Creative Commons Attribution-NonCommercial-NoDerivs 3.0 Unported License.

ment (Pager 2003), health (Massoglia and Pridemore 2015), and wealth (Harris, Evans, and Beckett 2010), as well as increased disadvantage for children of those experiencing criminal justice contact (Wildeman 2008), it is important to understand the factors that reduce future criminal justice contact.

Sociologists and criminologists emphasize the role of employment in reducing future criminal justice contact after release from prison. Employment has been theorized to reduce economic motivations for crime (Becker 1968; Freeman 1999), facilitate the achievement of normative societal goals (Merton 1938; Agnew 1985), act as an informal social control on parolees (Toby 1957; Sampson and Laub 1993), and provide a routine set of obligations that replace previous criminal activities (Cohen and Felson 1979). In particular, post-prison employment that pays well, is stable, and allows for future earnings growth is thought to be especially important in preventing future criminal justice contact.

However, previous research investigating the connection between post-prison employment quality and recidivism or other forms of criminal justice contact in the United States (Uggen 1999) has failed to adequately control for selection into employment quality, not just employment. This may pose a problem if those who find high-quality post-prison employment differ from those who find low-quality employment in dimensions that are also predictive of future criminal justice contact, such as age, human capital, or prior measures of criminal or antisocial behavior.

In this article, I estimate whether individuals who are first employed after prison in industries that offer relatively high-quality employment are significantly less likely than those who are first employed after prison in industries that offer relatively low-quality employment to be arrested or return to prison in the two years following the beginning of employment. I do so using comprehensive labor market information collected on all prisoners paroled in the state of Michigan in 2003 for six years after the quarter of release from prison, alongside an array of rich demographic, human capital, and criminal justice–related measures. I first measure employment quality within industries along four objective dimensions: average quarterly wages among the sample of parolees, average job tenure among the sample of parolees, average quarterly wages among all employees at employers who hire parolees in the sample, and union coverage among all Michigan workers. I then use inverse propensity score weighting to compare the future criminal justice contact of parolees who are equally likely (based on demographic, human capital, and criminal history variables) to find work in a high-quality industry but who find work in industries that offer a different quality of employment. This results in an estimate of the effect of employment quality on future criminal justice contact net of a wide variety of controls that may jointly affect both employment quality and future criminal behavior.

I find that those whose first job after prison is in an industry that offers relatively high-quality employment are, in general, less likely to be arrested or recidivate during the two years after hire. The results of the models that account for differential selection into employment based on observable characteristics provide mixed evidence about whether high-quality employment is associated with reduced future criminal justice contact. When comparing those who find employment in the industries that offer the highest job quality—namely, manufacturing and transportation or warehousing—to those who find it in those that offer the lowest—namely, the employment services industry—the relationship between employment quality and the likelihood of being arrested in the two years after hire is more clear.

Notably, when comparing employment of varying quality to the counterfactual of not finding employment, I find evidence that high-quality, but not low-quality, employment is associated with a lower likelihood of returning to prison.

## POST-PRISON EMPLOYMENT AND FUTURE CRIMINAL JUSTICE CONTACT

Researchers studying the connection between post-prison employment and future criminal justice contact have offered a variety of mechanisms through which employment after incarceration should reduce the risk of recidivism. Most obviously, employment may reduce the risk of reoffending by reducing the motivation to commit crime for economic gain (Becker 1968; Freeman 1999). Similarly, anomic theories of crime (Merton 1938; Agnew 1985), which posit that individuals become motivated to commit crimes when they are unable to achieve socially normative goals using methods considered legitimate by wider society, suggest that employment reduces criminal behavior because it is a way to achieving economic and social goals. Employment may also act as an informal social control that prevents parolees from reoffending by inducing a sense that they have a stake in society (Toby 1957) or by providing continued interaction with individuals at work who are not in contact with the criminal justice system (Sampson and Laub 1993). Finally, employment may also reduce the risk of future criminal justice contact by providing a set of routine activities for workers, making it less likely that they will spend time in more criminogenic environments (Cohen and Felson 1979).

In particular, these mechanisms suggest that it is not just employment after release from prison but also the quality of the employment—as measured by objective markers such as earnings, job stability, and earnings growth—that should have a significant effect on future criminal justice contact. For one, highly paid employment may reduce immediate economic motivations for crime. Further, the social control perspective holds that jobs that provide longer tenure or offer regular, full-time work may be especially likely to inhibit future criminal justice contact, by leading to interdependence with professional social networks (Braithwaite 1989) and to the creation of new and durable routines to replace associations and activities from before prison that may have fostered criminal behavior (Crutchfield and Pitchford 1997). Robert Sampson and John Laub (1990, 611) highlight that it is not just employment but also "employment coupled with job stability, job commitment, and ties to work that should increase social control and, all else equal, lead to a reduction in criminal behavior." Finally, employment that carries the potential for earnings growth over time is more likely to provide workers with a sense that they can achieve normative economic and social goals (Uggen 1999).[1]

However, Michael Gottfredson and Travis Hirschi (1990) argue that there is not a causal relationship between employment and future criminal justice contact. Specifically, they posit that both employment and crime are determined in part by the capacity for self-control. Individuals with low self-control will be less likely to find employment, much less high-quality employment, and will also be more likely to commit crimes. Under this logic, any effects of the quality of post-prison employment on future criminal justice contact would be spurious.[2]

Employment quality could also not affect recidivism if the pathway through which employment affects recidivism is decreased state surveillance. In *Poor Discipline*, Jonathan Simon (1993, 222) argues that parole officers often view any employment undertaken by parolees as a sign that they are on the right track and will thus be more lenient in supervising employed parolees or recommending parole revocations for violations such as occasional drug use. This,

---

1. Although this study focuses on job quality as measured by objective measures, it is also plausible that subjective markers of job quality, such as the desirability of an occupation (Uggen 1999) or a sense that a job is significant or allows the employee to do what they do best (Wadsworth 2006), lead to reduced future criminal justice contact for those who have been to prison. Jobs experienced subjectively as high quality may give these workers additional motivation to desist from crime so as to not jeopardize their employment. Further, routine activities and social control theories suggest that subjective job quality could lead to reduced future criminal justice contact if subjective job quality increases job tenure.

2. The claim that employment does not affect future criminal justice contact is supported by the meta-analysis conducted by Christy Visher, Sara Debus, and Jennifer Yahner (2008), which finds that experimental assignment to employment programs does not reduce recidivism. However, these results do not necessarily speak to how different types of employment may differentially affect recidivism. If, for example, these programs do not place those who have been to prison in high-quality jobs, and only high-quality jobs affect future criminal justice contact, we could still observe that employment programs do not affect recidivism.

in turn, could cause employed parolees—no matter whether their job is high or low quality—to face lower risks of recidivism than those who are unemployed. If this difference in supervision is the main route through which employment affects recidivism, then we may not see a causal relationship between employment quality and future criminal justice contact.

One way that researchers have examined the connection between the quality of available employment and the propensity to commit crime is by using aggregate measures of local labor markets as a proxy for the quality of available employment. For example, Emilie Allan and Darrell Steffensmeier (1989) estimate that state-level rates of underemployment and low-wage employment are positively associated with arrest rates for young adults. Focusing on samples of released prisoners, Steven Raphael and David Weiman (2007) and Xia Wang, Daniel Mears, and William Bales (2010) find a small but statistically significant relationship between local unemployment rates and the probability of returning to custody. Similarly, Crystal Yang (2017) finds that prisoners who are released to counties with higher wages for workers without college degrees see lower rates of recidivism. Roberto Galbiati, Aurelie Ouss, and Arnaud Philippe (2017) and Kevin Schnepel (2018) examine the effect of industry-specific job openings on recidivism in France and California, respectively. Both articles find that the county-level creation of jobs in relatively high-quality industries—manufacturing in France, and construction and manufacturing in California—is associated with lower recidivism rates for inmates released within the county, although overall county-level job creation has no effect.

These results are strongly consistent with the thesis that it is the quality of employment, not merely being employed, that matters for future criminal justice contact. However, the cited studies generally have individual-level data on criminal justice system involvement but not on employment. They therefore do not allow us to disentangle the degree to which changes in local labor market conditions affect the likelihood of future criminal justice contact directly by affecting the quality of employment of recently released prisoners (that is, that increases in available jobs in the construction industry cause recently released prisoners to be more likely to work in the construction industry, and thus less likely to experience future criminal justice contact), rather than indirectly through other mechanisms (for example, whether increased economic opportunity makes a local environment less criminogenic in general).

Other research examining the connection between the quality of employment and future criminal justice contact has relied on individual-level data that include information on both employment and criminal justice contact after release.[3] Christopher Uggen (1999) investigates the relationship between post-prison job quality and reoffending among a longitudinal sample of released prisoners using a sample selection model, which adjusts the relationship between job quality and reoffending among jobholders for unmeasured factors that jointly affect the propensity to enter employment and to reoffend. Based on this model, Uggen finds that job quality, measured using subjective job satisfaction scores from a nationally representative sample of workers, is a significantly negative predictor of recidivism, even after controlling for demographic characteristics and previous criminal history. However, the adjustment Uggen makes accounts for differential selection into any employment, not for differential selection into high-quality versus low-quality employment, and so does not necessarily disentangle any selection effects into high-quality versus low-quality employment

---

3. Although this study focuses on the effect of job quality on future criminal justice contact for those who have been recently released from prison, the literature on how job quality is associated with criminal behavior among a broader population of young adults is sizeable. For example, Jeff Grogger (1998) finds that wages are negatively associated with criminal activity among young adults, whereas Tim Wadsworth (2006) finds that subjective measures of job quality are more important than objective measures in predicting self-reported crime. Other work examines a population of those who have just been admitted to prison and considers how job quality covaries with self-reported criminal activity in the time before prison admittance (Apel and Horney 2017).

from the effects of high-quality employment on recidivism. In addition, by controlling for job tenure and wages in predicting the effect of job quality on crime, Uggen's analysis focuses on the effect of "the extraeconomic effects of job quality" (134). Although these extraeconomic dimensions of job quality are certainly important, this work does not test economic and anomic theories of crime, which explicitly suggest that the pecuniary rewards of employment are important predictors of future criminal justice contact.

Recent research by Anke Ramakers and colleagues (2017) uses propensity score techniques to account the probability that Dutch ex-prisoners who find employment in their first month after release do so in higher or lower occupational levels. These authors find a significantly negative effect of being in a higher (relative to a lower) occupational level on recidivism. However, given differences between labor market and criminal justice institutions between the Netherlands and the United States, generalizability of these findings to the United States context may be limited.

## DATA

I rely on longitudinal data on the employment outcomes of all prisoners paroled in the state of Michigan in 2003, collected from the Michigan Unemployment Insurance Agency and Workforce Development Agency. The benefit of unemployment insurance (UI) data is its comprehensive coverage: UI data capture virtually all formal employment undertaken in the state of Michigan for twenty-four quarters after the sampled individual's release from prison. In each person-quarter, the data contain individual-level information on total wages earned from each Michigan-based employer, alongside employer-level information on the average quarterly wages paid to employees in the given quarter and the employer's detailed six-digit North American Industry Classification (NAICS) Code.

I focus on the 10,794 individuals who are no older than fifty-five at the time of release. I estimate job quality using UI data from all these individuals; however, when I estimate the effect of employment quality on future criminal justice contact, I focus in particular on those who find employment, have not been arrested or returned to prison at any point between their sampled release from prison in 2003 and the end of the quarter in which they find such employment, and who do not have missing values for any covariates used in the estimation of the effect of job quality on future criminal justice contact.

### Job Quality

Because UI data do not include information about workers' occupations, only the industries of their employers, I measure job quality at the level of the industry, using four distinct measures of job quality.

First, I compare average industry-level quarterly earnings of workers to average quarterly earnings in all other industries. Earnings are clearly a central component of job quality: higher earnings make it easier for workers to meet consumption needs and to grow savings. For parolees in particular, higher earnings may reduce recidivism by reducing economic motivations for crime. Calculating industry-level earnings within UI data is complicated by the fact that UI data do not have information on hourly wage rates or the number of hours that employees work within a quarter. Further, differences in job tenure between industries could affect calculations of average industry-level wages, both because higher-tenured workers earn more and because workers are more likely to work only for part of quarter in low-tenure industries. Thus, I compare industry-level wages between workers who work only at one job, are in their second quarter of employment at that job, and work at that job in the next quarter.

Second, I compare average industry-level employment tenure to average employment tenure in all other industries. Tenure is also an important dimension of job quality, reflecting stability of employment as well as the ability of workers to have careers within firms. Further, employers that provide greater employment stability may curb recidivism by providing a set of routine activities to replace those that led to imprisonment and creating deeper ties to individuals who are not in contact with the criminal justice system. I measure employment tenure as the number of consecutive quarters in a given employment spell with a given employer.

Third, I compare average industry-level quarterly wages per employee to average quarterly wages per employee in all other industries. This measure may reflect in part the potential for wage growth for employees who advance within the firm. Thus, being employed at a firm with higher quarterly wages per employee may provide workers who have just been released from prison with a sense that they are able to achieve normative economic and social goals, and therefore reduce the probability that they will return to prison. Harry Holzer and his colleagues (2011) use a similar measure—firm-level earnings effects—in using national UI data to compare how job quality varies by industry, arguing that this measure captures differences in firms' contributions to pay due to capital holdings, compensating differentials, or human resources policies.[4] Although this measure does not directly capture dimensions of job quality such as fringe benefits, growth opportunities, or safety, evidence suggests that these other dimensions are positively correlated with firm-level earnings effects (Andersson, Holzer, and Lane 2005; Hamermesh 1998). I calculate industry-level quarterly wages per employee using the average across the last quarter of all employment spells within the industry reported in the UI data.

Finally, I compare industry-level statewide union coverage rates to the average industry-level statewide union coverage rate. I calculate industry-level union coverage rates in the state of Michigan using data from 2003 through 2009 from the Current Population Survey, downloaded from CPS-IPUMS (Flood et al. 2018). It is unclear from UI data which parolees are covered by unions at their work. However, industry-level union coverage is likely to improve job quality for low-wage workers because nonunion employers in highly unionized regions are compelled to raise job quality to forestall the threat of unionization. Research has found associations between region-industry union coverage and higher wages (Western and Rosenfeld 2011) and lower work hour volatility (LaBriola and Schneider 2019) for low-wage workers.

In sum, three of these four measures of job quality—average quarterly earnings, average employment tenure, and average firm-level quarterly wages per employee—are calculated from the sample of parolees in UI data and hence reflect the quality of the average job within each industry that sampled individuals might obtain after release from prison. The fourth measure—industry-level statewide unionization rates—reflects normative pressures that likely translate to better job quality for marginal workers. Although measuring job quality at the level of the industry has limitations (discussed in greater detail in the conclusion), the stark differences between industries in these measures of job quality strongly suggest that the measures meaningfully reflect how job quality varies between industries for individuals finding work after release from prison.

For each industry, I use two-tailed t-tests to determine whether average wages, average employment tenure, average quarterly wages per employee, and statewide union coverage are significantly greater than or less than average wages, average employment tenure, average quarterly wages per employee, and statewide union coverage in all other industries combined. I define an industry as offering high-quality employment if at least three out of four of these measures are significantly greater within the industry than in the rest of the sample, the fourth measure not being significantly lower. Conversely, I define an industry as offer-

---

4. In results available on request, I test the robustness of this article's findings to measuring the quality of industries via industry-level average firm earnings effects (calculated from Holzer et al. 2011, table 2.1). Using this measure to classify industry quality reveals largely similar results to those reported in this article—higher-quality jobs reduce future criminal justice contact. However, the industry groupings used in the study by Harry Holzer and his colleagues (2011) are not granular enough to capture the industry of employment services (temporary help agencies), which offers the worst job quality to parolees in the Michigan data set. These jobs are contained in the administrative and support services category, which Holzer and his colleagues do not rate as low in quality as other industries. Further, within-sample measures of industry-level job quality are more likely to capture parolees' experience of job quality than are national measures of industry-level job quality. Thus, I chiefly rely on these within-sample measures of industry-level job quality.

ing low-quality employment if at least three out of four measures are significantly lower than in the rest of the sample, the fourth measure not being significantly higher. Within high-quality and low-quality industries, I also identify the highest-quality and lowest-quality industries that are above or below average in all four dimensions of job quality.

Table 1 tabulates the percentage of quarters worked by individuals in the sample by industry classification, along with average quarterly gross wages, average job tenure, average quarterly wages per employee, and statewide unionization rates by industry. Boldface entries in the columns measuring dimensions of employment quality indicate that the average value for a given industry is significantly larger than the average value in all other industries; italicized entries indicate that the average value for a given industry is significantly smaller than the average value in all other industries (a significance level of .05 is used for both).

The highest-quality industries in which sampled individuals find employment are manufacturing (NAICS = 31xxxx, 32xxxx, 33xxxx; 18.78 percent of quarters worked) and transportation and warehousing (NAICS = 48xxxx, 49xxxx; 1.89 percent of quarters worked); both industries offer above-average quarterly earnings, job tenure, firm-level quarterly earnings per employee, and state-level union coverage. Among common industries, construction (NAICS = 23xxxx; 9.19 percent of quarters worked) is also a high-quality industry, offering both above-average earnings, firm-level quarterly earnings per employee and state-level union coverage.

In contrast, employment services (NAICS = 5613xx; 19.66 percent of quarters worked in the sample) is the lowest-quality industry in which individuals paroled in Michigan in 2003 found employment, coming in below average in every measured dimension of employment quality. Industries classified as offering low-quality employment include limited service eating places (NAICS = 7222xx; 7.82 percent of quarters worked), full service restaurants (NAICS = 7221xx; 6.09 percent of quarters worked), and services to buildings and dwellings (NAICS = 5617xx; 3.69 percent of quarters worked).

I code the treatment variable as an indicator variable, equal to 1 if a sampled individual obtains their first employment after the sampled prison spell in a high-quality or highest-quality industry, and 0 if in a low-quality or lowest-quality industry. To more closely study the relationship between employment quality and future criminal justice contact, I focus on respondents who find post-prison employment before experiencing arrest or a return to prison. I assign individuals who have their first record of employment in a high-quality industry in the same quarter as they have their first record of employment in a low-quality industry a value of 1 for the treatment variable.

I also report results from a similarly constructed treatment variable where 1 indicates that a parolee finds employment in a highest-quality industry before getting arrested or returning to prison, and 0 indicates a lowest-quality industry. I use this treatment variable to test for the existence of any discernible effects of post-prison job quality on future criminal justice contact: if models that account for differential selection into job quality find no significant difference in future criminal justice contact between those who find the highest-quality employment and those who find the lowest-quality employment, no such effect likely exists.

Finally, I create four treatment variables to test for the effect of finding post-prison employment in an industry offering a given level of job quality relative to not finding employment. For each of four industry quality classifications (highest-quality, high-quality, low-quality, and lowest-quality), I set an indicator variable equal to 1 if a parolee finds employment in that industry category within one quarter of the quarter of release from prison, and 0 if not. As with other treatment variables, I drop observations when a parolee is arrested or has returned to prison within the time frame.

**Post-prison Criminal Justice Contact**
I measure two types of criminal justice contact: arrests and returns to prison. Prison terms are certainly more consequential than arrests, and much of the literature on the effect of employment on future criminal justice contact focuses on recidivism as a dependent variable. Yet arrests are also an indicator of criminal behavior, and the various theories connecting employ-

**Table 1.** Within-Sample Measures of Employment Quality, by Industry Classification

| Industry Name | NAICS Prefix | Percentage Quarters Worked | Average Quarterly Earnings | Average Job Tenure (Quarters) | Firm Average Quarterly Earnings | State-Level Union Coverage |
|---|---|---|---|---|---|---|
| All industries | | 100% | 5,366 | 2.03 | 4,361 | 21.6% |
| **Highest-quality industries** | | | | | | |
| Manufacturing | 31–33 | 18.78 | **6,741** | **2.65** | **7,831** | **26.4** |
| Transportation and warehousing | 48–49 | 1.89 | **6,832** | **2.48** | **6,389** | **42.9** |
| **High-quality industries** | | | | | | |
| Construction | 23 | 9.19 | **7,407** | 2.06 | **6,724** | **27.2** |
| Educational services | 61 | 0.81 | 6,132 | **2.52** | **8,333** | **52.7** |
| Mining | 21 | 0.14 | **8,309** | 2.03 | **9,127** | **44.7** |
| **Medium-quality industries** | | | | | | |
| Retail trade | 44–45 | 7.47 | 5,299 | **2.13** | 4,759 | 10.9 |
| Health care and social assistance | 62 | 5.16 | *2,837* | **2.77** | *3,181* | 15.3 |
| Wholesale trade | 42 | 3.18 | **6,429** | **2.7** | **7,913** | 9.5 |
| Automotive repair and maintenance | 8111 | 2.46 | 5,302 | **2.4** | 4,299 | 2.4 |
| Other administrative and support services | 56 | 2.16 | 5,496 | *1.82* | 4,297 | 5.5 |
| Professional, scientific, and technical services | 54 | 1.96 | **7,826** | 2.11 | **5,637** | 2.9 |
| Missing NAICS code | . | 1.25 | 6,167 | *1.57* | 4,254 | NA |
| Real estate and rental and leasing | 53 | 0.91 | 6,052 | 2.21 | **4,947** | NA |
| Public administration | 92 | 0.56 | 6,456 | 2.25 | **10,360** | **55.5** |
| Agriculture, forestry, fishing, and hunting | 11 | 0.55 | 6,049 | *1.75* | 3,270 | 2.9 |
| Information | 51 | 0.50 | 5,302 | 2.36 | 6,219 | 18.1 |
| Finance and insurance | 52 | 0.45 | **6,904** | 2.59 | 6,475 | 5.3 |
| Management of companies and enterprises | 55 | 0.12 | 5,780 | 2.41 | **7,381** | 0.0 |
| Utilities | 22 | 0.01 | | 3 | **17,230** | **46.7** |
| **Low-quality industries** | | | | | | |
| Limited service eating places | 7222 | 7.82 | *2,852* | 1.98 | *2,241* | 2.0 |
| Full service restaurants | 7221 | 6.09 | *3,820* | 2.03 | *2,671* | 2.0 |
| Services to buildings and dwellings | 5617 | 3.69 | *4,976* | *1.92* | *3,660* | 6.3 |
| Other accommodation and foodservices | 72 | 2.73 | *4,067* | 1.99 | *2,837* | 6.0 |
| Other services | 81 | 1.56 | *4,434* | 2.06 | *3,684* | 4.6 |
| Arts, entertainment, and recreation | 71 | 0.90 | *4,260* | 1.99 | *2,908* | 10.7 |
| **Lowest-quality industries** | | | | | | |
| Employment services | 5613 | 19.66 | *4,205* | *1.59* | *2,677* | 4.2 |

*Source:* Author's compilation from data from the Michigan Unemployment Insurance Agency, the Michigan Workforce Development Agency, and the 2003–2009 Current Population Survey (Flood et al. 2018).

*Note:* Boldface entries indicate significantly higher job quality than in other industries ($p < .05$, two-tailed test). Italicized entries indicate significantly lower job quality than in other industries. Quarterly gross wages calculated among all workers in the sample working in the second consecutive quarter working for an employer, and who are still working for that employer in the next quarter. Average quarterly gross wages per employee calculated during the last quarter working for an employer.

**Figure 1.** Cumulative Likelihood of Criminal Justice Contact After Finding Employment, by Employment Quality

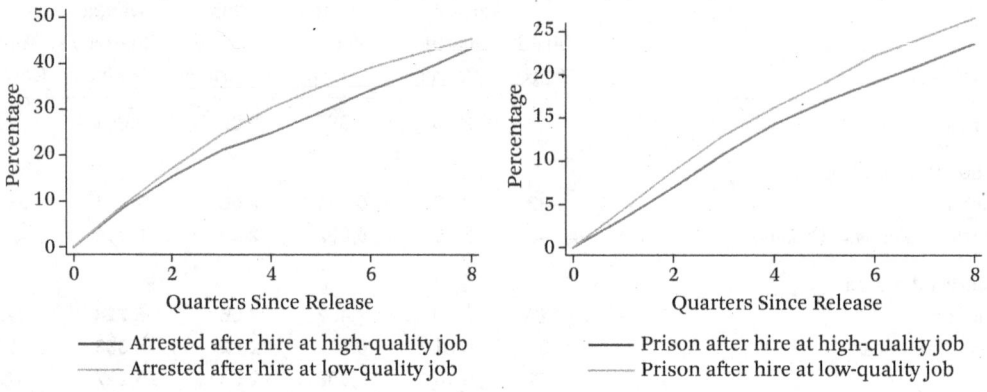

*Source:* Author's compilation from data from the Michigan Unemployment Insurance Agency and the Michigan Workforce Development Agency.

ment quality to recidivism all suggest that high-quality employment should reduce criminal behavior more generally. I measure each of these types of criminal justice contact in each of the eight quarters after the quarter in which an individual finds employment in a high- or low-quality job. Data on arrests come from the Michigan State Police, and data on returns to prison come from the Michigan Department of Corrections.

Figure 1 shows the cumulative percentage of sampled parolees who are arrested or return to prison in the eight quarters after beginning work in a high- or low-quality industry. Criminal justice contact is fairly common for both groups, more than 40 percent of each set of workers experiencing an arrest within two years from starting employment and more than 25 percent of each set of workers experiencing a return to prison over this time frame. Sampled parolees who find high-quality employment are slightly less likely to experience arrest or a return to prison over the period, and the gap in criminal justice contact between those who find high- and low-quality employment widens over time.

**Other Covariates**

Selection into a high-quality industry, relative to a low-quality industry, is a nonrandom process. Further, some of the same traits that predict this selection process are also likely to predict whether an individual is likely to recidivate. Therefore, to more closely estimate the causal effect of finding employment after release from prison in a high-quality industry (relative to a low-quality one), it is necessary to control for factors that could affect both the quality of industry in which parolees find employment and the likelihood that parolees experience future criminal justice contact.

I include as covariates several variables that measure parolees' demographic and human capital characteristics—age at time of release, sex, race (operationalized as white or black),[5] an indicator for being married at time of release, whether an individual has a high school degree or GED, and the logged maximum quarterly earnings recorded in the Michigan UI data between 1997 and the time of release. I also include as covariates the quarterly unemployment rate at the time that the parolee first found employment in the county in which the

---

5. The race of 98 percent of parolees captured in the data is white or black. The analysis focuses on these individuals because the small number of individuals of another race in the dataset does not allow for strong inference on the effects of job quality within this group. Analyses that dichotomize individuals' race as white or nonwhite produce similar results.

**Table 2.** Means of Model Covariates, by Post-prison Employment Quality

|  | Low-Quality Employment | High-Quality Employment |
|---|---|---|
| Age at release from prison | 33.3 | 35.1*** |
| Percentage white | 45.0 | 54.4*** |
| Percentage female | 10.1 | 5*** |
| Percentage married | 12.4 | 15.7** |
| Percentage with high school degree or GED | 57.8 | 60.2 |
| Logged max quarterly pre-prison wages | 5.4 | 5.7* |
| Number of prior arrests | 4.9 | 5.2 |
| Percentage with conviction for violent offense | 47.5 | 47.6 |
| Percentage with conviction for theft | 45.2 | 44.3 |
| Percentage with conviction for drug offense | 31.8 | 29.9 |
| Percentage with conviction for behavioral offense | 24.9 | 26.7 |
| Number of years in prison spell | 3.3 | 3.4 |
| Maximum management level during prison spell | 2.7 | 2.6 |
| Misconducts per year during prison spell | 0.8 | 0.6*** |
| Percentage time in solitary during prison spell | 1.1 | 0.8 |
| Percentage classified as sex offender | 8.3 | 8.1 |
| Percentage known to have mental illness | 18.6 | 18.0 |
| Percentage with known substance abuse history | 43.9 | 43.4 |
| Percentage subject to post-prison electronic monitoring | 8.9 | 11.3* |
| Unemployment rate in county to which parolee released, in quarter of release | 7.4 | 7.5 |
| Time to finding post-prison employment (quarters after release) | 2.5 | 2.5 |
| N | 2,529 | 1,026 |

*Source:* Author's compilation from data from the Michigan Unemployment Insurance Agency and the Michigan Workforce Development Agency.
*p < .05; **p < .01; ***p < .001

parolee first lived after release from prison (collected from the Michigan Department of Labor and Economic Growth), and the quarter after release from prison in which the respondent found employment.

Finally, I include a host of covariates collected by the Michigan Department of Corrections that reflect both parolees' exposure to the criminal justice system through the sampled release from prison and factors used in previous research to predict post-prison employment and criminal justice outcomes (Uggen 1999). Notably, given that Josh Seim and David Harding (2020) find that parole supervision may impel parolees into obtaining employment, I control for a proxy of the intensity of parole supervision: whether a parolee is subject to electronic monitoring.

Table 2 lists all model covariates and displays their mean values within the sample by employment quality. Parolees who found employment in high-quality industries are older, had higher pre-prison earnings, and are more likely to be white, male, and married than their counterparts in low-quality industries. Although those who found employment in low-quality industries committed more frequent misconducts during their sampled prison spell, these groups surprisingly do not otherwise appear to differ in the levels of variables reflecting their criminal justice history. The final analysis sample of those who have nonmissing values on all covariates consists of 1,026 individuals who found employment in high-quality industries and 2,529 who found employment in low-quality industries.

## METHODS

I first estimate the naïve treatment effect of employment quality on each of the measures of future criminal justice contact using a series of linear probability regression models:[6]

$$Prob(Y_{it}) = \alpha + \beta_1 HQ_i + \varepsilon_i, \qquad (1)$$

where $Y_{it}$ is an indicator variable equal to 1 if individual $i$ has experienced a given form of criminal justice contact in the $t$ quarters since finding high- or low-quality employment and 0 if not, $HQ_i$ is the treatment variable described, and $\varepsilon_i$ is a standard error term. These models estimate what the effect of post-prison employment quality would be on future criminal justice contact if selection into post-prison employment quality were random, and essentially capture the difference in probability of experiencing future criminal justice contact between those who find high-quality and low-quality employment. Negative values of $\beta_1$ indicate that those with high-quality employment are less likely to experience a given form of future criminal justice contact, whereas positive values indicate that those with high-quality employment are more likely.

Next, I compare these naïve estimates of effects of employment quality on future criminal justice contact to estimates that use inverse propensity score weighting (IPW) (see, for example, Morgan and Winship 2015, 226–66) to account for differential selection into employment of differing quality. To do so, I first estimate the propensity score—here, the probability that an individual in the final analysis sample finds employment in a high-quality industry—using the following logistic model:

$$\log\left(\frac{Prob(HQ_i)}{1-Prob(HQ_i)}\right) = \alpha + \beta_1 X_i + \varepsilon_i, \qquad (2)$$

where $X_i$ is the vector of covariates listed for individual $i$ and other variables are as previously defined. Then, I use the predicted propensity scores from the above regression to assign each individual $i$ weights as follows:

$$w_i = \frac{1}{Prob(HQ_i)} \text{ if } i \text{ finds high-quality employment}$$
$$w_i = \frac{1}{1-Prob(HQ_i)} \text{ if } i \text{ finds low-quality employment} \qquad (3)$$

Here, observations are weighted by the inverse of the probability of receiving the treatment (of high-quality or low-quality employment) they actually received. This weighting gives more weight to individuals who find high-quality employment and are more similar to those who find low-quality employment on covariates included in the propensity score model, and vice versa. In essence, this creates a pseudo-population where post-prison employment quality is uncorrelated with the covariates that affect both employment quality and future criminal justice contact.[7]

Finally, I include these weights in a weighted linear probability model predicting future criminal justice contact as a function of job quality and covariates listed above:

$$Prob(Y_{it}) = \alpha + \beta_1 HQ_i + \beta_2 X_i + \varepsilon_i. \qquad (4)$$

I specify this model to have robust standard errors. The inclusion of covariates in both the model predicting employment quality and the model predicting future criminal justice contact—known as "doubly-robust" regression (Morgan and Winship 2015, 234–37)—increases the likelihood that this modeling process obtains an unbiased effect estimate, because if either model is correctly specified, the estimated treatment effect will be unbiased.

I estimate the naïve and IPW models for two

---

6. I use linear probability models rather than logistic regression models to facilitate the comparison of coefficients across models, because doing so using the results of logistic regression models is inadvisable (Mood 2010).

7. For weighting to remove the association between covariates that affect the outcome and the treatment, the distribution of covariates must not vary between the weighted treatment and weighted control groups. In each model, I implement the test of Kosuke Imai and Marc Ratkovic (2014) to check whether covariates are balanced between treatment and control groups, and in all cases do not reject the null hypothesis that the propensity score model balances covariates between groups.

measures of future criminal justice contact—being arrested after finding employment and returning to prison after finding employment. For each measure, I estimate the effect on the cumulative probability of experiencing criminal justice contact between the time of finding employment and one to eight quarters afterward. Negative values of $\beta_1$ indicate that high-quality employment leads to lower risk of criminal justice contact; positive values of $\beta_1$ indicate that high-quality employment leads to higher risk of criminal justice contact.

I also replicate the analysis using a treatment variable that compares future criminal justice contact of parolees whose first post-prison employment is in a highest-quality industry (manufacturing and transportation-warehousing) to their counterparts in the lowest-quality industry. Finally, I use the same method to estimate the respective effects of finding employment in a highest-quality, high-quality, low-quality, and lowest-quality industry within the first quarter after the quarter of release from prison, relative to not finding employment in that time frame.

## RESULTS

I first discuss estimates of the effect of employment quality on future criminal justice contact. I then turn to discussing how estimates of the relationship between employment and future criminal justice contact vary by employment quality.

### Effects of Employment Quality on Future Criminal Justice Contact

Figure 2 presents both the naïve estimates (solid line confidence intervals) and the estimates from the IPW procedure (dashed line confidence intervals) of the treatment effect of finding high-quality post-prison employment (relative to low-quality) on future criminal justice contact. The left panel shows effects for the outcome of being arrested after finding employment; the right panel shows effects for the outcome of returning to prison after finding employment. The magnitude of the estimated effect on the probability of being arrested is shown on the x-axis. Estimated effects are ordered vertically by time such that the estimated effect on the probability of being arrested or returning to prison in the first quarter after finding employment is at the top of the figure and the estimated effect for within eight quarters is at the bottom.

The naïve estimates of the effect of employment quality on future criminal justice contact restate the findings in figure 1: those who find high-quality employment are less likely, and often significantly less likely, to experience future criminal justice contact in the quarters after starting employment. However, the IPW estimates, which account for differential selection into employment quality based on observable characteristics, are lower and less often significantly different from zero. For the outcome of being arrested, the cumulative risk is significantly lower for those who find employment in high-quality industries through the fourth and fifth quarters after finding employment; however, for the outcome of returning to prison, no significant causal effect of employment quality is evident. Overall, the effect of finding employment in a high-quality relative to a low-quality industry on future criminal justice contact appears to be positive, but the estimates are decidedly mixed.

Figure 3 presents the results of the naïve and IPW estimates of the effect of finding employment in one of the highest-quality industries—manufacturing, transportation, and warehousing—relative to finding employment in the lowest-quality industry—employment services—on future criminal justice contact. If employment quality does in fact reduce future criminal justice contact, the effects should be most apparent when comparing the highest- and lowest-quality industries.

Here we do see a more consistent effect of employment quality on future criminal justice contact, especially for arrests. After accounting for observable characteristics, those who find employment in the highest-quality industries are just over 4 percentage points less likely to be arrested between starting employment and eight quarters afterward; this corresponds to a roughly 10 percent decrease in the likelihood of being arrested over the period. Similarly, those who find employment in the highest-quality industries are almost 4 percentage points less likely to return to prison in the eight quarters after starting employment than those

**Figure 2.** Effect of High-Quality Versus Low-Quality Employment on Future Criminal Justice Contact

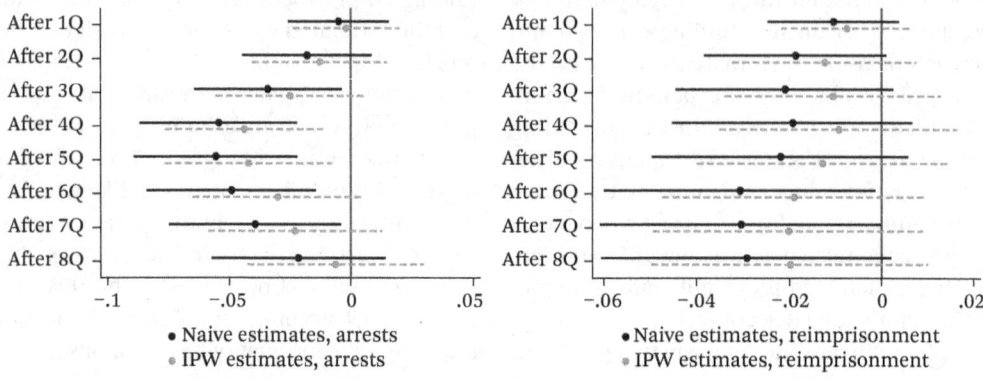

*Source:* Author's compilation from data from the Michigan Unemployment Insurance Agency and the Michigan Workforce Development Agency.
*Note:* These figures represent estimates of the effect of finding employment after release from prison in an industry that offers high-quality employment (relative to finding employment in an industry that offers low-quality employment) on the cumulative likelihood of experiencing an arrest (left panel) or returning to prison (right panel) in each of the eight quarters after finding employment. High-quality industries include manufacturing, transportation and warehousing, construction, educational services, and mining; low-quality industries include services to buildings and dwellings, employment services, arts-entertainment-recreation, accommodation and food services, and other services. Estimates are expressed in percentage points, with negative values indicating reduced future criminal justice contact for those who find high-quality employment. The estimates with solid-line confidence intervals represent the naïve difference in future criminal justice contact between those who find high- and low-quality employment. The estimates with dashed-line confidence intervals represent the estimated difference in future criminal justice contact between those who find high- and low-quality employment that accounts for differential selection into employment quality using inverse propensity score weighting.

who find employment in employment services; this translates to about a 13 percent decrease in the likelihood of returning to prison.

### Effects of Employment on Future Criminal Justice Contact, by Employment Quality

Figure 4 presents naïve and IPW estimates of the effect of finding employment by the first quarter after release from prison (relative to not doing so) on the cumulative risk of arrest in the eight quarters afterwards, by employment quality. Figure 5 presents analogous estimates for the outcome of the cumulative risk of returning to prison.

We see in figure 4 that employment in itself does not appear to have a robust effect on reducing future arrests, no matter the quality of employment. Interestingly, those who find employment in low-quality industries actually appear to be more likely to be arrested in the first two or three quarters after finding employment than those who do not find employment at all. Figure 5, however, shows strong evidence that high-quality employment reduces the cumulative risk of returning to prison in the eight quarters after beginning employment relative to not finding employment. Finding low-quality employment, on the other hand, appears to have no such effect.

### DISCUSSION

Social scientists have put forth several causal explanations for criminal behavior, including economic motivation, anomic isolation, lack of social control, and lack of routine activities. Each of these theories suggests that, for those who have had previous criminal justice contact, not just employment but employment quality should matter for future criminal justice contact. Although previous work has found an effect of employment quality on recidivism in the context of the United States, the question of

**Figure 3.** Effect of Highest-Quality Versus Lowest-Quality Employment on Future Criminal Justice Contact

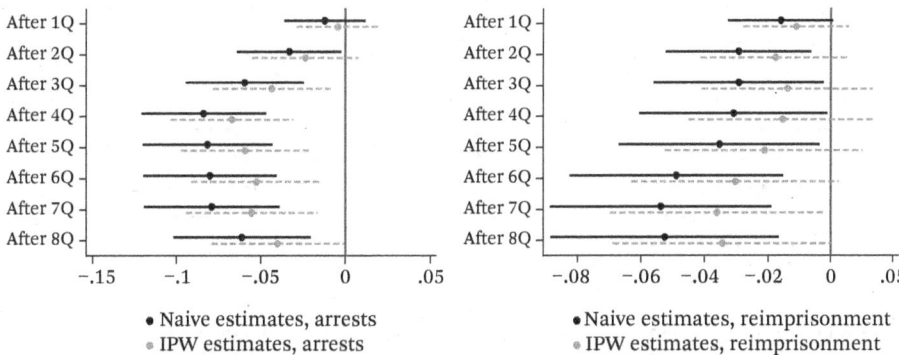

- Naive estimates, arrests
- IPW estimates, arrests
- Naive estimates, reimprisonment
- IPW estimates, reimprisonment

*Source:* Author's compilation from data from the Michigan Unemployment Insurance Agency and the Michigan Workforce Development Agency.
*Note:* These figures represent estimates of the effect of finding employment after release from prison in an industry that offers highest-quality employment (relative to finding employment in an industry that offers lowest-quality employment) on the cumulative likelihood of experiencing an arrest (left panel) or returning to prison (right panel) in each of the eight quarters after finding employment. Highest-quality industries include manufacturing and transportation and warehousing; lowest-quality industries include employment services. Estimates are expressed in percentage points, with negative values indicating reduced future criminal justice contact for those who find highest-quality employment. The estimates with solid-line 95 percent confidence intervals represent the naïve difference in future criminal justice contact between those who find highest- and lowest-quality employment. The estimates with dashed-line 95 percent confidence intervals represent the estimated difference in future criminal justice contact between those who find highest- and lowest-quality employment that accounts for differential selection into employment quality using inverse propensity score weighting.

whether this effect can be accounted for by selection into various types of employment is unanswered. Further, this work focused on extra-economic components of job quality, although economic aspects of job quality are also thought to be important for reducing motivations for crime.

I use matching techniques to compare otherwise similar parolees who find employment in industries characterized by varying levels of employment quality, as defined by average earnings, job tenure, firm-wide earnings per employee, and state-level union coverage. Some evidence indicates that high-quality employment reduces the risk of future criminal justice contact relative to lowest-quality employment, though this effect is most apparent when comparing the industries that offer the best employment quality to the industry that offers the worst.

I also analyze how employment in industries of varying quality affects the future likelihood of arrest or reimprisonment relative to those who do not find employment. I find that securing employment in high-quality industries reduces the risk of future criminal justice contact, but that in low-quality industries it does not. This may imply that, due to the increasing precarity of work in the United States (Kalleberg 2011), much of the employment available to parolees may not be able to provide economic benefits or social integration that are thought to link post-prison employment to reduced criminal justice contact. These results are consistent with the findings of Seim and Harding (2020), who use the same data as in this article to show that, among both those on parole and those who have been discharged from parole, employment appears to have negligible effects on recidivism. The most obvious explanation for these results is that most individuals who find work after prison do so in rel-

**Figure 4.** Effect of Employment on Future Arrests, by Employment Quality

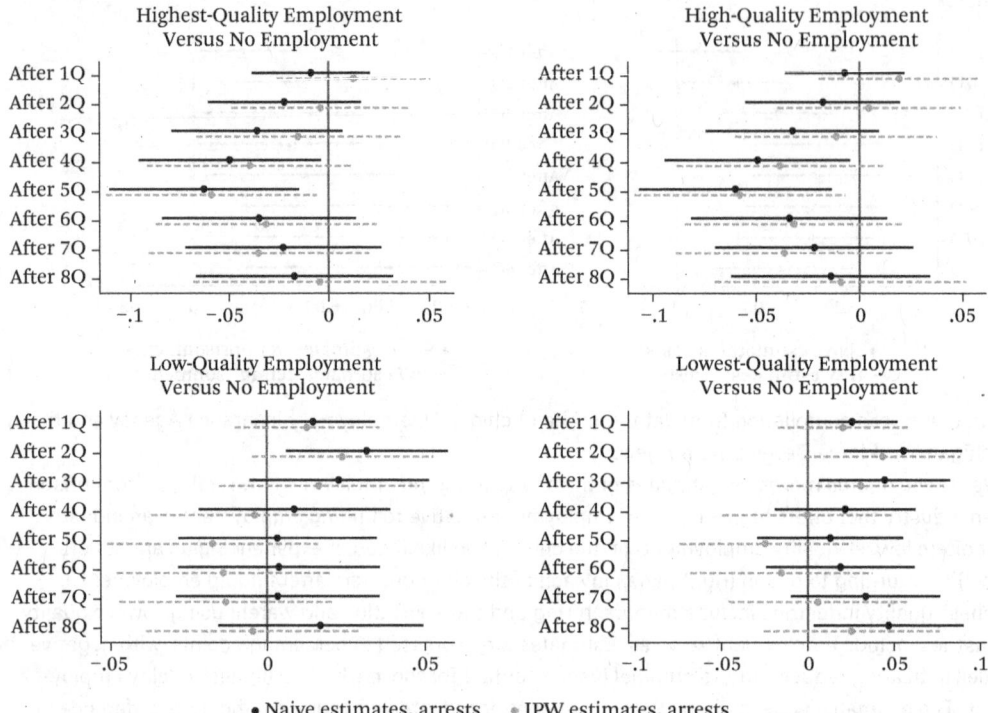

*Source:* Author's compilation from data from the Michigan Unemployment Insurance Agency and the Michigan Workforce Development Agency.
*Note:* These figures represent estimates of the effect of finding employment within the first quarter after release from prison in industries that offer varying qualities of employment (relative to not finding employment in this time) on the cumulative likelihood of experiencing an arrest in each of the eight quarters after this time. The estimates with solid-line 95 percent confidence intervals represent the naïve difference in future arrests between those who find employment within the first quarter after release from prison and those who do not find employment. The estimates with dashed-line 95 percent confidence intervals) represent the estimated difference in future arrests that accounts for differential selection into employment of varying quality using inverse propensity score weighting.

atively low-quality industries: the counts in table 2 suggest that parolees are roughly two and a half times as likely to find low-quality employment as high-quality employment after release from prison. Further, even high-quality employment does not forestall all future criminal justice contact, and many of the estimates of the effect of high-quality employment on criminal justice contact have confidence intervals that overlap with zero.

These findings should be qualified in several ways. Perhaps the most salient limitation is that the UI data do not include information about workers' occupations, which would likely give more precise information about workers' job quality than is available at the industry level. If there is heterogeneity in job quality within industries classified here as high-quality or low-quality, then this would attenuate the estimates of the effect of job quality on future criminal justice contact toward zero. Given the limitations of this data, it is impossible to determine the extent to which this is the case. However, despite variation in job quality within industries in general, those who have been to prison are likely to mostly be able to find employment in jobs that are among the lowest quality within industries, given their poor job prospects overall (Western 2006). This would imply relatively little within-industry heteroge-

**Figure 5.** Effect of Employment on Future Reimprisonment, by Employment Quality

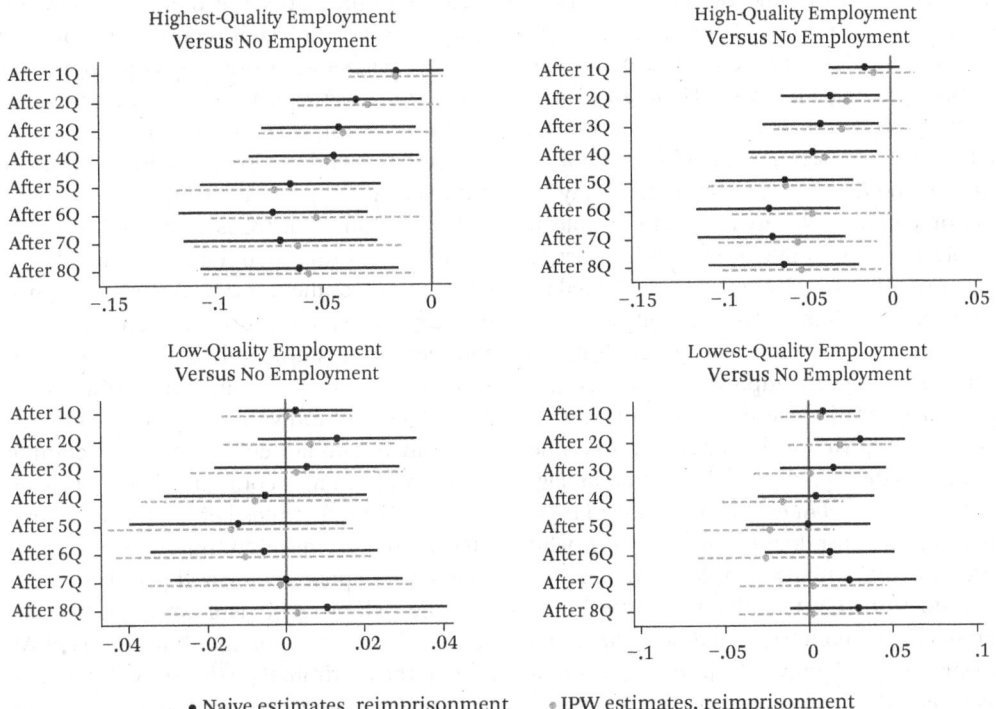

*Source:* Author's compilation from data from the Michigan Unemployment Insurance Agency and the Michigan Workforce Development Agency.
*Note:* These figures represent estimates of the effect of finding employment within the first quarter after release from prison in industries that offer varying qualities of employment (relative to not finding employment in this time) on the cumulative likelihood of returning to prison in each of the eight quarters after this time. The estimates with solid-line 95 percent confidence intervals represent the naïve difference in returning to prison between those who find employment within the first quarter after release from prison and those who do not. The estimates with dashed-line 95 percent confidence intervals represent the estimated difference in returning to prison that accounts for differential selection into employment of varying quality using inverse propensity score weighting.

neity in job quality in this sample. Future research that has access to detailed data on parolees' trajectories of occupations and criminal justice contact after release from prison could help test the extent to which post-prison occupational quality varies within industries.

A second qualification is that UI data do not capture informal employment, which some surveys have found is as common as formal employment within the first year of release from prison (Visher et al. 2008). Informal employment is likely to be of worse quality than the formal employment along dimensions of wages, job tenure, wage growth, and worker protections (Nightingale and Wandner 2011), and is likely associated with less structure than formal employment is. This implies that informal employment may be less likely than formal employment to prevent future criminal justice contact. However, with this data, this proposition cannot be tested.

Third, and relatedly, this study focuses on only a small sample of the population of those who have been released from prison. Most notably, formal employment is generally rare in this sample: fewer than one in three parolees are employed in the formal labor market in any given quarter after release (author's calculations). These low rates are similar to those found in previous research (Pettit and Lyons

2007; Sabol 2007), and are likely caused by several processes, including stigma against those with a criminal justice history (Pager 2003), state-level "hidden sentences" that hinder employment (Warner, Kaiser, and Houle 2020), and monetary sanctions, which interfere with the ability to maintain employment in several ways (Cadigan and Kirk 2020). Because this study focuses on parolees who are most employable, it cannot speak to how the future criminal justice contact of other parolees would be affected by finding employment of varying quality.

Fourth, it is possible that the relationship found here between employment quality and future criminal justice contact could result from those who are ready to desist from crime pursuing higher-quality employment as a "signal" (Bushway and Apel 2012) to others of their intentions to desist. In this scenario, those who search for high-quality employment may be disproportionately less likely to experience criminal justice contact, no matter their actual post-prison employment trajectory. Although this explanation cannot be completely ruled out with the data in this study, I am able to use a wide set of demographic, human capital, and criminal justice-related individual controls to account for selection into employment quality.

Finally, this study follows only one cohort of parolees who exit prison into a particular social and economic context, and so the external validity of these findings is limited. It would be useful to conduct similar analyses of the effect of job quality on recidivism in different times and places to build a more robust body of evidence about this relationship.

Although I find that employment quality reduces future criminal justice contact, it should still be emphasized that sampled individuals experience relatively short job tenures across all industries, and the difference in job tenure between high- and low-quality industries is often less than one quarter. Thus, any protective effects of relatively high-quality employment may be unlikely to last. Although those who have been to prison may be generally less likely than others to find and maintain stable, well-paying employment, it also seems probable that parolees are especially likely to experience precarious work, given that work has become more precarious generally in the United States (Kalleberg 2011), especially for workers of lower socioeconomic status. It is therefore plausible that increases in job quality and worker protection for all low-wage workers may facilitate the ability of those who have been to prison to maintain stable, well-paying employment, which may then have longer-lasting effects on future criminal justice contact.

Such a shift in the focus of research and policy interventions—from recidivism to the broader environment to which parolees return to after release from prison—echoes recent commentaries (Butts and Schiraldi 2018) that emphasize that recidivism is not reducible to the behavior of individuals alone. Recidivism is contingent on law enforcement's becoming aware of illegal acts committed by those who have committed crimes before; because state surveillance is more common in neighborhoods where poor people and people of color live, the risk of recidivism among otherwise equal individuals is not distributed equally. Although these criminal justice system inequalities have deservedly received increased attention as a site of intervention in recent years, labor market institutions are also important sites of intervention—not merely for the effects they may have on recidivism, but also for their potential impact on parolees' ability to positively participate in the social life of their community.

## REFERENCES

Agnew, Robert. 1985. "A Revised Strain Theory of Delinquency." *Social Forces* 64(1): 151–67.

Allan, Emilie Andersen, and Darrell J. Steffensmeier. 1989. "Youth, Underemployment, and Property Crime: Differential Effects of Job Availability and Job Quality on Juvenile and Young Adult Arrest Rates." *American Sociological Review* 54(1): 107–23.

Alper, Mariel, Matthew R. Durose, and Joshua Markman. 2018. "2018 Update on Prisoner Recidivism: A 9-Year Follow-up Period (2005-2014)." *Bureau of Justice Statistics* special report no. NCJ250975. Washington: U.S. Department of Justice.

Andersson, Fredrik, Harry J. Holzer, and Julia I. Lane. 2005. *Moving Up or Moving On: Who Advances in the Low-Wage Labor Market?* New York: Russell Sage Foundation.

Apel, Robert, and Julie Horney. 2017. "How and Why Does Work Matter? Employment Conditions, Routine Activities, and Crime Among Adult Male Offenders." *Criminology* 55(2): 307–43.

Becker, Gary S. 1968. "Crime and Punishment: An Economic Approach." *Journal of Political Economy* 76(2): 169–217.

Braithwaite, John. 1989. *Crime, Shame, and Reintegration*. Cambridge: Cambridge University Press.

Bushway, Shawn D., and Robert Apel. 2012. "A Signaling Perspective on Employment-Based Reentry Programming." *Criminology & Public Policy* 11(1): 21–50.

Butts, Jeffrey A., and Vincent Schiraldi. 2018. "Recidivism Reconsidered: Preserving the Community Justice Mission of Community Corrections." Papers from the Executive Session on Community Corrections at Harvard Kennedy School. Cambridge, Mass.: Harvard University.

Cadigan, Michele, and Gabriela Kirk. 2020. "On Thin Ice: Bureaucratic Processes of Monetary Sanctions and Job Insecurity." *RSF: The Russell Sage Foundation Journal of the Social Sciences* 6(1): 113–31. DOI: 10.7758/RSF.2020.6.1.05.

Carson, E. Ann. 2018. "Prisoners in 2016." Bureau of Justice Statistics bulletin no. NCJ251149. Washington: U.S. Department of Justice.

Cohen, Lawrence E., and Marcus Felson. 1979. "Social Change and Crime Rate Trends: A Routine Activities Approach." *American Sociological Review* 44(4): 588–608.

Crutchfield, Robert D., and Susan R. Pitchford. 1997. "Work and Crime: The Effects of Labor Stratification." *Social Forces* 76(1): 93–118.

Flood, Sarah, Miriam King, Renae Rodgers, Steven Ruggles, and J. Robert Warren. 2018. Integrated Public Use Microdata Series, Current Population Survey: Version 6.0 [dataset]. Minneapolis: IPUMS.

Freeman, Richard. 1999. "The Economics of Crime." In *Handbook of Labor Economics*, vol. 3, edited by Orley Ashenfelter and David Card. Philadelphia, Pa.: Elsevier.

Galbiati, Roberto, Aurelie Ouss, and Arnaud Philippe. 2017. "Jobs, News, and Re-Offending After Incarceration." Toulouse School of Economics working paper no. 17-843. Toulouse: University of Toulouse Midi-Pyrénées.

Gottfredson, Michael R., and Travis Hirschi. 1990. *A General Theory of Crime*. Stanford, Calif.: Stanford University Press.

Grogger, Jeff. 1998. "Market Wages and Youth Crime." *Journal of Labor Economics* 16(4): 756–91.

Hamermesh, Daniel. 1998. "Changing Inequality in Markets for Workplace Amenities." *Quarterly Journal of Economics* 114(4): 1085–23.

Harris, Alexes, Heather Evans, and Katherine Beckett. 2010. "Drawing Blood from Stones: Legal Debt and Social Inequality in the Contemporary United States." *American Journal of Sociology* 115(6): 1753–99.

Holzer, Harry J., Julia I. Lane, David B. Rosenblum, and Fredrik Andersson. 2011. *Where Are All the Good Jobs Going?: What National and Local Job Quality and Dynamics Mean for U.S. Workers*. New York: Russell Sage Foundation.

Imai, Kosuke, and Marc Ratkovic. 2014. "Covariate Balancing Propensity Score." *Journal of the Royal Statistical Society: Series B, Statistical Methodology* 76(1): 243–63.

Kalleberg, Arne L. 2011. *Good Jobs, Bad Jobs: The Rise of Polarized and Precarious Employment Systems in the United States, 1970s to 2000s*. New York: Russell Sage Foundation.

LaBriola, Joe, and Daniel Schneider. 2019. "Worker Power and Class Polarization in Intra-Year Work Hour Volatility." *Social Forces* soz032. First published online. DOI: 10.1093/sf/soz032.

Massoglia, Michael, and William Alex Pridemore. 2015. "Incarceration, Health, and Racial Disparities in Health." *Annual Review of Sociology* 41(1): 291–310.

Merton, Robert K. 1938. "Social Structure and Anomie." *American Sociological Review* 3(5): 672–82.

Mood, Carina. 2010. "Logistic Regression: Why We Cannot Do What We Think We Can Do, and What We Can Do About It." *European Sociological Review* 26(1): 67–82.

Morgan, Stephen L., and Christopher Winship. 2015. *Counterfactuals and Casual Inference: Methods and Principles for Social Research*, 2nd ed. Cambridge, Mass.: Cambridge University Press.

Nightingale, Demetra Smith, and Stephen A. Wandner. 2011. "Informal and Nonstandard Employment in the United States." Policy Brief no. 20. Washington, D.C.: The Urban Institute.

Pager, Devah. 2003. "The Mark of a Criminal Record." *American Journal of Sociology* 108(5): 937–75.

Pettit, Becky, and Christopher J. Lyons. 2007. "Status and the Stigma of Incarceration: The Labor

Market Effects of Incarceration, by Race, Class, and Criminal Involvement." In *Barriers to Reentry? The Labor Market for Released Prisoners in Post-Industrial America*, edited by Shawn Bushway, Michael Stoll, and David Weiman. New York: Russell Sage Foundation.

Ramakers, Anke, Paul Nieuwbeerta, Johan Van Wilsem, and Anja Dirkzwager. 2017. "Not Just Any Job Will Do: A Study on Employment Characteristics and Recidivism Risks After Release." *International Journal of Offender Therapy and Comparative Criminology* 61(16): 1795–818.

Raphael, Steven, and David Weiman. 2007. "The Impact of Local Labor Market Conditions on the Likelihood That Parolees are Returned to Custody." In *Barriers to Reentry? The Labor Market for Released Prisoners in Post-Industrial America*, edited by Shawn Bushway, Michael Stoll, and David Weiman. New York: Russell Sage Foundation.

Sabol, William J. 2007. "Local Labor Market Conditions and Post-Prison Employment Experience of Offenders Released from Ohio State Prisons." In *Barriers to Reentry? The Labor Market for Released Prisoners in Post-Industrial America*, edited by Shawn Bushway, Michael Stoll, and David Weiman. New York: Russell Sage Foundation.

Sampson, Robert J., and John H. Laub. 1990. "Crime and Deviance Over the Life Course: the Salience of Adult Social Bonds." *American Sociological Review* 55(5): 609–27.

———. 1993. *Crime in the Making: Pathways and Turning Points Through Life*. Cambridge, Mass.: Harvard University Press.

Schnepel, Kevin T. 2018. "Good Jobs and Recidivism." *Economic Journal* 128(608): 447–69.

Seim, Josh, and David J. Harding. 2020. "Parolefare: Post-prison Supervision and Low-Wage Work." *RSF: The Russell Sage Foundation Journal of the Social Sciences* 6(1): 173–95. DOI: 10.7758/RSF.2020.6.1.08.

Simon, Jonathan. 1993. *Poor Discipline: Parole and the Social Control of the Underclass, 1890–1990*. Chicago: University of Chicago Press.

Toby, Jackson. 1957. "Social Disorganization and Stake in Conformity: Complementary Factors in the Predatory Behavior of Hoodlums." *Journal of Criminal Law and Criminology* 48(1): 12–17.

Uggen, Christopher. 1999. "Ex-Offenders and the Conformist Alternative: A Job Quality Model of Work and Crime." *Social Problems* 46(1): 127–51.

Visher, Christy, Sara Debus, and Jennifer Yahner. 2008. "Employment After Prison: A Longitudinal Study of Releases in Three States." Justice Policy Center Research Brief. Washington, D.C.: The Urban Institute.

Wadsworth, Tim. 2006. "The Meaning of Work: Conceptualizing the Deterrent Effect of Employment on Crime Among Young Adults." *Sociological Perspectives* 49(3): 343–68.

Wang, Xia, Daniel P. Mears, and William D. Bales. 2010. "Race-Specific Employment Contexts and Recividism." *Criminology* 48(4): 1171–211.

Warner, Cody, Joshua Kaiser, and Jason N. Houle. 2020. "Locked Out of the Labor Market? State-Level Hidden Sentences and the Labor-Market Outcomes of Recently Incarcerated Young Adults." *RSF: The Russell Sage Foundation Journal of the Social Sciences* 6(1): 132–51. DOI: 10.7758/RSF.2020.6.1.06

Western, Bruce. 2006. *Punishment and Inequality in America*. New York: Russell Sage Foundation.

Western, Bruce, and Jake Rosenfeld. 2011. "Unions, Norms, and the Rise in U.S. Wage Inequality." *American Sociological Review* 76(4): 513–37.

Wildeman, Chris. 2008. "Parental Imprisonment, the Prison Boom, and the Concentration of Childhood Disadvantage." *Demography* 46(2): 265–80.

Yang, Crystal S. 2017. "Local Labor Markets and Criminal Recidivism." *Journal of Public Economics* 147(1): 16–29.

# Parolefare: Post-prison Supervision and Low-Wage Work

JOSH SEIM AND DAVID J. HARDING

*How might parole operate as a labor market institution, and how might it contribute to the governance of poverty and social marginality? Drawing on a series of correctional, employment, and arrest records for a cohort of parolees in Michigan, we show that parole generally supervises a jobless population, but also oversees a significant number of people who work. We also find evidence that parole, contrary to many expectations, increases the odds of employment. However, we do not find convincing evidence that parolee employment alleviates individual poverty or reduces the odds of recidivism. These results inspire a conceptualization of* parolefare, *another poverty regulating regime that successfully motivates worker-citizenship but does little to extend or protect the life chances of the poor.*

**Keywords:** parole, employment, recidivism, poverty governance

Research illustrating how the carceral state sweeps up those on the margins of the labor market and exacerbates their marginality in the process is more than ample (Apel and Sweeten 2010; Bushway, Stoll, and Weiman 2007; Irwin 2004; Pager 2007; Raphael 2014; Wacquant 2009; Western 2006). Accordingly, many elected officials, academics, and think tankers have of-

**Josh Seim** is assistant professor of sociology at the University of Southern California. **David J. Harding** is professor of sociology at the University of California, Berkeley.

© 2020 Russell Sage Foundation. Seim, Josh, and David J. Harding. 2020. "Parolefare: Post-prison Supervision and Low-Wage Work." *RSF: The Russell Sage Foundation Journal of the Social Sciences* 6(1): 173–95. DOI: 10.7758/RSF.2020.6.1.08. We thank the many people who provided us with feedback on earlier versions of this article. We are especially grateful to the participants in Berkeley Sociology's Race and Economic Inequality Workshop who critically evaluated our theory and method. A version of this article was also presented at the Pacific Sociological Association 2017 annual meeting and benefited from audience commentary. Chris Herring provided us with a detailed and constructive critique earlier in the development of this project. Heather Harris also assisted greatly with data cleaning and management. Collection and analysis of the data for this project were funded by the University of Michigan Center for Local, State, and Urban Policy, the National Poverty Center at the University of Michigan, the Russell Sage Foundation, the National Institute of Justice (2008-IJ-CX-0018, 2012-IJ-CX-0044), the National Science Foundation (SES-1061018, SES- 1060708), and the Eunice Kennedy Shriver National Institute of Child Health and Human Development (1R21HD060160 01A1) and by center grants from the Eunice Kennedy Shriver National Institute of Child Health and Human Development to the Population Studies Centers at the University of Michigan (R24 HD041028) and at UC Berkeley (R24 HD073964). Direct correspondence to: Josh Seim at jseim@usc.edu, Department of Sociology, University of Southern California, 851 Downey Way, Los Angeles, CA 900089–1059; and David J. Harding at dharding@berkeley.edu, Department of Sociology, University of California, Berkeley, 462 Barrows Hall, Berkeley, CA 94720.

Open Access Policy: *RSF: The Russell Sage Foundation Journal of the Social Sciences* is an open access journal. This article is published under a Creative Commons Attribution-NonCommercial-NoDerivs 3.0 Unported License.

fered a common prescription for reducing criminal justice contacts: put convicted felons to work (City of New York 2017; Finn 1998; Kachnowski 2005; Mead 2007; Western 2008). This recommended treatment is often packaged with other calls for behavioral and contextual interventions (substance abuse programming, cognitive behavioral therapy, and housing assistance), but employment remains a primary concern. It is not surprising, then, that so many programs behind bars and on the street tend to emphasize the promise of wage labor for justice-involved populations (Abrams and Lea 2016; Jonson and Cullen 2015; Miller 2014; Muhlhausen 2018; Seim 2016).

The intuition that hard work can be a good preventative for hard time does indeed find some support in evidence-based evaluations of job-training, transitional employment, work release, and so-called human capital investment programs (Drake, Aos, and Miller 2009; Redcross et al. 2012; Solomon et al. 2004; Uggen 2000). Yet evidence is also compelling that such interventions actually have little to no effect on future recidivism (Bohmert and Duwe 2011; Jacobs 2012; Moses 2012; Turner and Petersilia 1996; Visher, Winterfield, and Coggeshall 2005). Complicating matters even more, simple employment may matter less than quality employment. In general, working in the lower bulb of an employment hour glass—in the secondary labor market where most people who encounter police, courts, jails, prisons, and other correctional institutions tend to be found when they are not jobless or incarcerated—may do little to discourage criminal activity (Crutchfield 2014; see also Schnepel 2018; Uggen 1999).

Although insightful, much of the research that underscores these kinds of discussions neglect a significant sector of American criminal justice: parole. This omission is problematic. For one, the sheer size of parole suggests its significance among people caught in the belly of criminal justice processing. In Michigan, the focus of this study, more than 90 percent of state prisoners are released on parole supervision (Herbert, Morenoff, and Harding 2015).[1] Also, perhaps more than any major institution of criminal justice, parole is officially oriented toward shaping people's labor market participation. Indeed, parole officers usually mandate their subjects to work in the formal economy and apparently mix practices of policing with practices of social work to encourage compliance (Irwin 1970; Petersilia 2003; Werth 2013; West and Seiter 2004). These officers usually couple this frequently articulated, but rarely enforced, employment mandate with claims that labor can promote desistance and that wages can significantly challenge post-prison poverty (Seiter 2002).

To our knowledge, no convincing research suggests whether these claims are valid. Reasons have certainly been offered to suspect that parole may impel labor through surveillance, sanction, and aid (Rakis 2005). However, this is a far cry from what much of the scholarship on prisoner reentry tells us. Not only are formerly imprisoned people a notoriously difficult-to-employ population, but parole officers may actually impede labor by burdening their subjects with drug tests, check-ins, mandatory treatment programs, and other requirements (Patersilia 2003; Solomon et al. 2004; Travis 2005; Werth 2011). Accordingly, parole may paradoxically dampen its double mission of public safety and offender reintegration by building barriers to post-prison employment.

In this article, we turn to a unique dataset of longitudinal parole, employment, and arrest records for a cohort of working-age formerly imprisoned people in Michigan to address two questions. First, does parole affect the odds of employment? Second, does working while under parole supervision reduce the odds of recidivism? We first calculate the unadjusted employment rate and the wages earned for this population over five years. Then we assess the potential labor effect of parole. We deploy a fixed-effects approach to model the odds of

---

1. Fragmented across fifty-one departments (federal plus state) and often divided administratively by county, parole agencies in the United States collectively supervised an estimated 870,500 formerly imprisoned people at year-end 2015 (Kaeble and Bonczar 2017). So-called discretionary parole decisions may be increasingly replaced by mandatory release dates, but the regime that supervises former convicts and often facilitates their return to the penitentiary, what is typically called parole, remains.

quarterly employment. To check the robustness of our findings, we also model the odds of employment in five relatively common industries for formerly imprisoned people to work in (employment services, manufacturing, food services, construction, and retail). Again using fixed-effects modeling, we consider the consequences of parolee employment by estimating the odds of recidivism as measured by arrest or reincarceration (prison or jail).

Our results complicate what social scientists often assume about parole and parolee labor. Although employment is unquestionably low for parolees, we find that parole supervises a sizable number of formally employed people. We demonstrate that earnings are low for these workers, the median hovering around the federal poverty line. We also find, however, that parole exposure is positively associated with employment. By comparing individuals over time, we demonstrate that discharge from parole significantly lowers the odds of working in the formal economy. This association is not apparently driven by one industry, such as employment services (which includes temp work), but is also evident in manufacturing, food services, and retail industries. This finding directly counters commonly held assumptions that parole hinders employment. Last, in considering the effects of parolee labor, we do not find evidence that working while under parole is associated with decreased recidivism. This finding seems to be consistent with claims that so-called bad jobs are not reasonable deterrents of criminal justice contact and helps disrupt a false crime-employment dichotomy (Crutchfield 2014; Fagan and Freeman 1999; Harding, Morenoff, and Wyse 2019; Ramakers et al. 2017).

These findings inspire a conceptualization of *parolefare*, another poverty-regulating regime that motivates worker-citizenship but does little to extend or protect the life chances of the poor by way of increased employment. Like work-centric welfare programs, parole seems to encourage wage labor, but mostly for poor men instead of poor women. Similarly, parole does not apparently offer a convincing pathway out of poverty through formal employment. Such comparisons nevertheless account for only part of the story. Parole operates less like a workfare institution and more like a penal institution in that it supervises a population still largely outside formal labor. And, unlike some work-first welfare programing, parole does not apparently yield docility by way of mandated labor. We do not find evidence that holding employment while under parole lowers a person's odds of recidivism. This raises serious questions about the functions of employment mandates for parolees and other justice-involved populations.

## POOR DISCIPLINE OR DISCIPLINING THE POOR?

We understand parole to be part a splintered and contradictory state that governs, or regulates, relatively poor populations using a mixture of assistance and punishment (Piven and Cloward 1971; Seim 2017; Soss, Fording, and Schram 2011; Wacquant 2009). The technologies of American poverty regulation are numerous and specific, but two complementary strategies highlighted by Loïc Wacquant (2009) seem integral today: a *workfare* regime for processing mostly poor women who are also disproportionately women of color and a *prisonfare* regime for handling their male counterparts. Through workfare, the state reinforces the conditions for employers to exploit the poor by conditioning aid on labor-force participation (Collins and Mayer 2010; Hays 2003; Peck 2001; Soss, Fording, and Schram 2011). Through prisonfare, the state manages poor populations generally and historically excluded from labor, property, and civic life, amplifying their exclusion by containment and isolation (Alexander 2012; Irwin 2004; Western 2006).

We draw on two perspectives, one that preferences a more prisonfare-based explanation and one that preferences a more workfare-based explanation, to develop some hypotheses on parole and labor. These perspectives are mined from two similarly titled books: Jonathan Simon's *Poor Discipline* (1993) and Joe Soss, Richard Fording, and Sanford Schram's *Disciplining the Poor* (2011). According to Simon, the state, through the parole office, regulates an impoverished population largely excluded from labor. For him, contemporary parole officials recognize the futility of labor as a disciplinary force and do little to actually promote post-prison employment. Put another way, parole is part and parcel of a kind of prisonfare management of urban poverty. However, should parole actually impel more than impede labor, then Soss and colleagues analysis may be more useful. For those authors, the state regulates an impoverished population marginally included into the most exploitive segments of labor by way of the workfare office.

In *Poor Discipline*, Simon (1993) divides parole into three historical periods: disciplinary parole (circa 1890 to 1950), clinical parole (circa 1950 to 1970), and managerial parole (circa 1970 forward). During the first two periods, parole incentivized labor to varying degrees. Under disciplinary parole, the state coerced formerly imprisoned people into a tight labor market, subjecting them to the normalizing, punitive, and controlling conditions of work. Under clinical parole, the state decreased its focus on the employment of formerly imprisoned people. Less able to rely on a tight labor market to discipline their subjects, parole authorities intensified their supervision capacities to control and rehabilitate parolees therapeutically. The end of the clinical era was defined in part by a recognition of the "futility of enforcing a labor requirement on a population increasingly excluded from the labor market" (Simon 1993, 96). Work mandates were often underenforced, though most were preserved on paper. This ushered in the current regime. In partial reaction to mass incarceration and the hardening of urban poverty, so-called managerial parole shifted even further away from labor enforcement. This does not mean that all efforts to promote parolee employment have ceased. It does suggest, however, that parole is now generally oriented toward securing, containing, and isolating "a class excluded from the labor market" (Simon 1993, 259). From this point of view, the flourishing of contemporary employment-based programs for parolees might best be explained as an effort to neutralize and surveil a population of labor market outcasts.

In *Disciplining the Poor*, Soss, Fording, and Schram (2011) offer a comparable account of contemporary poverty governance in America, but they focus less on the penal state and more on its welfare analog. They argue that poverty governance in the United States has taken a "disciplinary turn," a mutation defined by the interaction of two political forces: neoliberalism (strengthening the state in service to the market and reorienting public and quasi-public institutions around market principles) and new paternalism (expanding state surveillance of unruly populations and conditioning public goods and rights on the demonstrable fulfillment of social obligations). When read with *Poor Discipline*, it becomes clear that the "neoliberal paternalism" detailed in *Disciplining the Poor* ascends concurrently with managerial parole in the late twentieth century.

Although these studies have much in common, one difference between *Poor Discipline* and *Disciplining the Poor* is clear. The managerial parole regime detailed in the first book aims to surveil and isolate a population largely omitted from the labor market. The neoliberal paternalistic regime detailed in the second, however, pressures its subjects "into accepting the worst jobs at the worst wages" (Soss, Fording, and Schram 2011, 7). These books inspire competing hypotheses regarding the employment effects of parole. From *Poor Discipline*, we might expect that in addition to supervising a largely jobless population, parole has no, little, or perhaps even a negative labor effect. From *Disciplining the Poor*, we might expect parole, should it operate like workfare, to significantly impel labor.

Our inquiry should not end with just a consideration of employment. As Soss, Fording, and Schram (2011) make clear, successfully promoting poor people's employment does not guarantee an extension of their life chances. In general, the employment incentivized by workfare does not adequately challenge poverty, and this may also be the case for employment incentivized by parole. Although, to be fair, that is not really part of the formal mission of parole or its labor mandate. As noted, these mandates are typically justified as a strategy to challenge future criminal justice contact. Thus, in speculating how incentivized employment may or may not extend the life chances of former prisoners, we should also consider the association between parolee labor and recidivism.

## METHODOLOGY

As noted, our study focuses on parole in Michigan. General parole requirements in the state include an explicit mandate to secure and maintain employment. Various exemptions aside, such as for those who are diagnosed with a disability, enrolled in school, or over the age of sixty-five, most parolees in Michigan are formally required to work. There is little reason to believe that parole officers are reincarcerating their subjects for being unemployed, but they seem to incentivize employment in different ways. As we learned from conversations with agency officials and former prisoners (Harding, Morenoff, and Wyse 2019), Michigan parole officers do not typically require employed parolees to report to them as often as unemployed parolees. Parole officers in the state are also supposedly more likely to allow their subjects with jobs to check in by phone rather than in person. For those who are unemployed and not in school, evidence of time spent searching for work is typically required by parole officers. It remains to be seen, however, whether incentivizing employment this way is effective or if working while under supervision significantly extends a parolee's life chances.

## Data

We draw on three primary data sources. First, we examine a longitudinal set of administrative data from the Michigan Department of Corrections (MDOC). These data include all people in Michigan who were paroled from a state correctional facility to Michigan communities in 2003 (n = 11,064). In addition to offering detailed demographic information such as dates of birth and county of parole, these records also detail the dates people started parole and, if applicable, the dates they were discharged from parole or died as well as the dates of certain post-prison events, including reincarceration. Second, we link our sample to data from the Michigan Unemployment Insurance Agency (MUIA) that contain employer-reported quarterly records of wages earned and industries worked according to the North American Industry Classification System. We matched 99.7 percent of the 2003 parolee cohort records to the MUIA data, leaving a cohort size of 11,032.[2] Although the employment data do not include informal work, they provide insight into parolees' participation in formal labor. Third, we also link to post-prison arrest records that local law enforcement agencies report to the Michigan State Police (MSP). These records capture incidents in which an individual was arrested by police (which may or may not lead to a parole revocation).[3]

Using the merged MDOC, MUIA, and MSP files, we constructed a dataset that nests quarterly records within individuals and limits the observation period to quarters between individual-specific prison release dates for the 2003 parole and December 31, 2007. This provided us with an observation period of up to a maximum of twenty calendar quarters per individual. During this period, Michigan experienced a relatively stable monthly state unemployment rate of 7 percent from January 1, 2003, through December 31, 2007 (Bureau of Labor

---

2. To match parolees with their quarterly employment statuses, all social security numbers (SSN) available in MDOC databases for the 2003 parole cohort were sent to the Michigan Unemployment Insurance Agency and Workforce Development Agency for matching. In some cases, more than one SSN was available for each subject. For thirty-two individuals, MDOC had no SSN, so these individuals have no UI data and are removed from the dataset. Returned UI records were matched with names from MDOC databases, including aliases, to eliminate incorrect SSNs. Approximately 5 percent of the sample had no UI data match their SSN, indicating that they had no formal employment in Michigan between 1997 and 2010. If more than one SSN that MDOC had recorded for the same person matched records in the UI data, project staff selected the best match by comparing employer names listed in the UI records with those listed in the MDOC records (from parole agent reports). This procedure resulted in one-to-one matches of individual records between MDOC and UI records for more than 99 percent of sample members. For less than 1 percent of the sample, a single SSN could not be selected after matching on the parolee's name and the name or names of that person's employer or employers. In such cases, UI data were retained for all SSNs listed in the MDOC records for a given individual, under the assumption that such people worked under multiple SSNs.

3. People placed in custody by a parole agent are not captured by the MSP arrest measure.

Statistics 2018). Because we are interested only in working-age parolees, we eliminated eleven individuals who were paroled as minors, forty-three who were paroled as elderly, and 468 quarterly records in which individuals aged out of the labor market during the observed period (turned sixty-five before the first day of the quarter). We then omitted sixteen individuals who died during the first quarter of their parole as well as three who were discharged during that same time. Next, we dropped 2,684 quarterly records in which individuals were listed as deceased during the observed period. To handle the remaining records with missing data, we dropped thirty-one individuals (less than 0.3 percent) who had no values on one or more of the variables used in our analyses. These procedures left us with an unbalanced panel dataset of 199,503 quarterly records across 10,928 individuals.

We draw on other data as well. We retrieved county-specific monthly records from the Michigan Department of Labor and Economic Growth, calculated average quarterly unemployment rates, and then linked these to individuals based on the initial county of parole. Across the overall dataset, the mean county unemployment rate was 7.4 percent, the minimum at 2.8 percent and the maximum at 22.2 percent (standard deviation = 1.4 percent). Because we do not have detailed information on where individuals lived over time, we are forced to assume that our subjects did not move between counties or out of the state. We also integrated state-level minimum wage data by adding a variable that codes each quarter as either $5.15 (majority of time observed), $6.95 (beginning in the fourth quarter of 2006), or $7.15 (beginning in the third quarter of 2007).[4] Last, we examined aggregate Temporary Assistance for Needy Families (TANF) data on caseload and work participation maintained by the Office of Family Assistance (U.S. Department of Health and Human Services 2018). These data allowed us to compare employment rates among Michigan residents governed by the state's primary workfare program, TANF, with employment rates among parolees.

### Variables

Our study uses three types of dependent variables. First, we constructed a dichotomous variable that captures whether an individual earned any money from formal employment in the quarter.[5] Second, we constructed five dichotomous variables that capture whether the individual was employed in each of the five most common industries observed in the data: employment services (which includes jobs assigned through temporary staffing agencies), manufacturing, construction, food services, and retail. Together, these five industries account for just over half of the employment records in the data. Third, we produced three related time-varying measures of post-prison recidivism: whether the individual was arrested in the quarter, reincarcerated in prison or jail in the quarter, or experienced either (or both) of these events.[6]

Our primary independent variable, which we

---

4. To capture quarter-specific changes, we relied on newspaper reporting of minimum wage law changes under Governor Granholm (Graboski 2006). We confirmed these changes with annual minimum wage rates as reported by the U.S. Department of Labor (2017).

5. We calculated an unadjusted employment rate by dividing the number of individuals who worked in a given quarter by the total number of individuals who are assumed to be "exposed" to the labor market during that period (that is, not reincarcerated, alive, and under sixty-five). Unlike the official employment rate, this method does not exclude from the denominator people who are not actively seeking employment.

6. Although the MDOC data reliably capture post-prison jail spells only for those under active parole supervision, it reliably captures prison spells for both parolees and those who have discharged from parole. To mitigate this potential for bias in jail reincarceration, we primarily compare employed parolees with jobless parolees in the recidivism models. We also assume that risks for both arrest and reincarceration depend on whether a formerly released person is on parole or discharged from parole. Parole violations probably substitute arrests for a significant number of parolees.

call *discharged*, codes each quarterly record as a period of either active parole or postparole discharge.[7] When examining the associations between discharged and our outcomes, we control for a lagged binary indicator capturing whether the individual experienced at least sixty days of the quarter in jail or prison. This ensures that comparisons between parole and discharge are focused on periods when the individual is in the community, without having to drop quarterly records when reincarceration is experienced, which would potentially introduce sample selection bias. Finally, our fixed-effects models also control for electronic monitoring, parole violation, county unemployment, season, and quarter since release. We lag most of our predictors to prevent problems with reverse casually in the fixed-effects modeling.[8] Table 1 provides descriptive statistics for all study variables (for time-invariant characteristics, see table A1).[9]

## Analysis

Our goal is to estimate the association between being discharged from parole and the labor market and recidivism outcomes described above net of potential confounders. We deploy a series of hybrid or between-within fixed-effects logit models. Leveraging strengths of both traditional fixed effects and random effects, the hybrid approach decomposes time-variant predictors in a panel dataset into a within-person component and a between-person component (that is, person-specific means) while estimating a random-effects model to account for clustering of periods within individuals (Allison 2009). The intuition is that the person-level means on key variables control for all between-person variation in the predictor, allowing the coefficients on within-person variables to be interpreted as fixed-effects coefficients. This hybrid method is ideal because it does not, like a standard fixed-effects model, eliminate individual cases with zero variation in the outcome over time (for example, individuals who are never employed or who never recidivate). Per Stephen Vaisey and Andrew Miles (2017), we interact our person-level mean variables with our set of indicator variables for time (quarter since release) to relax the common trends (parallel trajectories) assumption of fixed-effects models. We also test the endogenous selection assumption by examining whether lagged outcomes predict discharge from parole and find that assumption is not violated in our data (Vaisey and Miles 2017).[10]

---

7. For all applicable individuals, the first quarter discharged is the first full quarter after the date of discharge.

8. Because we lag most independent and control variables, we ran analyses with and without the first quarter of parole. In all cases, the results were effectively the same.

9. Although family status and education level are probably not time-invariant in reality, our dataset does not account for changes over time with these variables so we are forced to assume they do not vary within individuals during the quarters observed. Given the relatively short period over which we observe our sample, this assumption does not seem unreasonable. Moreover, we do not control for age as a time-varying factor (except when dropping individuals once they turn sixty-five years of age) because of its high correlation with quarter since release.

10. Paul Allison (2009), typically credited with producing the definitive summary of the hybrid method for social scientists, suggests constructing the between-person component as deviations from the person-specific mean. However, later, in a defense of the hybrid approach for logistic regression, Allison (2014) demonstrates that it is unnecessary to construct the deviations in logistic models as long as the corresponding person mean variables are included. We do not include cluster-level means for spring, summer, or fall season indicators because these are simply control variables. We also do not include person means for the "will discharge" indicators because these are very highly correlated with person mean for lagged discharge. We also follow Allison's (2014) advice to test the linearity assumptions of the hybrid logistic model by examining whether controlling for squared and cubic terms on the person-mean variables changes the fixed-effect estimates. These controls do not change the estimated coefficients in the model, indicating that we can safely exclude them.

**Table 1.** Descriptive Statistics

|  | Individual-Quarters | Individuals Ever Experiencing | Quarters Among Individuals Ever Experiencing |
|---|---|---|---|
| **Dependent variables** | | | |
| Employment models | | | |
|   Employed | 25.00 | 67.76 | 36.75 |
|   Employed in employment services | 5.49 | 34.09 | 16.12 |
|   Employed in manufacturing | 5.46 | 21.91 | 24.88 |
|   Employed in food industry | 3.78 | 18.44 | 20.42 |
|   Employed in construction | 2.57 | 12.55 | 20.24 |
|   Employed in retail | 2.13 | 11.66 | 18.35 |
| Recidivism models | | | |
|   Arrested | 8.57 | 69.20 | 12.32 |
|   Starting new reincarceration spell | 8.23 | 62.88 | 13.09 |
|   Arrested or starting new reincarceration spell | 13.11 | 78.70 | 16.61 |
| **Independent variables** | | | |
| Employment models | | | |
|   Discharged from parole, lagged | 28.00 | 58.60 | 46.85 |
| Recidivism models | | | |
|   On parole with a job, lagged | 14.49 | 62.17 | 23.35 |
|   On parole without a job, lagged | 57.51 | 100.00 | 58.02 |
|   Discharged with a job, lagged | 9.29 | 33.62 | 27.10 |
|   Discharged without a job, lagged | 18.71 | 51.69 | 35.49 |
| **Controls** | | | |
| Reincarcerated for sixty-plus days, lagged | 18.18 | 47.12 | 38.20 |
| Arrested, lagged[a] | 8.12 | 67.87 | 11.88 |
| On electronic monitoring, lagged | 15.21 | 18.94 | 79.14 |
| Absconded from parole, lagged | 10.96 | 38.28 | 28.61 |
| Winter season | 22.96 | 99.71 | 23.03 |
| Spring season | 24.43 | 99.75 | 24.46 |
| Summer season | 25.67 | 99.73 | 25.74 |
| Fall season | 26.94 | 99.65 | 27.07 |
| $5.15 State minimum wage | 73.27 | 100.00 | 73.57 |
| $6.95 State minimum wage | 16.06 | 97.79 | 16.23 |
| $7.15 State minimum wage | 10.68 | 97.51 | 10.82 |

*Source:* Authors' calculations.
*Note:* All numbers in percentages. N = 10,928 individuals, 199,503 records. Omits individual-quarters in which subjects are deceased or over the age of sixty-five on the first day of the quarter. The first column of statistics covers individual-quarters, the second column covers differences across individuals, and the third column covers differences inside individual cases overtime. For example, 25 percent of the employed variable are coded as employed. However, 67.76 percent of individuals have ever held employment during the observed period. And, of those individuals, 36.75 percent of their quarterly records were coded as employed.
[a] For employment models only.

**Figure 1.** Parolee Employment Rate by Year-Quarter

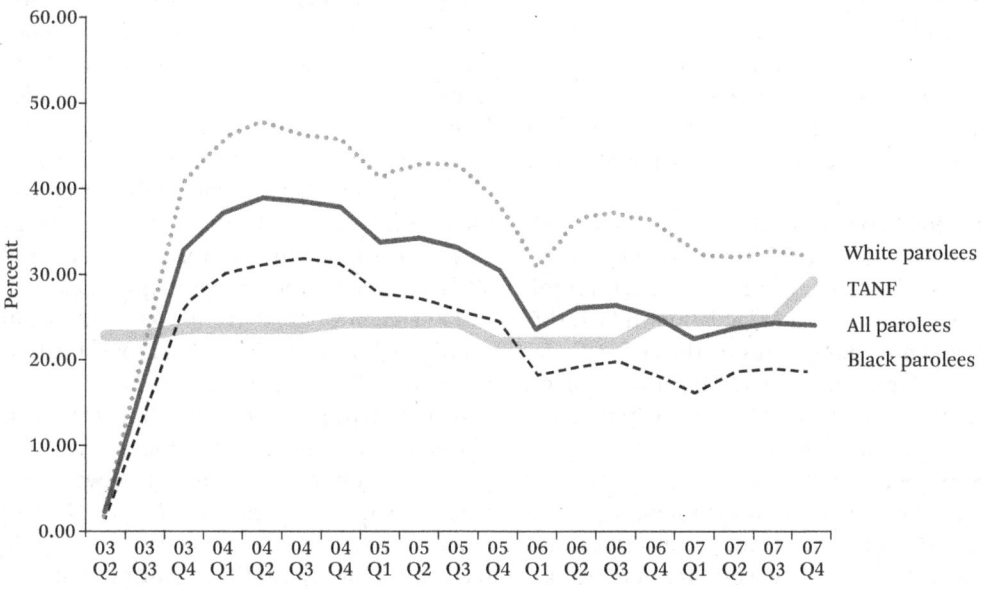

*Source:* Authors' calculations.
*Note:* Omits individual-quarters in which subjects are deceased, over the age of sixty-five on first day of quarter, or discharged from parole. TANF rate captures cross-sectional unsubsidized employment rates for all adult participants in Michigan's TANF program between fiscal year 2003 and fiscal year 2008.

As with any fixed-effects approach, this hybrid model essentially treats every individual as their own control when estimating within-person effects. Time-invariant factors, whether included in the model or not, are thus controlled by the fixed effects. This means that there is no reason to include predictors that do not vary within individuals in the period observed. This is why we do not include controls for race, gender, criminal history, and other variables typically used to predict employment and recidivism among formerly incarcerated individuals. This approach may be much less vulnerable to omitted-variable bias than cross-sectional analyses or even a traditional random-effects model, but it is potentially vulnerable to unmeasured time-varying confounders. Certainly imperfect, this method offers a powerful test for whether parole affects employment outcomes and whether parolee labor affects the odds of recidivism.

## RESULTS

We divide our results into three sections. First, we detail employment trends for parolees. We then consider how parole supervision might affect employment. Last, we examine the relationship between parolee employment and recidivism.

## EMPLOYMENT ON PAROLE

Figure 1 shows the proportion of parolees who are employed in the formal labor market between the second quarter of 2003 and the fourth quarter of 2007, including only quarters in which an individual is on parole and not reincarcerated for sixty or more days. This figure shows that parole in Michigan supervises individuals with a generally low employment rate, but a nontrivial portion of the sample experiences some employment. Averaged across these periods, the overall employment rate is 28 percent. Quarterly employment for this cohort begins at 2 percent in the second quarter of 2003, rises to nearly 39 percent in the second quarter of 2004, and then drops to hover around 25 percent until the end of the observation period. This temporal pattern is consistent with prior studies of formal employment among formerly imprisoned individuals (Bushway, Stoll, and Weiman 2007). African Americans have consistently lower post-prison employment than whites, although the over-time pattern is similar for both groups. Employment peaks in the second quarter of 2004 for whites at just under 50 percent. Among blacks, employment peaks in the third quarter of 2004 at just over 30 percent.

We conclude that Michigan parole manages a mostly but not entirely jobless population. In other words, parole governs a population primarily detached from wage labor. In fact, this indicates even more exclusion than what Simon (1993, 147) reports for his California parolees. He estimates that only 43.3 percent of parolees receive income from work.

Still, we should not just write off parole as just another penal institution for managing labor market outcasts. Evidence also indicates that parole is a bit like workfare in that it actively supervises a number of formally employed subjects. There is even reason to believe that people are more likely to work while on parole than before they went to prison. A separate publication drawing on the same data estimates that only 14 percent of the individuals in our study were employed in the year before the imprisonment spell that preceded their 2003 parole (Herbert, Morenoff, and Harding 2015).

A useful, albeit imperfect, comparison can also be made with Michigan's adult TANF recipients, a local population under the prototypical American workfare regime. Drawing on data from the U.S. Department of Health and Human Services, we divided the number of adult TANF recipients recorded as holding unsubsidized employment by the total number of adult TANF recipients during the same general period.[11] This provides a reasonable basis for comparing workfare and parole. Like the employment rate in our parolee sample, this does not account for adults who may replace their traditional work mandate with other activities (such as college courses and job search assistance programs). Drawing on these data, figure 1 plots the employment rate among Michigan TANF recipients, showing a generally similar rate of employment between parolees and TANF recipients. The average employment rate of 24 percent for TANF recipients in Michigan is only slightly lower than what is observed for the cohort of parolees over a similar period (28 percent). To be clear, we understand this is bit like comparing apples and oranges. TANF employment requirements can vary between single and two-parent families and the TANF data we draw on are cross-sectional. Moreover, TANF recipients may voluntarily exit the program, effectively stopping the clock on their five-year standard limit for enrollment, and then return later if eligible. Parole obviously does not operate this way. Nevertheless, in terms of the simple share of active subjects who hold formal employment, Michigan's parole and workfare programs are seemingly similar.

Although wage and benefit details are unavailable for the TANF data we retrieved, sociologists often note that the program fails to lift its subjects out of poverty, at least significantly or for long periods (Collins and Mayer 2010; Hays 2003; Soss, Fording, and Schram 2011). The same may be true for parole. This regime supervises a population that frequently, if not primarily, earns an income through the formal labor market. However, as seen in figure 2, which plots quarterly earnings from formal employment by race, these payments are low. The

---

11. This measure of employment among TANF recipients is a more appropriate comparison for the parole data than the commonly reported "employment participation rate," which can span an array of work activities (such as unpaid job training, employment searching, and select college programming) and typically depends on a minimum of thirty hours of such activities a week (Lower-Basch 2018). Because TANF recipients can combine work activities, we only examine unsubsidized employment when calculating an employment rate. On average, less than 0.08 percent of adult TANF recipients worked a subsidized job (either in a "public" or a "private" position) during the years we analyze. For the denominator, we use total number of adult TANF recipients rather than the total number of work-eligible individuals because we have no way of determining work eligibility among parolees.

**Figure 2.** Wage Profile of Employed Parolees by Year-Quarter

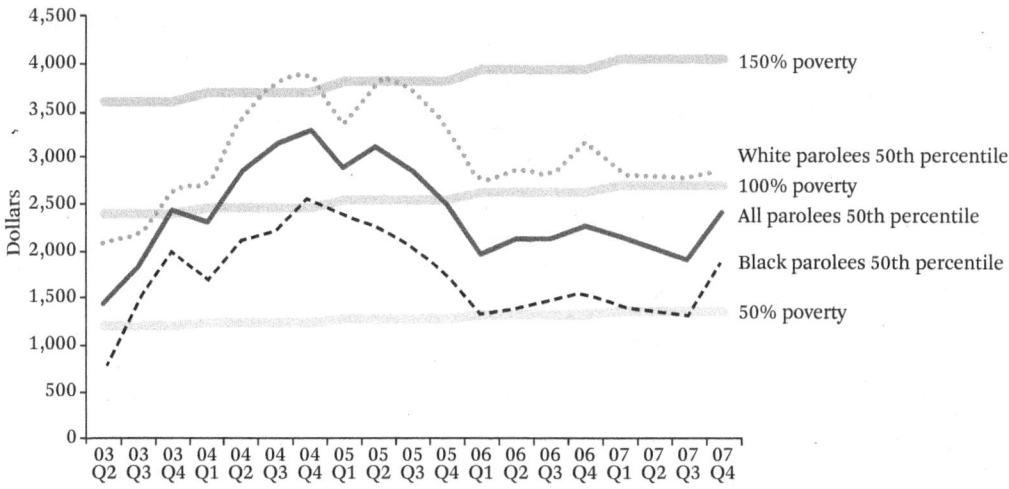

*Source:* Authors' calculations.
*Note:* Omits individual-quarters in which subjects are deceased, over the age of sixty-five on first day of quarter, discharged from parole, or jobless. Unadjusted dollar amounts and year-specific poverty thresholds.

average median earnings for all parolees during the observed period is $2,398 per quarter (about $184 per week). This peaks at $3,273 during the fourth quarter of 2004. Despite the clear racial disparity in earnings, the median earnings pattern over time follows a similar trend for both black and white parolees, the latter often earning about double what the former earn. Plotting the federal poverty line for a single adult, which begins at $2,393 per quarter in 2003 and increases to $2,697 per quarter in 2007, provides useful insight, as do the thresholds for 50 percent and 150 percent poverty. This suggests that black parolees tend to earn wages below the poverty line across most quarters, and that their white counterparts tend to earn below 150 percent of the poverty line. Black or white, the wages earned through employment while under parole are typically low.

In sum, our examination of employment while on parole shows that this institution manages a mostly jobless population. However, it also supervises people who work at a rate comparable to those governed by the local workfare regime. Moreover, when parolees do work, most earn little. It is unclear whether this is due to low-wage, part-time employment, sporadic work, or some combination of these conditions, but most working parolees garner earnings near the federal poverty level.

### The Employment Effects of Parole

We now turn to the association between parole and employment. We use discharged to distinguish periods of parole from periods of nonparole. Should parole discharge status be negatively associated with employment within persons when controlling for other pertinent time-varying factors, then we have evidence that parole increases the odds of employment.

Figure 3 graphs the share of individuals who have discharged from parole over time since release from prison. The proportion of subjects who have discharged from parole gradually increases over time until the ninth quarter, when it jumps dramatically from 12 percent to 42 percent. This dramatic jump occurs after two years on parole, a standard period of parole in Michigan during the period covered by our study. This jump is important for our ability to assess the effect of parole discharge because it indicates that a substantial portion of the variation in discharge status from parole over time is determined by the rules of parole rather than by

**Figure 3.** Parole Discharge Rate by Quarter Since Start of 2003 Parole

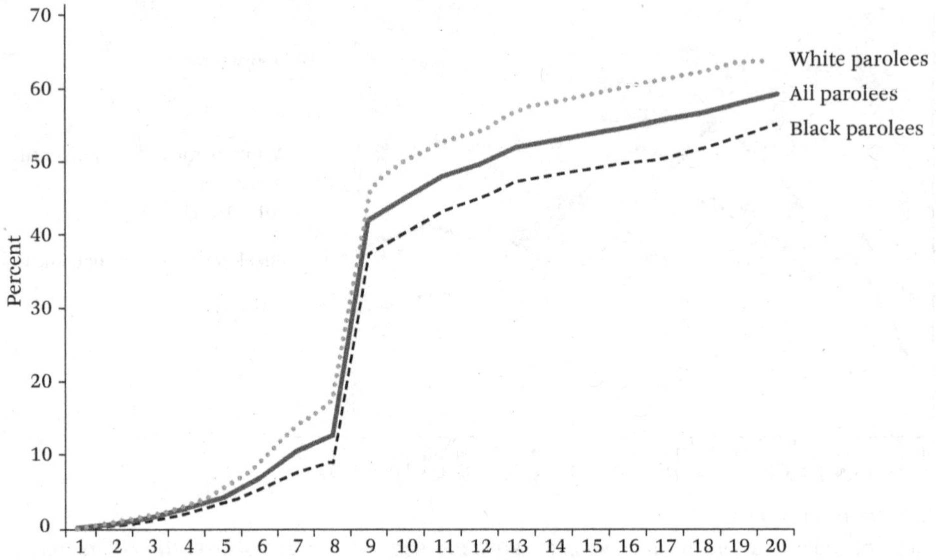

*Source:* Authors' calculations.
*Note:* Omits individual-quarters in which subjects are deceased or over the age of sixty-five on first day of quarter.

individual idiosyncrasies that might change over time. Following this dramatic jump, the probability of being discharged from parole increases gradually again through the end of our observation period, ending at about 60 percent of individuals.

Figure 4 examines the bivariate relationship between parole discharge status and employment by plotting employment rates over time relative to the discharge quarter among all individuals who eventually discharge during our observation period. Quarter zero is the individual's discharge quarter, negative quarters are before discharge, and positive quarters are after discharge. This graph shows a clear pattern of employment relative to the timing of discharge. Employment peaks in the quarters immediately before discharge and declines after that. Parolees experience maximum employment just before their discharge and then experience decreased participation in formal labor after their parole ends. This suggests that parole may increase employment.

To more rigorously examine the relationship between parole and employment, we now turn to the fixed-effects logit models with controls for the time-varying predictors discussed in the methodology section. Table 2 summarizes two fixed-effects models predicting any formal employment in the quarter.[12] These models answer our first research question: how does parole affect employment outcomes among formerly incarcerated individuals?

Model 1 estimates that discharging from parole lowers the odds of employment by more than 35 percent (odds ratio = 0.644). In other words, parole seems to increase employment. The average marginal effect for the lagged discharged variable in this model suggests that when the average parolee discharges, their probability of employment drops by five percentage points. Model 2 adds indicators for pe-

---

12. Given the difficulties in comparing coefficients across logit models (Mood 2010; Karlson, Holm, and Breen 2012), we caution against comparing coefficients across models. Instead, tables 2 and 3 should be understood as capturing seven indicators of the relationship between parole discharge and employment. For the full versions of the models, see the online appendix, available at: https://www.rsfjournal.org/content/6/1/173/tab-supplemental.

**Figure 4.** Employment Rates of Discharging Parolees, by Quarterly Distance to Discharge

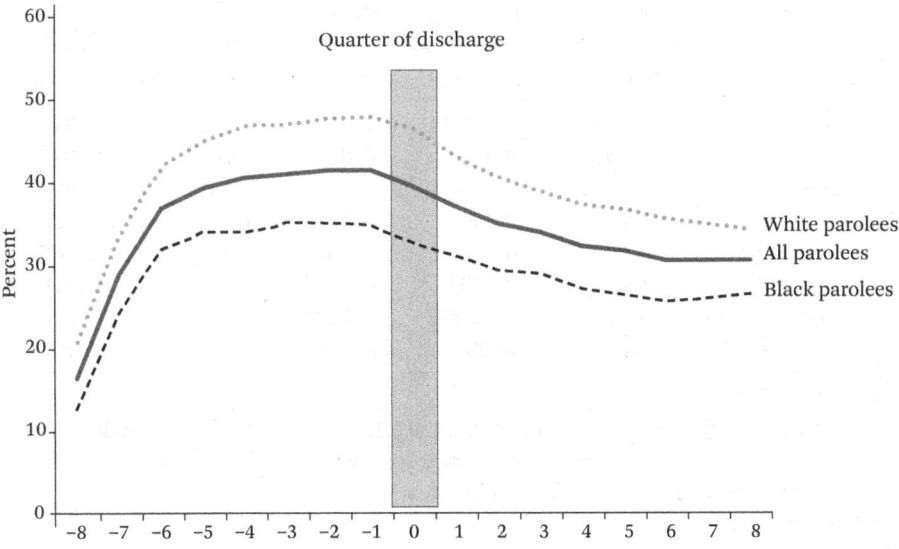

*Source:* Authors' calculations.
*Note:* Limited to individuals who discharged form parole during the observed period. Omits individual-quarters in which subjects are deceased or over the age of sixty-five on first day of quarter. Quarter 0 corresponds to individual-specific date of discharge.

**Table 2.** Any Employment, Fixed-Effects Logit Models

|  | Model 1 | Model 2 |
|---|---|---|
| Discharge, lagged | 0.644*** | 0.679*** |
|  | (0.02) | (0.03) |
| Will discharge in one quarter |  | 1.105* |
|  |  | (0.05) |
| Will discharge in two quarters |  | 1.122* |
|  |  | (0.05) |
| Will discharge in three quarters |  | 1.091 |
|  |  | (0.05) |

*Source:* Authors' calculations.
*Note:* Odds ratios and standard errors, 10,928 individuals, 199,503 records. All models include controls for reincarceration, arrest, electronic monitoring, absconding, county-level unemployment, seasons, and quarters. Full models reported in the online appendix.
*$p < .05$; **$p < .01$; ***$p < .001$

riods one, two, and three quarters before discharge. The odds ratios for each of these quarter indicators are higher than one and the first two are statistically significant, indicating that employment increases in the quarters leading up to discharge, which is consistent with figure 4.

The models in table 3 replicate the second model in table 2, except that they limit the outcome to quarterly employment in one of the five most common industries in our data. These models show that the patterns documented in table 2 are not driven by employment in particular industries. Instead, we see that parole

**Table 3.** Any Employment by Industry, Fixed-Effects Logit Models

|  | Model 1 Employment Services | Model 2 Manufacturing | Model 3 Food Services | Model 4 Construction | Model 5 Retail |
|---|---|---|---|---|---|
| Discharge, lagged | 0.647*** | 0.667*** | 0.812* | 0.853 | 0.678*** |
|  | (0.04) | (0.05) | (0.07) | (0.08) | (0.07) |
| Will discharge in one quarter | 0.956 | 0.972 | 1.300** | 1.070 | 0.999 |
|  | (0.07) | (0.08) | (0.12) | (0.12) | (0.12) |
| Will discharge in two quarters | 1.002 | 0.992 | 1.236* | 1.173 | 0.962 |
|  | (0.07) | (0.08) | (0.11) | (0.12) | (0.11) |
| Will discharge in three quarters | 1.058 | 1.028 | 1.299** | 1.143 | 0.846 |
|  | (0.07) | (0.08) | (0.11) | (0.12) | (0.10) |

*Source:* Authors' calculations.
*Note:* Odds ratios and standard errors, 10,928 individuals, 199,503 records. All models include controls for reincarceration, arrest, electronic monitoring, absconding, county-level unemployment, seasons, and quarters. Full models reported in the online appendix.
*p < .05; **p < .01; ***p < .001

discharge reduces the probability of employment in all five industries (although the coefficient is not significant in model 4 for construction). Increased employment in the quarters immediately before discharge is most clearly evident for the food services industry (model 3) and does not appear to be occurring in retail.

In sum, although we find evidence that parole governs a mostly jobless population, we also find evidence suggesting that it increases employment among its subjects.

## The Recidivism Effects of Parolee Labor

Parolee labor may not be a convincing program for combating poverty, but this is not the official goal of parole in the same way it is for workfare. Representatives from the latter regime often explicitly, although perhaps not very seriously, insist that they aim to lift their subjects out of poverty by promoting personal responsibility. Parole authorities, on the other hand, usually claim they want to promote personal responsibility for other ends, namely, for "offender reintegration" and "public safety." Reading between the lines, this seems to more accurately mean the separation of the offender from penal custody and the promotion not of an individual economic security but of a public security from activities deemed criminal. Parolee employment may yield these ends by reducing recidivism.

In considering whether this is the case in our data, we investigate the relationship between parolee employment and recidivism. Table 4 shows fixed-effects logit models in which the primary predictors of interest are based on a four-category variable that combines discharge status and employment. Its categories are on parole and jobless (the reference category), on parole and employed, discharged and jobless, and discharged and employed. As we did with the independent variable in the employment models, we lag this variable to avoid potential reverse causality in quarters in which arrest or reincarceration precede job loss.

If parolee employment helps prevent future criminal justice contact, we would expect that being on parole and employed (relative to being on parole and jobless) would be associated with lower odds of arrest or reincarceration. This does not seem to be the case, given that being employed while on parole is associated with greater odds of arrest (model 1) and no difference in the odds of reincarceration (model 2). In addition, the large odds ratios for discharged and employed and for discharged and jobless in model 1 indicate that discharge status itself is associated with greater odds of arrest, whereas the odds ratios below one on these

**Table 4.** Recidivism Outcomes, Fixed-Effects Logit Models

| (Reference = On Parole and Jobless) | Model 1 Arrest | Model 2 Reincarceration | Model 3 Arrest or Reincarceration |
|---|---|---|---|
| On parole and employed, lagged | 1.095** | 1.048 | 1.069* |
|  | (0.03) | (0.03) | (0.03) |
| Discharged and employed, lagged | 2.111*** | 0.248*** | 1.492*** |
|  | (0.12) | (0.03) | (0.08) |
| Discharged and jobless, lagged | 2.064*** | 0.392*** | 1.529*** |
|  | (0.09) | (0.03) | (0.06) |

*Source:* Authors' calculations.
*Note:* Odds ratios and standard errors, 10,928 individuals, 199,503 records. All models include controls for reincarceration, electronic monitoring, absconding, county-level unemployment, seasons, and quarters. Full models reported in the online appendix.
*p < .05; **p < .01; ***p < .001

variables in model 2 indicate that discharged is associated with lower odds of being placed in jail or prison. We interpret these estimates as consistent with the idea that the greater surveillance of parole supervision enhances the risk of being reincarcerated for parole violations while also substituting parole violations for some arrests by police.[13]

It is worth emphasizing that our results suggest that parole supervision is related to recidivism in complicated ways. Among employed subjects, being on parole seems to lower the odds of arrest (model 1) and increase the odds of reincarceration (model 2). Among those who are not employed, the effects are about the same. We assume that this discrepancy is largely explained by technical violations. Whether that is or is not the case, we find some evidence that parole reduces recidivism. This is also apparent in the third model, which collapses arrest and reincarceration into a single outcome. This finding is not unique (Ostermann 2013, 2015). We are, however, not particularly interested in how parole may or may not affect recidivism. Instead, we are interested in how working while under parole supervision might affect the odds of recidivism. Our findings clearly challenge the assumption that parolees who work in the formal economy are less likely to recidivate than their jobless counterparts. If parole lowers the odds of recidivism (and that is not demonstrated beyond question in this study anyway), we are at least skeptical that employment explains this effect.

In sum, we find evidence that parole's successful promotion of labor does not challenge the odds of post-prison recidivism, at least as indicated by the odds of being arrested or reincarcerated. Just as increasing the employment of welfare recipients does not seem to signifi-

13. To assess whether employment lowers recidivism after parole discharge, we tested the equivalency of the coefficients for discharged and employed and discharged and jobless for each recidivism model. These coefficients are not significantly different from one another in the arrest model (p = .632) but are significantly different from one another in the reincarceration model (p = .001). These coefficients are also not significantly different from one another in the arrest or reincarceration model (p = .593). Together, these tests suggest that being employed after discharge, versus being jobless after discharge, does not reduce the odds of arrest net of other time-varying confounders. In fact, the odds of arrest are positively associated with employment after discharge, albeit slightly. However, when recidivism is measured as either arrest or reincarceration, employment after discharge is associated with reduced odds of recidivism. Thus, to the extent that labor challenges recidivism at all, it seems to only do so after parole discharge (after the odds of any employment drops somewhat dramatically anyway). This may reflect a better average job quality for employment held after discharge.

cantly challenge their economic insecurity, parolee labor does not seem to facilitate offender reintegration or public safety.

## DISCUSSION AND CONCLUSION

Our findings motivate a reconceptualization of parole as an institution that blends the poverty regulating strategies of prisonfare and workfare (Wacquant 2009). First, parole seems to regulate labor in a way similar to prisonfare, by controlling a population largely detached from the labor market. When averaged across all observed quarters, only about 28 percent of the 2003 cohort of formerly imprisoned people in Michigan earned wages from formal labor while under parole supervision. This is powerful evidence that supports Simon's (1993) vision of managerial parole as a regime that largely governs people excluded from labor.

Second, parole seems to regulate labor in a way similar to workfare. The comparison is imperfect, but the average unadjusted employment rate for Michigan parolees is not unlike a similar statistic for adult TANF recipients in the same state around the same period. Extending the possibility that parole maintains parallels with workfare as Soss, Fording, and Schram (2011) describe, we predicted that post-prison supervision would impel formerly imprisoned people to work. Our study yielded a novel finding that supports this hypothesis. Fixed effects models showed that formerly incarcerated individuals have greater odds of employment while under parole than after they discharge from this supervision. This pattern conflicts with common assumptions that parole impedes employment. Additionally, the effect of parole on employment is not limited to just one or two industries.

But though it is similar to both prisonfare and workfare, we argue that parolefare is something distinct. On the one hand, post-prison supervision is the usual sequel to imprisonment and part and parcel of an expansive penal state that handles a mostly impoverished male population. Still, parolefare cannot be written off as yet another prisonfare institution for simply managing labor market outcasts. Parolefare not only supervises a substantial number of workers, it also impels employment.

On the other hand, this does not mean that parolefare is just workfare under a different name or for a different gender. Indeed, these regimes are perhaps permanently separated by two major conditions. First, parolefare, like prisonfare but unlike workfare, operates on official platforms of public safety and offender reintegration. Narratives of work first and poverty alleviation are peripheral (if not nonexistent) for parolefare but essential for workfare. Second, although both parolefare and workfare rely on carrots and sticks, they almost definitely do so in different proportions. Whereas workfare draws in clientele because of the rewards it offers to obedient subjects (for example, cash benefits), one of parole's primary incentive devices is the threat of punishment (that is, reincarceration).

### Limitations

Our theorization is ambitious, but our study is not without notable weaknesses. We examined only one cohort in one state more than a decade ago and are therefore reasonably concerned about external validity. And, although fixed-effects modeling controls for time-invariant factors, it assumes all relevant time-varying confounders are controlled in the model. We are potentially exposed to omitted-variable bias, including individual-level changes in residence, family status, supervision level, informal and supplemental income, and health. These shortfalls are not insignificant, but such omitted variables would need to change values at the same time as parole discharge to seriously challenge our conclusions.

Next is the issue of measurement. Our data limit us to a discussion of *formal* employment. Previous scholarship suggests a likely discrepancy between the unemployment insurance covered records (or paystub jobs) we examine and the self-reported employment of young men with histories of criminal justice involvement (Kornfeld and Bloom 1999). However, we assume that, like workfare recipients, the subjects of parole are pressured to demonstrate their participation in so-called legitimate labor. We also assume that parole would not, or at least would be much less likely to, impel informal labor. Unfortunately, we have no way of testing these assumptions.

Similarly, we recognize that life chances are

imperfectly, or at least incompletely, captured by our recidivism models. We assume that arrest and reincarceration tend to sever a former prisoner's life chances more than extend or protect them. Still, the case might be made that we would have been better off examining different life chance outcomes like mortality or morbidity. We do not necessarily disagree. However, we believe recidivism makes the most sense for an examination of parolee employment because it is an official policy focus of this institution and is frequently cited as a justification for the employment mandate. Even so, recidivism is not the only outcome of parolee employment we consider. We also examine quarterly earnings and show that they tend to hover around the federal poverty line, where life chances are typically low.

We also understand the obvious mismatch in our causal theory and our descriptive data. However, without any data accounting for the random assignment of parole discharge (or, better yet, parole admission) we are restricted to the types of analyses we performed. Ultimately, we do not test a parolefare theory, but instead develop and support it. We nevertheless think the parolefare framework we advance—that being the simple claim that parole impels some employment for a population still largely excluded from the labor market but that it does so without considerably extending their life chances—is useful.

This framework certainly faces some alternative explanations, especially for the observed patterns in employment. It is possible that employment participation dropped for our subjects as some sort of nascent effect of a worsening economy. However, we think this is unlikely due to both our controls for county-level unemployment rates and the fact that we limit our dataset to quarters before the Great Recession. Another possibility is that formerly imprisoned people experience a deterioration in hope and motivation that is independent of supervision status. According to this logic, by the time they reach parole discharge, people are so exhausted or defeated that they abandon the labor market, but not because they are excused from supervision. The employment drop after discharge would just be a coincidence. However, we doubt that best explains our findings because such discouragement is unlikely to be experienced by different individuals at the same time. Indeed, neither of these alternative explanations can account for the simple, and somewhat dramatic, drop in average employment at the moment of discharge, which varies significantly by individual subject (figure 4).

Far more concerning is our inability to speak to the mechanisms of parolefare. How, and under what particular conditions, parole impels the kinds of formal employment that do little to extend life chances remains a mystery. We can only speculate. Perhaps parolees feel compelled to work in the formal economy to simply satisfy their supervision conditions but then they ditch these likely mentally and materially underwhelming jobs following discharge. However, if true, that is probably only part of the story. The mere presence of a formal rule is likely insufficient. Parole officers probably play a critical role. They may surveil their unemployed subjects more intensively than their employed subjects, which may motivate some parolees to take any job they can find with clear plans to quit after discharge. Also, in executing their social work duties, parole officers may successfully broker their clientele to third-party services that increase employability (such as job search programs). Parolefare may also be mixed into their policing duties, and these officers may significantly impel labor with the threat of reincarceration. It is also possible the mechanisms are less direct. Maybe in imposing restrictions—such as in where to live, who to interact with, and how to behave—parole promotes an increase in personal stability that somehow makes a formerly imprisoned person more employable. Following this logic, it is possible that a kind of Durkheimian anomie follows a parole discharge. A sense of normlessness may spring from discharge and this might somehow promote joblessness and further instability. It is also possible that mandated employment does not fundamentally alter one's sense of self. There might be particular frustrations associated with more "forced" employment and this might somehow be associated with criminal activity. We simply do not know, but all of these imagined mechanisms are consistent with the broad vision of parolefare we develop in this article.[14] In the end, we hope that future research explores these possibilities in a deeper analysis of parole operations and the effects of parolee labor.

We also hope that future research moves beyond parole and considers how other forms of community corrections might complicate the proposed framework. The obvious alternative is the much larger institution of probation, for which we do not have data. Probation is typically imposed as an alternative to imprisonment and probation officers usually manage a larger case load than parole officers. We assume that our findings are most generalizable to supervision regimes that include explicit employment mandates, intensive monitoring, and similar sanctions (such as reduced check-in requirements for employed subjects). This assumption, however, should be put to the test. Just as we hope to see more considerations of parolefare outside of Michigan, we hope to also see inquiries into what might be called probationfare. For now, we can only surmise interesting, but understudied, similarities and differences between these regimes of poverty governance.

## POLICY IMPLICATIONS

This article fuels an ongoing policy debate regarding the benefits of formerly imprisoned people's employment. We struggle to identify the virtues of parolee labor. It does not appear to provide a pathway out of poverty nor does it convincingly reduce the odds of arrest or reincarceration in our data. We therefore find it difficult to recommend the policies and programs that seek to commodify post-prison labor. We are not alone either. Christy Visher, Laura Winterfield, and Mark Coggeshall (2005), in what arguably stands as the most comprehensive meta-analyses of employment programming for ex-offenders (not just formerly imprisoned people), conclude that such interventions do not affect the likelihoods of recidivism (see also Bohmert and Duwe 2011; Jacobs 2012; Moses 2012; Turner and Petersilia 1996). Despite the reasonable defenses of employment-focused programming post-incarceration (Bushway and Apel 2012; Drake, Aos, and Miller 2009; Redcross et al. 2012; Solomon et al. 2004; Uggen 2000), we add to more pessimistic conclusions.

Our vision of parolefare also has the potential to clarify and critique the policy discourse regarding employment and criminal justice contact. In this regard, we offer a timely contribution. Lawrence Mead (2007), a notorious advocate for mandating welfare mothers to work in the 1990s, has more recently turned his attention to formerly imprisoned men. He insists that the latter suffer from a similar "breakdown in work discipline," and he proposes a plan that first coerces jobless parolees into programs that broker low-wage employment before shoving more incompliant subjects into forced work crews (Mead 2007, 61). Although his proposal rubs against our findings as well as the scholarship showing that participation in the secondary labor market does little to promote criminal desistance (Crutchfield 2014; see also Schnepel 2018; Uggen 1999), such a labor the-parolee strategy seems to appeal to the convenient assumption that employment is the key to successful reentry.

Moreover, a work-first slogan orients many discussions of criminal justice policy, making our framework relevant beyond just a consideration of parole. For example, in New York, the mayor has introduced a Jail to Jobs program that promises transitional job opportunities to everyone leaving city jails (City of New York 2017). The mayor's office claims that such short-term (and presumably low-wage) employment can reduce recidivism by 22 percent. However, the evidence for this claim relies on an evalua-

---

14. Somewhat related to the issue of mechanism, we are not convinced that parolefare necessitates an instrumentalist vision of parole. Our insistence that parole helps commodify post-prison labor does not mean we are characterizing parole simply as an institution for serving businesses with cheap labor power in the interest of promoting capital accumulation. In fact, we think it is more plausible that parole is not a simple instrument of a ruling class but instead a relatively autonomous institution equipped with distinct logics for motivating worker-citizenship. It seems more likely that parole officers and their managers believe that post-prison labor promotes public safety and offender reintegration. Indeed, this seems to be the common sense opinion reinforced by scholars, elected officials, reentry-focused nonprofit leaders, and other correctional personnel.

tion of an employment-based reentry program that actually produced more complicated conclusions (Redcross et al. 2012). Three years following their engagement in the work crew–focused program, participants were less likely to recidivate but not more likely to hold formal employment, leading the study's authors to admit that the recidivism effects were puzzling (Zweig, Yahner, and Redcross 2010, 14). How else could a jobs-focused program for returning prisoners reduce recidivism if not by increasing their employment? Adding to the confusion, many of the same researchers evaluated another transitional jobs program—though one less likely to also mix in intensive reentry support and coaching—and found no recidivism effects despite also undergoing a rigorous case-control experimental evaluation (Redcross et al. 2010; see also Bushway and Apel 2012).

Our broad vision of parolefare can help us make sense of these empirical patterns and the often-mismatched policy prescriptions that follow. Pipelining formerly incarcerated people into precarious labor does not seem to yield especially promising challenges to recidivism. Still, like the large-scale implementation of workfare programming in the 1990s, an any-job-will-do mantra appeals to conventional values. Such a framework is also easily absorbed into a rationale of reentry that emphasizes personal responsibility (Seim 2016, 452–53; see also Abrams and Lea 2016; Miller 2014). Parolefare, we argue, is part and parcel of this rationality.

To be clear, we do not imply that parolefare would be justified if other researchers found evidence that low-wage work reduces the odds of arrest or reincarceration. In thinking about parole not just as criminal governance but also as poverty governance, we would be more impressed with research showing how post-prison labor can significantly reduce individual poverty for long periods. On a related note, we do not argue that work is automatically bad for formerly incarcerated people. We expect quality employment to be a crucial factor in directing people away from both routine criminal justice contact and material deprivation. Indeed, as seen in another article in this volume, Joe LaBriola (2020) examines the same dataset and finds that formerly incarcerated people who work in select industries with higher wages, longer tenure, and more unionization are less likely to be arrested or reincarcerated. Unfortunately, very few individuals in the dataset find work in such industries, and we have little reason to believe that parole does much to increases the odds of higher-quality employment. In the end, we are simply not convinced that the types of labor typically impelled by parole, and now increasingly by employment-focused reentry programing, constitutes the best course of action if the goal is to significantly extend the life chances of those caught in American criminal justice.

In closing, parole supervises a population generally, but not totally, excluded from labor. We find evidence that it also impels its subjects into formal employment. The real novelty of our study lies in our discovery that when someone discharges from parole his or her odds of employment are lowered. This association is significant across multiple industries. We also challenge assumptions that parolee labor is automatically "good" by questioning its ability to offer a livable income and reduce recidivism. Parolefare, a concept engineered for the findings presented and motivated by extant theory, helps us make sense of these otherwise perplexing results. We believe this concept has implications for a number of academic and policy discussions regarding employment after prison.

**Table A1.** Baseline Demographic Profile of Working-Age Parolees, 2003 Cohort

| | |
|---|---|
| **Age, race, and gender** | |
| Age at baseline (mean) | 35.02 |
| SD | 9.41 |
| Min | 18.00 |
| Max | 64.92 |
| Black (percent) | 53.44 |
| White (percent) | 44.75 |
| Other race (percent) | 1.81 |
| Male (percent) | 92.26 |
| **Education and employment** | |
| High school dropout or GED recipient (percent) | 72.75 |
| High school or more (percent) | 26.13 |
| Unknown education (percent) | 1.12 |
| Ever employed before 2003 parole (percent) | 62.17 |
| **Family** | |
| Any dependents (percent) | 59.58 |
| Never married (percent) | 66.48 |
| Divorced or separated (percent) | 20.19 |
| Married (percent) | 12.26 |
| Unknown or other marital status (percent) | 1.07 |
| **Judicial history** | |
| Non-assault convictions (percent)[a] | 45.85 |
| Assault conviction (percent)[a] | 28.49 |
| Drug convictions (percent)[a] | 25.66 |
| Number of pre-2003 prison terms (mean) | 1.46 |
| SD | 1.94 |
| Min | 0 |
| Max | 32 |
| Length of prison term leading to 2003 parole (mean years) | 2.96 |
| SD | 3.20 |
| Min | 0.16 |
| Max | 31.32 |

*Source:* Authors' calculations.
*Note:* N = 10,928. Omits individual-quarters in which subjects are deceased or over the age of sixty-five on first day of quarter.
[a] Mutually exclusive categories capturing most serious conviction (in terms of maximum sentence under state law) leading to prison sentence ending with 2003 parole.

# REFERENCES

Abrams, Laura S., and Charles H. Lea. 2016. "Becoming Employable: An Ethnographic Study of Life Skills Courses in a Men's Jail." *The Prison Journal* 96(5): 667–87.

Alexander, Michelle. 2012. *The New Jim Crow: Mass Incarceration in the Age of Colorblindness*. New York: The New Press.

Allison, Paul D. 2009. *Fixed Effects Regression Models*. Los Angeles, CA: SAGE Publications.

———. 2014. "Problems with the Hybrid Method." Philadelphia, PA: Statistical Horizons. Last modified September 2, 2014. Accessed July 23, 2018. http://statisticalhorizons.com/problems-with-the-hybrid-method.

Apel, Robert, and Gary Sweeten. 2010. "The Impact of Incarceration on Employment During the Transition to Adulthood." *Social Problems* 57(3): 448–79.

Bohmert, Miriam Northcutt, and Grant Duwe. 2011. "Minnesota's Affordable Homes Program: Evaluating the Effects of a Prison Work Program on Recidivism, Employment, and Cost Avoidance." *Criminal Justice Policy Review* 23(3): 327–51.

Bureau of Labor Statistics. 2018. "Databases, Tables & Calculators by Subject: Local Area Unemployment Statistics." Washington: U.S. Department of Labor. Accessed July 23, 2018. https://data.bls.gov/timeseries/LASST260000000000003.

Bushway, Shawn D., and Robert Apel. 2012. "A Signaling Perspective on Employment-Based Reentry Programming: Training Completion as a Desistance Signal." *Criminology & Public Policy* 11(1): 21–50.

Bushway, Shawn D., Michael A. Stoll, and David Weiman, eds. 2007. *Barriers to Reentry?: The Labor Market for Released Prisoners in Post-Industrial America*. New York: Russell Sage Foundation.

City of New York. 2017. "Mayor de Blasio Announces Re-Entry Services for Everyone in City Jails by End of This Year." Last modified March 29, 2017. Accessed July 23, 2018. https://www1.nyc.gov/office-of-the-mayor/news/187-17/mayor-de-blasio-re-entry-services-everyone-city-jails-end-this-year#/0.

Collins, Jane L., and Victoria Mayer. 2010. *Both Hands Tied: Welfare Reform and the Race to the Bottom in the Low-Wage Labor Market*. Chicago: University of Chicago Press.

Crutchfield, Robert D. 2014. *Get a Job: Labor Markets, Economic Opportunity, and Crime*. New York: New York University Press.

Drake, Elizabeth K., Steve Aos, and Marna G. Miller. 2009. "Evidence-Based Public Policy Options to Reduce Crime and Criminal Justice Costs: Implications in Washington State." *Victims & Offenders* 4(2): 170–96.

Fagan, Jeffrey, and Richard B. Freeman. 1999. "Crime and Work." *Crime and Justice* 25: 225–90.

Finn, Peter. 1998. "Job Placement for Offenders in Relation to Recidivism." *Journal of Offender Rehabilitation* 28(1–2): 89–106.

Graboski, Leah. 2006. "Granholm Approves Minimum Wage Hike." *The Michigan Daily*, March 29, 2006.

Harding, David J., Jeffrey D. Morenoff, and Jessica J.B. Wyse. 2019. *On the Outside: Prisoner Reentry and Reintegration*. Chicago: University of Chicago Press.

Hays, Sharon. 2003. *Flat Broke with Children: Women in the Age of Welfare Reform*. New York: Oxford University Press.

Herbert, Claire W., Jeffrey D. Morenoff, and David J. Harding. 2015. "Homelessness and Housing Insecurity Among Former Prisoners." *RSF: The Russell Sage Foundation Journal of the Social Sciences* 1(2): 44–79. DOI: 10.7758/RSF.2015.1.2.04.

Irwin, John. 1970. *The Felon*. Berkeley: University of California Press.

———. 2004. *The Warehouse Prison: Disposal of the New Dangerous Class*. Los Angeles, CA: Roxbury.

Jacobs, Erin. 2012. *Returning to Work After Prison: Final Results from the Transitional Jobs Reentry Demonstration*. New York: MDRC.

Jonson, Cheryl Lero, and Francis T. Cullen. 2015. "Prisoner Reentry Programs." *Crime and Justice* 44(1): 517–75.

Kachnowski, Vera. 2005. *Returning Home Illinois Policy Brief: Employment and Prisoner Reentry*. Washington, D.C.: Urban Institute.

Kaeble, Danielle, and Thomas P. Bonczar. 2017. *Probation and Parole in the United States, 2015*. Washington. U.S. Department of Justice, Bureau of Justice Statistics.

Karlson, Kristian Bernt, Anders Holm, and Richard Breen. 2012. "Comparing Regression Coefficients Between Same-Sample Nested Models Using Logit and Probit: A New Method." *Sociological Methodology* 42(1): 286–313.

Kornfeld, Robert, and Howard S. Bloom. 1999. "Measuring Program Impacts on Earnings and Employment: Do Unemployment Insurance Wage Reports from Employers Agree with Surveys of Individuals?" *Journal of Labor Economics* 17(1): 168-97.

LaBriola, Joe. 2020. "Post-prison Employment Quality and Future Criminal Justice Contact." *RSF: The Russell Sage Foundation Journal of the Social Sciences* 6(1): 154-72. DOI: 10.7758/RSF.2020.6.1.07.

Lower-Basch, Elizabeth. 2018. *Work Participation Rate: Temporary Assistance for Needy Families*. Washington, D.C.: Center for Law and Social Policy.

Mead, Lawrence M. 2007. "Toward a Mandatory Work Policy for Men." *Future of Children* 17(2): 43-72.

Miller, Reuben Jonathan. 2014. "Devolving the Carceral State: Race, Prisoner Reentry, and the Micro-Politics of Urban Poverty Management." *Punishment & Society* 16(3): 305-35.

Mood, Carina. 2010. "Logistic Regression: Why We Cannot Do What We Think We Can Do, and What We Can Do About It." *European Sociological Review* 26(1): 67-82.

Moses, Marilyn C. 2012. "Ex-Offender Job Placement Programs Do Not Reduce Recidivism." *Corrections Today* August/September: 106-8.

Muhlhausen, David B. 2018. "Research on Returning Offender Programs and Promising Practices." Washington: National Institute of Justice. Last modified June 21, 2018. Accessed July 24, 2019. https://www.nij.gov/about/director/Pages/muhlhausen-research-on-returning-offender-programs-and-promising-practices.aspx.

Ostermann, Michael. 2013. "Active Supervision and Its Impact Upon Parolee Recidivism Rates." *Crime & Delinquency* 59(4): 487-509.

———. 2015. "How Do Former Inmates Perform in the Community? A Survival Analysis of Rearrests, Reconvictions, and Technical Parole Violations." *Crime & Delinquency* 61(2): 163-87.

Pager, Devah. 2007. *Marked: Race, Crime, and Finding Work in an Era of Mass Incarceration*. Chicago: University of Chicago Press.

Peck, Jamie. 2001. *Workfare States*. New York: Guilford Press.

Petersilia, Joan. 2003 *When Prisoners Come Home: Parole and Prisoner Reentry*. New York: Oxford University Press.

Piven, Frances Fox, and Richard A. Cloward. 1971. *Regulating the Poor: The Functions of Public Welfare*. New York: Pantheon Books.

Rakis, John. 2005. "Improving the Employment Rate of Ex-Prisoners Under Parole." *Federal Probation* 69(1): 12.

Ramakers, Anke, Paul Nieuwbeerta, Johan Van Wilsem, and Anja Dirkzwager. 2017. "Not Just Any Job Will Do: A Study on Employment Characteristics and Recidivism Risks After Release." *International Journal of Offender Therapy and Comparative Criminology* 61(16): 1795-818.

Raphael, Steven. 2014. *The New Scarlet Letter?: Negotiating the U.S. Labor Market with a Criminal Record*. Kalamazoo, Mich.: W.E. Upjohn Institute.

Redcross, Cindy, Dan Bloom, Erin Jacobs, Michelle Mano, Sara Muller-Ravett, Kristin Seefeldt, Jennifer Yahner, Alford A. Young, and Janine Zweig. 2010. *Work After Prison: One-Year Findings from the Transitional Jobs Reentry Demonstration*. New York: MDRC.

Redcross, Cindy, Megan Millenky, Timothy Rudd, and Valerie Levshin. 2012. *More Than a Job: Final Results from the Evaluation of the Center for Employment Opportunities (CEO) Transitional Jobs Program*. OPRE report no. 2011-18. Washington: U.S. Department of Health and Human Services.

Schnepel, Kevin T. 2018. "Good Jobs and Recidivism." *The Economic Journal* 128(608): 447-69.

Seim, Josh. 2016. "Short-Timing: The Carceral Experience of Soon-to-be-Released Prisoners." *Punishment and Society* 18(4): 442-58.

———. 2017. "The Ambulance: Toward a Labor Theory of Poverty Governance." *American Sociological Review* 82(3): 451-75.

Seiter, Richard P. 2002. "Prisoner Reentry and the Role of Parole Officers." *Federal Probation* 66(1): 50-54.

Simon, Jonathan. 1993. *Poor Discipline: Parole and the Social Control of the Underclass, 1890-1990*. Chicago: University of Chicago Press.

Solomon, Amy L., Kelly Dedel Johnson, Jeremy Travis, and Elizabeth C. McBride. 2004. "From Prison to Work: The Employment Dimensions of Prisoner Reentry." Washington, D.C.: Urban Institute.

Soss, Joe, Richard C. Fording, and Sanford F. Schram. 2011. *Disciplining the Poor: Neoliberal Paternalism and the Persistent Power of Race*. Chicago: University of Chicago Press.

Travis, Jeremy. 2005. *But They All Come Back: Fac-*

ing the Challenges of Prisoner Reentry. Washington, D.C.: Urban Institute.

Turner, Susan, and Joan Petersilia. 1996. "Work Release in Washington: Effects on Recidivism and Corrections Costs." *The Prison Journal* 76(2): 138–64.

Uggen, Christopher. 1999. "Ex-Offenders and the Conformist Alternative: A Job Quality Model of Work and Crime." *Social Problems* 46(1): 127–51.

———. 2000. "Work as a Turning Point in the Life Course of Criminals: A Duration Model of Age, Employment, and Recidivism." *American Sociological Review* 65(4): 529–46.

U.S. Department of Health and Human Services. 2018. "Data & Reports: Caseload Data." Accessed July 23, 2018. https://www.acf.hhs.gov/ofa/programs/tanf/data-reports.

U.S. Department of Labor. 2017. "Changes in Basic Minimum Wages in Non-Farm Employment Under State Law: Selected Years 1968 to 2017." Last modified December 2017. Accessed July 24, 2018. https://www.dol.gov/whd/state/stateMinWageHis.htm.

Vaisey, Stephen, and Andrew Miles. 2017. "What You Can—and Can't—Do with Three-Wave Panel Data." *Sociological Methods & Research* 46(1): 44–67.

Visher, Christy A., Laura Winterfield, and Mark B. Coggeshall. 2005. "Ex-Offender Employment Programs and Recidivism: A Meta-Analysis." *Journal of Experimental Criminology* 1(3): 295–316.

Wacquant, Loïc 2009. *Punishing the Poor: The Neoliberal Government of Social Insecurity*. Durham, NC: Duke University Press Books.

Werth, Robert. 2011. "I Do What I'm Told, Sort of: Reformed Subjects, Unruly Citizens, and Parole." *Theoretical Criminology* 16(3): 329–46.

———. 2013. "The Construction and Stewardship of Responsible yet Precarious Subjects: Punitive Ideology, Rehabilitation, and 'Tough Love' Among Parole Personnel." *Punishment & Society* 15(3): 219–46.

West, Angela D., and Richard P. Seiter. 2004. "Social Worker or Cop? Measuring the Supervision Styles of Probation & Parole Officers in Kentucky and Missouri." *Journal of Crime and Justice* 27(2): 27–57.

Western, Bruce. 2006. *Punishment and Inequality in America*. New York: Russell Sage Foundation.

———. 2008. *From Prison to Work: A Proposal for a National Prisoner Reentry Program*. Washington, D.C.: Brookings Institution.

Zweig, Janine, Jennifer Yahner, and Cindy Redcross. 2010. *Recidivism Effects of the Center for Employment Opportunities (CEO) Program Vary by Former Prisoners' Risk of Reoffending*. New York: MDRC.

# PART IV
# Work and Identity in and After Prison

# Sandpiles of Dignity: Labor Status and Boundary-Making in the Contemporary American Prison

MICHAEL GIBSON-LIGHT

*This study investigates discursive strategies through which prisoners seek dignity. In particular, it turns toward the role of penal labor in such pursuits. Drawing on eighty-two in-depth interviews and eighteen months of ethnographic fieldwork conducted within one U.S. men's prison, it details the role of job status in prisoner dignity claims. In the scramble to the top of a shifting sandpile of dignity, prisoner appeals to legitimacy rely on downward-facing symbolic boundaries erected to distinguish from lower-status others. Participants in the highest-status work sites made moral claims against others by self-identifying as professionals rather than inmates. At the bottom reaches of the labor hierarchy, workers emphasized lateral distances from other low-status prisoners. These competitive processes serve to reify penal labor structures, inequity, and control.*

**Keywords:** prison, labor, dignity, symbolic boundaries

An emerging literature examines the relevance of dignity to developments in administrative and legislative approaches to prison operations (Demleitner 2014; Henry 2010; Simon 2011, 2017; Snacken 2015; Van Zyl Smit and Snacken 2009; Waldron 2012); yet dignity's role behind bars at the micro level has been less explored. To complement these top-down approaches, this article investigates strategies through which U.S. prisoners claim and assess dignity. In particular, it looks at the role of penal labor in such pursuits. Work is a core facet of punishment for most prisoners (Hatton 2018; Stephan 2008) and shapes "penal subjectivities" (Sexton 2015). That is, prisoners' experiences and understandings of work may affect the ways in which they orient to and make meaning of punishment and of self-worth more generally (Hatton 2018). For the prisoner, as for the free citizen, "life demands dignity and meaningful work is essential for dignity" (Hodson 2001, 3). Yet the penal institution is fraught with hurdles to its acquisition.

This study therefore asks about the discursive strategies prisoners use to assert, justify, or maintain self-worth behind bars. What role do perceptions tied to labor play in prisoners' understandings of their own and others' identities and worth? To address these questions, I draw on eighty-two in-depth interviews with

---

Michael Gibson-Light is assistant professor of sociology and criminology at the University of Denver.

© 2020 Russell Sage Foundation. Gibson-Light, Michael. 2020. "Sandpiles of Dignity: Labor Status and Boundary-Making in the Contemporary American Prison." *RSF: The Russell Sage Foundation Journal of the Social Sciences* 6(1): 198–216. DOI: 10.7758/RSF.2020.6.1.09. Special thanks to the prisoners and staffers of SSP and all who helped advance this work. Direct correspondence to: Michael Gibson-Light at michael.gibson-light @du.edu, 2000 E. Asbury Ave., Sturm Hall 446, Denver, CO 80208.

Open Access Policy: *RSF: The Russell Sage Foundation Journal of the Social Sciences* is an open access journal. This article is published under a Creative Commons Attribution-NonCommercial-NoDerivs 3.0 Unported License.

prisoners and staffers in a medium security men's state prison unit. Ethnographic observations help contextualize findings.

Work status offers one arena to assert worth relative to others. However, rather than a fixed "career ladder" with clear pathways to advancement and consistent understandings of status, prisoners instead face "opportunity sandpiles" (Giuffre 1999), in which stability is not guaranteed and perceived self-worth is often reconstituted with shifts in relative position. The world of penal labor is precarious and at times unpredictable. Prisoners face mass firings, frequent expressions of arbitrary authority and mistreatment, sporadic intra- and inter-institutional relocations, and other forms of instability. Findings suggest that working prisoners draw on moral rhetorics related to job status to assert dignity in this unstable context. In the scramble to the top of this shifting sandpile of dignity, they make claims to legitimacy in part by erecting symbolic boundaries between themselves and those of lower status to justify and reinforce their own standing—a form of "secondary adjustment" (Goffman 1961). Seeking to establish moral footing on the faults of others, participants regularly challenged the dedication, motivations, and work ethics of those in less desirable jobs than their own.

Although they shared a relatively consistent vocabulary of dignity, participants' boundary-making strategies were in part shaped by their positions within a tiered penal employment status hierarchy. Through distinction processes tied to work status, incarcerated workers reify structures of carceral labor and control. Although other group distinctions, such as those drawn along the lines of race (Walker 2016), age (Kreager et al. 2017), or gang affiliation (Skarbek 2014), remain important in the penal context, qualitative findings suggest that these and other social barriers may be cross-cut by labor distinctions, illuminating new class lines behind bars.

## DIGNITY AND PUNISHMENT
The definition of dignity has shifted both colloquially and legislatively over the years (Simon 2017). In assessing various usages throughout legal history, Leslie Henry (2010) identifies five key, overlapping components: institutional status, equality, liberty, personal integrity, and collective virtue. In a more general sense, we may understand dignity as "the ability to establish a sense of self-worth and self-respect and to appreciate the respect of others" (Hodson 2001, 3). It is a basic sense of value or belonging in the social world (Pugh 2009)—a sense that is confirmed when one's personhood is recognized (Fagan 2017, 317). In the penal context, human dignity is linked to personal identity (Liebling 2011). As Gresham Sykes (1958, 6) notes, "a man perpetually locked by himself in a cage is no longer a man at all; rather, he is a semi-human object, an organism with a number. The identity of the individual, both to himself and to others, is largely compounded of the web of symbolic communications by which he is linked to the external world," the stripping of which results in a decay of personality and worth. Likewise, Erving Goffman (1961, 21) highlights the "loss of identity equipment" upon incarceration, which may "prevent the individual from presenting his usual image of himself to others." The deprivation of identity expression coupled with the forced adoption of institutionally approved expressions actively "mortifies" the self. "In total institutions, such physical indignities abound" (Goffman 1961, 22). Thus "retaining an identity" is central to prisoner conceptions of dignity (Liebling 2011).

Nevertheless, the processes through which it is pursued in situ behind bars remain understudied. In the absence of equitable access to resources and outlets for expression, we may expect the nation's prisoners to turn instead to local "economies of dignity" (Pugh 2009)—that is, local meanings systems through which they may ascertain which characteristics are privileged, assert value, and maintain positive self-images. Dignity claims may be externally validated by incarcerated peers, staffers, or contacts on the outside.

Classical prison scholarship links prisoner identity to internal hierarchies. Twentieth-century accounts of prison social systems detail largely agreed-upon prisoner roles linked to the nature of the crime and, to a lesser extent, race, age, and masculinity (Sykes 1958). In this setting, dignity and respect were conferred to those who followed the "convict code" and filled particular roles. In later years, penal institutions grew more divided along ethnoracial and geographic lines. The value of outside criminal activity shifted as well, and noncareer criminals and drug users rose in the ranks of the social order (Irwin 1980). Through the 1960s and into the beginning of what became the era of mass incarceration, prisoner populations continued to develop a competitive "segmented order" (Irwin 1980, 127) in which gang affiliations outpace many strata.

Prison social order in the era of hyperincarceration continues to fractionalize, with ethnicity and criminal orientation intersecting in evolving ways. Status distinctions and assertions of worth today take various forms rather than reflect a single, unified "code" (Clemmer 1958; Sykes 1958). Following a gap in interest in prison social order (Simon 2000), recent research points to prison gang structures (Skarbek 2014), ethnoracial hierarchies (Walker 2016), and age distinctions (Kreager et al. 2017) as arenas of prisoner status struggles. And, although earlier prison research tended to discuss penal labor primarily in terms of its material benefit for the incarcerated (see, for example, Sykes 1958), contemporary scholarship notes that work is salient to how individuals today perceive their time and positions behind bars (Guilbaud 2010). Standing in prison labor systems represents an emergent source of identity and dignity behind bars (see, for example, Rhodes 2004, 109). In this manner, the retention or "remaking of identity" (Liebling 2011) through work is principal in prisoner dignity pursuits.

**Boundary-Making in Dignity Pursuits**
The ability to derive self-worth from work is shaped by the conditions of labor. Forms of control and supervision can have mortifying effects, limiting workers' ability to find meaning or satisfaction (Hodson 1996). In such contexts, dignity (and indignity) is often perceived relationally as individuals assess and assert worth along the lines of occupational divisions and access to power or resources (Crowley 2014).

The erection of symbolic boundaries is often central to securing and maintaining dignity. To this end, barriers between status groups may be erected in part to justify imbalances in the control of resources (Weber 1978). Such boundaries, according to Michele Lamont (1992, 11), "emerge when we try to define who we are: we constantly draw inferences concerning our similarities to, and differences from, others, indirectly producing typification systems," through which we "signal our identity and develop a sense of security, dignity, and honor." Moral positions, such as a strong work ethic, are central to workers' conceptions of self. Erecting boundaries along these lines "helps workers to maintain a sense of self-worth, to affirm their dignity independently of their relatively low social status, and to locate themselves above others" (Lamont 2002, 19). Those perceived as lacking work ethic or discipline are frequent objects of scorn. Frustrations with the moral deficiencies of others in part represent a response to challenges of low-status labor, which is often physically and psychologically strenuous and underpaid (Lamont 2002).

Positions in market hierarchies offer ready-made lines along which to erect symbolic boundaries. In navigating perceptions surrounding employment in low-status jobs, for instance, fast-food workers erect boundaries between themselves and the unemployed (Newman 1999). Workers may also assert distinctions from coworkers of different status levels. Competition is a consistent feature of internal labor markets—especially across occupational or departmental lines up the career ladder (Burawoy 1979). Yet, in some contexts, status and trajectories may be less clearly delineated or less stable. These environments may be conceptualized as "opportunity sandpiles" (Giuffre 1999). Amid such volatility, relative positions between workers may be insecure, resulting in a structure in which "each career can only be evaluated in relationship to other actors" (Giuffre 1999, 830). Perceptions of self-worth may be regularly reconstituted or challenged with shifts in one's or others' standing.

**The U.S. Penal Labor Context**
In today's state penitentiaries, approximately two-thirds of prisoners participate in work programs (Stephan 2008). They engage in textiles; data entry; and other light industry (Haney 2010); maintain and clean prison facilities (Hatton 2018; Solomon et al. 2004); are contracted

in public works projects, such as road and park maintenance, construction, and public lands upkeep; engage in agricultural work; work in call centers (Stephan 2008); and fight fires in the outside world (Goodman 2012). These are only some of the pervasive uses of penal labor (Pryor 2005).

Several factors distinguish the prison labor context from the free world sites in which other scholars have investigated boundary-making processes. First, the prison work environment is uniquely unstable and intensely competitive. Mass or unjustified firings are common; prisoners may be transferred to other jobs or facilities without notice; and wages may be reduced or seized with little oversight, generating uncertainty and ambiguity (Crewe 2011). Additionally, "The work [is] draining... and its very existence help[s] to stimulate intense competition for the better jobs among the inmates" (Jacobs 1977, 48). Second, the prison is more explicit in limiting the mobility of disadvantaged groups. The most valued assignments are often inequitably awarded along ethnoracial or gender lines (Crittenden, Koons-Witt, and Kaminski 2018). Finally, prisons house a particularly narrow range of social class. Whereas the free world is fraught with conflict between middle-class managers and working-class employees (Burawoy 1979) or workers and the nonworking poor (Newman 1999), the prison population is largely made up of poor labor market under- or nonparticipants (Wakefield and Uggen 2010).

In this environment, self-discipline and dedication to "a hard day's work" have emerged as central to how prisoners as well as prison staffers understand value (see Goodman 2012). Work is perceived as a disciplining or normalizing endeavor through which prisoners adopt new or renewed responsibilities (Simon 1993). By highlighting the importance of work ethic, contemporary prisoners not only signal virtue, but also inject meaning into their labors and hence their time behind bars. Shadd Maruna (2001) suggests that skilled or vocational work experiences may help bolster prisoners' perceptions of self-worth and the reconstruction of positive narratives about their lives. If, as Randy Hodson (2001) asserts, dignity is contingent on meaningful work, then dignity behind bars is hinged in part on the perceived relative worth of one's work.

## METHODS AND SITE

This article draws primarily on eighty-two in-depth interviews to investigate dignity pursuits on the inside. Sixty-nine were conducted with prisoners and thirteen with staff members at a medium security unit of a men's state prison, which I refer to as Sunbelt State Penitentiary (SSP).[1] Prisoner participants were drawn from four penal labor programs where I conducted ethnographic observations. The nature of the prison and prisoners' dominated schedules often made it difficult to secure time and space to conduct interviews. Because of this, they ranged from fifteen to eighty minutes. Questions inquired broadly into prisoners' experiences of life and work, including personal employment history inside and outside prison, perceptions of work, the dynamics of navigating prison life, and future plans for release. Influenced by the racial politics of the institution—informal rules governing and limiting interactions between racial-ethnic cliques (Goodman 2014)—white prisoners were quicker to consent to recorded interviews in the early weeks of collection, increasing final participation rates. The reluctance of other groups eventually faded but resulted in fewer interviews overall.[2] No clear trends emerged along ethnic or racial lines in regard to the focus of this article.

Ethnographic field notes are drawn on for context and added detail. I conducted eighteen months of fieldwork across 2015 and 2016 at SSP. Following approval from the state Department of Corrections (DOC), I entered the field during daylight hours to observe and participate in penal labor tasks alongside prisoners of diverse ages, ethnic groups, and criminal histories. I explored many work programs but, to better focus observations on consistent processes and themes over time, I spent most days

---

1. All names, including that of the institution, are pseudonyms.

2. The final prisoner interview sample included twenty Latino (twelve Mexican American, eight foreign national), thirty-four white, fourteen black, and one Native American.

at one of four sites. These were selected on the basis of their divergent desirability to workers and included the "worst" prison job, one "decent" job, and the two "best" jobs, in the language of participants.

The site first was the food factory, a derided food prep warehouse in which approximately eighty men rolled bologna, wrapped sandwiches, and engaged in a range of other mostly deskilled tasks. The second was the fleet garage, a fully stocked auto garage at which a small crew of four to seven men performed regular maintenance on the institution's vast vehicular fleet. The third was the call center, the highest paying and one of the two most lauded work programs onsite, in which a staff of approximately thirty prisoners made cold-call telemarketing sales to the outside world. The fourth and final work program was the sign shop, the second of the two "best" work programs, in which around thirty working prisoners produced street signs and other signage to fulfill state and rarer private orders. At times, I observed the comings and goings of nonworking prisoners on the prison yard—or "Idle Men" (Sykes 1958)—though I did not interview them. I also occasionally shadowed staff performing various duties within and beyond prison walls.

The site of this research, SSP, is located in the U.S. Sunbelt—defined as the region below the 36th parallel (Browning and Gesler 1979). Home to several thousand male prisoners, this institution is in the top quartile of U.S. prisons in terms of average daily population size (Stephan 2008).[3] It is a state prison, meaning that it is managed by a state DOC. Administrative and security staffers are state employees; however, many civilian staff members are employed by private firms contracted to oversee services like food production or medical care, or manage certain work programs like the call center. As is typical of contemporary U.S. penal facilities, most SSP prisoners engage in some form of labor, whether in programs overseen by private firms or—most commonly—directly for the state in a facility support capacity (Stephan 2008).

## WORK AT SUNBELT STATE PENITENTIARY

Approximately two-thirds of SSP prisoners worked in some form of labor program. Those participating in morning education programs (around 10 percent of prisoners) were exempted from mandatory labor, as were those deemed physically or mentally unfit. The institution housed an expansive list of work programs of different types and levels of appeal in the eyes of the incarcerated. The four sites on which observations were focused were selected purposively to allow insight into each tier of this hierarchical employment system. Early insights from working prisoners as well as facility staff helped me identify the selected sites.

### The Hierarchical Penal Employment System

Work programs regarded as the best within the unit shared characteristics with "good jobs" (Kalleberg 2011) in the free world. These positions—the call center and sign shop—were classified by the institution as "skilled positions" and offered the highest wages, paying up to approximately $1.00 per hour or higher. Further, good jobs also promised greater degrees of autonomy (allowing smoke breaks at prisoners' leisure, for instance), relative stability (lower levels of turnover), and opportunities for internal mobility (allowing workers to move between stations within the work site). In addition, they were commonly less exposed to the institution's security apparatus (for example, by not having correctional officers [COs] stationed onsite) and facilitated work experiences that reportedly felt "more like a real job," where men could "escape prison in their mind." I refer to these positions as top-tier prison jobs.

At the opposite end of the spectrum, positions regarded as "bad prison jobs" conferred lower pay, many offering less than $0.20 hourly on average. These sites also offered deskilled tasks, little autonomy, pronounced instability, and few opportunities for internal mobility. Examples include scrubbing tiles on the floor crew, cleaning toilets as a porter, or collecting cigarette butts across facility grounds. These sites were often despotically managed—deemed

---

3. Specific information about the facility, such as particulars regarding its location and the size and characteristics of its prisoner population, have been minimized to help secure participant confidentiality.

prison-within-the-prison—and featured repressive oversight from the penal security system via constant CO surveillance, pervasive security cameras, or more regular police dog unit searches. The quintessential bad prison job was the food factory, which was overwhelmingly derided by participants. Workers often reported feeling "trapped" with little hope of advancement. One CO related that these jobs were "for troublemakers. It's like an informal punishment." I refer to them as bottom-tier prison jobs.

Finally, certain positions possessed a combination of desirable and undesirable characteristics, eliciting ambivalence from many. Examples included the outside highway cleanup crews, heavy equipment operators, or carpenters in the wood shop. As another example, working as a mechanic in the fleet auto garage offered the opportunity to engage in skilled labor with a higher degree of autonomy than many prison spaces; however, this site was also home to a permanently stationed CO, offered few opportunities for internal advancement, and offered only average prison pay. As such, it was often described simply as a "fine" or "decent" position. I refer to these as middle-tier prison jobs.

For the most part, jobs at SSP were plentiful and nearly everyone who was deemed able to work was slotted somewhere into the labor system. However, certain DOC policies limited the prospects of particular groups. For instance, coveted sites such as the call center and sign shop required a high school diploma or equivalent. Because approximately 70 percent of the nation's incarcerated have no such certifications (Wakefield and Uggen 2010), most remained unable to secure the most lucrative positions. These jobs also formally excluded noncitizens, further restricting the pool of eligible workers. Such exclusions applied to work sites beyond prison walls as well, disqualifying foreign nationals and the less educated from working on the highway cleanup crews, for example. Some jobs featured other criteria for entrance—such as a clean disciplinary record over recent months—though these were at times more selectively enforced.

The vast majority of prisoners worked in the middle and bottom tiers of the labor hierarchy, receiving between around $0.05 and $0.50 per hour. The mean wage was approximately $0.20 per hour. At six- or eight-hour workdays, many might expect to earn $4.00 to $6.00 weekly before deductions for different fees and services. Such fees included charges for medical and dental visits, steadily rising charges for each minute of telephone use or letter mailed, commissary costs for food or hygiene products like toilet paper or denture cream, monthly utility fees for anyone possessing an electrical appliance like a radio, and other "pay-to-stay" expenses (Gipson and Pierce 1996; Gottschalk 2010; Levingston 2007; Von Zielbauer 2007). After all deductions were accounted, many reported quite meager earnings. Although the difference between $0.20 and $1.00 per hour might seem minimal to an outsider, prisoners and staffers alike attested that this gap could generate divergent carceral experiences as men relied on wages for necessary goods and services. As one man put it, "Some of these jobs pay fifteen cents [hourly], then they take out for gate fees, electrical, medical—in the end, you get a check for a dollar-twenty. A soda costs one-nineteen!"

## Indignity and Instability at Sunbelt State Penitentiary

At SSP, workers scrambled for jobs in a frequently shifting opportunity sandpile. Officially, the job application and assignment process at SSP was straightforward. Prisoners had simply to fill out an application indicating their preferences and wait for an opening in their work site of choice. In practice, however, this process rarely if ever played out as described. Paper job applications were inexplicably difficult to locate. After applying, it could take weeks, months, or years to hear back from the preferred work program, if at all. The most desirable top-tier programs relied on additional steps to vet applicants. Being accepted into the prison sign shop required completing a short educational assessment. The onsite manager of the shop, Mr. Edwards, described this as a way to narrow down the applicant pool by assessing knowledge of "basic middle school things—shapes, colors, et cetera. Things that you and I could do with ease." Those who passed the test were then interviewed regarding their work history, skills, and general outlooks toward work. Similarly, applicants to the call center had to pass a computer test—demonstrating their ability to log in and dial a call using the automated system. On completing this, they then had to perform a mock sales call to be assessed by the call center manager, Dennis.

Race was intertwined with these processes in different ways. For instance, during the mock sales call portion of the call center application process, minority applicants were often penalized for "sounding ghetto" (in the words of one staffer) or exhibiting a non-American accent over the phone. For reasons such as these, ethnicity often directly limited one's ability to secure desirable prison work (Crittenden, Koons-Witt, and Kaminski 2018; for a more extensive examination of the process and racial dynamics of getting a prison job, see Gibson-Light 2019).

Few managed to reach higher-status positions and many reported feeling "stuck" at the bottom reaches. The system was indeed competitive and at times chaotic. According to one staffer, "[We] don't have to have a paper trail to fire somebody." Many prisoners were fatalistic in the face of this precariousness. As one man said with a shrug, "We're in prison. Things come and go."

Although volatility was felt in all tiers of the work hierarchy, top-tier positions did promise a slight reduction in transfers between sites. Participants in these jobs were often placed on institutional hold, making it more difficult for administrators to transfer them, save for security or disciplinary interventions. As CO Bush, who oversaw work assignments, said, "You don't want these guys moving from skilled jobs—the sign shop, call center. . . . So, I'll place a work hold on the skilled workers. They [DOC] can still move them, but it won't be part of daily movement. There better be a [good] reason." Conversely, labor-force churn and instability typically increased in lower-status sites. The food factory, for example, reported a turnover rate as high as two workers daily. Demotions were also frequent, typically without explanation. When one participant was moved from the freezer section to meat prep, a derided entry-level position, he exclaimed, "That bitch [manager] fired me." When asked why, he responded, "I dunno—she wouldn't tell me. Fucking bullshit!"

Prisoners also had to cope with unreliable grievance systems. Such systems are often convoluted, slow, and outmoded, with prisoners reporting feelings of powerlessness and frustration at their inability to make their voices heard (Calavita and Jenness 2015). Responding to the suggestion that he approach his managers with concerns, one participant scoffed, "One of them? No way! . . . They don't care about grievances unless it comes from the warden." When asked whether appealing to the warden was effective, he shrugged: "Not that I've ever seen." Writing a letter to the warden's office was a slow process, removed from the actual workplace. Furthermore, it entailed risk as it required prisoners to link their name to institutional criticisms.

In addition to challenges within the workplace, the actual trek to work was also dehumanizing for many. Those who had to be transported to a secondary site away from the housing units had to pass through the strip shack before and after each workday. This plagued workers in a variety of jobs, ranging from the low-status food factory to the high-status sign shop. Here, they were stripped naked in groups and inspected for hidden contraband. Lemmy, from the sign shop, described the experience: "They strip you butt-ass naked, seven guys at a time. 'Spread your cheeks, lift your sack'—that sort of thing. That's for anybody that leaves the yard. Lotta guys don't like leaving the yard and dealing with that. . . . It's a pain in the ass. Sometimes literally." The call center and other sites housed inside the fencing surrounding the housing units were excepted from such encounters.

These conditions culminated in a general sense of indignity for incarcerated laborers. One man exclaimed, "They're just trying to punish us! They show authority instead of showing gratitude for us working here." Another declared, "There's no appreciation for what we do in here." Many dreaded work. According to one man from the food factory, "I feel better as soon as I get home. But when I'm here I don't feel well." Shaking his head with a distressed expression, he added, "Ugh. It wears

**Figure 1.** Downward-Facing Boundary-Making in a Sandpile of Dignity

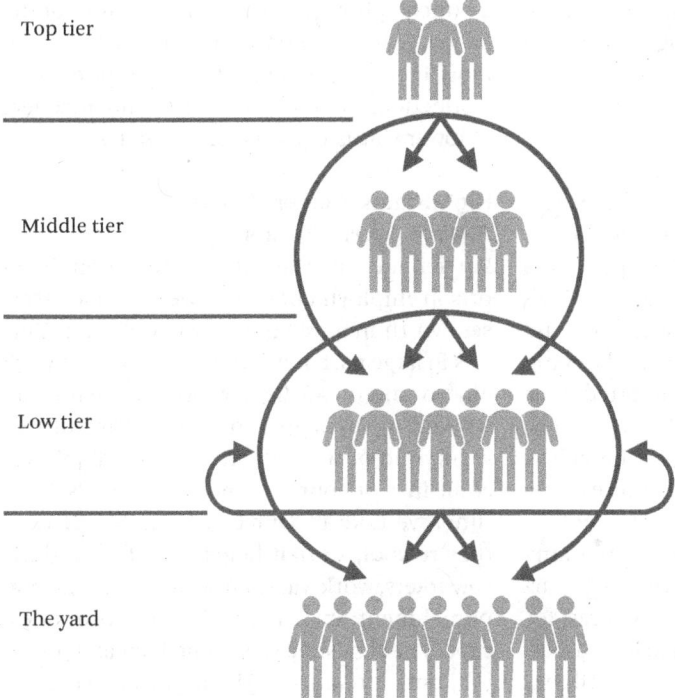

Top tier

Middle tier

Low tier

The yard

*Source:* Author's illustration.

me down." Such sentiments are confirmed by the formerly incarcerated, who emphasize three distinctly punitive characteristics of prior prison work: "their lack of remuneration, their lack of autonomy in choosing whether to work and in negotiating the terms of their labor, and their mistreatment and degradation on the job" (Hatton 2018, 181). These concerns were compounded by the fact that DOC policy barred prisoners from freely quitting their work assignments. (On occasion, some willingly sought termination; however, this entailed risk because it necessarily involved receiving several disciplinary tickets, which typically brought additional sanctions.) What is more, most relied on their meager wages to purchase food, medical care, and other things necessary for survival (see, for example, Smoyer and Lopes 2017).

Staff members largely rejected worker assertions of legitimacy. Work, according to one CO, was important solely for managing the prison population, "otherwise, they sit in the yard all day, getting in trouble." James Jacobs (1977, 46–47) recounts similar outlooks in the mid-twentieth century, noting that officials relied on carceral labor to "coerce the inmate into a conformity that would ultimately produce a respect for the rules" as well as "reinforce control by keeping inmates busy rather than providing job training." Penal labor has thus remained central to the management of the prisoner population.

Nevertheless, staffers and prisoners frequently drew on rhetorics valuing cultural narratives tied to work ethic and discipline when discussing captive laborers themselves. As the following sections will detail, prisoners at different tiers of the penal employment system sought to affirm their own identities in these terms. In the context of the opportunity sandpile of the prison, they often framed worth in contrast to others' perceived failings along valued lines. As such, symbolic boundaries were commonly erected downward as workers sought to distinguish themselves from their lower-status counterparts (see figure 1). At the bottom of the sandpile, challenges were also turned inward.

## THE TOP TIER OF THE PRISON EMPLOYMENT SYSTEM

The sign shop and the call center shared the honor of being called the best jobs at SSP. Securing a seat in one of these coveted programs was, to many, a signal of superior skill and—vitally—morality. By discursively casting the larger prison body as less qualified and lacking a strong work ethic, these men asserted their worth. In the process, they sought to supplant dehumanizing labels of *inmate* or nameless DOC prisoner numbers with other, more dignified distinctions as *worker* and *professional*.

The actual workspaces of these programs helped make this possible. Neither was surveilled with institutional security cameras, for instance, and each was designed to look different from other cold prison spaces. The call center was lined with cubicles and plastered with posters. In addition to printouts of the sales script, prisoners adorned their desks with pictures of loved ones, uplifting slogans ("Never give up!"), or other decorations. Although their computers lacked open internet access and phones were restricted to business numbers preloaded into the computer, these connections nevertheless elevated prisoner experiences. Similarly, the sign shop was modeled after shops on the outside and managed by a man with decades of industry experience. Prisoners had access to tools, including sharp implements such as box cutters. This access—and the implied trust—was rare behind bars. Such features distanced workers from many other institutional indignities, save for unexpected reminders like the crackle of a staff radio. As one sign shop worker, Luther, put it, "You feel like you're at a company, in society. Until you hear that radio! But it's peaceful—not like on the yard."

On rare occasions, workers in the two top-tier programs would cast dispersions at one another. One man working in the sign shop, for instance, once said of his counterparts in the prison call center: "Buncha prima donnas over there." He would add, "You ask me, they're just a buncha phone salesmen. The bottom of the barrel." Such claims were, however, uncommon. Instead, workers in both sites prioritized distinctions between themselves and prisoners of lower status in the labor hierarchy.

### High-Status Workers Defined Against Other Workers

Participants at the top of the hierarchical prison employment system were able to assert self-worth in a way that most could not. This was in large part due to the nature of their work environment. As Ben, a prisoner who had worked in the sign shop for upward of two years, said of the site, "It's like a real job. We come in, work our eight hours. If there's down time, we take it. Our bosses are civilians—they're cool, so that helps." For Ben and his coworkers, work was far from a facet of carceral punishment; instead, it offered a form of escape. The sign shop was framed not as a prison job, but a "real job." The overseers were not COs, but civilian bosses. As another shop worker, Jon, attested, "People forget—this ain't no [typical prison] job. This is a business. If you don't like somebody, you gotta set aside your differences. You gotta do that for the company." That the sign shop shipped orders to customers in the free world further contributed to the image that it was a business in some way removed from the penal facility—enabling workers to distance themselves to an extent as well.

The call center, which was in fact managed by a private firm, evoked similar assertions from its workers. Jake would insist, "When we're in here—[despite] wearing orange—working in a telemarketing place, we're telemarketers in our mind." According to another incarcerated salesman, Javi, the highlight of his job was that "It feels like a real job. You come in here and it's a professional atmosphere. You're on the phone and you're talking to other people—you have to be on a professional level here. You're representing your company." These sites were deemed professional because they resembled work environments in the free world in some ways, distinct from the identity-stripping, overtly punitive conditions of most prison sites. Affiliation with the call center helped provide a new, more dignified identity in this way. Javi attested that he operated not merely as a contracted prisoner, but also as a representative of the company. He added that the job "prepares you psychologically, mentally. And you wake up at a certain time because you have to be at work by six o'clock. You have to work your forty hours a week. So, you've got these obligations and you have to fulfill the obligations like a regular job."

Dedication to fulfilling such duties was central to the identity of professional and associated relative perceptions of worth. Unlike lower-status workers, said Franklin of the sign shop, "We're professional men. We appreciate our jobs." Related to such claims was the assertion that others—the "unappreciative"—were merely lazy. According to Marino, "If you are just sitting around all day not doing anything and they need you in the kitchen, the food factory . . . they're going to force you to work because no one wants to work that. So, it's the lazy guys who get those bad jobs because they're not putting forth the effort to look for the good jobs. And they get locked in the bad jobs."

Receiving the highest hourly wage in the prison, workers in the call center were sometimes defensive about their status. Clay expressed this in reference to a middle-tier job site at SSP, the outside highway cleanup crew: "This ain't a job like the highway crew, you know what I mean? They told us, 'Well, [that crew] doesn't make [as much as you]. And they're outside. They're getting dirty. They're working hard. You guys are sitting in air conditioning at computers.' While that job has no skill set. . . . The [people in the] best job are going to have hate from those people." To Clay, the higher pay, perks, and resources from which top-tier workers benefited were deserved in part because the position demanded particular capabilities.

To these men, dedication to the "company" and possession of valued skills were central to "professional" identities. They embraced the institutional designation of skilled laborers to this end. Beyond erecting these identities through contrasts to other workers, they also often cited nonworkers who spent their days on the prison yard as well.

## High-Status Workers Defined Against Nonworkers on the Yard

To many penal laborers, those who did not work were seen as taking advantage of the system. Although some were legitimately unable to perform labor tasks, others reportedly exploited the system to evade assignment. Jake, a call center salesman, attested that "A lot of guys just don't want to do nothin'," he said. "They just want to sit at home, just like they are on the streets. They just—pshh—just stay home. Some of those guys can't work for medical reasons, but most of them just avoid it. . . . A lot of guys don't want to work, bud." According to Marino, the DOC repeatedly failed to adequately reward those who did work hard. In particular, he contested the departmental policy that required the highest-paid (which in this unit only included sign shop and call center workers) to pay a room-and-board fee out of a percentage of their pay. "Here I am working," Marino said, "and [they] charge me rent, when the dope fiend next to me—who does nothing all day but sleep all day and get high all day—doesn't have to pay rent! . . . [While I'm] actually doing a grind and doing what's supposed be done."

This sentiment was common at the top reaches of the employment hierarchy. Many cited their willingness to work—to "do what's supposed to be done"—as a source of pride. "There are some of us—the more mature men—we want to work," said Franklin. "We don't want the drama of the yard. It [work] gives you something to do, gives you integrity. That's what we all strive for." Hoke would also situate his own self-image along these lines. "You got a lot of guys [on the yard] sitting around. They don't do nothing. They don't even want a job." Distancing himself from these lower-status men, he added, "Well, I've always supplied for myself. You know what I'm saying? I've always taken care of myself."

Participants also related frustrations with how they believed nonworkers perceived them. "You got to understand a prison," said Marino. "They hate on me, man. If somebody's trying to do good, they hate on it. If somebody's doing good, they going to hate on you because they don't want you doing as good as them." Jon recounted facing contempt for having secured his coveted position in the sign shop. The best strategy, he advised, was avoidance. "On that yard, with all those angry dudes, mad that they in prison? Starting fights? Uh-uh," he exclaimed, shaking his head. "It's no good. That's why this job is good—I go here, then straight to school after. So, then I only have three hours in the yard before I can sleep." Many associated the yard, in contrast to the workplace, and those who spent their days there with unstructured volatility—with idleness, drama, and potentially violence, which were best avoided through attending work.

**THE MIDDLE TIER OF THE PRISON EMPLOYMENT SYSTEM**

Like the call center and sign shop, the fleet auto garage resembled similar sites in the outside world in several ways, including being home to civilian bosses, Graham and Boyle. Yet other features of this site made it difficult for its workers to fully reframe it as a "business" beyond prison walls. For instance, it was home to a permanently stationed CO, Officer Peña, who patrolled the garage and closely surveilled tool use. Additionally, every corner of the site was monitored by visible security cameras. From time to time, some garage workers referenced "professionalism" similar to top-tier workers. Occupying more liminal positions, however, they instead typically focused on erecting boundaries between themselves and the (more limited supply of) lower-status workers in bottom-tier sites as well as nonworkers on the prison yard.

**Mid-Status Workers Defined Against Low-Status Workers**

Danny, an imprisoned mechanic who worked primarily on heavy equipment like tractors and buses, suggested that differences between skilled workers in the fleet garage and men working in low-tier work programs designated as unskilled by the institution were observable. To him, this was evident in the mechanics' dedication to approaching work earnestly and with positivity: "I think generally, I would say the biggest thing is that most of the guys here are going to work hard every day [and] are probably a little bit more upbeat and happier." Many of Danny's opinions on the matter were formed early in his prison sentence when he was assigned to work on the general maintenance crew, a low-status work site at SSP. It was here that he said he encountered frequent issues he attributed to prisoners lacking dedication to the job:

DANNY: Usually it's somebody that just doesn't know what they're doing or somebody who just doesn't give a shit about their job. I mean . . . they're just making it harder for everybody else. Dragging their feet, or just causing some kind of issue that's making everybody else's job harder. That's usually what I think is the common problem.
INTERVIEWER: So, when that sort of thing happens, how does it get resolved?
DANNY: Usually they pretty much just stop coming to work. [laughter] You know what I mean?

Against these undedicated workers, Danny framed himself and his coworkers as men who "work hard every day." Additionally, they "give a shit" about work and remained "a little bit more upbeat" in the face of laboring in the prison context, signaling the importance of attitudinal performance in addition to commitment to task completion.

Another central characteristic that these mid-status workers highlighted was the skilled nature and designation of their tasks. Directly tied to this were participants' (or their assessments of others') work experiences, illustrating the relevance of pre-prison employment to dignity pursuits. According to Seth, the newest of the mechanics to be stationed in the garage following a stint in the low-status food factory, "a lot of them guys [in the food factory] never worked anywhere but McDonald's or Jack in the Box or some shit." Gael, a senior mechanic, insisted that many prisoners "don't know what they're doing" when it comes to work. Despite this, Gael said, many falsely claimed various skills. "That's one thing about being in prison," he told me, "is that you see these guys that say they know what they're doing, [but] they don't have no idea. They just do it [lie about their skills] to try to get out of the yard or get into something they might have a little bit experience in."

Beyond their level of skill (or lack of skill), other features distinguished low-status workers from the mid-status mechanics, according to Gael:

INTERVIEWER: So, do you think there's a difference between [workers from] a skilled job and an unskilled job?
GAEL: Oh, yeah. You can tell when you're over there at the food factory, you can tell the difference in a person's demeanor. . . . The guys over there or other jobs like that, you'll notice they aren't able to stay focused on things a lot. And with these [skilled] jobs you have to stay focused, you have to have an understanding of professional relationships.

Workers in the food factory and other low-tier sites, according to Gael, lacked an understanding of "professional relationships" between peers or between workers and management. He later detailed the unwillingness of lower-status workers to build trusting working relationships with the staffers overseeing them: "The people who are less educated, they seem to really misinterpret things that are being presented to them. Like when [a staffer] says, 'Oh, this is the way we're going to implement these types of rules or regulations,' and it's going to be beneficial, they think that there's something trying to go against them."

**Mid-Status Workers Defined Against Nonworkers**

Fleet garage workers were also quick to define themselves in contrast to nonworking prisoners at SSP. As one mechanic said, "Most motherfuckers don't want to work. They just want to sit on the yard all day. Fucking bums." One man, Seth, was particularly adamant that his work ethic, which he learned at a young age, was what put him above these other men:

I think it was my dad instilling the work values into me. . . . He could tear apart a motor of a car and fix it. He could tear apart anything, a fucking generator, whatever it was, man. He could fix it. I think the thing that I really took away from it was the work ethic. And I think I get a lot of that from him, because I'd like to think I'm a pretty good worker. . . . Without him, I would be like some of these jackasses that the only thing they got to look forward to is [unskilled work] or janitorial shit or whatever.

According to the mechanics, laboring in the garage each day offered an opportunity to actually escape interactions with nonworkers. After work, "I've got to go back to the yard and deal with a bunch of freaking idiots," exclaimed one mechanic. "Just completely stupid people, you know what I mean? We don't have to come out here [to work] and deal with that." Another shop worker, Ethan, said he, too, sought to limit interactions: "I'm really doing my best in here and staying away from all the riff-raff." Danny suggested that he and his coworkers were above the pursuits occupying the time of nonworkers on the yard. He also advised avoidance:

We're tired when we get back. We can just go home and chill and relax. You know what I mean? Our minds are tired. Our bodies are tired. We just wore ourselves out. Not really worried about what else is going on in the yard. Don't really give a shit. I just want to go to work the next day. We have a routine. You know what I mean? These guys are fucking nitpicking everything that's going on. "Man, this sucks. This sucks." We're like, "Whatever, dude." You know what I mean?

Defining themselves in opposition to the nonworkers on the yard, mechanics' professed dedication to labor mapped on to a desire to avoid distractions. Despite—or perhaps motivated by—their liminal standing, they demarcated stark distance from those lower in the hierarchy.

**THE BOTTOM TIER OF THE PRISON EMPLOYMENT SYSTEM**

Prisoners confined to the bottom of the internal labor hierarchy of Sunbelt State faced magnified indignities of prison life. To them, work was not an escape, but instead one more facet of punishment. The work environment of such sites reflected this. The food factory, for instance, was unmistakably a prison labor site. The walls were the same drab gray stone as the housing bays. An onsite CO, Byrne, made regular patrols of the large warehouse. Although a civilian crew oversaw most work tasks, they were often quite punitive and did not seek to recreate the atmosphere of outside workplaces like their counterparts in top- and mid-tier jobs. Overseers regularly referred to workers as *inmate* rather than by name. Work was regularly interrupted for "count time," with prisoners ordered to line up and be accounted for.

On occasion, food factory workers referenced failed attempts to break into the top labor tier. Vin, for instance, related that he had once attempted to get a job in the prison call center but failed. With a shrug, he said, "Eh, but I don't really want to sit there and do that all day long anyway." More commonly, these participants drew on distinctions from prisoners who spent days on the yard—much like the working poor Katherine Newman (1999) studied, who asserted worth in opposition to nonworkers. Moreover, they also engaged in lateral distinctions, erecting boundaries between stations within their site in a manner much rarer at the mid and top tier.

## Low-Status Workers Defined Against Nonworkers

Occupying the bottom of the worker hierarchy at SSP, the men of the food factory had few workers against whom to assert their relative value. Despite poor working conditions, participants often insisted that the job remained an improvement from the yard. According to one man, Dread, "I don't really care what [job] I do. Anything is better than being stuck on that yard all day.... It's just too much stuff going on there." By "stuff," Dread referred to the general perception of "drama" of day-to-day yard life, including gossiping and time spent dwelling on outside relationships or other concerns. Soto said,

> I like leaving the yard because I don't like all that drama. There's a bunch of grown-ass men who are nosier than these teenagers out there on the internet. Straight up, man. [If] something happens over here in Building 1, in about 15 minutes it'll be known in Building 4. You know what I mean? So, I'm not trying to be a part of that. That's why I want a job, because I don't want to be in there.

Others lamented the violence that occurred outside of work. Pedro, for instance, claimed, "I'm always a respectful person, and just neutral. But I see a lot of people . . . since I've been here, and some people are just, like, real hardheaded. You know what I mean? They just want to fight every time or pick a fight with you." When asked whether "hard-headed" individuals were often encountered at work, Pedro shook his head and said, "Usually it's not at work. . . . They [workers] just try to stay busy." He reiterated, "But in the yard it is [common]."

One food factory worker, Bobby, suggested that the men on the yard possessed entirely different values, lacking dedication to labor and instead emphasizing "appearances":

BOBBY: I like to be around people that like to work. Sometimes the environment [at work] is kind of less stressful, less strange. We can laugh and joke. And you meet interesting people. People with the same kind of mindset that I have.
INTERVIEWER: More so than you do on the yard, you mean?
BOBBY: Yeah. Because it seems like on the yard, most people are just trying to put on appearances for their friends or whatever.

Men preoccupied with appearances and other distractions were sometimes called youngsters. In prison, both biological age and the length of sentence are important to social organization (Kreager et al. 2017). However, at Sunbelt State, to be labeled a youngster was often less tied to these criteria than to perceived maturity. Men who did not work, regardless of birth year or sentencing date, were seen as immature and therefore referred to with this moniker. Cliff, a worker in his twenties, made such a distinction:

> I've told everybody, all the youngsters on the yard, I'm saying like, "Dude, get a job." I'm

saying, "Your time will go like that [snapping his fingers]." Know what I'm saying? And they're like, "Oh, well, da, da, da—." I get it. I've gotten quite a few people in here a job. Know what I'm saying? But most people can't [do it]. "Oh, I don't want to wake up before seven in the morning." And we wake up—I wake up at four-thirty. I go eat breakfast about—they open the yard about four-forty-five, four-fifty for workers to go eat early chow. And we go eat early chow, come back, and it's probably like five-ten, five-twenty. I sleep for about another forty-five minutes, and I get up and come to work.

Cliff's insistence that youngsters on the yard lacked the willingness or discipline to "get up and come to work" was not unique. Lonnie, for instance, referred to himself as a "high-quality worker." When I followed up, asking, "Would you say there's a lot of high-quality workers in prison?" he quickly responded,

LONNIE: No. No, sir.
INTERVIEWER: What makes you sure?
LONNIE: Three-fourths of these guys in here—and I mean this has been on every yard I've been on. Three-fourths of the people that come to prison, it's a vacation for them. . . . Nobody can stand on their own two feet, man. But it's just a fact of you got to—sometimes you just got to stand up and be grown. Get some sense. Get some morals about yourself.

Drawing such overtly moral boundaries between themselves and their nonworking counterparts enabled food factory workers to overcome low status by reframing themselves as principled men—dignified in their dedication to eschew violence and drama and to spend time working. To them, they may be prisoners, but at least they are workers; they may sit at the bottom of the employment hierarchy, but at least they are not sitting idly in their bunks.

## Low-Status Workers and Lateral Distinctions
Some food factory workers also erected boundaries in opposition to others in the same low-status site. For instance, drawing on a rhetoric similar to that used to describe nonworkers, Bobby insisted that many food factory workers lacked work ethic. With a chuckle he said,

BOBBY: Some people don't like to work a lot. So, they try to find the jobs where you do the least amount. I like to work—whatever to keep me busy.
INTERVIEWER: Do you think that's common in here? That outlook of liking to work, I mean.
BOBBY: No. I think statistically—and this is just me—I think nine out of ten of the guys that actually come into work, they don't really come in to [do] work. They just find it as a way to eat extra or play around with their friends or whatever.

Without dedication to hard work, Joe suggested, most food factory workers would not succeed in the free world: "I mean, they wouldn't last long in the streets like that. Especially at a [decent] job. I mean, especially if I was the boss. If the production ain't there, why keep them?"

These distinctions were most salient between workstations. In this site, where most labor was classified as unskilled, a few rare positions were deemed semi-skilled. The most prized of these was special diet cook. This station employed only three or four prisoners at a time and turnover was low. Diet cooks prepared special meals for prisoners with recognized dietary restrictions, including those with allergies, vegans, and men on dialysis. In a separate area, they also prepared kosher meals. When I asked one diet cook, Adam, how he managed to secure this competitive position, he attributed it to his dedication to work: "[The manager] saw drive in me. I stayed and cleaned while everyone else went outside to wait for the bus." Alexey, the most senior of the diet cooks, made similar statements when asked about the process of moving from an entry-level food factory position to the diet cook station: "Well, first you got to start in the sandwich shop and work really hard in the sandwich shop without getting in any trouble. And then they deem you as a trustworthy and a good-enough worker to work in the kosher area, which is a privileged area to work in here at the food factory."

Several cooks were explicit in distancing themselves from other food factory workers. According to one man, the cooks were "the guys who do something every day. We have an important job here. These guys?" he asked rhetorically, gesturing to a nearby cluster of prisoners wrapping sandwich ingredients, "[Their work] doesn't matter. But we have an important task every day." Alexey told me that most food factory workers "just want to bitch" about their work situations, suggesting that many were jealous of the special diet cooks. "I mean, to come to work [in prison] and expect to get a meaningful job?" he asked, laughing. "It ain't going to happen.... But I think a lot of people just—[it's a] misery-loves-company type of thing. They just want to sit around and bitch about it and yadda yadda."

Most often, diet cooks kept to themselves, sometimes even working with their backs to the rest of the food factory crew. One cook, Josh, expressed that the attitudes of unskilled food factory workers made work more difficult for those in semi-skilled stations:

JOSH: You're working with people that don't want to work. Most of them don't want to work. They're just there to F around and steal stuff. And you're trying to get the work done, and you got to make up where they're messing it up. What they're not doing, you got to do their stuff. It kind of sucks.... You can tell the ones that don't want to work.

INTERVIEWER: How can you tell?

JOSH: Some of these guys, they take all day long when they roll the sandwiches, just one rack. They'll just roll like [miming slow motion].

Workers at the bottom of the prison labor status hierarchy endured indignities from the institution, its staff, and higher-status carceral laborers. Unlike other workers, however, many also faced criticism from men working right alongside them. Crushed beneath the sandpile of dignity of the prison employment system, these workers were forced to erect "defensive shields" (Viggiani 2012) in every direction. Upward mobility, it seemed, may offer the only escape.

## DIGNITY AMID REPOSITIONING IN THE SANDPILE

A key aspect of the instability characterizing the prison labor system is the regular churn of workers. The unpredictability of hiring, firing, and promotion practices was a source of regular frustration for the workforce, though its effects were somewhat less for those at the top. Nevertheless, even these workers remained aware that their prized positions could disappear. Reflecting on this, Lester, in the sign shop, noted, "You never know. Any of us could be gone any day. There's no security—you think you're secure, but . . . this is prison. They could roll any of us up at any moment." Similarly, Jake from the call center once remarked, "I mean, this is the bottom line: we're in prison. There's nothin' else to it but that. [I've] been lucky for as long as I been here, but it's no surprise that that could change, you know?" Such changes—for example, when top-tier laborers lose their positions or when others move up the hierarchy—reveal the contours of how unpredictability influences prisoners' senses of worth and dignity.

Although it was somewhat less common for top-tier workers to be fired (at least relative to those further down the hierarchy), it did occasionally happen. One such incident occurred in the sign shop during fieldwork. Alec, a man with a well-known "side hustle" drawing portraits, was fired after only a few months on the job. The pretext for his termination, by his account, was that he used the shop photocopier one too many times to scan his artwork. Rather than challenge the apparent arbitrariness of his firing—indeed, it was common for workers to use this equipment during slow periods—workers in the shop made sense of Alec's forced departure using the same vocabulary with which they critiqued lower-status laborers. Suggesting that it had come as no surprise, one man said, "He simply doesn't want to work. He has absolutely no ambition!" Lemmy, who had trained Alec when he first joined the crew, lamented, "If he paid half as much attention to this [the screen-printing supplies] as he does to his drawings, he'd be good."

In enduring the sort of arbitrary authority and instability characteristic of lower-tier positions, Alec revealed parallels between the sign shop and lesser positions in the occupational sandpile. The durability of the logics underlying prisoner dignity claims is highlighted in how his former coworkers pivoted to lump him in with the larger working prisoner body against whom they situated their self-worth. For his own part, Alec sought to decouple his sense of worth from his evidently unstable position in the shop. "To tell the truth," he said, "I can be making more doing my portraits anyway."

Rhetorics also shifted when workers moved up the sandpile, such as when Seth transitioned from the food factory, where he and I first met, to the fleet garage. Not long after this move, I asked whether he missed anything about his old job. "No," he replied emphatically, "I hated it over there. That's the worst job I ever had. They treat everyone like shit! I mean, a lot of them guys got it coming—lot of idiots in there. But still." Along with gaining an improved work environment and other perks of the middle tier, Seth also quickly adopted the practice of erecting symbolic boundaries between his new job and the bottom tier. Although scorning the conditions that all faced in the food factory, he nevertheless distanced himself from his former coworkers after ascending the ranks, adapting to his new position in the sandpile.

As was true of Alec's, Seth's experiences reveal the durability of these logics of dignity as well as the apparent firmness with which they are linked to different tiers of the employment system. Although individual workers may be repositioned, the rhetorics that they adopt (and that others adopt in assessing them) map on to status levels in the labor hierarchy.

## DISCUSSION AND CONCLUSION

All prisoners, regardless of work status, are subject to the mortification processes of prison life (Goffman 1961; Sykes 1958). The despotic labor processes, deskilling, lower pay, heavy restrictions on movement, and other undesirable features of "bad" prison jobs magnified such challenges. "Good" jobs, on the other hand, offered greater autonomy and skilled, engaging tasks in environments that participants deemed more like the outside world. Where the latter better facilitated claims to dignity, the former often stifled them. Across tiers, participants shared a common vocabulary of dignity—evoking "discipline" and "hard work" against "laziness" and "drama." For workers generally, labor participation was a dignified endeavor, especially in contrast to the unstructured volatility that accompanied perceived idleness on the prison yard.

As noted, race and ethnicity influenced the job search process at SSP. Minority applicants faced added hurdles in ascending the labor hierarchy, disadvantaging them in terms of access to more desirable workplace environments and hence the identity reconstruction strategies that such positions enabled. As a result, the ability to assert the identity of worker—to contest the label of inmate—was racialized (see Crittenden, Koons-Witt, and Kaminski 2018; Gibson-Light 2019).

The relative rarity of upward-facing dignity projects—for example, lower-tier participants asserting that they deserve to move up the labor hierarchy—was initially unexpected. However, this appears consistent with other strategies of incarcerated men seeking legitimacy. For instance, prisoners erect downward-facing boundaries between their own criminal charges and those deemed more objectionable. Of his English prison field site, Nick de Viggiani (2012, 281) notes, "Some prisoners strove to legitimize their offence by contrasting it with what they viewed as more heinous or unacceptable offence types. . . . Drug-related offences were castigated by nondrug related offenders, and 'petty theft' that exploited vulnerable victims was viewed more negatively than that defined as 'corporate theft.'" By shaming alleged inferiors, prisoners construct "defensive shields" to manage prison identities. Further, given the visible inequities of the prison job search (Crittenden, Koons-Witt, and Kaminski 2018), those lacking resources to succeed in this market may consciously avoid focusing attentions upwards, lest they risk embarrassment at immobility.

Some of the trends reported here parallel those in other, free-world labor settings. The shifting nature of dignity and status as well as the persistence of downward-facing legitimation processes, for instance, have been investigated in diverse sites (Giuffre 1999; Newman 1999). More important, however, is the observation that the carceral context amplifies many negative outcomes of these and other features of labor stratification. Today's prisoners are already disproportionately "drawn from the lowest rungs in society" (Western and Pettit 2010, 8) and prisons overwhelmingly "house the jobless, the poor, the racial minority, and the uneducated, not the merely criminal" (Wakefield and Uggen 2010, 393). The discursive strategies that emerge here—in conjunction with their material bases—further stratify this already disadvantaged population. What is more, they may reinforce underlying conditions of captive labor.

In general, labor may promote prisoner competition (Jacobs 1977). When distance from other worker groups becomes a central focus (fueled by the thirst for dignity), it displaces competition between overseers and prisoners writ large (see Burawoy 1979). As the incarcerated scramble to maintain value via work status, carrying out the mandatory labor assignments upon which the institution relies—and doing so with enthusiasm—becomes framed as virtue. By moralizing dedication to penal labor, prisoners' "economy of dignity" (Pugh 2009) reproduces values benefiting this institution. As such, the rhetorics on which incarcerated participants drew often mirrored those espoused by staffers. For instance, CO Peña openly boasted that his auto garage workers "have more integrity. The guys here, they like to work." Of men in bottom-tier positions like the food factory, he said, "Those guys don't want to work.... Whereas these guys, they grew up working. They like coming here and working on cars." Some prisoners acknowledged the benefits of this agreement with staff. "If they [COs] see you want to work," said Franklin, "they treat you good." Similarly, many prisoners working in positions designated as skilled by the institution frequently cited skill level when making distinctions. Beyond merely keeping prisoners busy (Jacobs 1977), then, work is an arena of penal discipline that provides an opening to shape the very outlooks of carceral populations.

Future work should examine how the dynamics reported here shift on reentry. Erin Hatton's (2018) work advances an understanding of general patterns in ex-prisoner discourse relating to work; scholars should additionally explore how varying labor experiences on the inside may map on to divergent rhetorics post-release. For instance, how do top-tier prison laborers experience the transition back into the formal labor force as they, like others with criminal records, struggle to acquire good jobs in the free world (facing the bottom of a new labor hierarchy)?

Finally, this article has examined the discursive strategies of working prisoners pursuing dignity. Although in the minority, nonworkers deserve additional study along these lines. I had some access to nonworkers on the yard; however, my project design precluded me from investigating their experiences as systematically as was possible with their laboring counterparts. Such individuals often engage in informal labors, which may provide alternative sources of dignity. Recall Alec, who noted the value of his informal job drawing portraits. How might such prisoners' perceptions differ from workers in the formal penal labor market? What boundary-making patterns emerge among so-called Idle Men (Sykes 1958) as they navigate in and out of informal and formal work?

## REFERENCES

Browning, Clyde, and Wil Gesler. 1979. "The Sun Belt–Snow Belt: A Case of Sloppy Regionalizing." *The Professional Geographer* 31(1): 66–74.

Burawoy, Michael. 1979. *Manufacturing Consent*. Chicago: University of Chicago Press.

Calavita, Kitty, and Valerie Jenness. 2015. *Appealing to Justice: Prisoner Grievances, Rights, and Carceral Logic*. Oakland: University of California Press.

Clemmer, Donald. 1958. *The Prison Community*. New York: Rinehart & Company.

Crewe, Ben. 2011. *The Prisoner Society*. London: Macmillan.

Crittenden, Courtney, Barbara Koons-Witt, and Robert Kaminski. 2018. "Being Assigned Work in Prison: Do Gender and Race Matter?" *Feminist Criminology* 13(4): 359–81.

Crowley, Martha. 2014. "Class, Control, and Relational Indignity: Labor Process Foundations for Workplace Humiliation, Conflict, and Shame." *American Behavioral Scientist* 58(3): 416–34.

Demleitner, Nora. 2014. "Human Dignity, Crime Prevention, and Mass Incarceration: A Meaningful, Practical Comparison Across Borders." *Federal Sentencing Reporter* 27(1): 1–6.

Fagan, Jeffrey. 2017. "Dignity Is the New Legitimacy." In *The New Criminal Justice Thinking*, edited by Sharon Dolovich and Alexandra Natapoff. New York: New York University Press.

Gibson-Light, Michael. 2019. "The Prison as Market: How Prison Labor Systems Reproduce Inequality." PhD diss., University of Arizona.

Gipson, Frances, and Elizabeth Pierce. 1996. "Current Trends in State Inmate User Fee Programs for Health Services." *Journal of Correctional Health Care* 3(2): 159–78.

Giuffre, Katherine. 1999. "Sandpiles of Opportunity: Success in the Art World." *Social Forces* 77(3): 815–32.

Goffman, Erving. 1961. *Asylums*. New York: Anchor.

Goodman, Philip. 2012. "'Another Second Chance': Rethinking Rehabilitation through the Lens of California's Prison Fire Camps." *Social Problems* 59(4): 437–58.

———. 2014. "Race in California's Prison Fire Camps for Men: Prison Politics, Space, and the Racialization of Everyday Life." *American Journal of Sociology* 120(2): 352–94.

Gottschalk, Marie. 2010. "Cell Blocks and Red Ink: Mass Incarceration, the Great Recession, and Penal Reform." *Daedalus* 139(3): 62–73.

Guilbaud, Fabrice. 2010. "Working in Prison: Time as Experienced by Inmate Workers." *Revue Française de Sociologie* 51(5): 41–68.

Haney, Lynne. 2010. "Working Through Mass Incarceration: Gender and the Politics of Prison Labor from East to West." *Signs* 36(1): 73–97.

Hatton, Erin. 2018. "When Work Is Punishment: Penal Subjectivities in Punitive Labor Regimes." *Punishment and Society* 20(2): 174–91.

Henry, Leslie. 2010. "The Jurisprudence of Dignity." *University of Pennsylvania Law Review* 160: 169–232.

Hodson, Randy. 1996. "Dignity in the Workplace Under Participative Management: Alienation and Freedom Revisited." *American Sociological Review* 61(3): 719–38.

———. 2001. *Dignity at Work*. Cambridge: Cambridge University Press.

Irwin, John. 1980. *Prisons in Turmoil*. New York: Little, Brown.

Jacobs, James. 1977. *Stateville*. University of Chicago Press.

Kalleberg, Arne. 2011. *Good Jobs, Bad Jobs*. New York: Russell Sage Foundation.

Kreager, Derek, Jacob Young, Dana Haynie, Martin Bouchard, David Schaefer, and Gary Zajac. 2017. "Where 'Old Heads' Prevail: Inmate Hierarchy in a Men's Prison Unit." *American Sociological Review* 82(4): 685–716.

Lamont, Michele. 1992. *Money, Morals, and Manners*. Chicago: University of Chicago Press.

———. 2002. *The Dignity of Working Men*. Cambridge, Mass.: Harvard University Press.

Levingston, Kirsten. 2007. "Making the Bad Guy Pay: the Growing Use of Cost Shifting as an Economic Sanction." In *Prison Profiteers*, edited by Tara Herivel and Paul Wright. New York: The New Press.

Liebling, Alison. 2011. "Moral Performance, Inhuman and Degrading Treatment and Prison Pain." *Punishment and Society* 13(5): 530–50.

Maruna, Shadd. 2001. *Making Good*. Washington, D.C.: American Psychological Association.

Newman, Katherine. 1999. *No Shame in My Game*. New York: Vintage Books.

Pryor, Frederic. 2005. "Industries Behind Bars: An Economic Perspective on the Production of Goods and Services in U.S. Prison Industries." *Review of Industrial Organization* 27(1): 1–16.

Pugh, Allison. 2009. *Longing and Belonging*. Berkeley: University of California Press.

Rhodes, Lorna. 2004. *Total Confinement*. Berkeley: University of California Press.

Sexton, Lori. 2015. "Penal Subjectivities: Developing a Theoretical Framework for Penal Consciousness." *Punishment and Society* 17(1): 114–36.

Simon, Jonathan. 1993. *Poor Discipline*. Chicago: University of Chicago Press.

———. 2000. "The 'Society of Captives' in the Era of Hyper-Incarceration." *Theoretical Criminology* 4(3): 285–308.

———. 2011. "Editorial: Mass Incarceration on Trial." *Punishment and Society* 13(3): 251–55.

———. 2017. "The Second Coming of Dignity." In *The New Criminal Justice Thinking*, edited by Sharon Dolovich and Alexandra Natapoff. New York University Press.

Skarbek, David. 2014. *The Social Order of the Underworld*. New York: Oxford University Press.

Smoyer, Amy, and Giza Lopes. 2017. "Hungry on the Inside: Prison Food as Concrete and Symbolic Punishment in a Women's Prison." *Punishment and Society* 19(2): 240–55.

Snacken, Sonja. 2015. "Punishment, Legitimate Policies and Values: Penal Moderation, Dignity and Human Rights." *Punishment & Society* 17(3): 397–423.

Solomon, Amy, Kelly Johnson, Jeremy Travis, and Elizabeth McBride. 2004. "From Prison to Work: The Employment Dimensions of Prisoner Reentry." A Report of the Reentry Roundtable. Washington, D.C.: The Urban Institute.

Stephan, James J. 2008. "Census of State and Federal Correctional Facilities, 2005." NCJ 222182. Washington: U.S. Department of Justice, Bureau of Justice Statistics. Retrieved September 24, 2019. http://www.bjs.gov/index.cfm?ty=pbdetail&iid=530.

Sykes, Gresham. 1958. *The Society of Captives*. Princeton, N.J.: Princeton University Press.

Van Zyl Smit, Dirk, and Sonja Snacken. 2009. *Principles of European Prison Law and Policy*. Oxford: Oxford University Press.

Viggiani, Nick de. 2012. "Trying to Be Something You Are Not: Masculine Performance within a Prison Setting." *Men and Masculinities* 15(3): 271–91.

Von Zielbauer, Paul. 2007. "Private Health Care in Jails Can Be a Death Sentence." In *Prison Profiteers*, edited by Tara Herivel and Paul Wright. New York: The New Press.

Wakefield, Sara, and Christopher Uggen. 2010. "Incarceration and Stratification." *Annual Review of Sociology* 36(1): 387–406.

Waldron, Jeremy. 2012. "How Law Protects Dignity." *Public Law and Legal Theory* working paper no. 317. New York: New York University.

Walker, Michael. 2016. "Race Making in a Penal Institution." *American Journal of Sociology* 121(4): 1051–78.

Weber, Max. 1978. *Economy and Society*. First published 1922. Berkeley: University of California Press.

Western, Bruce, and Becky Pettit. 2010. "Incarceration and Social Inequality." *Daedalus* 139(3): 8–19.